# CRITICAL REFLECTIONS ON ECONOMY AND POLITICS IN INDIA, VOL. 2

# *Studies in Critical Social Sciences Book Series*

Haymarket Books is proud to be working with Brill Academic Publishers (www.brill.nl) to republish the *Studies in Critical Social Sciences* book series in paperback editions. This peer-reviewed book series offers insights into our current reality by exploring the content and consequences of power relationships under capitalism, and by considering the spaces of opposition and resistance to these changes that have been defining our new age. Our full catalog of *SCSS* volumes can be viewed at https://www.haymarketbooks.org/series_collections/4-studies-in-critical-social-sciences.

# CRITICAL REFLECTIONS ON ECONOMY AND POLITICS IN INDIA, VOL. 2

## A Class Theory Perspective

### RAJU J. DAS

Haymarket Books
Chicago, IL

First published in 2020 by Brill Academic Publishers, The Netherlands
© 2020 Koninklijke Brill NV, Leiden, The Netherlands

Published in paperback in 2021 by
Haymarket Books
P.O. Box 180165
Chicago, IL 60618
773-583-7884
www.haymarketbooks.org

ISBN: 978-1-64259-429-4

Distributed to the trade in the US through Consortium Book Sales and
Distribution (www.cbsd.com) and internationally through Ingram Publisher
Services International (www.ingramcontent.com).

This book was published with the generous support of Lannan Foundation and
Wallace Action Fund.

Special discounts are available for bulk purchases by organizations and
institutions. Please call 773-583-7884 or email info@haymarketbooks.org for more
information.

Cover design by Jamie Kerry and Ragina Johnson.

Printed in the United States.

10 9 8 7 6 5 4 3 2 1

Library of Congress Cataloging-in-Publication data is available.

# Contents

# Acknowledgements

I have benefitted from my conversations (online and offline) with many scholars in different parts of the world who take the class perspective seriously. I have discussed with them various issues, including fascistic tendencies and Left politics. They include: Greg Albo, Himani Bannerji, Tom Brass, Patrick Bond, Joseph Choonara, Kevin Cox, Jamie Gough, Kevin Hewison, Sándor John, Robert Latham, David Laibman, Deepak Mishra, Bertell Ollman, Hira Singh, Murray Smith, Mohanakumar S., Steven Tufts, and many others. My current and former graduate students at York University, have been, of course, a permanent source of comradely suggestions, criticisms and encouragement. Yvonne Yim at York University has kindly provided assistance numerous times.

A grant from Canada's Social Sciences and Humanities Research Council in 2006 (*grant* number: 510441) made it possible for me to collect some of the empirical evidence reported in the book to illustrate its theoretical arguments. This is gratefully acknowledged. I am grateful to the men, women and children in various localities in India who have freely shared with me their thoughts about their lives and about their struggles.

I made rough drafts of the diagrams used in the book, but it was Ashley Chen, a former graduate student of mine and now a teacher, who deciphered these drawings and who converted these into their publishable form. I do not know who else can do this. She also produced the graphs based on the statistical data I supplied to her, and she has saved me from many typographical errors as well. I cannot thank her enough.

I imagine this book as a concrete 'application', theoretically and empirically, of the ideas laid out in my *Marxist class theory for a skeptical world* published in 2017. I have wanted to write a book on India from the theoretical perspective of class, but I would not have written that book at this moment, if it was not for the constant encouragement received from Professor David Fasenfest, the editor of Brill's Critical Social Science Book Series. He encouraged me in part because he saw my desire to write such a book. He is incredibly patient, kind and supportive, and like a true comrade, he is never unwilling to offer criticisms when they are due and in my own interest. I am extremely grateful for his unflinching support for unfashionable ideas in my work (and in the writings of many others in the world). I hope that the book meets David's expectation to some extent.

Finally, I am grateful to all those who have kept alive class analysis, both theoretically, and politically.

# Illustrations

## Figures

## Tables

## Maps

# Preface

*Critical Reflections on Economy and Politics in India* is a book on political economy and the politics of the Right and the Left in post-independence India. Originally published in 2020 by Brill as a single volume (658 pages), this book is now being published by Haymarket as two volumes for the convenience of the reader. Volume 1 of this edition contains chapters 1-7 from the original, and Volume 2 covers the remaining chapters 8-14. All in-text references to different chapters can be found in the respective Haymarket volumes. The Introduction to the complete work is found in Volume 1, and the Conclusion in Volume 2 refers to all the material in the Haymarket paperback volumes.

These two volumes present a class-based interpretation of the economic and political situation in contemporary India within a globalizing world. The first Haymarket volume deals with such topics as: the importance of class analysis of the Indian society and the state, the specificities of India's capitalism and neoliberalism, as well as the dynamics of poverty, geographically uneven (and combined) development, technological change, and nature-dependent export-oriented production.

Volume 2 concerns itself with more explicitly political matters. Given the sufferings of workers and petty-producers, it is not surprising that India has had one of the strongest Left movements in the world. Indeed, Left-led struggles in the form of workers' strikes in urban areas and the Naxalite/Maoist movement in rural areas have been a long-standing part of the political landscape of India. But all is not well with Left theory and practice, so this book offers a critical discussion of the Left. Interestingly, and dialectically speaking, the political-economic processes that have adversely impacted the masses which therefore necessitated Left-led struggles at local, regional and national scales, have also been the ones that are responsible for the emerging politics of the Right. There now exist in India 'fascistic tendencies' (i.e. the mechanisms that *can* produce a fully-fledged fascist state), part of a global trend, which are nurtured and supported by certain political and so-called cultural organizations. Right-wing politics is blatantly pro-big-business and against the fundamental interests of the exploited masses. India's right-wing politics reflects the identity politics of the ruling classes materialized in the form of Hindu nationalism and supremacism. It seeks to preserve a crisis-ridden capitalist system through physical coercion and ideological manipulation by the fascistic elements both from within and outside the state. In India, the democratic rights of religious minorities (especially, Muslims), democrats, Leftists, trade union leaders, progressive intellectuals, and millions of ordinary secular-minded workers and petty-producers are increasingly under attack; millions live in fear or intimidation. The world's largest democracy has become a 'half democracy' even by the traditional standards of capitalism. Not surprisingly, the politics of the Right is explicitly anti-Left, raising the question of 'what is to be done' by the Left. Volume 2 takes up this question in greater detail.

If class relations, especially under capitalism, are behind the problems of the masses, as is the case in India and elsewhere, then the response should be a political project. The goal of this political project must be to create not a more democratic, more egalitarian and more developed *capitalism* but a society that practices popular democracy and operates without the rule of capital and other forms of class relation. The political mobilization for such a project as a protracted process requires workers and small-scale producers to militantly combat the identity politics of the Right, and to defend democratic and economic rights.

The two volumes apply *abstract* theoretical ideas to the *concrete* situation in India, prompting a rethinking of certain abstract ideas. In general terms, the analysis in these volumes demonstrates the necessity of abstract theories for the study of concrete situations undersstood as 'the concentration of many determinations'. More specifically, this analysis applies a materialist and dialectical class theory (see my *Marxist Class Theory for a Skepitcal World*, Brill 2017 and Haymarket 2018) to the Indian context in a manner that takes seriously the matter of the 'tyranny, oppression, violence, and abuse' that have become the fate of ordinary men and women belonging to religious minorities and lower castes in India.

The struggle of the masses in defense of hard-won democratic rights and for a secure and sustainable livelihood is quite literally a matter of life and death. People are dying because of hunger, malnutrition, economic insecurity, poverty and poverty-inducted illnesses, and they are dying because of lynching and riots orchestrated by fascistic elements. Given India's growing global importance, the success or failure of the struggle of the masses in India will influence the success and failure of such struggles elsewhere. Theoretically-informed critical reflections on the current situation are a necessary tool in such struggles for a just society, in India and in other countries.

Raju J Das
Professor
York University, Toronto
April 19, 2021

# Class Dynamics of Poverty, State Failure, and Class Struggle

Historical materialism views human society through the lens of class struggle, a concept that, unfortunately, is unfashionable today.[12] This historical materialist view conjures up several significant ideas. One is that: humans *make* their own history, as Marx asserts on the opening page of his *Eighteenth Brumaire* (Marx, 2000: 329). But what does making history (and geography) really mean? It means, among other things, creating something that would not otherwise exist, in the absence of purposeful (collective) human interventions (Callinicos, 2004). A more specific instance of intervening in the world is fighting against its various forms of injustice. Though a critic of most tenets of historical materialism, Giddens (1981: 224), echoes Marx, to some extent, when he says: 'unless drugged or beaten – and usually not even then – human beings fight back [against oppression], for a part of being a human agent is to know that ... one has the capability of exercising agency'. Marx and Engels had a more explicitly *class-specific* version of this view, when they wrote in 1847 in the *Communist Manifesto*, emphasizing *class* rather than just *human* agency: the oppressed classes – plebeians, slaves, serfs and workers – 'stood in constant opposition' to their oppressors, in the quest for justice (Marx and Engels, 1977: 108–109). This is an idea repeated in a letter written in 1879 to German activists: 'For almost 40 years we have emphasized that the class struggle is the immediate driving power of history ... we, therefore, cannot possibly co-operate with people who wish to expunge this class struggle from the movement' (Marx and Engels, 1982: 307). For historical materialists, therefore, making history means that existing conditions of life are not acceptable because they are exploitative and oppressive, and that new and better conditions of life can, and must, be created, and that they can only be created through political struggles against the class/classes responsible for the existing conditions. The act of making history (and geography) in a class-society *is*, ultimately, class struggle. In this precise

---

1   An earlier version of this chapter appeared as Das (2009).
2   Historical materialism includes what David Harvey famously calls historical-geographical materialism, which is a geographically-inflected historical materialism. The latter takes seriously the issues of space (geographical unevenness), place and scale (Harvey, 1996).

sense is the history of society the history of class struggle, as stressed in the opening lines of the *Communist Manifesto*.

Implicit in the class view of society is an interesting dialectical connection. This connection is between the conditions of existence and class struggle. Conditions of existence include what Marx (2000: 425), in *Preface to the Critique of Political Economy*, referred to as 'material productive forces' and 'relations of production' (and the empirical effects, such as various forms of deprivation emerging partly from the contradiction between the two). Because these conditions are exploitative, they *require* (necessitate) class struggle for their transcendence, and they *prompt* (make possible) class struggle for this purpose. The second aspect of the dialectic is that: these conditions not only prompt class struggle, but also condition, or set limits on, class struggle (i.e. class struggle from below, the class struggle of the oppressed). For, humans make history not as they choose but under the historical-geographical conditions transmitted from the past (Marx, 2000: 329; Harvey, 2000: 47).

The conditions under which people live can now be interpreted more broadly than usual. They must be seen as encompassing not only material conditions, but also ideas that people produce in the process of living under, reflecting on, and struggling against, the material conditions. These ideas can include the ideas that signify disrespect towards certain groups, and ideas that prompt people to support or to fight oppression. An idea can act like a material force when many people have it, as Marx said. Plekhanov, widely regarded as the father of Russian Marxism, said: 'once the forms of [people's] consciousness have sprung from the soil of social being, they become a part of history' (1971: 116), a history that 'weighs like a nightmare on the brain of the living' (Marx, 2000: 329). The conditions of existence include not only ideas but also the state that seeks to create order (Lenin, 1977b: 11). As discussed in the previous chapter, the state seeks to create an order not only by interventions in support of the dominant classes, but also by *repressing* exploited classes and seeking to elicit their consent to the system's reproduction, including through selective bribes. State policies often take the form of 'development', on the ground and on paper. These must be construed partly as a form of class struggle from above, launched on behalf of the propertied. The chapter focuses on the first aspect of the dialectic, in the historical-geographic context of India (i.e. how conditions of existence create political spaces for class struggle). It will only briefly discuss the second aspect.

The anti-imperialist struggle in the less developed world embodied a great dream. This was a dream that *post* independence, the unjust conditions of existence created by colonialism would be removed, and that people would live a better life. They would eat more and better. They would live a life of dignity.

This dream remained unfulfilled, more or less, at least for the most disadvantaged classes, groups and regions. 'Spaces of hope' that millions of villages represented, became spaces of despair. New exploitative conditions were produced, while old conditions were left intact by the post-colonial state and new ruling classes (in a way not dissimilar to what Fanon feared). The cross-class nationality struggle soon gave way to class struggle from below, 'now hidden, now open fight' (Marx and Engels, 1977: 109).

The struggle by common people takes different forms in different countries and places. In the Indian context, one of these is the Naxalite movement. It is so called because it started in the Naxalbari region of the West Bengal province. The Naxalite movement is a part of the worldwide Maoist movement.[3] Even if one is broadly critical of the movement, it is possible to say that 'it has been the principal defender of the poorest and most deprived against their class oppressors and the politicians, bureaucrats, police and paramilitaries backing them at various levels' (Vanaik, 2011: 102). Since the late 1960s, it has undergone a scalar transformation: from a local flare-up to a regional, and some might say, a national-scale movement. It has spread to 40% of the country's geographical area. Some form of the movement exists in about 20 of the country's 29 provinces, including 223 districts out of a total of 640; in 2003, only 55 districts were affected (Ismi, 2013) (see Map 8.1).

Sumanta Banerjee (2017), a sympathetic commentator on the Naxalite movement, says that the Naxalite/Maoist armed struggle is the longest surviving revolutionary movement in the history of peasant resistance in India. Shah and Jain (2017: 1215) say that: the Naxalite movement is 'the world's longest standing revolutionary struggle' (see also Mukherji, 2012: 5). The former Prime Minister of India, Dr. Singh, of the centrist Congress Party, the traditional party of the Indian proprietary classes, called the Naxalites the single biggest national security threat.[4] The BJP government, the right-wing government in power now, is very aggressive towards Naxalism. The study of radical movements claiming to *change* the conditions of existence in the world is an opportunity to *interpret* the conditions that prompt them in a way in which lessons can be drawn to facilitate the act of changing the world, even if the lessons might not be liked by participants and supporters of a given movement. The Naxalite movement, including its geography, is also a window on an Indian countryside in perpetual developmental crisis.

---

3  Often, by the term 'Maoist', some refer to the activities of the CPI (Maoist). I use the term 'Naxalite' and 'Maoist' as a generic category to refer to the class-based social movement in India that is ideologically informed by Maoism, which originated in Naxalbari, and which includes activities of CPI (Maoist).

4  This prompted The Financial Times to say 'A spectre is haunting South Asia – the spectre of Maoism' (quoted in Callinicos, 2010).

MAP 8.1     Geography of the Maoist Movement
            Note: The darker the areas, the more active is the Maoist movement.
            SOURCE: HTTP://WWW.SATP.ORG/SATPORGTP/COUNTRIES/INDIA/DATABASE/
            LWE_CONFLICTMAP2015.HTML

This chapter briefly looks at some of the material conditions in India's rural areas in relation to Naxalism, from the 1960s to the present time. The remainder of the chapter has four sections. Section 1, which follows this Introduction, discusses how relations of class and social oppression have created difficult conditions of living for the rural poor. I also briefly consider the failure of the post-colonial capitalist-landlord state to counter these conditions, thus suggesting that state's failure itself is an aspect of poor people's life. It is the unjust conditions of living that have created a situation 'ripe' for class struggle, one instance of which is the Naxalite movement. Its growth and spread are dealt with in Section 2. Section 3 presents a critique of the movement. A final section concludes the chapter.

## 1    Class Dynamics, State Failure and Poverty in Rural India

The material conditions of existence of the rural masses are structured by re-lations of production including relations of unequal distribution of land, the main means of production. They are also influenced by relations of social op-pression based on gender (partly signifying the relations of reproduction) and caste/ethnicity. During colonial times, the British imperialists created highly unequal agrarian class relations. A significant aspect of this was an extremely unequal distribution of land: by the time they left, fewer than 12% of families owned 65% of all land.[5] During the nationalist movement and after, there was a demand for a more egalitarian agrarian order from peasants, many of whom were organized by the communists. But to maintain the class unity of the movement, nationalist leaders did not pay serious attention to this demand. After formal independence, the post-colonial state sought to implement land reforms that would make agrarian relations more egalitarian. The policy did not achieve much success. More than a decade after the British left, about 40% of India's land was owned by 5% of rural households, who did not farm their plots personally. Pauperized small holders began selling plots of land to meet their subsistence expenditures. Inequality in the ownership/control over land continues: in 1995–96, approximately 7% of families operated 66% of the land (GOI, 2007: 109), and in 2003, less than 10% of families owned more than 56% of land (Bhalla, 2006: 34). On the other hand, the number of landless households, or families who were near-landless (owning less than 5 acres) has been in-creasing (albeit rather slowly): in 2003, these families constitute 90.4% of rural households, an increase of more than 20% since the mid-1950s (Bhalla, 2006: 34). Lack of land, the basic source of subsistence, is particularly severe in the case of socially marginalized groups, the Scheduled Castes (SCs) and Sched-uled Tribes (STs): 90% of the former and 70% of the latter possess less than 5 acres, or are landless. Land ownership is a major determinant of income (and power): in the 1990s, a large farmer (owning more than 25 acres), who is likely to earn most of their income by using tenants for a rent and/or who employs daily-wage laborers, earned more than 7.5 times the income of a landless wage-earning household (which is approximately 11,000 Rupees) (Shariff, 1999: 28).

---

5   The data are for 1953–54, the earliest year for which data on land distribution are available.

Those who deny the significance of private property (specifically, private property that allows its owner to exploitat the labor of others) as the major determinant of material conditions should take note of this simple statistic. It is not without reason that the demand for the abolition of capitalist private property is the factor that distinguishes Marxists from all other progressives, as Marx argued.

Associated with an unequal land distribution is the presence of rental exploitation. In the 1960s, many landlords cultivated their land by leasing it to poor peasants (i.e. those who did not own much land and who had to work for others as tenants and/or for a wage). Landlords demanded high rents. Landowners would also impose levies on tenants to bear the cost of ceremonies in their houses. Peasants performed free forced work on landlords' land and for their households. Many of these practices still exist, although on a smaller scale. There are still at least 40 million bonded laborers, and close to 90% of them are Dalits or tribals (Human Rights Watch, 1999); there are also close to 100 million child laborers (who are effectively unfree laborers, many of whom are subjected to physical violence by their employers) (Das and Chen, 2019). The bonded laborers cannot choose who they work for, how long, and for how much.

In the 1960s, landowners also had their land cultivated by nominally free, hired laborers, paying below-subsistence wages. Hired labor is now occurring on a much larger scale than in the 1960s in most States. More and more people depend on the sale of their labor power for living, although they rarely have paid employment for more than 200 days in a year. They live as long as they work, and they work as long as they live. For, there is neither personal saving nor pension for old age. On the other hand, minimum wage laws are hardly implemented. In 1989, in Bihar's Jehanabad district, a hotspot of agrarian struggles, minimum wages were paid in only 16% of the 933 villages (Louis, 2005: 5372). In 1999–2000, the real wages of agricultural laborers was only 25.48 rupees for males, which was lower than the average minimum wages of 14 States (Rupees 44.13) (Singh, 2002: 70). Agricultural laborers, like poor peasants, and all those involved in petty production (e.g. tribals), are the most food-insecure. This is partly because food prices have increased relative to their earnings, while the Public Distribution System (PDS) of the government, which is supposed to provide subsidized food, has been ineffective (Singh, 2002: 72). The collapse of the PDS has recently prompted villagers in Bihar's Bhojpur district, another area known for class struggle, to burn their ration cards protesting the fact that they are not receiving subsidized food. There are many places, such as Orissa's Kalahandi district, where millions of tonnes of food are stored in government food-stores, while locals are forced to eat mango seeds. One does not need to employ the strategy of deconstruction to construe that these seeds are not good for health. Of course, state officials with university degrees, including of the coveted IAS (Indian Administrative Service), maintain that the local indigenous population eats these seeds because of poor eating habits. What is to be questioned is these officials' own habit growing out of their responsibility to manage the unjust social system, the habit of adding insult of salt to already festering class-inflicted wounds. This is a habit that coexists with another habit, that of being subservient to the property-owning classes and their political masters, partly, in their own career interests.

Indeed, in some places, people eat the rats that fatten themselves by eating the grains stored in government stores overflowing with food. Monkeys feast at some of these stores, while humans starve nearby. It seems that animals are better off than millions of human beings in India.[6] This, of course, might not be extra-ordinary to academics, including many fascinated by ANT (actor network theory), and other theoretical gimmicks of the comfortable petty bourgeoisie, who deny ontological dualities.[7] The situation described above points to this irrefutable inference from a Marxist standpoint: continued separation of direct producers from means of production (e.g. land) and means of consumption (e.g. food) is necessary in reproducing their dependence on capital (including landed capital), and this dependence lies at the heart of class relations.

It is true that wages of agricultural workers have risen somewhat. But their wages are much lower than what is required for a decent living. The rate of growth of their wages is also lower than that of wages in the rural non-farm sector. More importantly, it is also lower than the rate of growth of labor productivity which benefits landowners (Singh, 2002: 70). Thus agricultural workers not only live in a condition of absolute poverty, but also in relative poverty, relative to other workers and to property owners. And their poverty – and indeed, poverty of other categories of the toiling mass – are partly because the price of labor power is low, the price of the product of labor sold by small-scale producers is low. All this is in a situation where there is much uneven development between areas and sectors (see Sainath, 2001: 158) and where there are few welfare benefits from the state.[8]

Low agricultural wages, lack of suitable and plentiful non-farm employment, and poor income on tiny holdings, mean that peasants must depend on private moneylenders for their credit needs. The annual rate of interest charged by them is 50% or more. In the 1960s, 'of the estimated total number of 16.3

---

6   That in recent times, under the patronage of right-wing groups and their government, cows in India have higher status and respect than some of the oppressed groups in the country is an interesting development.

7   This is the idea that human beings are qualitatively different from non-human animals, even if they are both living beings, and that human beings' needs must be prioritized over the animals'.

8   In fact, because wages are low, many people are forced to work as small-scale producers.

million agricultural labor households..., 63.9% of the estimated were indebted'
(Banerjee, 1984). In 2003, the figure was still high at 49% (GOI, 2007: 73). An
average farmer's debt was equal to her/his household's total spending over two
years (ibid.). Since 1983, the percentage of the total debt incurred from private
moneylenders has been increasing (Bhalla, 2007: 317). To the extent that there
was institutional credit (e.g. from government owned banks) for rural areas,
most (close to 90%) was monopolized by larger farmers, rather than made
available to poor peasants and landless laborers (Varma, 2002: 65). In recent
times, institutional sources of credit are drying up under neoliberal capitalism.
This is why private moneylenders are more important as a source of credit
than in the 1960s, when Naxalist movement began. Apart from large landowners and moneylenders, traders are another class, on which poor people's lives
are dependent, including in aboriginal areas. They buy farm and forest products from tribals, as well as economically insecure peasants, at a cheaper-
than-market rate, and sell them at a higher rate. Enjoying the support of many
politicians, traders hoard the essential commodities such as rice, wheat, pulses
and sugar, and increase the prices way beyond the level workers and poor peasants can afford. Unable to pay their loans due to crop failure and/or decline in
profitability of farming, thousands of peasants, including many from the better-off section, are committing suicide: 182,936 between 1997 and 2007 to be
precise (Sainath, 2009). This means more than 18,000 a year. In other words,
one farmer commits suicide every half an hour. (Note that these figures ex-
clude female farmers committing suicide: because they do not own land (their
husbands do); they are not considered farmers in the official statistics.) Many
farmers are jailed because of default on their loans.

Conditions of life are, dominantly, but not exclusively, determined by class
relations. The charge that historical materialists reduce everything to class is a
most disingenuous ideological propaganda by academic pluralists and relativ-
ists, whose main motive is to under-value class, and banish class struggle from
intellectual and political practice by playing identity politics. Marxists maintain that class relations are experienced through, and reproduced by, caste (or
race), ethnicity and relations of reproduction or gender (Callinicos, 1993;
Gimenez, 2005) that compound the injurious effects of class. All Dalits, tribals
and women are not landless laborers. But when someone is a Dalit, a woman,
and a landless laborer, or a petty producer from an economically backward and
politically neglected region, her condition of life is even more miserable. In
addition to suffering class-based exploitation and dispossession from the land,
the toiling masses – poor women, tribals and low caste people, including *Dalits* –
are also subjected to social discrimination and political marginalization. Poor
people live under constant threat to their dignity (*izzat*) and political rights.
Caste oppression is rooted in class exploitation (e.g. agrarian class relations)

and contributes toward the reproduction of class relations, sometimes more directly and sometimes less so. Until recently, low caste people, even if they had the money, could not buy the clothes they want, cannot walk in upper caste neighborhoods wearing footwear or carrying an umbrella, and cannot sit on a cot in the presence of upper castes. Nor can they take upper caste surnames. Nor can students of lower castes sit on front benches in class-rooms (Nathan, 1999). In July 2009, upper caste people in a village near Patna beat up a Dalit woman for listening to popular Hindi songs on a mobile phone. Caste influences the division of labor and access to assets. This is seen in the 'continuing confinement of lower castes to the ranks of agricultural laborers' (Nathan, 1999: 162).[9] In many villages, low caste people (mainly women) have to trudge long distances to fetch water, for they are not allowed by the upper caste people to take water from the public ponds or wells near their huts. This creates a difficult situation in times of drought: low caste women are not allowed to use wells located in upper caste hamlets. India remains a caste society or, more accurately, a class-caste society.

Poor people are not only oppressed by caste, but also gender relations. In rural areas, the economic disparity between men and women appears to be greater than in urban areas. Not only are women more likely to be unemployed. Their daily wage rate is also much less than that for males. Given the continuing preference for male children in a patriarchal society without provisions for old age security, female feticide and infanticide, as well as the neglect of female children, continue. The result is that the female male ratio for the population as a whole is well below unity (Dreze and Sen, 2002: 230) and that the ratio for children (0–6 years), in particular, is extremely low and declining (945 in 1991, to 927 in 2001, and 919 in 2011).

Women from lower castes and from poor peasants and working-class backgrounds have little control over their own bodies. Their body is a means for the cheap production of wealth for the landed and for their sexual enjoyment. Their body is also a means/weapon of class struggle in their hands. When low caste laborers demand higher wages from higher caste landlords, the latter feel 'threatened that a "low man" [is] ... challenging their privileged position' (Frankel, 1990: 122). This explains why they commit atrocities against the Dalits, including Dalit women. An ideological condition of existence of the class system is that the exploited class 'looks upon the requirements of [the existing] mode of production as self-evident natural laws', as Marx remarked towards the end of *Capital*, vol. 1 (1977: 899). This ideological precondition for reproduction of the class system begins to be undermined when exploited people view the existing conditions of life (i.e. the class relations and the state that reproduces these) as changeable and challengeable, and actually start

---

9   This conclusion is based on Prasad's study of Bihar villages under the influence of Naxalites.

challenging them. This, in turn, prompts a counter-challenge, class struggle from above, which uses caste and other non-class relations to intensify the offensive. Let me cite just two instances. A Dalit farm worker in Tamilnadu was forced to drink urine for complaining to the police about trespass against a caste Hindu; in another case, two Dalits were forced to feed each other human excreta because they stood by another Dalit in his battle with a local elected leader (Kumar, 2002: 157). Between 1981 and 1999, on average, an atrocity (e.g. rape, murder, arson, etc.) was committed against three Dalits every hour.[10] In the State of Bihar, the response of upper caste landlords to the political assertions of Dalit laborers and poor peasants has taken the form of private landlord armies that ruthlessly suppress the low caste poor fighting for their legitimate rights.[11] Massacres of the lower classes of low castes by landowners of upper (and sometimes middle) castes are highly gendered, showing how class, caste and gender are interconnected at a concrete level, *within the context of class relations*.[12] For example, landlords subject low caste women to the most barbaric mutilation and murder, to stop them from giving birth to children who, landlords fear, would become Naxalites (*Liberation*, 2003).

Thus millions of people who depend entirely or partly on the sale of labor power suffer from multiple forms of deprivation and live under the clutches of capitalists, landlords, usurers and merchants, who make use of caste and other forms of non-class oppression. The state has sought to intervene in four major areas in addressing problems of rural distress and deprivation. These are: land reforms (1950s–), the Green Revolution (1960s–), cheap credit to the poor (1970s–), and providing wage-employment (2006–). These policies have failed in most places, for most of the people who need them.

In terms of land reforms, the state failed to restrict the amount of land owned or controlled by the larger landowners, including the pre-capitalist landowners. It could not reduce the rental exploitation of peasants. The total amount of land distributed in the whole country amounted to less than 5% of total gross cropped area. The agrarian question – social obstacles (e.g. non- or pre-capitalist class relations) acting as a barrier to capitalist development – that was to be

---

10    Interestingly, 'The conviction rate of cases of atrocities against the SCs/STs [is] less than 30 per cent against the average of 42 per cent for all cognisable offences under the Indian Penal Code' (Dhar, 2009). This shows the casteist nature of the Indian state.

11    One of these, the Ranvir Sena (army), was formed in 1994 to respond to the new assertiveness of the farm laborers with more effective repression, through the creation of a professional militia with better training, weaponry and leadership. The Sena enjoys the protection of much of the political elite across party lines (Kumar, 1999).

12    Intersectionality is definitely not the tool with which to examine the relation between class and social oppression, and one reason why, as I see it, is that the intersectionality approach does not have any theory of inter-section (see Science & Society's symposium on intersectionality) (Science & Society, 2018).

resolved at the national scale, through state interventions, remained unre-
solved. Having failed to destroy landlordism, the state resorted to a technological fix to the agrarian question in the mid-1960s. It did so by providing technological support in the form of the Green Revolution in specific areas. Much of
the benefit from this policy, which was in no small measure prompted by US
imperialist interests in the sale of modern inputs in India, was monopolized by
the same larger landowners whose power the land reforms policy was supposed
to undermine but left intact. This class used the technology to increase productivity. The smaller owners did not have much financial capacity. Nor did they
have a sufficient amount of land to benefit from the new technology. Capitalist
landowners resorted to mechanization. This deprived laborers of any gains they
might have otherwise enjoyed. Representing a technological fix to India's rural
distress, the Green Revolution came to be associated with multiple forms, or
layers, of social-spatial inequality. These included: inequality between employers and laborers; between larger owners (i.e. capitalist farmers/landlords) and
smaller owners; between landlords and semi-proletarians/tenants; and between Green Revolution areas (in which the state deliberately concentrated its
efforts at promoting agrarian capitalism) and non-Green revolution areas.

As the Green Revolution could not reduce poverty, in the late 1970s – early
1980s (a topic explored in a previous chapter), the state launched the Integrated Rural Development Policy (IRDP). This aimed at giving small loans to poor
people to start income-generating activities – setting up small shops, starting
dairy businesses, using improved farm implements, etc. This policy, more or
less, was also a failure. In the capitalist system, the use of its resources must be
justified mainly on the basis of the profit-logic. This logic put severe limits on
the amount of money the capitalist state could commit in the form of pro-poor
policies, such as the IRDP or PDS, *relative* to (a) the massive need of the tens of
millions of the poor whom the system marginalizes (e.g. peasants increasingly
losing access to land; people without secure employment for a living wage),
and (b) the massive need to appease, bribe and subsidize capitalists to invest
in specific areas and sectors. It is also not easy for 'penny capitalists' – semi-
proletarian entrepreneurs to whom the state gives a small loan to invest in
business – to accumulate 'capital' and benefit from it. Given a choice between
converting a meagre state loan to 'capital' (or a means of creating self-
employment, more accurately) and using it to buy food just to live, they would
just choose the latter. This they did (Das, 2000). The law of dialectics says that
Rs. 500,000 can be capital but not Rs. 500. The fact that it is difficult for starving
poor people to be entrepreneurs did not occur to the apologists of capital and
anti-poor officials and politicians, sitting in far-away and comfortable places,
who were, and still are, eager to promote market relations in every nook and

cranny of the country. And, the limited money that the state could commit did not even reach the intended beneficiaries. Officials and politicians work in an utterly undemocratic manner and have unscrupulous links to traders and landowners. Therefore, much of the IRDP money ended up in the pockets of the local officials, or with the traders supplying the assets needed for the income-generating activities (e.g. animals; farm implements) (Das, 2000). That small bits of money given to individuals or to groups of individuals (especially women), and possibly via NGOs, can be empowering has become conventional wisdom, including among so-called critical social scientists. This shows the extent to which the fetish of the market has colonized the consciousness of the politicians, bureaucracy and petty-bourgeois intellectuals.

Partly due to the pressure from the parliamentary left, the state started, in 2006, a new policy of employment creation, known as National Rural Employment Guarantee Scheme or NREGS. Its aim is to provide at least 100 days of guaranteed waged employment a year to every household whose adult members volunteer to do unskilled manual work at the legislated minimum wage. Reports suggest that, like the IRDP, a large part of the money meant for this policy has gone to the politicians, officials and property owners (e.g. contractors), except in those few areas where the poor people are able to exercise constant vigilance over the implementation of the scheme (Khera, 2008; Liberation, 2008; Rai, 2007). Because the policy, if properly implemented, can hurt the economic elite a bit by tightening the labor market, it seeks to sabotage the policy (Roy, 2015). Provisions of the act are routinely violated. For example, the delay in the payment of wages lasts for weeks and months; laborers are not paid the mandated unemployment insurance if they are not provided wage-work when they demand. There is also not enough money provided for the policy to work (to give *everyone* wage-work at a decent living wage as and when they need it): once again, the capitalist system puts limits on how much can be committed in the form of any anti-poverty policy. The actual amount spent on the poor depends on the balance of class forces. But there are severe structural limits, ideologically expressed through such constructs as 'budget deficits go up' or 'government assistance makes people lazy'. Note that these are expressed by the members of same class, directly or through their spokespersons, who have no qualms about milking the state (the fiscal stimulus as a bribe, or corporate welfare, from the state) to get out of an economic rut that is entirely of their own making. This signifies that hypocrisy, like most things in life, has a class character.

The major interventions of the post-colonial state have failed to significantly improve the conditions of life of the poor created by class (and other) relations. The main, if not the sole, reason for this is the class character of the state itself. For example, the abysmal failure of the land reforms legislation can be attributed to two major factors connected to class relations (Das, 1999c). First, as in other similar post-colonial countries, and as discussed in Chapter 7, large landowners in India share state power with the urban bourgeoisie: this means that state policies were dominantly in the interests of these classes and their international patrons. *Given* the absence of alternative opportunities to make profit, caused by the overall imperialist framework in which the country oper- ates, these landowners' class interest was in the ruthless exploitation of people with little or no land: exploitation of poor peasants via rental extractions and (increasingly) of laborers at via the payment of below-subsistence wages, sometimes under unfree conditions. Heavy rental extraction meant that peas- ants had insufficient resources to invest in land. Super exploitation of peasants (and laborers) also reduced the size of the home market. Besides, given the opportunity to earn revenue through these means of super-exploitation, prop- erty owners had little incentive to invest in land to increase labor productivity. Thus, to the extent that one can at all isolate national-scale factors of under- development from imperialism,[13] class relations acted as a fetter on the devel- opment of productive forces, at least in specific regions.[14] This under-develop- ment of productive forces contradicted capitalists' interests in higher rates of profit which would have come from a higher level of the development of pro- ductive forces resulting in the production of cheaper farm products for food and raw materials combined with a growing home market allowing large-scale production in the cities. So, landowners were potential 'enemies' of the urban capitalist class. The *economic* interest of the capitalist class, domestic and for- eign, was such that it would not have had any problem if the land reform legis- lation had completely or significantly destroyed the pre-capitalist class (except that some elements of the urban capitalist class were also involved in forms of exploitation in villages that were not quite capitalist). Such legislation would also have improved the material conditions of peasants and rural laborers. But the *political* interests of capitalists were such that they could not go against the feudals type. What Marx said in 1852 (in an article in New York Daily Tribune) about the then-British bourgeoisie, is relevant to their Indian counterpart now: 'They prefer to compromise with the vanishing opponent [i.e. the feudals] rather than to strengthen the arising enemy [i.e. the working class], to whom the future belongs, by concessions of a more than apparent importance.

---

13    Imperialism is defined here 'as a form of class relations: relations between metropolitan bourgeoisie and Third World workers/peasants', as it is enabled by the powerful states of the imperialist countries and by the actions of the elements of the bourgeoisie of the less developed countries (Das, 2001c: 168).

14    This does not mean that the dominant reason for India's under-development lay in the so-called pre-capitalist or semi-feudal class relations per se. Indeed, many of the so-called feudal relations are not semi-feudal but capitalist at a lower stage of development.

Therefore, they strive to avoid every forcible collision with [them]' (Marx, 2000: 361). The landowners, including the *pre-capitalist* elements of this class (e.g. former *rajas, zamindars,* etc. who were supporters of imperialism) were powerful in specific regions. They perform the important role of controlling the rural masses, including laborers, whose anger against landlordism could be potentially directed at the bourgeoisie of the country as well as at the imperialists. So, the bourgeoisie, and the state on its behalf, could not afford to hurt the landowners' interest too much by implementing land reforms. Second, those who were directly or indirectly responsible for the implementation of the legislation, including judges, came from the landed class or represented their interests.

If large landowners' farms were broken and their land was consequently redistributed among poorer peasants and the landless, and if the latter were provided technological and financial support by the state through cooperatives, land productivity would have increased, putting money in their hands creating a home market. This did not happen. This could not happen. This is because of the overall balance of class forces, within the country and internationally (i.e. influence of imperialists). Promises of land reforms on paper (and insignificant material benefits here and there) were just used to quell the resentment of the masses. These must be seen as what they are: as class struggle from above, to pre-empt any class struggle from below.

The Green Revolution, in a sense, represented a continuity with the earlier program (i.e. the land reforms), although these two programs are seen by many as different. This continuity reveals the class character of the state. The land reform legislation protected the class interests of the propertied families (landlords, capitalist farmers, rich peasants), who were allowed to possess land beyond the legal ceiling-limit (i.e. any amount of land they could hold on to). The Green Revolution placed new means of production (e.g. the new technological package; state capital in the form of subsidized loans, etc.) *precisely* in the hands of the same class and allowed it an opportunity to accumulate capital, unfettered *and* untaxed. Neither the land-reforms nor the Green Revolution did anything to undermine the economic and political power of large property owners (many of whom also invested in non-farm activities such as transportation, trading, etc.). They continued to govern the conditions of existence of the poor. That radicals had expected otherwise (that bureaucratic land reforms would be progressive and the Green Revolution would bring about technological change, and empower poorer peasants with proper state support), without any radical change in balance of class forces, signifies their fascination with the national progressive bourgeois thesis and the idea that the nation-state in an imperialized country can help bring about radical long-term rural transformation in property relations and in the level of development of productive forces. On the other hand, given the state's class character, the daily activities of the state must be insulated from the constant monitoring of it by the masses. Without their popular participation in the everyday workings of the state, including ways in which pro-poor policies are implemented, government funds meant for the poor are squeezed on their way from the national and provincial scale state apparatuses, to the local government officials/politicians. Like landlords, government officials and politicians are utterly insensitive to the problems of the poor (Corbridge and Harriss, 2000: 201–202; Subramanian, 1998).

In the post-1991 period, not only have the newly introduced government programs for the poor largely failed, but also earlier programs have been diluted (in several States). There is a clear connection between this and neoliberal capitalism, partly imposed by imperialism. For, one of the (contradictory) aims of the latter is to shrink mass income and consumption at home in order to enable cheap exports and repayment of debt to imperialist finance capital (see Patnaik, 1999) and to reproduce India as a low-wage platform of global capitalism.[15] Since the inception of neoliberalism, rural development expenditures, as a ratio of the net national product, have dropped, as mentioned earlier (Patnaik, 2007: 155). Among other things, this has led to a reduction in the creation of employment opportunities. The little help available from the government in the name of the economic reforms with a *human* face[16] has not been enough to counter the inhumane effects of neo-liberalism (on rural income, employment and access to land). The dilution of the development program is also seen in the case of the land reforms laws. The legal restriction on land ownership is considered by domestic and foreign capital and their political and ideological supporters to be an institutional constraint on the flow of agribusiness investment to rural areas of the country. Indeed, India is known for its wide diversity of climates favorable to the production of various commodities which cannot be economically produced in cold climates of imperialist countries (Patnaik, 1999). The existing ceiling on land is seen as a constraint also on acquiring agricultural, homestead and forestlands for a variety of agricultural as well as non-agricultural purposes including export-oriented capitalist industrialization (Special Economic Zones or SEZs) (Pushpendra, 2000).

The SEZ phenomenon, which has even infected the Left governments, signifies a pattern of peripheral capitalist industrialization which requires both (a) *dispossession of peasants* and (b) extra-ordinary level of *exploitation of laborers*,

---

15    Shrinking income and consumption of the toiling classes is the characteristic aspect of neoliberalism *everywhere* (including in imperialist countries), not just in peripheral countries. This means that there is a potential basis for international solidarity of working class and peasants against capital, including its neoliberal *avatar*, everywhere and at all scales.

16    The fact that ruling class and the state use this phrase indicates that they admit that economic reforms are inhumane.

including some of the erstwhile peasants, now rendered landless, who work in these SEZs for low wages and without the usual façade of legal rights. Land is acquired minimally as a space on which to put constant capital. It is acquired more for speculation by predatory capital. To the extent that land is used for actual production process, the existing land reform legislation is being diluted to facilitate the transfer of land from peasants to big business, who invest capital to produce commodities for export and for local elites (e.g. golf courses; holiday resorts; luxury houses; 'luxury crops' such as flowers), the commodities that the rural masses cannot afford to consume, thus immensely contributing to inequality. Global capitalism is producing new needs, and new means of satisfying these needs, as it must. It is also (re)producing a class of poor peasants and workers which cannot meet these needs. With no land for household production, with no/little social security from the state, and with not much alternative and regular employment opportunities within a reasonable commuting distance for a living wage, vast sections of the rural and semi-rural (as well as urban) population are subjected to ruthless exploitation including the use of coercive labor relations. The degree of exploitation increases with the extent to which commodities are produced for export. Export-production, especially of luxury products, generally, means that the local workers and semi-proletarians are not a market to rely on. Anyone who has actually observed areas of export agriculture or SEZs will know this to be true.

The unequal land distribution, mentioned earlier, to which the land grab under neoliberalism contributes, means that, in the absence of plentiful non-farm employment at a decent wage, the majority of the landless and near-landless population represents the vast reserve army of labor for domestic and foreign capital. The reserve army of labor has been produced from colonial times through the devastating impacts of British manufactured exports to India on her industries. It has been swelling, thanks to new imperialist mechanisms imposed by World Bank, WTO, etc. (e.g. liberalization of trade). The reserve army, which Harvey (2003), unfortunately, treats as capitalism's other, has far-ranging implications: it contributes to the backward nature of peripheral capitalism. For, a disproportionately large reserve army (without any social security from the state) undermines conditions of class struggle against low wages and long hours of those employed, especially when workers are divided along lines of caste, gender, ethnicity and location (migrants vs locals).[17] In turn, this, more or less, dampens the normal imperative on the part of

---

17    The reserve army also raises the level of exploitation of the currently employed through the mechanisms of low wages and overwork, despotically imposed by capital, and this reduces employment opportunities of those who are a part of the reserve army, as Marx

capitalists to go for technological innovation. The implication is that millions of people remain in technological backwardness with extremely low level of labor productivity and of cooperation at work, as well as spatial isolation. For every Bangalore, there are thousands of under-developed villages and small towns which are literally in darkness. People work with rudimentary technology on farms and in factories and without the benefits that large-scale production provides. The vast majority have been living in half a million villages. 63% of villages with a population of 1000 or less are not even connected by a road (GOI, 2005: 199). If the spatial system is a productive force (Cohen, 2000: 51), one can imagine how under-developed India's villages are.

The effects of class relations and relations of oppression and state's failure to counter these have created a situation of declining food availability for the poor,[18] land alienation (especially in aboriginal areas) and farmers' suicide.[19] Available statistical data on poverty reveal some crucial aspects of rural living conditions from the early 1960s.

1.  The official poverty line is based on 'inadequate absolute standards' which do not reflect 'norms of dignified human living' (Mehta, 2002: 34). It is best seen as a 'line of hunger'. Even so, the percentage of poor people in the total population went from 38% in 1960–61 to 54% in 1968–69, years of the original launch of Naxalism. In the 1970s and 1980s, as many as 320 million, on an average (more than 40% of the total population and close to half of the rural population), were in official poverty in any given year (GOI, 2003: 92). Thousands have perished from starvation or starvation-related illnesses. Close to 6 out of 10 children are malnourished (Shariff, 1999: 94). The life of villagers is cut short due to lack of proper food and medical help. In the 1980s–1990s, rural life expectancy was not even 60.

2.  As late as 1999–2000, there were 260 million people living below the official poverty line, including 193 million rural poor: this means that more than one in every four Indians, and nearly a third of its rural population, was in official poverty (GOI, 2003: 92).[20] Utsa Patnaik's (2007) very useful

---

argued in chapter 25 of *Capital* volume 1. What follows is that those who are employed *and* those who are not, are both impacted by the capitalist system.

18   The daily net availability of foodgrains (food production plus import minus export) per person has gone down from 510 grammes in 1991–92 to 470 grammes in 1994–95 to 434 grammes in 2001–02 (Patnaik, 1999: Table 12; 2007: Table 4).

19   The incidence of farmer suicide in Andhra Pradesh is one of the highest in many of its districts most associated with Naxalism.

20   In 2011, there were 276 million poor people in India (they lived on $1.25 a day in PPP terms).

analysis lays bare the class nature of poverty statistics and the class-prejudice of its ideological producers, the apologetics for big capital, who are dressed up as professors of the science of economics.[21] She shows that in 1999–2000, the per capita rural poverty-level expenditure which commanded food quantities giving 2400 calories (the minimum necessary for the normal functioning of the body) is Rs. 19 a day, and that 74.5% of the rural population consumed below this level (2007: 141, 189). (The figures for 1983 and 1993–94 were 70% and 74.5% respectively). 3 out every 4 Indian villagers have been in absolute poverty according to her. And, this means that the potential support base of movements for justice among poor people is simply huge and potentially threatening to the state which is why the state is increasingly turning coercive.

3. A villager is more likely to be poor than an urban person. A villager also does not have access to the collective consumption items (e.g. hospitals and educational institutions) that a city dweller has.[22] This partly explains why rural areas are so explosive politically.

4. The percentage of the rural population that is poor in the States affected by moderate or heavy Naxalism is generally above the all-India average (Table 8.1; column 3).[23]

5. The average monthly per capita expenditure of rural poor households and the overall level of rural development tend to be lower in all major Naxal-affected States than the all-India average (Table 8.2).

6. The official poverty level for Dalits and tribes, the groups Naxalites are most closely associated with, tend to be higher than for others; this is the case both at the all-India level and in the major Naxal-affected States (Table 8.1; column 1–2).[24]

---

21  Her scrutiny of official numbers suggests that the number game is not totally useless and that one can challenge the conventional analysts by playing their own rules of the game.

22  The percentage of the rural population that is officially poor is 27.09; the urban figure is 23.62 (GOI, 2005: Table 3.1). The rural infant mortality is 66 while the urban infant mortality is 38 in 2003 (GOI, 2007: 19). The relative infant mortality gap between rural and urban areas – the ratio of the rural infant mortality rate to the urban infant mortality rate – indeed increased between 1995 and 2003.

23  The united Andhra Pradesh is an exception. Before its division in 2014, it was the largest among all Naxal-affected States. It should be noted that poverty level is expected to be very high among the indigenous population in Andhra districts where the Naxalite movement is strong.

24  Of course, there are numerous areas where the level of developmental distress is high (e.g. higher than the national average) and, yet, there is no Naxal activity. Naxals have been active only in *some* of the distressed areas. The point is that where the level of distress is low, the Naxal-type movement is likely, showing that the Naxalite movement does

TABLE 8.1    Rural poverty (1999–2000) among most oppressed groups in selected Indian
States

| | Percentage of the poor among | | |
| --- | --- | --- | --- |
| | *Dalits* | *Scheduled Tribes* | *All groups* |
| Andhra Pradesh | 16.5 | 23.1 | 11.05 |
| Bihar (1) | 59.1 | 58.7 | 44.03 |
| Madhya Pradesh (2) | 41.2 | 57.1 | 37.06 |
| Orissa | – | 73.0 | 48.01 |
| West Bengal | 34.9 | 50.1 | 31.85 |
| All States (3) | 35.3 | 44.2 | |
| All-India (rural) (4) | 26.5 | | |

Notes: (1) includes Jharkhand; (2) includes Chhattisgarh; (3) all states = % of poverty among
SCs or among Tribes in rural India as a whole; (4) poverty ratio for rural India as a whole.
SOURCE: RADHAKRISHNAN ET AL., 2004, IN GOI, 2005

## 2    The Naxalite Movement as a Form of Lower-Class Struggle

> Maoism is spreading very rapidly across the Indian subcontinent. Genu-
> ine Marxists should be studying this phenomenon and drawing appropri-
> ate conclusions from it.
>
> JACOB SECKER (in a letter to *Socialist Worker*, UK, 2006)[25]

Thus a large proportion of the national population has not enjoyed a life of
economic security and dignity since independence from colonial rule. Because
of the unjust conditions created by class reproduced through, and reinforced
by, highly undemocratic relations of caste and patriarchy, and because of the
failure of the so-called *democratic* state, often praised by imperialist states as a
model for the Third World, to significantly mitigate the effects of these
conditions, a massive political space for potential radical movements for justice has been created. The Naxalite movement is a particular instance of radicalization of exploited masses, which will be discussed below. Indeed, given
the conditions of existence, as described above, one really wonders: why it is

---

not hang in the air: it is materially rooted. But objective conditions do not guarantee that
a radical movement will occur, least of all, a given *type* of movement (e.g. Naxalism).

25    https://socialistworker.co.uk/art/8691/Letters.

TABLE 8.2    Monthly average per capita expenditure of poor people (Rupees) in 1999–2000 in selected States

|                     | Poor | Composite Index of rural development |
|---------------------|------|--------------------------------------|
| Andhra Pradesh      | 215  | 99.3                                 |
| Bihar (1)           | 269  | 70.1                                 |
| Madhya Pradesh (2)  | 250  | 86.8                                 |
| Orissa              | 248  | 93.2                                 |
| West Bengal         | 281  | 103.2                                |
| All India           | 282  | 115.8 (unweighted average of all States) |

Notes: (1) includes Jharkhand; (2) includes Chhattisgarh.
SOURCE: GOI, 2005

that people do not revolt more often, more intensely, and in more areas, than has been the case? There is not enough space in this chapter to consider this question in any detail. An important question: what are the proximate factors behind its occurrence and continued existence? A correct understanding of the second, more specific, question may throw some light on the more general, first question.

The northern parts of India's West Bengal province[26] have a long history of peasant and worker struggles. Although short-lived, the first peasant organization in the country was formed in north Bengal itself at the All Bengal Peasant Conference of 1925 (Samanta, 1984: 21). From the early 1950s, a radical section of the Communist Party of India (CPI) organized peasants, most of whom were sharecroppers, in the Naxalbari area of West Bengal's Darjeeling district. In the period 1958–62, local peasants' associations, led by the Communists such as Charu Mazumdar, called for the harvesting of crops by peasants, arming them to protect their crops, and self-defense against police attacks (Banerjee, 1984). Such peasant activities in Naxalbari coincided with simmering troubles within the then-undivided communist party. In 1964, the party split into the 'pro-Soviet' CPI and the 'pro-China' Communist Party of India (Marxist) or the CPI(M). In 1967, these parties formed a United Front government in Bengal in coalition with some bourgeois parties. The formation of a Left-led state government increased the peasants' expectations for immediate relief.

---

26    This area is strategically important as it is not far off from Bangladesh, Nepal, and China.

On March 2, 1967, in Naxalbari, Bigul Kishan, a sharecropper, armed with a court order, had gone to till his land. He was attacked by the landlord and his hoodlums. The police did not take any action. The fact that the incident occurred just a month after the formation of the United Front government was seen as indicative of the futility of hoping that a Left-oriented government would help the peasants. This perception fueled further militancy. Fifteen to twenty thousand poor peasants, in about two thousand villages, were enrolled as full-time activists, supported by the urban educated youth (Jalal, 1995). Peasant committees were formed in every village. They were transformed into armed guards carrying traditional weapons such as bows, arrows and spears. They occupied land. They seized the crops from landlords' land. They burned all land records which had been used to deceive them. Peasant committees also passed death sentences on oppressive landlords, looted guns from them, and set up a parallel administration in the villages. They cancelled debts owed to moneylenders who were asked to return the mortgaged properties to the original owners. They established daily wages for farm laborers. They also fixed prices of essential goods in the big shops (Banerjee, 1984). From March to May 1967, feudalism was driven out of a 300-square mile area. Peasants' control over the area was complete: no outsider could enter without their permission. The exercise of political power, and control over territory, went hand in hand. With some justification, Naxalbari could be considered India's little Paris Commune.

The peasant movement turned violent when landlords resisted the seizure of their land and crops. Police action followed clashes between landlords and peasants. Following the killing of a policeman on May 23, 1967, a major police action was launched on 12 July by the State government, with full support from the Central government. The police killed nine people, including two children, as well as six (aboriginal) women, who played an important role in the movement (Damas, 1991: 84). The Naxalbari movement in the area was temporarily defeated.

Places stand for processes (Pred, 1984). What happens in a place triggers similar processes in other places. Even if what happened in Naxalbari was temporary, it became a beacon for class struggle in many other places. Naxalbari as a place multiplied itself, so to speak. Unlike other peasant movements, Naxalbari had a wider significance. It was a product of and a catalyst in a conscious process of building a new Marxist-Leninist party. The building of a new party was a consummation of the process of the 1964 split within the undivided communist party, and this in turned ensured that the tiny spark in Naxalbari that lasted only for three months developed into a prairie fire across much of India for decades (Sen, Arindam, 2017).

According to Government reports, 5424 agrarian agitations occurred between 1967 and 1970 (Shah, 1990: 291). A Coordinating Committee, and later a party, called the CPI(ML) – Communist Party of India (Marxist-Leninist) – was formed on April 22, 1969 by dissidents from the CPI(M). It got encouragement from the then Chinese Communist Party. Its aim was to coordinate localized struggles into a mass movement. Thus the CPI(M) was split into the CPI(M) and the CPI(ML). Naxalism is associated with the latter, CPI(ML). Government repression continued. By 1973, nearly 40,000 members or sympathizers were in jail.

All social movements[27] are informed by one or another ideological framing, consciously or not. The Naxalite movement is a part of a larger trend in which social movements are shaped by Maoism in the global South (Dirlik, 2014; Kumbamu, 2019). The CPI(ML) itself split many times into multiple factions, each claiming to be the true party. In post-Naxalbari times, the movement split into some 40 M-L groups engaged in fights for the expansion of their areas of influence. These groups have now consolidated into three main M-L streams, although a large number of other groups still remain outside. All M-L groups owe their origin to events in Naxalbari and are guided by their interpretation(s) of Marxism-Leninism-Maoism. They all view Indian society as semi-colonial (i.e. as under clutches of imperialism) and semi-feudal. According to them, the Indian state is controlled by imperialists, comprador bureaucratic bourgeoisie and feudal landlords. They agree on the need for a democratic revolution to destroy feudal economic and social-cultural relations, because for them the main contradiction in society is between feudals and the masses (and not between capital and labor). Therefore, their political mobilizational energy is spent dominantly on peasants (although they do make references to workers in their literature) who would geographically encircle the cities and capture power. The M-L movement is divided mainly on the basis of their tactical approach towards the balance between parliamentary and extra-electoral politics. Some [e.g. CPI (Maoist)] almost exclusively focus on armed struggle and are underground;[28] while others, such as Kanu Sanyal's group, use mainly over-ground methods and run mass organizations. Groups such as CPI(ML) Liberation use a combination of both underground and overground methods; they participate in elections (Banerjee, 1999: 203–204).[29] CPI(ML) (Liberation), a registered political party, is now cooperating, in electoral and extra-electoral struggles, with mainstream communist parties.

---

27    I am using (radical) social movements and class struggle interchangeably in this Chapter.

28    CPI (Maoist) has spread itself from the Telengana region of Andhra Pradesh to the tribal-dominated districts of adjoining Maharashtra, Chhattisgarh, Jharkhand, and Orissa.

29    Liberation has its bases primarily in Bihar and pockets of influence in Uttar Pradesh, West Bengal, Assam, Tamilnadu and Punjab and Orissa.

In terms of the Naxalite leadership, it is traditionally in the hands of petty-bourgeois or middle class people (see Routledge, 1997). They include: school teachers, students and skilled workers. Some of the leaders (including Mazumdar himself) do indeed come from peasant background. Women and Dalits are less likely to be in leadership positions. Many of the Naxalite leaders come from urban areas and are of younger age (this was especially the case in the 1960s in West Bengal). They have a sense of self-sacrifice. They speak the language of the poor and live like, and with, them. Naxalites dream of a better society. Shah (2017: 53) writes: 'It is, perhaps, the very hierarchies of Indian society that have produced some of the world's most committed pursuers of a more equal society'. Shah says the Naxalites 'came across with dignity, as equal human beings, over time making them a part of an extended family in the region' (p. 54).

Although the movement has been heavily repressed by the state, it exists in large number of almost a third of India's districts. One reason for this are the objective material conditions discussed in section 2, including dispossession.[30] Another reason is that Naxalites are able to provide some help to the poor to cope with, and fight against, many of these conditions. They have tried to ensure justice through direct means. The dedicated cadres have initiated 'social changes in their areas of control' (Banerjee, 2006: 3159).[31]

## 3     A Marxist Class-Theoretic Critique of the Naxalite Movement

Yet, as Banerjee (1999: 222) says, '[I]n terms of spatial growth', the Naxalite groups have 'virtually lost their original pockets in West Bengal', and 'have failed to extend their influence beyond their traditional bases', mainly located in the eastern half of the country. Why? Why is there a gap between (a) the potential social and spatial influence of a movement for justice such as that led by Naxalites, given the widespread unjust conditions of existence, and (b) its actual sphere of influence? Could it have a *larger* following, socially (in terms of classes, for example) and geographically, than it has traditionally had? What are its limitations, including of that segment which exclusively focuses on the

---

30    Braud (2015) says that in the contemporary round of globalization, the forcible seizure of land from the Scheduled Tribes in a process similar to primitive accumulation, explains the Naxalites' continuing appeal.

31    Naxalites' developmental activities will be discussed in more details in the next chapter.

armed struggle? The critique presented below will be from a Marxist class perspective.[32]

Focused on the oppression and exploitation of peasants by landlords, the movement is, generally speaking, not powerful in the areas of strong rural capitalism, where wage-workers are subjected to a high level of exploitation both within agriculture and outside (retail, transportation, construction, etc.). It is generally confined to areas where the development of capitalist relations of exploitation is relatively stunted. A certain segment of the Naxalite movement (CPI Maoist) is almost totally confined to the areas demographically dominated by tribals, who constitute less than 10% of the total population of the country. This strategy is not sufficiently sensitive to class differentiation in the aboriginal population (Duyker, 1981). It also leaves out vast sections of economically distressed people, especially the non-aboriginal poor peasants and laborers. The Naxalite mobilization is also generally absent from urban areas (Banerjee, 2017; Sagar, 2006: 3178). This means that the movement is weakly integrated into the class struggle of the non-agrarian working masses.

There is, in my view, a major theoretical reason for all this, which I will *briefly* discuss and aspects of which are ignored in the critical assessments of the movement. Firstly, Naxalites view what are in effect *capitalist relations at a low level of development of productive forces* as some kind of feudal relations of exploitation (or 'semi-feudalism'). This explains why the extent of feudal-type exploitation is overestimated and why, therefore, politically, the movement is confined mainly to economically backward agriculture-dominated areas, ignoring vast swathes of the country reeling under *capitalist*, and increasingly, neoliberal capitalist, exploitation. The Naxalite movement, *like the mainstream communist* movement which it criticizes, believe in a two-stage theory of revolution (a pre-1917 Leninist strategy transcended by Lenin's own *April Theses*, that is systematically ignored by most Indian marxists): a democratic revolution (against feudals) first, and a socialist revolution sometime in the future. The Naxalite movement and the mainstream communist movement are more similar that most people think. The Naxalite movement, like the mainstream Marxist movement from which it separated, is *not* a socialist movement; it is not a movement for socialism. The Naxalites' fight, effectively, amounts to a fight for a better bourgeois society cleared of vestiges of feudalism and without unfree labor relations. Their struggle is for an authentic system of (liberal) democracy, one without autocratic and bureaucratic

---

32    For a critical discussion on Naxalism from a post-colonial perspective, see Seth (2006).

distortions, before any fight against capitalist relations as such can begin.[33] Their ideological-political focus on what they call semi-*feudalism* will continue to keep millions of toiling people outside of their influence, including the reserve army of labor under capitalism. Their lives are adversely impacted by the bourgeoisie, including its so-called 'national' faction.[34] Naxalites' influence – and indeed, the influence of any movement – will be limited *unless* the fight against localized feudal practices (which the Naxalites are right to point to) becomes a part of the fight against the capitalist system *as such*, whether the 'bearers' (Marx, 1977: 92) of that system are national, monopoly or imperialist capitalists. Places where unfree/bonded laborers are used by property owners to make money, leaving ordinary people to starve, and places where employers use modern technology to make large profits, are both parts of the same system. These two kinds of place represent spatially uneven development *under capitalism* (discussed in Chapter 3) and do not require a *temporally uneven* (i.e. two-stage) political strategy. A correct and non-teleological understanding of capitalism and uneven development *within* poor countries such as India is at the heart of the matter here. This understanding Naxalites seem not to have. They seem not to have understood this: capitalism does not promote modern progressive development always and everywhere, so the low level of economic development cannot be automatically seen as existing because of pre-capitalism, or because of relations that are not really capitalism (see Chapter 3). Of course, the Naxalite movement uses such terms as the working class as the agent of revolution, socialism, Leninism, etc. but these terms are used more as an *ideological justification* for their inadequate theory and inadequate practice than anything else.

I have said earlier that conditions of existence have an important influence on the fundamental ideas about these conditions which in turn become a part of conditions of life. And ideas created under certain conditions in one place can travel to another place where these ideas are applied by people without giving due thought to the conditions in which they think and intervene. In

---

33    According to a major Naxalite stream – CPIML (New Democracy): 'The Indian Revolution, taken as a whole, passes through *two distinct stages* of historical development, i.e. the people's democratic and the socialist revolution'. This is the two-stage theory. And in terms of who will participate in the first stage of the revolution:
    'The people's democratic revolution under the leadership of the working class will establish a democratic dictatorship of the working class, the peasantry, the urban petty bourgeoisie and the *national bourgeoisie* under the leadership of the working majority of the Indian people'. The new, people's democratic state will ensure the '*Protection of Industry and trade of national bourgeoisie*' (http://www.cpimlnd.org/party-documents; italics added) (accessed on August 10, 2009).

34    The 'national' faction will be a part of their people's democratic state.

Chapter 1 of *Capital* volume 1, Marx (1977) says that Aristotle said great things about exchange but given the unequal slave society he lived in, he could not develop his ideas about value that underlies the equal exchange of commodities.[35] The Maoist thought that underlies Naxalism commits a kind of 'Aristotelian error' (or, a semi-Aristotelian error). This involves creating ideas about world-society based on what is happening within the narrow confines of a given society. Let me explain.

Consider the following conditions. Capitalist production co-exists with a vast peasantry which is exploited on the basis of rental and usurious extractions. Capitalist property owners resort to unfree labor relations including those based on extra-economic coercion. They also make use of vulnerability of migrant workers. Some of them make use of unfree labor, because it is can be cheaper and can be subjected to discipline more than free labor.[36] It is these sorts of conditions, when not seen in relation to what is happening globally and when not interpreted on the basis of adequate Marxist theory, that give rise of what is called Maoism, including the idea of semi-feudalism.[37] As a set of ideas, Maoism can then travel to another place and another time (for example, modern capitalist India), in the minds of some people. It has. The material conditions in Mao's peasant-dominated China (along with some conjunctural political conditions such as defeats in the city) might have prompted him to not think about (a) the urban wage-labor as the agent of revolution and (b) the idea of revolution against the rule of the capitalist class as opposed to

---

35    Marx (1977) writes in *Capital* vol. 1: 'What is the homogeneous element, i.e. the common substance', which, for example, 'the house represents from the point of view of the bed, in the value expression for the bed? Such a thing, in truth, cannot exist, says Aristotle. But why not? ...Aristotle himself was unable to [understand the fact that in] the form of commodity-values, all labour is expressed as equal human labour ...because Greek society was founded on the labour of slaves, and hence, had as its natural basis, the inequality of men and of their labour powers. The secret of the expression of value, namely, the equality and the equivalence of all kinds of labour' required a new material condition which was 'a society where the commodity-form is the universal form of the product of labour, hence the dominant social relation is the relation between [persons] as possessors of commodities' (pp. 151–152).

36    Marx's general theoretical assumption was that capital-as-a-whole (or capitalism) requires nominally free labor, but surely, *specific capitalists* do not mind at all using unfree labor if by doing so they can reduce the cost of production.

37    Of course, one should not think that mere observation of material conditions can explain the emergence of a specific theory that explains such conditions adequately. If that were the case, everyone in capitalism would become a Marxist armed with the theory of value and surplus value. But it is true that unless capitalism is fully developed, a theory of revolutionary scientific socialism would be impossible. Theory intervenes between material conditions and one's understanding of those conditions.

the revolution against feudal oppressors. These conditions might have, in part, given rise to the over-emphasis on peasants or small-scale self-employed property owners (in isolation from the urban working class) as the main agents of revolution.[38] Perhaps the specific conditions made him commit the Aristotelian error of sorts.

Now, these *ideas* have been influencing what are called Maoist political strategies in our times. One might ask: what makes India's Naxalites – and Indian communists as such – not to see that there is a much greater prevalence of wage-labor in modern-day India, which is a part of a world that is decisively capitalist. And does such recognition (dominance of wage-labor and of capitalist form of private property and of exploitation) not have serious implications for communist politics, including the fact that wage-workers allied with the non-exploiting peasants on coming to power, cannot but transcend capitalism, which means that a process of democratic revolution cannot be separated from socialist revolution? Aristotle did not live in a society dominated by value relations, so he could not theorize value. But Indian Naxalites live in India which is dominated by the capitalist law of value, and where the vast majority of direct producers are exploited on the basis of the appropriation of surplus value (in absolute or relative form) and yet, the central focus of their politics – like that of mainstream communist politics – is not fighting capitalist class relations (wage-slavery) as such.

So, Naxalites do not say 'no' to capitalism as such (they do not intend to and they do not need to abolish capitalist class relations, although they use anti-capitalist and socialistic terminology), for according to them, India lacks the dominance of capitalist production relations. India, for them, is still a semi-*feudal* (and semi-colonial) country.[39] They must then agree that the suffering of the masses is not fundamentally caused by capitalist class relation. A *democratic* capitalism, i.e. a capitalism which is free from neo-colonialism and feudalism and which uses free labor always and everywhere, is yet to exist, according to them. Such a capitalism must first be made to exist under the tutelage of Maoists. Many 'conscious capitalists', capitalists with a conscience, and

---

38    When the movement began, the Chinese communist party praising it said this in July 1967: 'The Indian revolution must take the road of relying on peasants, establishing base areas in the countryside, persisting in protracted armed struggle and using the countryside to encircle and finally capture the cities. This is Mao Tse-tung's road' (quoted in Bagchi, 2017).

39    As mentioned earlier, the Naxalite view that Indian society is semi-colonial/semi-feudal is conceptually inadequate (Basu and Das, 2013; for a critique of this view from the standpoint of concrete conditions in parts of the red corridor, see Shah, 2013). Yet, it cannot be denied that feudal practices persist within state apparatuses and within civil society and that India is increasingly under the onslaught of imperialism.

their ideologues (e.g. Amartya Sen; Vandana Shiva; many Aam Aadmi party supporters) would like to address the problems which Naxalites talk about and fight against: social and geographical inequality, corruption, poverty, landlessness, illiteracy, social discrimination, fraudulent practices of businesses, crony-capitalism, etc.[40] For example, a part of their protest against mining capitalists taking away people's land is the idea that they can control capitalist businesses in a more people-friendly way. Even Arundhati Roy, who is an enthusiastic supporter of Naxalites, and who believes in going beyond communism and capitalism, and who is no Marxist, thinks that Naxalites' industrialization policy is 'woolly' (2011: 210). Thus, in terms of Marxist class theory, Naxalism is very problematic.

Associated with their problematic view of the class character of India is their view of revolutionary agency, which is their second big theoretical problem: if capitalist exploitation is not the dominant form of exploitation, then wage-labor cannot be main agent of revolution. For them, rural oppressed classes (peasants, including Adivasi peasants) can lead a revolution. This view mistakenly conflates the capacity for revolutionary action with the degree to which a group is oppressed and poverty-stricken (e.g. peasants and adivasis). They seem oblivious of the fact that: the most oppressed group may not be the most revolutionary group (against capitalism). They also forget that: the peasantry are stratified into different classes including a class which exploits poor peasants/laborers and that the peasantry are geographically dispersed in thousands of villages. The non-exploiting independent peasants do have the ability to fight against exploitation and oppression by landlords, moneylenders and state officials but they cannot lead a revolution against the system of private property relations as such. Peasants' class instinct is generally proprietary; it is not coherent and collectivist as the class instinct of the urban proletariat potentially is. This fact is demonstrated by cadres of the Naxalite movement. Kunnath's Maoist respondent, Raju Bhai, very much wanted a piece of private property, as did the hero of the celebrated Indian novel, *Godaan* (the Gift of a cow). Any future success of the movement will be limited by its denial of the dominance of, and therefore, the need to remove, capitalist class relations as such. Its success will also be limited by its actual neglect of the role of the wage-earners in factories and offices as the pre-eminent anti-capitalist force, whose interest lies in their political independence vis-à-vis all sections of the business-class (compradore or not). In class terms, the Naxalite movement is *not* as

---

40    Mazumdar said in 1970 that the majority of the business-people would support the People's democratic revolution as they are a large part of the national bourgeoisie (in Banerjee, 1980).

threatening, as the state and some intellectuals think it is. However, by producing the image that it is the single biggest security threat and by labelling *any* movement for justice as Naxalite, the state is using its fight against movement(s) such as Naxalism as an excuse to eliminate any opposition to class rule, including the possibility of the Naxalites' fight for democratic capitalism from becoming a fight against capitalism as such.

There is some relation between Naxalite's theory of class society and their view of how to launch class struggle. Naxalites emphasize extra-economic coercion aspect of exploitation, and not economic-coercion that is the hallmark of the capitalist value relation. This view – coupled with their view of liberal democracy (discussed below) – is partly behind the stress on military struggle within a segment of the movement. The violence practiced by Maoist revolutionary squads, as a part of the Naxalite movement, must be seen as problematic. The ruling class and its state are not Gandhians. So the class struggle below cannot be Gandhian. It is true that the Indian state uses violence to crush people's movements for justice. This is the reality. 'Indian Maoists have at least addressed this reality, even if inadequately, and their very success in sustaining themselves among the poorest is testimony to the partial efficacy of taking up arms. However, for a segment of the Naxalite movement, what should be at best a defensive posture, politically subordinated to a more sophisticated strategy for long-term transformation, has unfortunately become the main strategy itself' (Vanaik, 2011: 107). The issue, therefore, is not whether violence can be used for a defensive cause. The issue is whether violence – and that too, secretive violence by individuals – can be the central method of class struggle. It cannot be.

The Naxalites' armed action is being used by the state as a justification for killing Naxalite supporters who are among the organic leaders of the exploited classes.[41] Such killings by the state are weakening the movement (Banerjee, 2017). The practice of violence affects the political culture of the movement. First, in many areas, anyone who challenges the government about its inactions and who fights for legal rights (e.g. payment of minimum wages), runs the risk of being labelled a Naxalite. And, the 'Naxal label' means punishment. Once one is labelled a Naxalite, it is difficult to return to normal life, relatively free from suspicion, fear and death. So people depend on the party to help them deal with the police and the courts. Thus, many people may remain in

---

41    They are killed by landlord armies supported by mainstream political parties. They are
      also killed by state's military forces or by state-sponsored civilian militias.

the party because they need its protection, and not necessarily because of ideological commitment (Bhatia, 2006: 3181). In the absence of ideologically committed cadres, the social and geographical expansion of the movement suffers. Secondly, there is a culture of intolerance amongst Naxalites towards those holding a different political view, including parties and leaders of the parliamentary left and even those of fraternal Naxalite factions. And the tension is often resolved through violent encounter. This strategy undermines conditions under which intellectual and political efforts can be made towards broad and principled 'Left unity' (a united front within which movements of proletarians and semi-proletarians march separately but strike together) that the radical resolution of the unjust material conditions demands (I am here abstracting from the fact that even if such a united front happens, the two-stage theory of revolution that binds all the elements of the front, including the Naxalites, and the political practices that theory will inform, will be an enormous obstacle to a socialist revolution) and constitute a crisis of revolutionary leadership.

Continuous armed conflicts between state forces and a part of the Naxalite movement have also drastically reduced the space for other forms of struggle (non-violent struggles) and thus compounds the problem that arises out of the movement's neglect of the urban working class. The stress on violent methods on the part of certain sections of the movement does dilute the emphasis on whatshouldbedone:democraticallyorganized,proletarian,political-ideological education and organization (see Haragopal, 2017).[42] As Lenin (1978: 11) said in *Revolutionary Adventurism*: '*without* the working people all bombs are powerless, patently powerless'.

Political power of the masses to challenge the whole capitalist system does not come from the Maoist 'barrel of the gun'. Nor does it come from 'semi-spontaneous consciousness' (of peasants, etc.) (cf. Guha, 1983). The latter is, more or less, a reaction to desperate conditions needing some urgent change. But revolutionary consciousness is a different matter: it reflects the imperative of destroying the relics of capital's history (e.g. feudal landlordism) and of transcending the capitalist system along with undemocratic and imperialist ways in which that system operates. Such a consciousness, including among sections of the peasantry, has to be *actively* worked for, both through education and

---

42    Speaking about the section of the Naxalite movement that prioritizes armed struggle, Haragopal (2017) says that whether the movement will succeed in achieving its goal (i.e. new democracy) will depend on whether it prioritizes political mobilization over its military strategy (see also Murzban, 2014; and Mukherji, 2012 for critiques of Maoist strategy of using violent methods of struggle). Interestingly, like most commentators on Naxalism, Haragopal does not challenge Naxalism's two-stage theory of revolution.

struggle. Such a process must not at all denigrate class consciousness (of peasants and others) in its 'embryonic form' (Lenin, 1977a: 113), including the consciousness which is the raw material of, and which is expressed in the form of, the Naxalite movement.

As I have said, Naxalites' view of liberal democracy is linked to their view of class struggle and the use of arms. A sympathetic analyst of the movement, Professor Mohanty (2006) says that a part of the Maoism-inspired movement has not fully recognized the importance of the liberal democratic process. One can also say that the movement – especially, the segment that emphasizes arms struggle – has not fully understood the *educative* role of practice (i.e. struggle). Liberal democracy is a form of bourgeois-class rule and yet it exists because the masses struggle for it and demand it. It is not a mere concession from the ruling classes; they would be happy to suspend it when doing so is in their interest. This is in fact happening now, as we will see in our discussion later on fascistic tendencies. To paraphrase Marx's second famous Thesis on Feuerbach (Marx and Engels, 1977: 13), whether the state and the ruling classes can meet the radical demands of the exploited classes cannot be (just) a '*scholastic* question'.[43] It is to be resolved in practice, i.e. through their own struggles for radical demands, and, therefore, it is 'a *practical* question'. Democratically-organized mass movements are necessary in struggling to get some material concessions from the state and the propertied classes. Naxalite areas are among the poorest in the country. There are, therefore, numerous things to struggle for, including: publicly provided schools, electricity, water and health centers (Bhatia, 2006: 3181). There is a need for struggles for a living wage and the right to employment and for free transportation. 'However, these issues get eclipsed since most of the Naxalite groups do not wish to engage with the present government except as an enemy' (Bhatia, 2006: 3181). This is because, in my view, Naxalite leaders possibly assume that the *theoretical* knowledge about the state (what it can and cannot do) that *they* possess is shared by the *masses*. This is a serious epistemological lapse. The bourgeois democratic process, within limits, offers to social movements for justice, some limited possibilities for exposing the patently undemocratic practices and developmental failures of the state and ruthless exploitation by the ruling classes (domestic and foreign). It is useful in educating the masses about the limits to what is possible

---

43    Some feminists and anti-caste thinkers believe that the state is not as inflexible as Marxists think because it can meet a variety of *their* demands (see Gudavarthy, 2005: 5417).

　　　Marxists have made the theoretical argument that: the state will not cross some well-defined limits in terms of meeting the demands of exploited classes. Those who are not convinced by this *theoretical* answer may find the answer in and through *practice* (= struggle).

within the system and about alternative anti-capitalist, anti-feudal demands. The process of struggle for concessions creates a condition for building solidarity and promoting class-consciousness, at multiple scales, among the exploited classes. They must emerge as agents of their self-emancipation *in the process of* fighting for these concessions at multiple scales. One, of course, does not have to believe that the state can or will meet these demands, but the masses must discover the limits to what the state can do partly in practice, i.e. in the process of making their demands.

Finally, the movement has been said to have paid in-adequate attention to gender and caste issues *in practice*. It has sought to respond a potential problem here. Celebrating the 50th anniversary of the movement that began in Naxalbari in 1967, and presenting a history of the movement, Bhattacharya, who is a major ideologue of the Naxalite movement and a leader of the CPI(ML) says:

> Naxalbari was a great moment of radicalisation of the Indian communist movement. It gave rise to a new paradigm of class struggle that is not confined to the economic realm or the parameters of parliamentary politics, but committed to fight out oppression and injustice in every sphere of social existence. Issues of caste and gender, race and nationality, language and culture found their rightful place in this new praxis of class struggle.
>
> BHATTACHARYA, 2017

The Naxalite movement does emphasize the fight against non-class oppression. Yet, some critics say, patriarchal attitudes and practices persist within Naxal organizations (Mohanty, 2006: 3164). Women are almost negligible in leadership positions. The movement seeks to 'create new casteless, classless communities where women will be equal to men' but it is 'most often led by men from elite backgrounds' (Shah, 2017: 55). Shah adds: 'In the Maoist case, although many Adivasis and, in some areas, women joined the revolutionaries, the higher-caste leaders not only failed to give sufficient space for the nurturing of lower-caste, Adivasi and women leaders, but also seemed to neglect the fact that the societies they worked amidst had more egalitarian gender relations than the ones from which they had come' (ibid.). The hard and dangerous work of handling guns is mainly done by Dalits or people from the lower castes, and those who get killed belong mostly to these sections (Bhatia, 2006: 3180). Tribals, Dalits and other low caste people comprising the bulk of their support base 'are not [yet] adequately represented in the upper echelons of the party leadership' (ibid.). Culturally, while 'song writing, tune setting and writing of poetry [generally] ...centred around the SC (Scheduled Castes) and OBC

(Other Backward Classes) *wadas* in the villages, ...writing theory and speech making still remained an upper caste phenomenon' within the movement (Il-aiah, 2004: 238).

## 4    Conclusion

Making history, from a class standpoint, means that existing conditions of life are not acceptable because they are exploitative and oppressive, and that new and better conditions of life can, and must, be created through political struggles against the class/classes responsible for the existing conditions. The act of making history (and geography) in a class-society *is* class struggle. This chapter is about class and class struggle in the historical-geographical context of post-colonial India. It discusses how relations of class as well as caste- and gender-based social oppression have created extremely difficult conditions of living for workers and peasants in rural and aboriginal areas, which the post-colonial capitalist-landlord state has, more or less, failed to significantly mitigate. The conjunctural combination of unjust conditions of living and the failure of the state to significantly alleviate these conditions has created a situation ripe for *class* struggle, one instance of which is the Naxalite movement, a part of the world-wide Maoist movement.[44] Its growth and spatial spread have been uneven in time and space. The movement has much appeal among the poor in many areas. This, like other similar movements, 'are explicit rejections of both the right to commoditize and appropriate natural resources and the exclusion from development of peoples in poor areas containing natural resources' (Herring, 2013: 131). The Naxalite movement, along with other such instances of political action by the masses (e.g. trade union struggles mentioned earlier), suggest, once again, that the masses are not passive victims of exploitation and oppression.

The Naxalite movement is rooted in material conditions of existence, social-cultural as well as economic. It has fruitfully combined class politics (albeit in a rather limited manner) as well as those of cultural oppression. Thus the Naxalite movement shares important characteristics of what Veltmeyer (1997) calls 'new peasant movements' in his research on peasants in Latin America. Many people within the state agencies, and many middle class people, do not

---

44    Gomes (2015: 106) says: 'the story behind the Maoist Conflict in India is a story of grievances arising out of feelings of exclusion of various forms. We see how the underdeveloped districts and districts with higher land inequality are more prone to conflict'.

fully understand Naxalites' pro-poor ideological significance. Partly influenced by a militaristic thinking, they homogenize the movement associating it exclusively with violence, and treating Naxalites merely/mainly as armed thugs, without any political and socio-economic program of development for the poor.[45]

However, the Naxalite movement does suffer from serious problems which emanate from its inadequate class-based understanding and class-based practice. The material conditions of deprivation are produced dominantly by the specific ways in which capitalism works in the concrete conditions of India, which include remnants of feudalism, and liberal democracy, within the system of global capitalism. The Naxalites have not fully and consistently understood this: that the most important reason for rural distress, and indeed the distress of the majority of the country's population, is the *capitalist* character of the system, which is also mainly responsible for state's failure to mitigate some of the adverse effects of the system on the poor. Because of the Naxalites' inadequate understanding of the system's dynamics, their dominant focus has been mistakenly on the rural/agrarian issue (in backward regions) and on its so-called 'semi-feudal' shell. This has meant that the movement has, more or less, been disconnected socially from the working class and spatially from urban areas, the main theatres of accumulation and exploitation by both domestic and imperialist bourgeoisie.

It is not popular to say this, but the reality is this: class is the most fundamental determinant of life. The ways in which class relations work in a historical-geographical situation, including through relations of gender and caste/ethnicity, etc., tend to create unjust conditions of existence. These conditions necessitate, prompt as well as influence class struggle, whose success in any given time and place is not guaranteed. Inspired by Maoism, the Naxalite movement, like other movements for justice, originated and continues to exist because of the extremely unjust material conditions of existence of millions of ordinary working people. The continuation of the movement is due also to the Naxalites being able to provide some relief to the suffering masses and help them stand up for their rights (as discussed in the next chapter). Yet, inadequate class-analysis and inadequate political practice, along with state repression, have limited the success of the movement.

---

45    Of course, a segment of the movement is itself no less responsible for such a perception as it too seems to be eager to propagate armed struggle (Gupta, 2006: 3172).

# State Repression as Class Struggle from Above

When the state is not responsive to ordinary people's needs, and when the normal operation of the economic system does not meet their needs, what do they do?[1] They engage in struggles, small or large, covert and overt, legal or illegal, against the state and against the economic system, protected by the state. India is known not only for the dual failure – state failure and economy's or market's failure – and associated poverty and inequality and social oppression. India is also known for its history of popular struggles against all forms of injustice.

Rural class struggle informed by Maoism is one of these struggles, as we have discussed in the previous chapter. It has mobilized poor people against sections of the propertied class (e.g. landlords, traders; mining companies) for social justice in India. The movement has conferred limited benefits upon the poor in some places. It is not averse to using violence to get these benefits and to stop them from being taken away. The Indian state seeks to violently repress it, killing thousands. Anyone suspected of having any links with the Naxalite movement, and especially, with that faction of it which the state has banned, can be jailed or killed. This raises wider conceptual questions about the relation between social movements (movements against injustice) and the state. Why does a liberal-democratic state kill its own citizens?

It must be made clear at the outset that a critique of the Indian state's violent response to the Maoist movement does not *at all* mean an endorsement of how Maoists understand society and seek to change it. This chapter takes the position that: long-term structural changes in society require active self-emancipatory participation of politically conscious masses in cities and villages in social-political mobilization against exploitation and injustice, and that emphasizing violent methods of destruction as a strategy, cannot construct conditions for social justice, even though such methods may yield short-term localized results.

The first section of the chapter briefly and critically discusses the existing conceptual literature on state repression of social movements, and presents a preliminary attempt at an alternative approach to the topic. The next two sections provide some empirical evidence, including from newspaper reports,[2]

---

1 An earlier version of this chapter appeared as Das (2017).
2 The use of newspaper reports in the social movements research has become a popular source (Earl et al., 2004); their online availability as a 'cyber-common-property resource' has

which supports this approach: while the second section looks at the state's ideological-repressive response to the movement, the third section examines why the state deploys violent means against it. The final section draws out some conceptual implications of the discussion.


1        State Response to 'Social' Movement: A Conceptual Discussion

There is a large literature on why social struggles/movements occur in rural areas (Anderson and Seligson, 1994; Castells, 1983; Houtzager, 2000; Oslender, 2004; Page, 1975; Skocpol, 1982) and in society at large (Auvinen, 1997; Dudley and Miller, 1998; MacCulloch, 2005; Miller, 2000; Morris, 2000). This chapter focusses on the state's response to social or people's movements: in particular, its violent response (della Porta, 1996, 2014; Hess and Martin, 2006; Ondetti, 2006;[3] Fominaya and Wood, 2011; Ortiz, 2013). Among the various explanations, I will deal with two: state form (i.e. whether it is liberal-democratic) and social nature of protesters.[4]

Lack of democracy – democratic state form – is said to cause state repression. In democracies, agents of repression are less able to function without some form of civilian oversight, which compels them to exert greater effort in justifying their action (Davenport, 2004: 542).[5] Repression may hurt politicians'

---

contributed to this trend. Of course, this common property resource is increasingly in danger of being controlled by capitalist companies in their own interest.

3   The last two sources consider how unjust state repression can engender social mobilization.

4   There are other explanations as well. For example: it is argued that repression can also make individuals realize that the state has the monopoly of force within society and thus pre-empt future anti-state resistance (Davenport, 2004). Also argued is that state's repressive activity in the past enhances its possibility at present. '[O]nce specialized agencies of state coercion are in operation, elites are likely to calculate that the relative costs of relying on coercion are lower... Moreover, directors [of repressive agencies] may ... recommend [or initiate] violent "solutions" to suspected opposition... as a means of justifying ... [their] continued existence' (Gurr, 1986: 160). It has also been said that elites who have used violence to gain power (or for national consolidation) will use violence to remain in power, as they believe that their past success in the use of violence will repeat itself (Gurr, 1988: 52). Thus state's (state actors') interests and state structure (especially its repressive structures) explain state's repressive activity. This view has some merit, but it is problematic. Just the fact that specialized agencies and methods of coercion exist does not mean that the state will use these against a given social movement.

5   It should be noted that: in some cases where mass movements have used peaceful means to challenge the state, and succeeded in changing public opinion in favor of the movement and against state policy, particular governments have had to exert greater effort in justifying their repressive actions, because the social movement has been a kind of educator of the public, and a shaper of public opinion.

prospect of returning to office. Democracy creates spaces for non-violent methods of resolving conflicts through political parties and elections (Henderson, 1991). Effective democracy also provides citizens – at least those with political resources – the tool to oust potentially abusive leaders from office (ibid.). The democratic state can also use non-coercive measures – concessions/reforms – to meet challenges from internal opposition (Gurr, 1988: 55). '[T]he more libertarian a state is, the less intense its violence can and tends to become' (Rummel, 1984: 443; 1985). A libertarian state guarantees not only basic civil liberties and political rights but also economic freedom. Indeed, if the state regulates economic affairs less, there will be less violence: 'the more government, the more violence' (Rummel, 1984: 461).[6]

In sum, the liberal argument is that: democracy pacifies. But this argument suffers from several problems. That democracy provides citizens the tool to oust potentially abusive leaders from office (or to force them to change their policies significantly) assumes the following: people's resistance is in a form that is approved by the state, and that electoral participation is an effective way of redressing inequalities. But most importantly the 'democracy pacifies' argument fails to properly recognize the constraining effect of private property relations (combined with a market-mode of resource allocation and use) on the exercise of democratic rights of ordinary people and on state's power to address their problems by giving meaningful material concessions. State repression of those protesting austerity points to this fact. As Dryzek (1996) argues, business demands on the state, whether in India or the USA, restrict state's political options, more or less, to those that support capitalist interests, even if these are anti-democratic and hurt the interests of the majority. Further, repression may not hurt chances of returning to office if *all* major political parties agree on the legitimacy of repression of given movements for social justice, and they *will* agree if they believe in the sanctity of private property and free markets. Further, to say that a state which controls economic affairs less will be less violent is to suggest that we should expect a saintly state and peaceful society. Instead, the 'more' capitalist the state becomes in its day-today activities, the less scope it has, to meet the demands of ordinary people, and therefore the more violent it tends to be in response to these demands.

People's democratic right is a valuable gain (Bobbio, 2005) obtained/sustained through struggle. A capitalist society with liberal democracy is better

---

6  Thus democratic institutions eliminate the desire for repression by opening up the political system to citizens, the need for repression by providing other mechanisms of influence, and the capacity for repression by curtailing the freedom of coercive agents (Davenport, 2004: 539; also Schatzman, 2005).

than one without.[7] But democracy, which is a form of class rule, generally does a good job of amicably resolving material-ideological conflicts that are *internal* not only to the ruling classes (e.g. conflicts among various fractions of ruling classes over access to state support for them or over how to manage the capitalist system) but also to the political elite of different political parties, an elite that is broadly supportive of these classes. Democracy may cause a time lag between a movement's beginning and onset of repression. But it is unlikely to stop the state from using repressive measures against a radical social movement that challenges certain aspects of class relations (e.g. unequal distribution of land) and certain effects of these relations (e.g. poverty, etc.).[8]

In the second explanation of state violence, protesters using non-institutional and confrontational tactics[9] are seen by the state as a greater threat, so they face greater repression than the dissidents not using these tactics (Davenport, 2004; Poe and Tate, 1994). These kinds of protest provide authorities with a legitimate mandate to sanction them as a law and order measure. But this explanation is also inadequate: peaceful protests (e.g. Occupy protests) have been routinely repressed, if they go beyond the limit of what the state and the ruling class will tolerate.[10]

An alternative explanation of state repression of people's struggles must these two approaches as points of departure. It must, at the minimum, look at the class character of the state and of mobilizations/protestors. First the latter. One must recognize two things here. For one thing, it is the subordinate strata of proletarian and semi-proletarian *classes,* who have little (informal) access to state power, that tend to use non-institutional tactics. For another, these classes or class-strata are considered a serious threat not just because of the *way* in which they rebel (i.e. the non-institutional method of protest) but because of *what* they rebel against: the fact that they rebel against what the state must

---

7    Maoists (and others) realized this during the mid-1970s when civil liberties were suspended in India.

8    On contradictory empirical effects of capitalism on human rights, see Burkhart (2002).

9    The word 'non-institutional' refers to direct action and extra-electoral methods.

10   Further, the chances of repression are said to be greater when the threat comes from subordinate protestors because they are said to collapse under pressure owing to their limited retaliatory power (Stockdill, 1996 in Earl, 2003). Failure of the attempt to repress will invite public ridicule, so easy targets – subordinate protestors – are more prone to repression. Thus, protests that are threatening (because they use non-institutional tactics) and that are weak (because they cannot retaliate easily) will be most prone to repression (Earl, 2003: 54). Research indeed shows that events in which subordinate groups participate are more likely to invite police action (Earl et al., 2003). But the reason for this may not necessarily be that that they are weak and have limited retaliatory power (India's Naxalites have much retaliatory power). Instead of their weakness, we must stress the class character, and therefore, class power, of the subordinate protestors.

protect (i.e. aspects of the private property system such as dispossession, super-exploitation, etc.).

In understanding why the state represses social movements, one must stress the class character of the state as well.[11] Whatever else it may be, 'the state is an organ of class rule, an organ for the oppression of one class by another; it is the creation of "order", which legalizes and perpetuates this oppression' within a given territory (Lenin, 1977b: 11). Its most fundamental objective is to protect exploitative private property relations and sustain/promote the associated mechanisms of accumulation (Das, 2006; Draper, 1977: 251). Class relations are fundamentally coercive, even under capitalism which celebrates individual freedom. For example, the reproduction of capitalist class relations (including the market-imperative) is based on the continuing separation of laborers from means of production. This separation has to be reproduced continuously. People are dispossessed of their land (and indeed access to common property and state's limited benefits), and often through state and private force. This happened during Marx's times (Marx, 1977: 874–876), and this happens now (Donnelly, 1989; Farid, 2005; Harvey, 2003).[12] People have to work under the 'despotic' control of property owners as well (Marx, 1977: 477, 548–550), surrendering much of the fruit of their labor to capital. This despotism often takes the form of violence against the masses, including proletarian and semi-proletarian women.

Every movement or mobilization is not directly against the existence of private property relations as such. A movement can fight against the ways in which these relations work or against the actual effects produced by these relations. For example, they can be against property owners not paying (minimum) wages or against the extension of the working day much beyond the normal. When laborers have the right to get minimum wages and employers

---

11    By state I refer to a set of institutions which exercise monopoly over the means of violence and whose main aim is to control the subordinate classes and protect the private property rights of the exploiting classes. The state, which appears to be neutral and to represent political equality, is rooted in substantive inequalities. This does not mean that all institutions of the state (e.g. police, army, judiciary, legislature, executive, various local branches of the state) work necessarily in tandem at a given point in time, nor that every single action of the state is pro-capitalist (in an immediate sense). There is a wide range of views on the state. Some have debated the state as an autonomous entity (Skocpol, 1985), a tool for the powerful classes (Domhoff, 1990; Mills, 1959), and as a structure of relations that work to create conditions for accumulation (Poulantzas, 1968). Others have discussed the state as an ensemble of representations, processes, and practices (e.g. Lemke, 2007; Mitchell, 1999; Sharma and Gupta, 2006). For recent reviews of ideas about the state, see Pressman, 2006.

12    Capitalism is also coercive in another sense: having been separated from access to means of production, people must depend on the uncertain labor market to find work, and if they don't, they starve; and this reliance on property owners must be reproduced by the state through coercive enforcement of private property relations (Marx, 1977: 272–273).

have the right to set the wage the way they want, or whenever peasants have a right to live and work in an area and companies want that area for factories or to extract minerals, it is often the case that '[b]etween equal rights, force decides' (Marx, 1977: 344). And, this force is generally (and in the last instance) the force of the state used on behalf of the property owners. The regime of low-wages is coercively reinforced. If lower classes challenge the right to private property, or the ways in which property owners accumulate wealth/income, this would be framed by the state as non-negotiable or difficult-to-negotiate. So, the movement faces violence. Whether the *mode/form* of such a movement is non-institutional/confrontational/violent is generally immaterial as far as the cause of state violence is concerned. The *content* of the movement, its class content, is moot. And the state being democratic or not is largely beside the point.

It would be inaccurate to state that the state rules only by coercion. It does not, as Gramsci has suggested. Sometimes it does introduce measures to alleviate the negative *effects* of private property relations and of mechanisms of class-based accumulation. Decentralized governance which moves the government administration to people's doorsteps, some redistribution of income and assets, employment creation through public works, and so on *are* implemented by the state. The state does this often in response to (violent and non-violent) movements.[13] Development measures of the state are a relatively cheap means of earning legitimacy. Legitimacy comes from the mere introduction of the measures (measures on paper, the very discourse of measures or of development). It also comes from their limited implementation, the actual concessions (e.g. developmental benefits). Many measures do remain on paper or under-implemented because their implementation will hurt the economic elite (for example, a significant rise in wages that is mediated/enforced by the state will adversely affect profits of capitalists, and state-enforced land redistribution without compensation to big landlords will affect the interests of landlords).[14] If a movement of subordinate strata fights for the implementation of pro-poor policies beyond a *given limit*, the state tends to make the movement a target for attack. Whether there is liberal democracy and whether protesters are violent is, once again, beside the matter. These two factors can, generally, only shape the magnitude of state violence and how quickly the state violence comes as a response.

---

13    The relatively autonomous role of an enlightened state leadership cannot be ruled out.

14    This is the case, according to some, even if in the conflict between the government and the Naxalite movement, the government programs make 'civilians more willing to support the police because it improves the relationship between the government and the people' (Khanna and Zimmerman, 2017: 132) and can, if effectively implemented, potentially mitigate violence (Dasgupta et al., 2017).

And finally, we must bear in mind the scalar character of the state in relation to effects of democracy on repression. Both economic reproduction of class relations and state's support for these relations happen at different scales. There are property owners (e.g. landowners; mining business) whose economic operations are more locally oriented, and others which are more nationally and globally oriented. State activities also exist at different scales: local, provincial and national (Cox, 1990). Challenge to capitalist relations and the state happen at different scales, therefore. A *nation*-state may be liberal-democratic as indicated by its national constitution and by social-political practices at the national scale, but at the *local* scale state institutions may be much less democratic. This partly reflects interests of ruling classes at the local-scale and the ways in which their interests support, and are supported by, undemocratic relations of gender, racial and caste inequalities. The argument that democracy reduces violence must be tempered by the fact that at the local scale there may be very little democracy in practice and therefore any resistance against the state, violent or not, will tend to meet with violent response from the state. Of course, the actual level of violence depends on the place-specific balance between state power and the power of the subordinate classes/class-strata.

This power balance is often upset in many places. The northern region of West Bengal State in India was such a place. Like many other regions of India, it has a long history of peasants' and workers' movement (Kennedy and Purushotham, 2012). From the early 1950s, a radical section of the Communist Party of India (CPI) organized peasants in West Bengal's Naxalbari subdivision of Darjeeling district. This is when the Maoist movement began and spread to other parts of the country. We have discussed some aspect of the movement in the previous chapter. In this chapter, the focus is on state's response to the movement.

## 2        The Indian State's Response to the Naxalite Movement

The Indian state has responded to the Naxalite movement by mainly two means: a developmental means which aims to produce consent of the affected masses to the legitimacy of the state, and a non-developmental (coercive) means. The deployment of the non-developmental means is supported by the third form of state response: an ideological struggle against the Naxalite movement. Ideologically fighting against the movement, the state is keen on 'bracketing the Naxalite movement with the terrorism of ... different religious, ethnic or linguistic varieties' (Banerjee, 2002). At one time, the Home Ministry described Naxalism as a 'more formidable threat than (posed by) Islamic fundamentalist groups'.[15] The state describes the movement: as a 'menace', and as 'left-wing *extremism*'. It engages in the domestic othering of the Naxalite area of influence ('the Red Corridor') as 'unpatriotic', 'undemocratic', a 'diseased zone' (Malreddy, 2014).[16] For the state:

> The perversion of Naxalism has to be traced to its very roots in the ideological concepts like class struggle and class violence and a demonology created by them. It is this demonology that then leads to terrorist acts...It is easy to understand that these concepts and the acts of violence that flow from these concepts have no sanction whatsoever ... in Indian philosophy and culture... Naxalism is a crime against humanity.
>
> GOI, 1998

In a speech in 1998, India's Home Minister belonging to BJP (Bharatiya Janata Party), a Hindu Right party, said that Naxalism is a 'particularly dangerous challenge to the rule of Law, to the Constitutional order, to the nation's *internal and external security* and to the supremacy and legitimacy of the Indian State itself' (GOI, 1998).[17] He added: Naxalism 'has blurred the distinctive nature of a war on the borders by making every street and every home a frontier of the nation. ... Naxalism is an enemy of the Indian dream [dream of an India free from hunger, fear and corruption]' (ibid.). In April 2006, addressing a day-long meeting of chief ministers of the provinces hit by Naxalism, the then Prime Minister, Mr. Singh, of the Congress Party, said: 'It would not be an exaggeration to say that the problem of Naxalism is the single biggest internal security challenge ever faced by our country' (quoted in *Rediff*, 2006). It is also a threat

---

15    http://www.dcrcdu.org/dcrc/Navalakha.doc.

16    Malreddy (2014) says that Indian state's response to the Maoist insurgency has been ideologically shaped by the 'new terrorism' discourse of Western powers, following the absolutely condemnable terrorist attack on the US; this discourse 'others' Islamic terrorism as a trope of a 'civilizational clash' between East and West.

17    Given the fascistic right's deep antagonism towards left forces, the onslaught against Naxalites continues under the Hindu-nationalist government in power now, which is a major threat to democratic rights of ordinary people (Das, 2016). BJP's Home Minister Rajnath Singh says he can finish the Maoists in '3 years' (by 2016) by flooding Chhattisgarh with troops. The Rightwing BJP government will not be any less authoritarian than the centrist securalist government of earlier times. 'The only change from the so-called "security and development" approach of the [earlier] regime, is the "securitise and communalise" approach of the BJP and its associates, illustrated by the recent announcement that "non-Hindus" would not be allowed into Bastar villages and the plan to develop sangh parivar-scripted "local histories" of adivasi areas'. (Sundar, 2014b). Sundar adds: 'what we have is not an anti-Maoist plan but an anti-adivasi plan since it is they who will bear the brunt of the government's onslaught'.

to democracy and to 'our way of life' (ibid.). Thus in the eyes of the state, the Naxalite struggle is ideological and is against the nation's cultural tradition. According to both of the biggest parties of the capitalists and landowners (the Congress and the BJP), Naxalism is a threat not to the oppressive practices of certain property owners but a threat to the *nation as a whole*, and one that exists every*where* within the national space. In other words, the Naxalite threat is scaled up: it is 'nationalized'. This allows the state to exaggerate the level of threat it poses, so that consent can be produced to the national-scale mobilization of military forces against the movement.[18]

Extraordinary police powers and the draconian laws have been used against Naxalites (SAHRDC, 2002). The Prevention of Terrorism Ordinance (POTA) of 2001 was promulgated during the BJP rule. It has now been repealed under public pressure. When civil society activists toured six districts of Jharkhand State between January 29 and February 3, 2003, they found that most of those arrested under POTA were cultivators, students or daily wage-earners. A majority of them were booked because they had provided food to Naxalites or possessed Naxal literature. When asked how a Naxalite is identified, a senior police official told reporters: 'Anyone caught with a copy of the Communist Manifesto or Mao's Red Book becomes a suspicious character. We then watch him and often find clinching evidence'.[19] A police officer said to Arundhati Roy (2009): if people in the forests have malaria tablets and Dettol (an antiseptic and disinfectant liquid) bottles which come from outside, they must be Maoists, and his 'boys' kill them. State killing of Naxalites continues (Figure 9.1 below). Between 1994 and 2014 (October end), security personnel have killed 29,904 Maoists/Naxalites, producing an annual average death of 1424, or 4 deaths a day (one every 6 hours).

'Encounters' are usually faked by the police to cover up the torture and subsequent murder of Naxalite suspects and sympathizers. These are extra-judicial killings by the liberal-democratic state. In many areas, hundreds of young men attend the police stations every week. Sympathizers of Naxalites are picked up at midnights (Murali, 2003). The state has deployed civilian militias which have been involved in rape, torture and displacement of aboriginal people. The Operation Green Hunt – a massive mobilization of paramilitary forces – is on. Militarized zones are produced in parts of India: 'Today Jharkhand [a province in eastern India] is a fully militarized zone. There are over a hundred bases

---

18    In more recent times, the state has threatened intellectuals who sympathize with Naxalism.

19    A Human Rights Watch Briefing Chapter for the 59th Session of the United Nations Commission on Human Rights March 25, 2003 available at: http//hrw.org/un/chr59/counter -terrorism-bck4.htm.

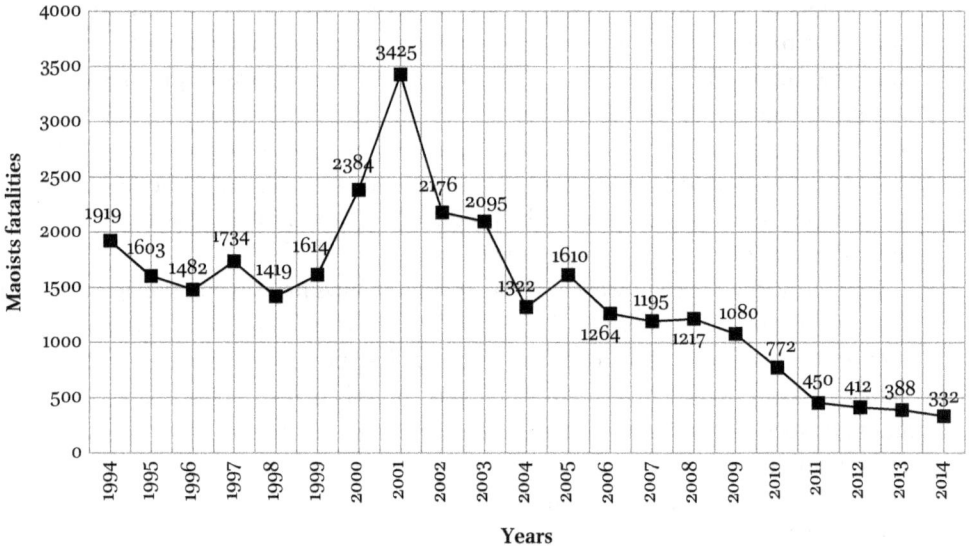

FIGURE 9.1   Fatalities of Maoists in India (1994–2014)
SOURCE: DATA FROM AN AUTHORITATIVE SOURCE, HTTP://WWW.SATP.ORG/

with a total of 50,000 official paramilitary troops involved in military action. There are Indian Army bases, too, but these are not involved in direct action yet' (Dias, in Ismi, 2013).

State violence is reinforced by, and complements, the direct violence of the wealthy class. In many parts of the country, members of this class hire private force (including goons) to attack anyone who challenges their super-exploitative practices (and upper-caste hegemony). They also have easy access to the police which is often bought with money and/or political connection. If industrial and mining businesses have private security force, landlords have their own armies. Violent activities of landlords and business people are often not penalized by the state. The legal process is more or less on sale: if one does not have money, it is impossible for one to get justice from the courts.

3        Why Does the State Repress the Naxalite Movement?

Why is there so much state repression, in a society which claims to have, and which, undoubtedly, does have, some elements of a liberal-democracy and which boasts of a spiritual culture of non-violence? One answer is that Naxalites use violent methods. This is to some extent *true*. Naxalites squarely place violence – armed agrarian struggle – on the agenda as a justifiable means to fight the Indian state with the objective of a radical transformation (Banerjee, 2002). They challenge the state's monopoly of violence, and assert the right of its opponents to resort to violence against the propertied classes and the state.[20] Some Naxalite groups (e.g. CPI-Maoist) have continued their near-absolute commitment to violence. But this is not true about other groups. For example, the CPI-ML (Liberation), says: 'we do not subscribe to any theory of "excitative violence" and still less to "individual assassination"'. But 'the rural poor cannot be denied their right to organise their own resistance forces to counter the attacks of landlord armies' (Arvind Das, 1997).

The Naxalite violence is real. In many areas of the country, 'The local administrators, especially the policemen are afraid to venture out of the main towns or their homes and offices' (Ray, 2002). And, in other areas, local level officials pay Naxalites money out of the development funds (e.g. 30 per cent or so) in exchange for peace (Shah, 2006; Srivastava, 1997). Numerous members of the legislature, and regional and local politicians are provided round the clock security in view of the Naxalite threat. Apart from rich traders and landlords, more than 225 political leaders, including those of parliamentary Marxist parties, were killed by a Naxalite outfit (People's War Group or PWG) only in Andhra Pradesh between 1993 and 2003 (Hindustan Times, 2003). As Figure 9.2 shows, security personnel have been regularly killed by Naxalites. Between 1994 and 2014 (end of October), Naxalites have caused 9424 security personnel deaths, producing an annual average of 452 (or more than one a day).[21]

That the Naxalites use violence, and therefore the state is violent towards them, is only a part of the story, however. There is another reason for state violence: Naxalites' political-development activities and political mobilization of people through these activities constitute an economic threat to certain types of private property owners, and a political-ideological threat to capitalist state power, as explained below. In many areas, poor people (especially, aboriginal people) are either led by Naxalites, or receive sympathy from them (see Harriss, 2011a). Naxalites articulate grievances against what the state has done (e.g. expropriation of people's land) and against what it has not done (e.g. its failure to satisfy people's basic needs). Naxalites construct an alternative

---

20    Charu Mazumdar, the architect of the movement, said that distributing land of 'feudal classes... among the landless and poor peasants... cannot be done peacefully. ... In today's era ... we cannot organize peaceful mass movements. ... Because the ruling class will not, and is not giving us any such opportunity' (in Banerjee, 1980: 26–27, 78).

21    As in the previous figure, this number excludes the civilian deaths in the incidents, for which Maoists/Naxalites must be co-responsible along with security personnel. The number of security personnel killed is one fourth the number of Naxalites/Maoists killed by security personnel.

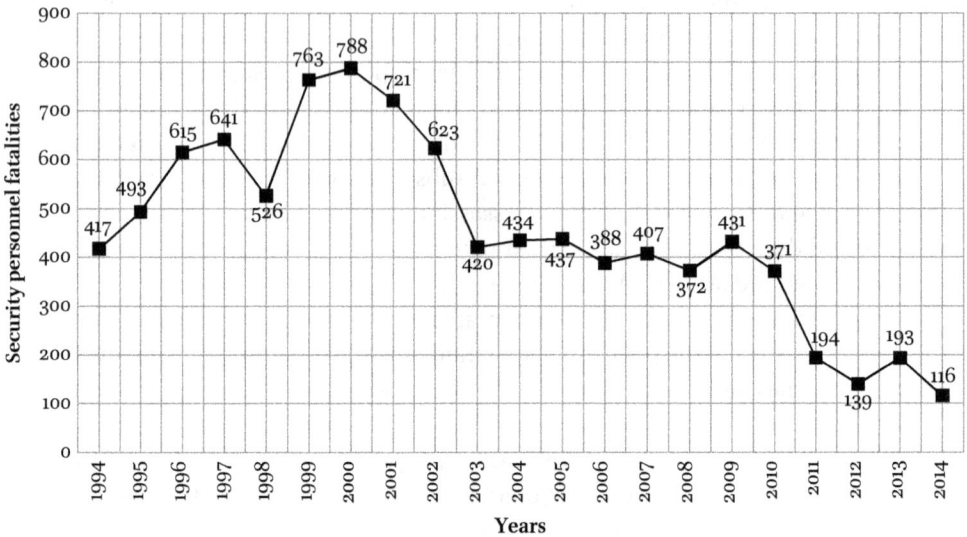

FIGURE 9.2  Security personnel fatalities in India (1994–2014)
SOURCE: DATA FROM AN AUTHORITATIVE SOURCE, HTTP://WWW.SATP.ORG/

landscape of development in socially-spatially marginal areas, within their limited means (Table 9.1). This landscape includes a variety of developmental activities which might put many NGOs to shame.

Where domestic or foreign big business is seeking to control the natural resources (e.g. minerals; land), Naxalites mobilize the aboriginal[22] peoples, as a part of a broader coalition of forces, against the land grab. The Naxalite left mobilized the tribals against land grab for the Posco steel project in Odisha (CPI-ML, 2011) Odisha. In some non-aboriginal areas as well, where attempts have been made to trample on the land and water rights of poorer people to promote capitalist development, Naxalites have fought against such attempts (e.g. the SEZ cases in West Bengal). In my own research I have seen the CPI(ML) Liberation mobilizing the fishermen castes around Orissa's Chilika lake, where the traditional fishing rights are being violated by rich investors of

---

22   Although I have stressed the aboriginal status of the people that Naxalites have mobilized, it is my view that the aboriginality itself is not necessarily the main cause of their sufferings. The cause of their suffering is their class background (e.g. the fact they are property-less or are gradually losing their property through market and extra-economic mechanisms; their reliance on a precarious labor market where wages are low). Their experience of class relations is reinforced by their aboriginal status which explains their discrimination in the economic sphere and the fact that the state has failed to give them the benefits that they deserve and that are claimed to be provided to them.

TABLE 9.1    Naxalite development activities

| | |
|---|---|
| – Building/maintaining irrigation infrastructure | – Education |
| – Community kitchen | – Health-services |
| – Land distribution among the poor | – Crime-control; administration of justice |
| – Abolition of bonded labor | – Implementing minimum wage policy |
| – Stopping exploitation of aboriginal women | – Punishing corrupt officials |
| – Fighting for fishing-community's right to fish | – Relief-measures |
| – Protection of peasant-tenants against eviction | – Making politicians declare their assets |
| – Protesting displacement of (aboriginal) people caused by capitalist development projects | |
| – Making sure low caste laborers/peasants can vote without fear | |

SOURCE: VARIOUS NEWSPAPER REPORTS AND ACADEMIC SOURCES

non-fishermen caste.[23] They provide protection to forest-dwellers against oppression by government officials who themselves behave as coercive landlords (Balagopal, 2006: 2185–2186; Roy, 2011). With their help, aboriginal people can enjoy access to state-controlled forests in some areas. The Naxalites also mobilize the masses against the destruction of their environment by capitalist development (see Kujur, 2006).

Naxalites have taken up issues of fixing prices for forest produce collected and sold by aboriginal communities, including by mobilizing them to strike for a higher price. In many areas under their influence, the price of *tendu* leaves (that are used to make country cigarettes), for example, did increase from Rs. 2–3 for 100 bundles (each bundle has 50 leaves) in the early 1980s to Rs. 80–100 by the mid-1990s.

In some places, the granaries of landlords are ransacked, and records of peasants' debts to moneylenders burnt. Naxalites occupy the ceiling surplus land (the land owned by landowners beyond the legal limit) and defend it by using force, if necessary, and distribute the land among the poor.[24] Naxalites have also secured minimum wages fixed by the State government for laborers

---

23    That the traditional Left has also played some role in slowing down neoliberalization (and in forcing the state to implement some pro-poor measures) is un-deniable.

24    By early 1990s, a group of neo-Naxalites formations in Bihar had distributed 14,000 acres among the poor (Sunday, 1992). In Andhra Pradesh alone, PWG is believed to have distributed half a million acres of land to poor people according to Prakash Singh (1995: 108). Naxalites have also taken land from the government (e.g. Forest department) and given it to the poor as well. The CPI Maoist itself has distributed 300,000 acres of forest land between 1986 and 2000 (Roy, 2011: 74).

(Behera, 2002; Louis, 2005; Wilson, 1999: 340). They are involved in the protection of rights of agricultural tenants and have fought to abolish bonded labor.

Naxalites have worked against social oppression. The viciously patriarchal dowry system has become less of a problem in many Naxalite areas (Bhatia, 2006). In Andhra Pradesh, PWG campaigns against gambling and prostitution (Singh, 1995: 112). Kunnath (2006: 116) reports that from the mid-1970s the Naxalite movement took up Dalit grievances and organized struggles against caste and class oppression. Not surprisingly, Dalit communities, along with those from the aboriginal communities, formed the primary support base of the movement. Naxalites have managed to roll back powerful upper caste militias in some areas. The social basis of CPI-ML (Liberation), in Bihar, has been centered on the Dalits' struggle for dignity (as well as for land and wages). They have organized separate anti-caste mass organizations, and fought for socio-economic benefits, including the reservation of jobs for lower castes in the private sector (Gudavarthy, 2005). Inter-religious and inter-caste marriages are being promoted. Parents and relatives who oppose such alliances are educated about the need to change their outlook (Bhelari, 2003). One Naxalite outfit (MCC) arranged at least 2,000 such marriages in Chatra District (in Jharkhand State).

Many Naxalite groups participate in elections. As Arvind Das (1987) writes, the setting up of Voters' Protection Committees by CPI-ML (Liberation) aims to ensure that the low-caste, poor people can vote without fear. Naxalites also mobilize people to demand that politicians announce publicly their assets both before and after becoming members of legislature, a demand that has led to the police shooting down many Naxalites (Misra, 1994). Punishing corrupt state officials, who eat up the government money meant for the poor, is another part of the Naxalite development agenda. They have organized rallies against crimes, corruption and communalism.[25] They run schools, health systems, and community kitchens (Navlakha, 2006: 2188; Chaudhuri, 2001). They propagate progressive ideas and educate people about the ills of the system (e.g. corruption; anti-people nature of development) through cultural activities (e.g. dance and songs). They force doctors to attend to patients, and make truant teachers teach classes.

---

25    One reason why the Hindu fundamentalists are against the Naxalites is that they are an obstacle to the Hindutva forces trying to Hinduize the aboriginal people and turn them against, say, Christians.

Thus Naxalites have produced an alternative landscape of development at the local/regional scale, however limited the developmental benefits for the poor may be. This landscape is an economic, political, and ideological threat to the state, and therefore *this* fact is a major explanation of state violence. The alternative landscape of development hurts the economic interests of ruling classes (e.g. when employers are forced to pay minimum wages or to surrender land), whose interests the state is to protect.[26] They also hurt the economic interests of the state directly when, for example, state-owned forests are taken over by poor people. Nearly 10.03 million hectares of forests in the country – which is about one seventh of the forest land – are said to be under the Naxalite political-military control. This has caused a loss of revenue. Naxalite 'disturbances' happen in a large area which is rich in minerals, which are worth billions of dollars (bauxite deposits in Odisha State only are worth $4 trillion, and this is more than three times India's entire annual gross domestic product). Any restriction imposed by the Naxalite on the use of this area – whether Naxalites are stopping the entry of mining companies or whether they are 'taxing them'[27] – hurts the economic interests of big business and of politicians/ officials associated with it. Interestingly, on 18 June 2009, Indian Prime Minister told the parliament: 'If left-wing extremism continues to flourish in parts which have natural resources of minerals, the climate for investment would certainly be affected' (quoted in Roy, 2009). Economic interests of rural property owners are also hurt: this occurs when the ceiling-surplus land of landlords is taken away for redistribution among the poor, when individual oppressive landlords who lease out land to poor peasantry for high rent and/or employ rural laborers at low wages are disciplined and are forced to grant concessions.

In all these ways, the Naxalite developmental activities are an economic threat to the state and ruling classes, which is why the state responds to it in a violent way, irrespective of the political party that is in power. When ruling classes fight to defend their interests (e.g. mining rights; payment of low rural

---

26    Consider how police killed 16 Dalit laborers on March 9, 2001 in Bhawanipur village in Mirzapur district, Uttar Pradesh province. The demands around which they fought under the Naxalite leadership were access to land, minimum wages and work. All the 16 had come from neighboring villages and were shot dead by police. A senior police officer told the People's Union for Democratic Rights that 'it is justified if they die or get killed. They are criminals'. Their crime was that as Dalit agricultural workers they dared to organize themselves and fought for their rights and that they, of course, were organized by Naxalites. Indeed, calling/labelling any democratic radical social movement Naxalite has become a convenient way of justifying state repression. http://www.dcrcdu.org/dcrc/ Navalakha.doc.

27    The movement levies 'taxes' on companies, which are used for development and possibly on arms.

wages and high rents, etc.), or when the state fights in defense of ruling class interests, Naxalites fight back, which invites (further) state violence.[28]

Naxalites' alternative development landscape is not just an economic threat; it is also a political threat. This is in two ways. One is the fact that the alternative development landscape can cause – and has caused to some extent – a potential transformation of the poor from being passive citizen-subjects to active class-subjects or from being merely local-scale political actors to political actors at provincial and national scales.[29] This happens when the movement makes demands that are legitimate/legal, but given the class character of the state (as discussed in an earlier chapter), the state finds it 'difficult' to implement these demands (e.g. land redistribution; irrigation of farm-land; payment of minimum wages). Such a political transformation can happen and does happen when, for example, the movement actually constructs an alternative development landscape by mobilizing common people to construct irrigation reservoir or to force local traders to pay more for the forest produce, or to take ceiling-surplus land from landlords and distribute it among the poor, and so on, and when it uses political power to defend that alternative landscape. Politically, Naxalites have tried to 'help the adivasi peasantry or Dalit laboring classes in some very backward regions to emerge as an independent political force' freed from the influence of landlords and traders (Gupta, 2006: 3173). While the Naxalite developmental activities can potentially organize the poor, and transform them politically, the state's agenda, however, is different: the state de-politicizes (and divides) the exploited classes (as Poulantzas, 1968 argued decades ago). The state does this by converting citizens to passive clients of its limited benefits/services and which citizens, the majority of whom have limited economic ability to pay, have to pay for. Or, when the state promotes any politicization, it is very limited 'politicization', in which people join voter-queues once every few years. They do so, as atomized individual citizens (groups of citizens divided on the basis of their loyalty to this or that bourgeois party), not as class-subjects, and the best that they as voters can achieve is to get rid of one party of the minority (the property-owning class) for another

---

28    The laws with which repression occurs bear the stamp of class. The colonial legal system
       set up to repress the anti-colonial resistance is used against radical social movement now.
       33% of Indian Penal Code provisions (designed during colonial times) pertain to offences
       against property (Kannibaran in Subramanian, 2004).

29    If peasants have a 'merely ... local interconnection', and if 'the identity of their interests
       forms no community, no *national* bond, and no political organization among them, [and
       thus if] they do not constitute a class' (Marx, 1967), they are not so much of a threat to the
       state. Note that strictly speaking, Marx is not right: to be a class, it does not have to be
       politically organized. Classes objective by virtue of objective relations and processes, and
       irrespective of whether they engage in politics.

party of the same minority. Any greater politicization which challenges the proprietary classes and politicians/officials about their undemocratic actions is not, and cannot, be on the state's agenda, given state's own class character.[30] To the extent that Naxalite developmental activities can cause a high level of politicization of the masses, it attracts state violence.

There is another threat from Naxalites' development activities, which is closely related to the threat from the politicization issue. The idea that the capitalist state is formally separated from the proprietary classes (Wood, 1995) does not hold in many areas. India may be a liberal democracy in Delhi and on the pages of the constitution, with its characteristic separation of political power from economic power. At the local scale, things are different: businesses and landowners directly use political power and means of violence in order to enforce exploitation, making a mockery of the bourgeois separation of the economic from the extra-economic. Here the authority of the state is that of, for example, the landlords, mining businesses, and other businesses. Their class interests are fixed in geographically circumscribed areas and cannot be moved. The state machinery often comprises of a non-official apparatus of moneybags and landed interests, traders, and their private armies. In this case, 'the local state' generally sides with the rich upper caste property owners in their dispute with the lower caste (or aboriginal) landless poor (Roy, 2002) and with other sections of the propertied-class. The Naxalites undermine the political (= extra-economic) power that the ruling class utilizes to enforce *economic* exploitation. For example, in many districts in Bihar where Naxalites are active, 'The price of labor [power] in the "flaming fields" is determined by the balance of forces between the armies of [landlords of] the upper castes (usually with police support) and the armies of the laboring poor' (Corbridge and Harriss, 2000: 206; the last bracket is in original). Naxalites side with the laboring poor in their political struggle. What all this means is this: any struggle against property owners and moneybags, for economic benefits (e.g. lower rents; higher wages; higher prices of commodities produced/sold by poor people) tends to become an extra-economic or political (and often military) struggle against the state which, however, claims monopoly over extra-economic coercion, and any struggle against the state for some economic gains hurts the interests of property owners.[31]

---

30    It should be noted that: the alliance of proprietary classes that holds state power includes landlords and urban bourgeoisie, and that landlords play an important political role of keeping the rural masses under control, and any direct threat to landlords will not easily be tolerated (see Chapter 7).

31    Landlords appropriate a large share of the state-resources supposed to be used for the poor. The more the poor claim, the less the landlords get, so the latter lose economically. And the more the poor receive from the state, the less favorable becomes the balance of

That the Naxalite movement, including that part of it which has been banned, is doing something for the masses is widely shared, even by agencies of the government. Sundar (2006), who is a Sociology professor at Delhi University and who does not support Naxal violence, says that the movement does show 'more commitment to people's development than the government' (p. 3190). Prakash Singh, who worked in Naxalite areas as a senior police officer, wrote: 'shorn of polemics, it (Naxalite movement) represents the struggle of the ...social and economic survival [of the poor]'. As Sarkar and Sarkar (2016: 891) say:

> Even the rudimentary services established by insurgents frequently outstrip those provided by the state. For instance, the Naxalites have attempted to address historical issues such as caste-based discrimination and landlessness that the Indian state has ignored, suppressed, or exacerbated.

As well, an expert group appointed by the erstwhile Planning Commission of India said that in terms of day-to-day activities, the movement 'is to be looked upon as basically a fight for social justice, equality, protection, security and local development' (in Banerjee, 2008a).

The Naxalite alternative development landscape – the fact that the movement has tried to help the poor – has posed, potentially and in reality, an ideological threat to the state as well, and not just an economic and military threat. The late Samir Amin (2005) says: 'in spite of tactical errors of judgment' the Naxalite offensive, 'has reawakened revolutionary awareness among the peasantry in vast areas ... of India'. As mentioned, Naxalites make 'difficult demands' on the state. Most of their demands – including the demand that aboriginal communities' land be not alienated without the consent of the people – are *legal* from the standpoint of the bourgeois laws. They are bourgeois-democratic demands, which, if met, would make the system a little more tolerable for some time. Through the national constitution and through its laws at national and provincial scales, the state has promised various measures for the poor (e.g. education, land redistribution, freeing bonded labor, and minimum wages) which, more or less, remain on paper. The implementation of these measures by the state will hurt the ruling class interests in one way or the other. But Naxalites demand that the state implement these. And when the state fails, they implement the legal measures, and if/when necessary, through the use of force. By forcing the state to implement its own measures and sometimes implementing these measures themselves where necessary by force (e.g. claiming

---

power between them and the propertied class in the class struggle, so landlords lose politically.

land held by landlords beyond the legal limit and giving it to poor people), Naxalites show in practice that the state, the so-called trustee of development (Cowen and Shenton, 1996), is no longer able to derive legitimacy and pacify poor people merely from its discourse, i.e. from the fact that it can write/utter a pro-poor development policy. Written or spoken words do not satisfy the need for food, for that need is not just an idea. Naxalites' development activities – and those organized by other progressive groups – indicate to some people that there is an agency which is somewhat anti-state but which can do things that the state is supposed to do but fails to do. The movement is forcing the state to see that the poor will not always accept the gap between 'development proper'[32] (that the post-colonial state has been promising), and 'development on paper'. The movement is taking steps to ensure that the poor will use arms to wrest concessions and to defend the limited gains that they have achieved through struggle. By providing palpable benefits to those who are poor, dispossessed, disrespected and neglected, however limited these benefits are, the movement gets their support (their consent), including to their violent means. And the state is in danger of losing poor people's consent in many areas.[33] What is the state's loss is Naxalites' gain. The state does not and will not tolerate the Naxalite movement gaining consent of the people, however. If the state loses consent of people to it, then its claim over (and actual practice of) monopoly over violence, its dominant form of survival, is undermined, and with that the control of the ruling class over economy and society is gone. There is an inverse relation, in many areas, between the amount of consent the state gets and that which the Naxalite forces (and indeed other such forces) get. If the geographical territory of the country is seen as an ideological surface indicating the distribution of support for the state as opposed to anti-state forces, that surface has numerous potholes, representing anti-state sentiments. These hidden potholes are more powerful than hidden land mines (that some Naxalite forces use – and once again, I do not support this at all). Their size and number can expand very quickly, given the right conditions. That is the fear of the state and of the ruling class.

In Naxalites' areas of influence, common people do believe that Naxalites are doing something for them, something that the state has not been able to do. For example, the Dalits of Dumari village in Bihar, where Kunnath (2006) conducted his fieldwork, did not object to the militant character of the Maoist campaign against the landlords and the local state, and they indeed 'wanted the Maoist armed squads to remain in the area as they feared that

---

32     This refers to promises of development in government documents.
33     The traditional Left, which, when in power, has pursued similar policies to the mainstream parties at least since the 1990s. So it is losing people's faith and consent too.

the landlords would re-establish their domination if the Maoist arms were withdrawn' (p. 205). Once a landless laborer bonded to a middle-caste land-lord family in Dumari, Rajubhai (Kunnath's respondent) grazed his master's cattle in exchange for 25 rupees per month and food. Daily 'humiliation, over-work and abusive words' were the staples on which he was compelled to sub-sist, yet he felt that 'silence was the best option' (p. 112). However, once the Maoists arrived, Rajubhai attended their secret meetings in the paddy fields, led the Dalits against a particularly oppressive landlord, and eventually be-came the commander of a Maoist armed squad (p. 113). The Maoist squad fought pitched battles with the landlords' army and were able to beat the landlords into submission so landlords could not be as violent as before (pp. 113–115). Interestingly, district-level econometric research shows that Naxalite activity has a dampening effect on the level of violence (violent crime and crimes against women), and that poverty attracts Naxalism (Borooah, 2008).

Because of their pro-poor material interventions, the Naxalites are able to mingle among masses and get their support, thus multiplying the effect of their revolutionary violence against injustice and state violence, which is why they are a threat to the state. They have a degree of support of the ordinary people in the areas of their operation (Haragopal, 2017). As Sarkar and Sarkar (2016: 891) say:

> By addressing these issues [people's problems], the Naxalites are able to project themselves as the champions of oppressed communities, while highlighting the state's apathy or antagonism, and effectively cultivating the perception that the state is the enemy. In such conditions, even if the state successfully stems insurgent activity, persisting and unresolved lo-cal grievances and popular support for insurgents are likely to bring about a re-emergence of insurgency.

That there is a threat of an alternative development landscape by Naxalites – the idea that a war is going on over consent/legitimacy – is inadvertently cor-roborated by none other than the Police Chief in charge of a region most guarded by the militarized Naxalite movement: 'I can fight the Naxals but not *Naxalism*. That has to be done only through development' (quoted in Chakrabarti, 2009, p. 376; italics added).[34] One can gauge the depth of ideological – discursive – conflict between the state working on behalf of the

---

34    Some part of the security establishment is unwilling to accept that Naxalites are winning people's consent through their good deeds. 'It is wrong to say that they have taken up people-oriented schemes' said Neeraj Sinha, senior police officer in Garhwa district in Bihar province. 'They are changing their strategy only to save their skin' (in Bhelari, 2003).

ruling class in the name of development, etc. and common people living in aboriginal areas. The state has been heavily investing in the construction of roads. Ordinarily, roads are an ordinary thing – who can be against roads? But roads have become a political thing. Without roads, natural resources cannot be extracted by the ruling class, nor can the state fight the Naxalites who have some control over the areas where resource extraction is happening or can happen. Roads are justified as a development work, as something that will benefit the masses by bringing schools and hospitals, etc. Ordinarily, roads should. But consider this report on how some people in Chhattisgarh see the roads in Naxalite areas, and in particular how and why they show their opposition to state's view of development via road construction:

> The villagers here ... are vehemently opposed to the state's definition of development. *"Humare paas na gaadi hai na ghoda, sadak humare kiss kaam ke?*(We neither have an automobile or a horse, why do we need concrete roads?)" asks the *sarpanch* [an elected leader] of one village... The villagers claim the entire focus on roads has been to further militarise the region. "Earlier it was Salwa Judum, now the vigilante group has manifested itself into an even more offensive District Reserve Guards (DRG). They come here, loot our ration, and ill- treat the villagers. Almost every house has at least one man or in some case even women arrested from our village".
>
> SHANTHA, 2018

The fact that an alternative development landscape posing a multi-pronged threat to the state is an important reason for state's violence is performatively proved by the state itself. Not only does the state burn villages and kill/harm Naxalites and their (academic) sympathizers. It also *destroys* the landscape of development constructed by them. An observer noted: the 'police and paramilitary forces destroyed a big irrigation bund [an embankment] near Mahboob Nagar ... [in Andhra Pradesh] built by voluntary labor *since the inspiration came from the Naxalites*. Police also destroyed five bus stops in Karim Nagar and Warangal district *since they were built by sympathisers of the Naxalite movement*' (reported in Frontier, undated). Such an act of destruction allows the state to continue to frame the movement (and other similar movements for justice) merely as a violent and anti-people movement. But the same act of state-led destruction is also strongly suggestive of the ideological (not – or not just military) threat that Naxalites pose and indeed, any similar radical movement against injustice inflicted by the system on common people would pose – to the capitalist state the main job of which is to protect the fundamental interests of the property-owning, exploiting class.

4      Conclusion

Let us briefly see the Naxalite movement through the lens of the literature on social movement/protest, which uses the language of *cultural frames*, *mobilizing structures* and *political opportunity* structure (McAdam, McCarthy and Zald, 1996). Clearly, ideological framing, or representation of the Naxalite movement as terrorist, as a menace, as a security threat, as ultra-left extremism, along with state's own democratic shell (liberal-democratic form), give some legitimacy to the state to repress.[35]

And this is not just specific to India (see Pion-Berlin, 1989 on Latin America). A part of the state's ideological framing is the coercive agencies' ethos that Gurr (1986) had identified. In the Naxalite case, this is the fact that they are a communist movement and that a communist movement is automatically seen as a threat to security of the capitalist state (Subramanian, 2004). This ethos, supported by many middle class people, helps state repression. Further, the state has access to its own expanding *mobilizing structures:* network of police and paramilitary agencies, police informers, anti-Naxalite civilian militias that the state supports, all of which, of course, complement the private coercive means available to the propertied classes. Here it is important to mention how state-supported research calls for more state violence against Naxalism. For example, Gupta and Sriram's (2018: 339; cf. Sarkar and Sarkar, 2016) publicly-supported research (from police headquarters) says that:

> at lower levels of security expenditure in the violence affected area, an increase in security expenditures leads to an increase in violent incidents (rather than a decrease); and only at higher levels of security expenditure in the area, an increase in security expenditure leads to a decline in violent incidents. Therefore, it is useful for the policy makers to start with higher security contributions than lower. However, if higher contributions are not forthcoming immediately, then security contributions should be continuous for long enough to see the desired impact.

In other words, the relation between the magnitude of state's violence (as indicated by the security expenditure) and the incidents of Naxal violence follows an inverted U-curve. Most importantly, the political-economic-ideological threat from Naxalites offers the *political opportunity* for repression.

There is no doubt that Naxalites use violent methods. One should also remind oneself that: landlords and some business houses use daily violence

---

35      See Thomas (2012) for a discussion on how the Naxalite movement has been framed in different ways (including as a law and order problem).

against ordinary people whether through their own security agencies or through state's coercive forces used as their own private property; Hindu mobs burn Christians' houses, destroy mosques and massacre Muslims, and Islamic terrorists kill innocent Hindus in a society where bourgeois democracy is turning to the right; landowners from higher castes also kill toiling men and women from lower castes (see Nandy, 2003: 124–125). Yet, Naxalite violence is seen as *the greatest* threat to the state by both of the biggest parties of the bourgeoisie, and to the class order that the state must protect. This is *because* their violence is against: actions of specific sections of the property-owning class (e.g. landlords, traders, mining companies), the excesses of the capitalist class system, and functioning of state personnel and laws that *support* the exploitative property owners, including by violent methods. It has been argued that 'repressive forces are themselves the most consistent initiators and performers of collective violence' (Tilly, 1978: 177; della Porta, 2014). In the case of the Naxalite movement, its violence is prompted by state violence (and by violence from the sections of the property-owning class itself).[36] If this is the case, then the idea that the state is violent towards Naxalites just because they are violent is inadequate, if not entirely untrue. State violence is rooted in its own class *content* and in the class content (character) of the Naxalites. It does not primarily come from their *mode* of fighting. The physical threat from Naxalites is not the only reason for state violence. The state uses, and will use, violence against the Naxalite movement because the state must defend the interests of sections of the propertied class that the movement is fighting against. And state violence, in turn, prompts Naxalite violence in certain cases, and which in turn prompts state violence.

Holloway advocates the 'emphasis ... on saying "No", refusing, puncturing capitalist command and (within that) constructing *alternative ways of doing things*', '*the immediate creation of an alternative society*', the creation of 'autonomous spaces', and thus saying 'yes' as well (Holloway, 2005: 271–272; 269; stress added). The Naxalite movement says both no and yes. They say no to *some* aspects of dominant power relations. They say yes to constructing alternative modes of living *within* capitalism. And that is a threat to the state.

In terms of its actual practice, the alternative development landscape that the Naxalites seek to produce conforms to the post-Marxist (e.g. Gibson-Graham, 2006) idea of production of post-capitalist spaces within capitalism. Arguably, the movement is a part of worldwide tendency of lower classes in

---

36    Mohanty (2017) says that violent reaction by the state might make the elite feel less insecure, but eventually such a strategy will be counter-productive because the people at the receiving end – those who have been alienated, exploited and displaced – take up arms against the state. Rather than being intimidated and killed, the oppressed communities (e.g. adivasis) need autonomy and support from the government, Mohanty says.

the capitalist periphery struggling for land, culture, democracy and employment (Chatterton, 2005; Hristov, 2005). They are not just an agency of *resistance*
(backed by *force* where necessary); they also play a positive, albeit limited,
developmental role. In a sense the Maoists are mimicking state practices of
governmentality (Sundar, 2014a), or rather what one might call 'state's developmentality'. The latter can be seen as developmental governmentality, which
signifies the deployment of developmental activities and state's developmental discourse (false promises of development) to discipline people and shape
their consciousness that in turn legitimizes the capitalist state. Naxalites promote an alternative developmentality which produces consent of common
people to Naxalism, and thus potentially enhances their politicization. This
can produce a serious threat to the state. State violence is partly directed at
*destroying* this threat.[37]

The state generally functions as one arm of the structure of private – property
relations, and intervenes on behalf of the propertied classes. Whatever else
the state is, it is, above all, an armed body of people, separate from ordinary
toiling masses who are the majority (workers and poor peasants). The state is
basically an institution of class violence, functioning on behalf of the ruling
classes, and against these ordinary people.[38] The state uses violence against
ordinary citizens if they fight against: (a) this *structure of private property relations*, (b) the *mechanisms* through which this structure works (e.g. competitive
drive for profit, rent and interest; dispossessing people of their land in order to
ensure access of the business world to people's resources), (c) and the *concrete
effects* of these mechanisms (e.g. extreme poverty; ecological destruction). The

---

37    For Sarkar and Sarkar (2016): 'Even the rudimentary services established by insurgents
      frequently outstrip those provided by the state. For instance, the Naxalites have attempt-
      ed to address historical issues such as caste-based discrimination and landlessness that
      the Indian state has ignored, suppressed, or exacerbated. By addressing these issues, the
      Naxalites are able to project themselves as the champions of oppressed communities,
      while highlighting the state's apathy or antagonism, and effectively cultivating the per-
      ception that the state is the enemy. In such conditions, even if the state successfully stems
      insurgent activity, persisting and unresolved local grievances and popular support for in-
      surgents are likely to bring about a re-emergence of insurgency. Counterinsurgencies
      must provide the services and address the issues that insurgents have taken up. In addi-
      tion to larger development initiatives, these efforts must include attention to small-scale
      local grievances. If the state is unable to address this range of grievances at least as effec-
      tively as the rebels, it is less likely that counterinsurgencies will be successful in the long
      term' (p. 891).

38    It is true that the state also contains workers and that many of its day-to-day activities
      (including non-military) are run by ordinary people. But these people have very little au-
      tonomy: they are constrained by state's policies which are structurally 'designed' to serve
      the ruling class interests. As well, the ordinary state workers usually have to do as the
      higher echelons of the state ask them to, and the higher echelons, which share ruling
      classes' interests and/or ideologies, work generally in the interest of these classes.

state uses violence against ordinary citizens if they fight against the powerful *agents* of the state (e.g. parties; officers, police) who support these relations/ mechanisms. The form of political movement of the masses does not matter much. Its content – its class content – does. That is: whether ordinary people are engaged in peaceful mobilization or whether they use a degree of violence (in self-defense), is generally beside the point. This is always the case. And when inequality level rises, the mask of democracy that a state wears is increasingly difficult to wear. There are 245,000-dollar millionaires in India, while 92 per cent of the adult population has wealth below $10,000. In this country a farmer kills himself every half an hour because he cannot pay the bills, and a child under five dies every 15 seconds because of lack of food and health-care, and the economic elite regularly kills/harms people for exercising their democratic rights including fighting against low wages and dispossession of the only thing they have (a small piece of land). In such a country, state violence against ordinary people and those who politically mobilize them *is* an intervention on behalf of the ruling classes and their political spokespersons, whether or not the mobilization of ordinary people is violent.

Launching class struggle from above on behalf of the propertied classes, the state impersonates guerilla tactics of a section of the Naxalite movement to fight it (Sundar, 2014a). By doing so, it is turning what I would call the 'homo sufferer' (working masses) into Agamben's 'homo sacer': those people who one could kill without being guilty of committing murder. In India's so-called red corridor,[39] there is an important contradiction: the red corridor's monetary value is multiple times the nation's annual income, and yet it contains the world's most impoverished people (especially among low castes and aboriginal communities). The state is trying to 'resolve' this kind of exceptionally intense contradiction, and the contradiction between a small elite and the majority of the population, by creating a (quasi-) 'state of exception', 'a legal civil war that allows for the physical elimination not only of political adversaries but of entire categories of citizens who for some reasons cannot be integrated into the political system' (Agamben, 2005: 2). This civil war is the class struggle from above, launched by the state, against the masses, i.e. the lower classes (workers and poor peasants, including those who are from the adivasi and Dalit backgrounds).

As Spacek (2017), a Canadian researcher, says: 'force and development have become conceptually blended and hybridised in practice, leading to a colonisation of statecraft by policing and violence' (p. 176). The consequence of

---

39  This part of the red corridor may represent an 'emergent system of dual authority in which the demarcation between official and insurgent governance is blurred' (Spacek, 2014).

development as war is the emergence of architectures of force across the conflict zone; architectures which have become, metaphorically, the forward operating bases of the state. The result has been a significant increase in the construction of policing facilities in previously ungoverned spaces as well as the fortification of existing police infrastructure. Throughout the [Naxal] region, the roads and towns have become dotted with barricaded, walled police compounds replete with sentry posts. Large areas of land in the major cities have been turned over for the construction of police cantonments and police lines. The government has also established, modelled on centres in the North-East, "schools of jungle warfare and counter-insurgency" directly in the conflict zone. Civil infrastructure is in the process of being colonised by the state. Educational facilities have become sites of war-making and, in many instances, have been physically altered, reflecting a hybrid logic of social service delivery and violence (p. 176).

As a result of all this:

> the state's presence has become more visible and militarised. Development and the spread of the state is materialised through architectures of force that function both as militarised nodes of state power and sites from which to dominate space. On the surface, it would seem that the militarisation of space fundamentally clashes with the developmental and constitutional frameworks that structure the official rhetoric of the state on insurgency. Arguably, however, it does not.
>
> Ibid.

The reason for this is that: 'The police have become the developmental agents in the [Naxal] region, responsible for carrying out infrastructural and social service delivery. They are the primary agents of the state', a state that is operating on the basis of 'architectures of force and spaces of violence' (p. 176). So, in so far as carrying out developmental activities is about producing consent to the legitimacy of the state and to the class rule that the state defends,[40] and in so far as the coercive organs are the agents of developmental activities, the boundary between coercive and consent-making state activities is blurred.

The state is able to engage in violence against Naxalites by producing an epistemological exaggeration: a political-geographic overestimation of the threat to the state, a knowledge-claim, a ruling class ideology, which would justify the increased level of violence by the state. By saying that the Naxalite threat can be anywhere anytime, the state of exception can potentially be

---

40    Singhal and Nilakantan (2016) say that state's developmental activities are about the battle over hearts and minds (of the oppressed).

produced anywhere anytime within the nation. The border moves inside, so the military can be engaged.[41] That this feeds into, and is supported by, right-wing, hyper-nationalist groups and individuals, is another matter.

There are three forms of violence (Zizek, 2008). Symbolic violence is 'embodied in language' and which is imposed through 'a certain universe of meaning' (Zizek, 2008: 1–2). The state labelling the Naxalite movement as a menace, as criminal, as unpatriotic, etc. is symbolic violence. The state's tendency to see any social justice movement as Naxalite or as having some Naxalite influence, and therefore as (potentially) violent that needs to be repressed, is also an act of symbolic violence. In September 2018, the state arrested five well-known social justice activists, labelling them 'urban Naxals'[42] for their alleged connection to the Naxalite movement (The Hindu, 2018a). The deployment of the construct of 'Urban Naxal' is a means of expanding state's battle against the Naxalite movement to the cities. This urbanization of state's fight against Naxalism is also a form of an all-out war against *any form* of dissent that the state cannot cope with or tolerate.[43] Someone who is seen as an enemy of *the state* is equated to an enemy *of the people* in order to justify penal interventions. This seeing does not see that the state works on behalf of the fundamental interests of a tiny minority of the population, propertied classes, and that it even works at the behest of certain individuals or fractions belonging to the propertied classes. This way of seeing things does not see that the act of exploitation by the capitalists and landowners – this act deprives the toilers of their right to the product of their labor and subjects them to unceasing miseries – is not a crime, while fighting against such exploitation in ways that the state sees as inappropriate is a crime. Why? The state must create its enemy, its other, to justify its own existence, the main purpose of which is to keep in check the state's real enemy (nation of workers and peasants, the majority of the population), whose interests are antagonistic to the ruling class-minority which the state must protect. The state cannot *overtly* declare the majority of the nation as its enemy

---

41    Azam and Bhatia (2017) say that the level of violence by the state against Naxalites has a significantly positive impact on violence committed by Naxalites themselves and that the provincial governments trigger an insurgency with the intention to acquire control of some economic assets with the help of the central government. As a result, India democracy seems to face a serious challenge in reconciling its thirst for natural resources and the economic growth sustained by these resources, with its founding humanistic values (ibid.).

42    Urban Naxals are supposed to supporters of Naxalism while active Naxals are actually engaged in struggles in rural areas.

43    The construct Urban Naxal supports, and is supported by, another right-wing construct: anti-national (anyone who asks difficult questions about the undemocratic and pro-capitalist character of the state is branded as anti-national).

but its actions treat the majority as the enemy or as if it is the enemy: *anyone* who resists the class rule and its effects is labelled a Naxalite and can be harmed, whether or not they have anything to do with Naxalism. So the state has *de facto* launched a war against the enemy within, against the majority of the people, via its war against the localized Naxalites (and similar others sites of radical resistance). Just as the state is generally a false protector of common people's interests, the enemy it constructs is also false, or not as true as portrayed by the state.

Symbolic violence can create a condition for what Zizek calls "subjective violence", which is the violence performed by "a clearly identifiable agent" (Zizek, 2008: 1, 10). This agent can be the agent of the ruling classes (their security agents or hired hoodlums) or of the state apparatus. State's subjective violence is reinforced by, and complements, the subjective violence by the ruling class, and to which Naxalite movement responds by its own subjective violence.

Systemic violence refers to the 'catastrophic consequences of the smooth functioning of our economic and political systems' (Zizek, 2008: 2). This is the violence that prompts the other two forms of violence. Class rule is behind systemic violence and the state supports the class rule. The state is launching a violent war on people because they are fighting against systemic violence (i.e. they are fighting against a war on their livelihood and on their democratic right to protest injustice). State violence against Naxalites is an instance of a general violence, a violence that is necessary to thwart all forms of actual/potential opposition to systemic violence (i.e. to class rule). The government claims that its troops are there to counter the Naxalites, but in actuality its aim is to intimidate into silence all kinds of democratically-organized movements such as people resisting land grabs or fighting police repression. By creating drastic panic among people and curtailing common people's freedom, the state makes it possible for corporations to be free to 'suck out the minerals and forest resources' (Dias, in Ismi, 2013).[44] One form of freedom (bourgeois freedom) comes at the expense of another (freedom of the toilers). Between two equal freedoms, it is the freedom that can be backed by greater violence that wins.

What state violence – the *de facto* 'everywhere-endless-war' against its own people fighting for justice – means is this: while a 'society' will not tolerate violence against the state, it will very easily tolerate violence against the body and soul of its common citizens, including little children who are malnourished, who have to work as bonded labor abused by labor contractors and employers (see Das and Chen, 2019), and who are assaulted by security people, in Naxalite

---

44     I am grateful to Professor Sheila Delany for drawing my attention to this article.

areas.[45] Why do the counts of security personnel killed while fighting against some segments of the Naxalite movement more important than the counts of the little children dying premature death because of the failure of the state to provide for better conditions of life?

Someone can argue that all states, when challenged by non-state forces, will behave the same way as the Indian state is doing in response to the Naxalite challenge. He/she might ask: would a socialist state (a state that comes to exist just after a revolutionary overthrow of capitalism) allow people to challenge it in the way that the Naxalite movement does? The answer is no. But there is a difference. All societies have a minority and have a majority. In class divided societies, the minority are the ruling class and the majority are the exploited classes.[46] All states of class societies, including capitalism, are states of, and for, a minority (the class of exploiters that controls society's productive resources) and against the majority. The capitalist states use violence to suppress the toiling exploited majority. That is very undemocratic. A socialist state is different, however: it would be the first state that is the state of the majority (workers and peasants) who need the state to stop overthrown classes from returning to power. Therefore any challenge from the overthrown properties classes, who constitute a tiny minority, will need to be crushed by the state on behalf of the people. That response of the state is not comparable to the fact that a capitalist state violently crushes an opposition from the masses (the majority) to it in the interest of the minority (exploiting property owners). The question is not: how does the state respond when it faces a challenge? The class character of the state and the class character of the challenge to its power are important to keep in mind. State violence to preserve the privilege of a minority is not the same violence that may be necessary to preserve the economic and political power of the vast majority.

This chapter has been critical of state violence in India, the scope of which has been *expanding*. There is another aspect of the reality which cannot be denied. This is that the Naxalite theory and strategy are self-*limiting* (Das, 2010, 2015). This is for various reasons, as we have discussed in the last chapter.

---

45    'Due to increasing police combings and diminished accountability, news of security forces burning villages or sexually assaulting children have become all too common... A survey by the Ministry of Women and Child Development also found that 38 percent of aboriginal children below 5 year of age are underweight and 44 percent have stunted growth' (Chowdhury, 2018).

46    'The owners of capital, the owners of the land and the owners of the factories in all capitalist countries constituted and still constitute an insignificant minority of the population who have complete command of the labor of the whole people, and, consequently, command, oppress and exploit the whole mass of laborers, the majority of whom are proletarians, wage-workers, who procure their livelihood in the process of production only by the sale of their own worker's hands, their labor-power' (Lenin, 1919).

Firstly, there is the fact that the Naxalite movement is *not* fundamentally against the totality of capitalist class relations. The Naxalite movement is also problematic in that, whether or not it uses violence, it mistakenly treats the peasantry (or, the rural poor) as the main revolutionary agent rather than an ally of the urban working class. The deployment of anarchic and secretive violence by certain segments of the movement, whom Jal (2014: 76) calls 'born-against anarchist', is against the principle that the masses can only self-emancipate themselves and that they will do this on the basis of their political organization and organized action, and not on the basis of secretive violence.[47] But if the state can inflict violence on a movement which is not particularly anti-capitalistic and if it does not mobilize urban workers, one can imagine how violent the state will be in relation to a movement that is fundamentally anti-capitalistic and that mobilizes the main revolutionary agent (the working class) to fight for a socialist society characterized popular democracy in every sphere of life, and not for a better – more democratic – form of capitalism.

We have seen that state repression is particularly likely when social movements target private property relations and accumulation projects of the property-owning class that cause ordinary citizens to suffer. Whether these movements are violent, and whether the state is a liberal democracy is a contingent matter. The liberals' argument that democracy pacifies the state collapses when one considers how repressive the liberal-democratic state is towards a movement such as the Naxalite movement, even if this movement is not seeking to go beyond capitalism. The response of the state to the Naxalite movement is symptomatic of a wider tendency across countries, including India: states are turning to authoritarian methods to suppress dissent. This is because with rising inequalities and given the crisis-tendencies of capitalism, states are increasingly unable to buy legitimacy by granting benefits, however limited, for the benefit of the majority. The states are increasingly unable to respond to the fact that there is a fundamental contradiction between big business's interests in profit and interest, and working masses' interest in obtaining access to food, shelter, health-care, education, culture and sustainable environment. The pacifying effect of democracy that some social movement theorists stress will work if the ordinary people remain pacified and do not exercise their (class-)agency and their right to dissent, in word and action, in the face of exploitation and oppression and wait indefinitely for some benefits from above

---

47    Much recent research draws attention to the fact that Naxalites kill many civilians based on their assumption that they are police informers (Vanden, 2018). There is a parallel between this and the fact that: 'The government's bid to crush Maoism has involved a frontal assault on sections of the latter's social base, which remains the most oppressed in Indian society' (Vanaik, 2011: 106).

(e.g. state, NGOs, etc.). But, if ordinary people have to remain pacified, what value does democracy indeed have?

The Indian state sees the Naxalite movement, especially, the activity of the more militant section of it (CPI-Maoist), as the greatest threat to itself and to democracy, and this is in part because the Naxalite movement does use physical force against oppressive elements where necessary and possible. But is the Naxalite movement really the main danger to democracy? It is not. The main anti-democratic force is not the Naxalite movement (sometimes called the Far Left) but it is the Far Right. So when the government labels the Naxalite movement as a force against democracy, it is taking a dangerous stance:

> The government's stance is ... dangerous because it receives legitimation from a whole array of intellectuals, academics and media figures, endorsing the idea that armed Maoism is "enemy number one". This is plainly ludicrous. The principal danger to Indian democracy comes not from Naxalism but from the forces of Hindutva, which have carried out violence and brutality on a scale that dwarfs anything armed Maoism has done. The forces of the Hindu right have succeeded in institutionalizing themselves within Indian civil society in a way unmatched by the whole of the left, mainstream or Maoist; its political and cultural vehicles have been legitimized as an acceptable part of the mainstream. For example, the instigators and apologists for the 2002 anti-Muslim pogrom in Gujarat – figures such as Chief Minister Narendra Modi – are not only unpunished, but lauded as statesmen.
>
> VANAIK, 2011: 106

Therefore, we must turn to the Far Right now, which is the real threat to democracy and an obstacle to lower-class struggle, and to much more. Indeed, this is how those who are associated with the Naxalite movement see – and must see – the Far Right.[48]

---

48    A major ideologue and leader of the Naxalite movement, Bhattacharya (2017) said this: 'Today when the Sangh brigade in power with their Hindi-Hindu-Hindustan agenda is desperate to bulldoze India under the twin wheels of corporate plunder and communal polarisation, the radical energy and resilience of Naxalbari could perhaps never be more needed'. A former Naxalite leader, V. Rao, said: 'We had fought against feudal lords and a bourgeois system to create a class-less society. We did not achieve success, but our objectives are more relevant in the present context when a BJP-RSS government is trying to divide the country and society on religious lines', adding that they are 'real enemies of class struggle' (quoted in Indian Express, 2017). Abhijit Mazumdar, a leader of CPI(ML) Liberation and son of Charu Majumdar who was the founder of the Naxalite movement, said: 'From the class struggle of 1960's, the focus has shifted to the RSS-BJP combine. If we have to fight against the communal divide, we have to widen the class struggle' (ibid.).

# Capitalist Development and Liberal Democracy under a Right-Wing Regime

Thus far we have talked about the capitalist character of India's political economy and of its politics.[1] A simple fact is that India's political system and its political economy have failed to meet the needs of the masses. Such a failure has prompted struggles from below: these have included not only trade union struggles and numerous political protests but also the Maoist struggle that has been going on in a quarter of the country's territory. This is the context in which to examine the threat to the democratic and social rights posed by right-wing forces in India, as a form of ruling class struggle 'from above'.

The Bharatiya Janata Party (BJP), an extreme right-wing party led by Narendra Modi, won India's 2014 general election partly by promising development or *vikas* for all (and also by stoking hatred against non-Hindus). On May 25, 2018, Mr. Modi, the supreme leader of BJP, said this on Twitter: 'On this day in 2014, we began our journey of working towards India's transformation'. He added: 'Over the last four years, *development* had become a vibrant *mass movement*, with every citizen feeling involved in India's growth trajectory. 125 crore Indians are taking India to great heights' (italics added).

Major promises made by the party in power – about bringing back black money (unearned money), creating 10 million jobs a year, and so on – have turned out to be false promises, but the government keeps repeating them. The government spends millions on publicity to make common people believe to be true what is not true, and, in particular, that good days (achhe din) are upon them.[2] Yet, many have started understanding the real intentions of the right-wing government, which are both communal (religious-sectarian) and pro-business, and therefore, against the toiling classes. Among those who initially fell for emotionally-charged appeals from the right-wing forces supporting the government, to national and religious pride based on distorted representations of the past (and present), many are now understanding that what is really important is access to decent employment and standard of living, social peace, and so on, and that false pride cannot meet such needs. One should ask, and many *are* asking: To what extent has development really happened under the

---

1   An earlier version of this chapter appeared as: Das (2018a).
2   The party's 2014 slogan was '*Achhe din* aane waale hain' (good days are coming).

right-wing government? If Mr. Modi says he and his people began their 'journey of working towards India's transformation', one might ask: how exactly has India been transformed? Transformed from what into what?

This chapter is the first in the series of four chapters on the extreme rightward turn in India's political economy and politics, characterized by the rising strength of political-social forces exhibiting certain fascistic traits. Using data from media, and national and international institutions, this chapter empirically examines India's economic, social and political development under its right-wing regime. The remainder of the chapter has 5 sections. In Section 1, I discuss the economic development record of the BJP government. In Sections 2 and 3, I show, respectively, how the ultra-rich are gaining enormously, and how the poorer segments are, more or less, losing under this government (2014–2019). In Section 4, I show the government's record of political development, including democracy and social harmony. In Section 5, based on the information from a national survey and other data, I discuss how the dismal record of development is slowly getting registered in the minds of common people who are getting disillusioned with the government. This disillusionment is an embryonic consciousness against right-wing thinking and policies, but whether it will further develop and how, no one can tell. In the final section, I provide some conceptual and general reflections on the government: in particular, I reflect on whether its dismal record of development is coincidental or whether it stems from its inherent right-wing nature. I also reflect on the internal connection between government's economic and non-economic character. I reason that the Right-wing government is right-wing for a reason: it is right for the business class.

## 1 BJP Government's Record on Economic Development at the National Level

Economic growth – increase in per capita Gross Domestic Product, or GDP per capita – is one of the indicators of economic development. Other things constant, a situation of rising GDP per capita is better for common people than one where it is not rising. There is little to suggest that economic growth has been stellar since 2014 (even if the calculation of GDP has been mired in controversy). If anything, the numbers have declined. The lackluster performance in terms of economic growth is in spite of the fact that the new government, installed in May 2014, enjoyed three advantages: a recovering global economy post 2008 crisis, and falling oil prices, due to which the country received a bonanza of 6 lakh crores in revenue; as well, the government has also had an absolute majority in the parliament.

An important aspect of development is physical infrastructure, which the government has rightly stressed. The number of electrified villages has increased since 2014. Of course, that does not mean that all or even the majority of people in a newly-electrified village have access to electricity: barely 7% of the villages newly electrified under the new government have 100% household connectivity. A village may be connected to the electricity grid but may not have access to power for most of the day, and even if there is power, all villagers may not be able to afford to buy power. Similarly, 36 million Liquefied Petroleum Gas (LPG) connections have been issued over the last two years; yet, millions of families do not have the resources for refills. The picture with respect to the construction of national highways has been generally positive: 4,410 kilometers in 2014–2015 and almost 10,000 in 2017–2018. Of course, one should bear in mind that while the target was to construct 41 kilometers a day, the actual achievement has been no more than 23 per day. 120,000 kilometers of rural roads were built during the 2014–2017 period, and this is a remarkable achievement, but it is a false claim made by BJP that this achievement is an all-time high.[3]

Development is more than about an increase in income/wealth or about an increased availability of infrastructure (including *bijli, sadak* and *pani*)[4] although it is necessary. An alternative indicator is the Human Development Index (HDI). HDI takes into account income as well as education and health conditions. India's index did not improve significantly (in spite of the fact that the previous government had made some social sector investment): on a scale of 0 to 1, the index was 0.609 in 2014 and 0.624 in 2015, and increased to only 0.636 and 0.640 in 2016 and 2017 respectively. Relative to other countries, India's HDI rank was 130 in 2014, and it remained the same in 2017.

2      **The Winners under the BJP Regime: The Capitalist Class (and the Richer Elite)**

Where the government is generally doing a good job is for the business class, which played a critical role in installing it, including through secretive election funding and the dissemination of pro-BJP ideas through the compliant and communalizing media that the business class controls. Consider the World

---

3   'In the period 2008–11, rural road construction was 157,631 kms with 2009–10 being a peak year with 60,117 kms of roads constructed. Year 2008–09 was also higher than 2016–17' (Jawed, 2017).

4   *Bijli, sadak* and *pani* are respectively electricity, roads and water.

Bank's Ease of Doing Business Index. This index indicates improvement in the business environment in terms of whether regulations for business activities, including labor-related regulations, are simpler for business and are in its interest. India's rank has moved up from 142 in the 2015 report to 100 in 2018 and 77 in 2019 (the years refer to the years of publication of the World Bank reports) (Figure 10.1). India's performance during the first four years of the right-wing pro-business government in terms of easing business regulations has been spectacular: India jumped 65 spots during this period. This means that the business people find it easier to do business without having to worry about government restrictions. The fact that the business class is benefitting from the government is also indicated by the fact that India's stock markets have been doing rather well.[5] More than any other section of the population, it is the business class which is experiencing *achhe din* (good days).

In serving the business class, the ultra-nationalist government has been giving away the nation's financial resources in the form of loans from public-sector banks to the private sector (Figure 10.2). The loans issued from nationalized banks are becoming non-performing assets (NPA): by mid-2018, the total size of bad loans had ballooned to nearly 10 trillion Rupees, three times more than in 2015. Like its predecessor, the BJP government continues to write off the loans that the big business owes to public-sector banks; the number of write-offs has increased substantially between 2014 and 2016 (Figure 10.3).[6] As well, the government's watch on capitalists is so relaxed that bank fraud has become standard practice. For the period from 2013 to March 1, 2018 there were 23,866 cases of fraud, each of 100,000 Rupees or more (*The Hindu* May 2, 2018). In addition to the write-off of loans and the abuse of the nationalized banking system by the big business allowed by the government, is the fact that the Income Tax Department has begun writing off 500,000 billion Rupees of tax arrears by corporate defaulters, on the ground that their economic health is not sound.

---

5  Sensex and Nifty are stock market indices in India, which, respectively, represent Bombay Stock Exchange (BSE) and National Stock Exchange (NSE). Now, 'Equity benchmarks BSE Sensex and NSE Nifty have advanced nearly 40 per cent since Modi took over as Prime Minister. The 30-share Sensex jumped to trade at 34,344 on May 23, 2018 from 24,716.90 on May 26, 2014. During this period, the index hit an all-time high of 36,443 on January 29 this year, while the Nifty surpassed the 10,000 mark for the first time ever' (Oberoi, 2018).

6  Note that the NPA problem has arisen at least in part because the current BJP government – like Congress-led governments – has made banks keep lending to India's business houses (including the businesses that are politically connected to them) to support a flagging economy (Kumara, 2018a).

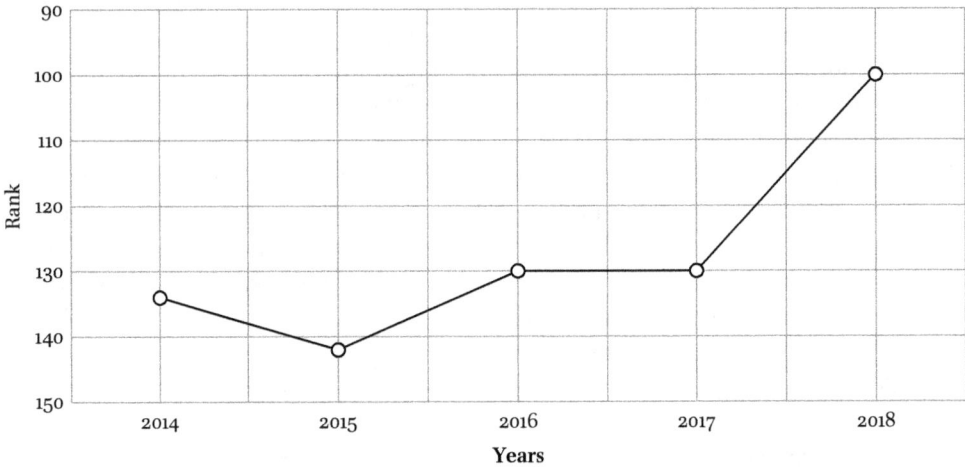

FIGURE 10.1      Ease of Doing Business Index 2014–2018
SOURCE: DATA FROM HTTPS://EN.WIKIPEDIA.ORG/WIKI/
EASE_OF_DOING_BUSINESS_INDEX

All these pro-business actions have adverse implications for the country's overall economy. The banking sector woes have indeed 'caused a collapse in availability of credit to industry which then spiraled into low investment by the private sector and consequently low fixed capital formation' (Chakravarty, 2018). This will not have a positive effect on employment-creation. Writing off unpaid loans means socializing them. When businesses make money, it is theirs. When they incur losses and cannot return the loans taken from society, the losses belong to society! The fact that the government gives all kinds of presents to the big business (write-offs of loans or tax arrears, etc.) means making the toiling masses 'pay through increased taxes' (including through the regressive GST) as well as 'social-spending cuts for the cash infusions needed to strengthen the banks' balance sheets and preparing them to be sold off to big business (Kumara, 2018a). When the nationalized banks' resources dry up in the fraudulent way that they are, these banks' ability to serve the ordinary people (both in terms of amount of lending and the cost of sending) will be compromised.[7] While the loans to the big business are waived, any talk of loan waivers to farmers in distress is seen as a threat to India's credit-worthiness by the rating agencies. The story does not end there. Farmers are being sent to jail

---

7   Besides, such frauds will have a serious impact on the economic health of the banks, and this
    will be used as a justification to privatize them, i.e. to hand them over to the business class
    which is responsible for the bad economic health in the first place.

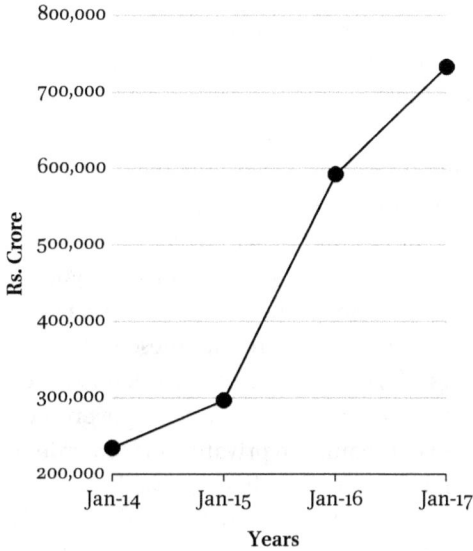

FIGURE 10.2    Public sector banks' gross NPAs in Rs. Crore, 2014–2017
SOURCE: DATA FROM HTTPS://WWW.FIRSTPOST.COM/
BUSINESS/BANK-NPA-TREND-IN-7-CHARTS-BAD-LOANS-
AT-STATE-RUN-BANKS-MAY-BE-PEAKING-SELECT-PRIVATE-
PEERS-SEE-RISE-4218813.HTML

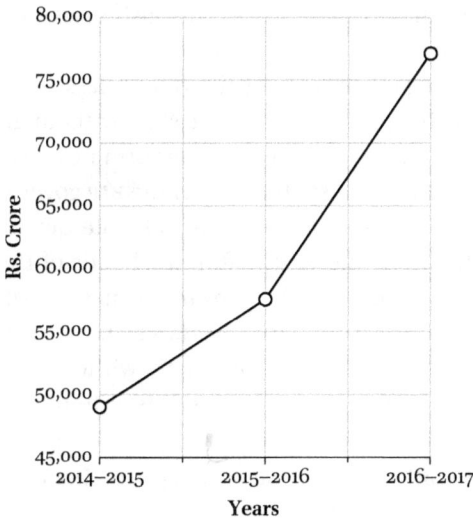

FIGURE 10.3    Loan write-offs (Rs. Crore), 2014–2017
SOURCE: DATA FROM HTTP://INDIANEXPRESS.COM/ARTICLE/
BUSINESS/BANKING-AND-FINANCE/PSU-BANKS-WRITE-OFF
-RS-55356-CRORE-IN-SIX-MONTHS-BAD-DEBT-4966594/

for defaulting on their loan repayment. Arvind Subramanian who served the BJP government as the former Chief Economic Advisor for almost 4 years, declares that writing off the corporate sector's bad loans makes good economic sense, saying 'this is how capitalism works' (cited in Sharma, 2017).

It is widely known that India's ruling elite has been pursuing a policy of privatizing state-owned companies since the early 1990s. But as with many other pro-business measures, the current right-wing BJP government with its brute electoral majority, has gone much further than the Congress governments. BJP even targets for privatization highly-profitable companies. Even if workers have had little say in how these companies are run, these companies are products of the labor and savings of millions of common people; these companies also provide some security to their employees. Yet, the government seeks to sell off government-controlled companies to private hands in order to allow the latter to make huge amounts of money on them. As well, an aim of the right-wing government is to dismantle whatever social protections the state-owned companies 'provide against low-wages, mass-sackings and deleterious working conditions so as to further undermine the social position of the working class as a whole and thereby make India even more attractive to investors' (Kumara, 2018a). By selling off state-owned companies, the government will also reduce the fiscal deficit and make the international rating agencies happy. It will also use the money from the sale of the companies for investment in cash-starved state-owned banks so they can lend to private businesses, and for building infrastructure as per the needs of the capitalist class.

In any case, there is a massive looting of the state by the ruling class going on.[8] The business class is not only taking resources from the state without an equivalent (consider cheap sale of state companies, or non-performing assets of state-owned banks). The blatantly pro-business character of the BJP government is indicated by the ways in which it goes about selling off state-owned companies to private businesses: the whole matter is left in the hands of the private businesses themselves.[9] This means that the *private* businesses will decide how they will loot *society's* resources. The ruling class is also using society's resources to produce and to protect its own private wealth, without paying the full cost of those resources (consider tax rebates and tax-write-offs by

---

8   One can call it 'looting of the state by the state' which is the state of the capitalist class, working on its behalf and in its interest.

9   'The rapacious big business interests animating the Modi government's privatization drive are exemplified by its appointment of Reliance Mutual Exchange Traded Fund, an investment fund owned by the billionaire Anil Ambani, to serve as the "consultant" and "expert" overseeing the quick, partial or complete privatization of ten giant and highly profitable [public-sector companies]' (Kumara, 2018a).

the government). If Britain looted Rupees 91 lakh crores (Rupees 91 trillion) at current rates over 300 years from India, one can compare very well the amount of loot of India's resources by the Indian (and foreign) capitalist class, fully assisted by politicians and bureaucrats, in the name of development and transformation (Shankar, 2018). The process of such a loot, which began under Congress with the full support of BJP-in-opposition, has intensified under the current BJP government, whose major policies are a package of presents for the business class.

The package provided for business by the government includes the things just mentioned. It also includes the government's anti-labor policies such as allowing employers to hire and fire freely (more on this below), not increasing minimum wages, using coercion to break unions and social resistance, and so on. This allows business to super-exploit workers by paying them minimal wages and benefits. So, the BJP's promise of *sabka saath* and *sabka vikas* (Together with all, Development for all) is in reality *corporates ke saath, corporates ke vikas* (Together with corporates, Development for corporates). It is no surprise that the number of India's dollar billionaires was 109 in 2014 and this has increased to 136 in 2017 (Figure 10.4). The BJP regime has made little difference to the continuing tendency towards the concentration of wealth, with the share of India's wealth held by the top 1% growing under the BJP government, from 49% to 58.4% between 2014 and 2016 (Figure 10.5). The richest people are increasing their share of the nation's health faster under this government than before: in 2017, a whopping 73% of the new wealth generated went to the richest 1% of the population. This means that under this so-called nationalist government, only 27% of the wealth created in 2017 went to the bottom 99% of the nation. OXFAM (2018) observed: 'In the last 12 months the wealth of this elite group increased by Rupees 20,913 billion. This amount is equivalent to [the] total budget of Central Government in 2017–18'. It is clear which nation, or which part of the nation, the nationalist government really cares about.

The BJP's populist claim that it would bring back black money from overseas and deposit 1.5 million Rupees in every citizen's account has melted into thin air. Of course, many of the super-rich have black money abroad.[10] But the strong ties between the government and the business class – through electoral funding mechanisms, for example – protect the rich. One of Mr. Modi's promises was: 'I have decided if you bless me and give me the opportunity I will bring back all the black money'. This lofty promise has melted into thin air.

---

10    'A report by US-based think tank Global Financial Integrity (GFI) estimated that $21 billion in black money was taken out of India in 2014 alone' (quoted in Arun, 2017).

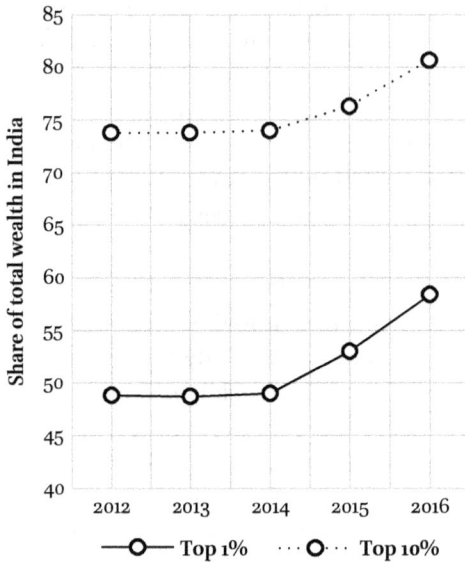

FIGURE 10.4     Share of wealth held by Top 1% and 10% in India,
                2012–2016
                SOURCE: DATA FROM HTTPS://WWW.LIVEMINT.COM/
                MONEY/MML9OZRWAACYEHLZUNIMNO/THE-RICHEST-
                1-OF-INDIANS-NOW-OWN-584-OF-WEALTH.HTML

One should note that the ultra-rich stratum, including the business class, and
the political class (law-makers/politicians) overlap: the ultra-rich become politicians, and politicians become the ultra-rich. According to the Association for
Democratic Reforms (ADR): 'the average assets of the 46-member Council of
Ministers [which was sworn in 2014] is Rupees 13.47 crore...Of the 44 ministers
analysed, 40 (91 percent) are *crore patis*'. Note that more than 92% of Indians
have assets that are worth Rupees 600,000 or less. ADR further reveals: 'Four of
Modi's ministers have declared more than Rupees 30 crores worth of assets'
(Pereira, 2014).

One might briefly refer to a few policies of the right-wing government to
show its pro-business character. One is demonetization. At 8 pm on November
8, 2016, the government made a sudden announcement invalidating all Rupees
500 and Rupees 1000 currency notes as of midnight of that day. It set a December 31 deadline for depositing the withdrawn currency bills into bank accounts.
It fixed a daily Rupees 4,000 limit (later reduced to Rupees 2,000) for the exchange of old notes for new currency. Explaining the demonetization scheme,

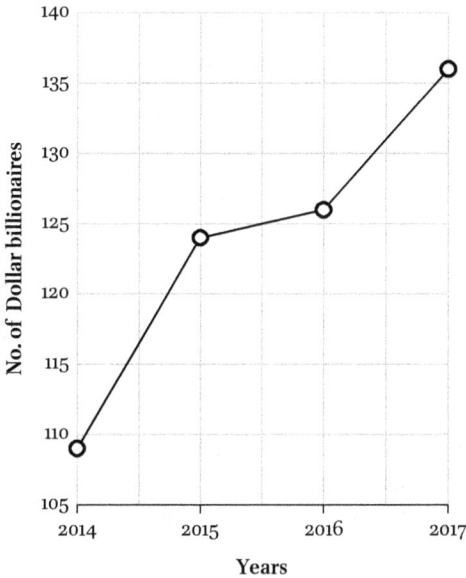

FIGURE 10.5    Number of U.S. Dollar billionaires in India,
2014–2017
SOURCE: DATA FROM HTTPS://WWW
.STATISTA.COM/STATISTICS/324237/
INDIA-NUMBER-OF-BILLIONAIRES/

Modi said: 'To break the grip of corruption ... we have decided that the currency notes presently in use will no longer be legal tender from midnight tonight' (quoted in Financial Express, 2018). The government had said that Rupees 5 lakh crores (Rupees 5 trillion) of illegally-held money, or black money, would be eliminated. Yet, 99.3% of demonetized currency returned to the banks. The rich people – 148,000 account holders – deposited more than Rupees 8 lakh of demonetized currency each, amounting to a total of Rupees 4.89 lakh crores into the banks. No action has been taken to ensure that these rich people's money is legally acquired.

The aim of demonetization is not really to fight corruption but to ultimately help the business class. How? First, demonetization has allowed the government to inject the desperately needed cash into the banking sector which will lend to the private sector. Note that the banking sector is burdened with non-performing assets because of defaults by the business class, and has therefore cut down on new business-lending, producing adverse effects on economic growth. Besides, the demonetization scheme has forced millions to open bank accounts. This constitutes a method of modernizing India's backward capitalist economy, by strengthening the Indian bourgeoisie's banking system and its reach; note that the BJP government has already made clear that one of its principal goals will be to privatize large parts of the banking system (Kumara and Kumar, 2016). As well, this policy has benefitted a segment of *the capitalist class* that deals in e-transactions (digital money). While demonetization has been broadly (even if not straightforwardly) in support of the business class, it has hurt the laborers and farmers (as mentioned below).[11]

Another major pro-business intervention is in the area of labor laws. Bypassing the parliament, the BJP government issued a notification in the government *Gazette* that 'Fixed Term Employment has now been introduced irrespective of the industry', thereby amending the 'Industrial Employment (Standing Order) Act, 1946' (Kumara, 2018a). This regressive change in labor laws means that Indian businesses can hire workers on a 'non-permanent' basis, for any length of time, whether for days, months, years, or the duration of a project. The 'fixed-term' does not mean any job security: an employer can indeed terminate a worker's contract at any time on the ground of changed business conditions. The laid-off worker is not entitled to severance pay or compensation. The government justifies such a regressive change by saying that companies can now hire workers on short-term contracts without having to use outside labor contractors and that workers hired on 'fixed-term' contracts will receive the same wages and, on a pro-rata basis, the same benefits (except severance benefits) as permanent employees. These are supremely spurious claims. First, the government has not prohibited employers from using labor contractors and temporary work agencies to hire casual workers by paying them wages and benefits far below those paid to regular workers. It has simply broadened employers' options for hiring workers who can be easily dispensed with. Second, the Indian Labor Ministry hardly enforces minimum wage, health and safety and other work standards anyway, which means that the legal guarantees of equal pay are essentially meaningless (Kumara, 2018a).

## 3     The Losers under the BJP Government: The Toiling Masses

In a capitalist society such as that of India, wealth is, ultimately, generated by the labor of common people who have to work for others for a wage and who receive only a small part of what they produce. The extraction of wealth is also based on the use of the nation's natural resources. Not only is the environment

---

11     This is the case even if some of them may have had a sense of satisfaction seeing and/or thinking that the demonetization has hurt the rich more, including by members of them having to stand in queues for depositing and withdrawing their money.

depleted as existing environmental regulations are dismantled, but there has been little improvement in the conditions of workers. The employment situation is simply desperate. According to *IndiaSpend,* an average 213,000 jobs have been created every year in the 2014–2017 period. This is a far cry from the 10 million jobs a year promised by the BJP government.[12] That the government has failed on the job front is corroborated in a national survey in May 2018 where 57% of voters said that finding jobs in their area had become more difficult during the past 3–4 years; this figure was 49% in January 2018 (Lokniti, 2018).

A wage-earner's economic living standard depends, more or less, on the number of hours and days employed, and the wages received per hour or per day. Not only are employment opportunities scarce and jobs precarious, but nominal and real wages have remained also low, showing little sign of improvement under the BJP government. According to a recent Reserve Bank of India report, rural wage laborers experienced high wage growth between 2007 and 2013, partly due to improvements to the rural employment program under the previous government (which was under the Congress), but that growth rate in rural wages has declined during the 2014–2018 period under BJP's rule, in part because the momentum of the rural employment-generation program has been dampened (Kundu, 2018). This is confirmed by data for rural wages: from 2008 to 2013 (prior to BJP's rule), in nominal terms, wages increased by 15%, but during the BJP's tenure, this rate has fallen to just a third of the previous rate (*Indian Express,* 2018).[13]

The promise of creation of self-employment through schemes such as the Mudra Yojana (Money Scheme) which provides small loans to small-business people is simply deceptive: the average amount of loan has been less than Rupees 50,000; with such a small amount one can never set up an enterprise that will generate revenue for a family to lead a life beyond poverty. Barely 1% of all

---

12    It should be noted that, during the 2014 general election campaign, the BJP had criticized the Congress Party for '10 years of jobless growth' and promised jobs and development, if voted to power.

13    During the latter period, the average number of person-days for each household employed under MGNREGS dropped, as did the number of households getting 100 work days a year.

51.7 lakh families got 100 days of employment in 2012–2013 and 46.6 lakh families got 100 days of employment in 2013–2014. But it has drastically come down to 24.9 lakh families in 2014–2015 and a dismal 20.45 lakh families in 2015–2016.

The Modi government has cut the financial allocation under MGNREGA. While the Congress-led government spent Rupees 39, 778.27 crore and Rupees 38, 552.62 crore on the scheme in 2012–2013 and 2013–2014, respectively, the spending went down to Rupees 36, 033.81 crore and Rupees 34, 226.80 crore in 2014–2015 and 2015–2016 respectively (INC, 2017).

mudra loans are substantial amounts (i.e. at least 5 lakh Rupees) (Mohammad, 2018).

Given the highly unsatisfactory situation with respect to employment and wage growth, it is not surprising that the majority are not doing that well. With more than 70% of the new wealth generated going to the richest 1%, the 670 million Indians comprising the poorest half of the population saw a paltry 1% increase in their wealth. While the richest 10% of Indians controlled 80.7% of nation's wealth in 2016, the bottom 50% owned a mere 2.1% (Chakravarty, 2016). According to the Indian brokerage firm Ambit Capital, while India's annual per capita income is a miserable $1,850, for the poorest half of the population, it is just $400. By contrast, the top 1 percent (i.e. 13 million people), earns $53,700 annually (Kumara, 2017). The per capita income of India's poorest 50 percent is substantially lower than the per capita income of Afghanistan ($561), a country devastated by decades of US imperialist-fomented wars, including the current 16-year American occupation (ibid). While the trend of increasing inequality preceded the Modi regime, the control of the ultra-rich over the nation's wealth has increased faster after 2014. With the ultra-rich doing as well as they are, there is no sign of the relative position of the majority improving at all.

The BJP government has emphasized the importance of development in the form of: *sabka saath and sabka vikas*, or in other words, inclusive development. This is a laudable goal. But does the government promote this? Luckily, there is a new development index that seeks to capture this interesting idea. Designed by the World Economic Forum as an alternative to GDP, the Inclusive Development Index (IDI) reflects more closely the criteria by which people evaluate their countries' economic progress. The IDI is based on: growth and development (GDP per capita; labor productivity; life expectancy and employment); inclusion (median household income; income and wealth inequality, and poverty rate); and intergenerational equity and sustainability (public debt level; carbon intensity of GDP, etc.) (World Economic Forum, 2018). India's IDI score was 3.38 in 2017 and slipped to 3.09 in 2018 (Norway, the top country, has a score of 6.08). Among the developing economies only, India's IDI rank was 60 in 2017 and it slipped to 62 in 2018.

When unemployment continues to be a major issue and when wage growth is slow, it is not surprising that millions cannot meet their basic needs. According to the Lokniti 2018 survey (referred to earlier), the percentage of people who are not able to fulfil all of their needs and face some or much difficulty has increased from 53% to 67%, just between January and May 2018. Another indicator of the miserable situation of the vast majority is the agrarian crisis: in rural areas, where most people live, the agrarian distress continues, with farmers not getting a remunerative price for their crops. Between 2014 and 2016, 36,362 farm-dependent people committed suicide, meaning two cases of suicide every hour. So, on the agrarian crisis front, there has been little improvement.

Conditions of farmers and workers were made worse due to demonetization. It paralyzed single-worker 'businesses', which are owned by numerous poor families, comprising 80% of the country's 52.85 million enterprises (Kumara, 2017). It also caused millions of urban workers in small businesses to be thrown out of work, at least temporarily, as the small businesses rely mainly on cash transactions (ibid.). Demonetization affected rural areas badly. A Ministry of Agriculture report said: 'India's 263 million farmers live mostly in the cash economy' (meaning that they do not use electronic transactions), and that demonetization came at a time when they were selling autumn crops or sowing winter crops, and that that is when they needed a lot of cash which demonetization removed from the market. The report also said that 'millions of farmers were unable to get enough cash to buy seeds and fertilizers for their winter crops. Even bigger landlords faced a problem such as paying daily wages', so workers suffered (quoted in Nair, 2018).

A country that aspires to be an economic power must meet the most basic needs of its poor, and especially, the need for food. Yet, hunger is rampant. The Global Hunger Index (GHI) study combines indicators that measure the extent of undernourishment in the population and the extent of undernourishment and mortality of children under five. The GHI ranks countries on a 100-point scale, with 0 being the best score (no hunger) and 100 being the worst, although neither of these extremes is reached in practice. The hunger index and scores for India are getting worse. In 2018, India was ranked 103 out of 119 countries.

## 4    BJP Government's Record on Protection of Democratic Rights

There is an *undeclared* emergency in India. This is an undeclared war on freedom of speech and assembly, in the name of *vikas*, patriotism, nationalism, Hindu pride, and so on. Journalists or indeed anyone who dares to criticize the BJP government and the militant-communal forces which support it, are subject to verbal or physical assault or online-trolling from their supporters. There is an attack on scientific attitude towards nature and towards society, including its history.

Consider the 'Democracy Index'. This index is based on five categories: electoral process and pluralism; civil liberties; the functioning of government; political participation; and political culture. Based on their scores (on a scale of 0 to 10, where 10 = best) on a range of indicators within these categories, each country is given a composite score. Although there is still a democratic tradition in India, the degree of the country's democratic character is shrinking, as seen in changes in this index (Figure 10.6). A free press is an important part of democracy. The degree of press freedom is, more or less, decreasing as well (Figure 10.7). This is corroborated by the assault on journalists who dare to speak the truth and to criticize wrong actions/thinking of the government and of the (militant-communal) forces.

The new government had promised to eliminate corruption through increasing public awareness, e-governance, etc. What is the reality? Corruption is reduced when, other things constant, common people have the freedom to keep an eye on politicians (especially of the ruling party) and government officials. A society where the rule of law is not well adhered to, where the rule of law is whatever the right-wing forces think it is, and where there is a threat to freedom of press and secular civil society organizations, from right-wing violent mobs and from the state institutions steeped with right-wing ideas, such a society will not lower the level of corruption within the government institutions and at the interface between them and the business-world. As far as everyday corruption is concerned, a survey – by the Centre for Media Studies – reports in 2017 that 43 per cent of households feel that the level of corruption has increased in the preceding year. This is petty corruption, something that households face in their day-to-day life.

The Transparency Corruption Perception Index uses a scale of 0 to 100, where 0 is highly corrupt and 100 is very clean. India's corruption score has remained unchanged at 40. In 2015, the score was 38. India is among the 'worst offenders' in terms of graft and press freedom in the Asia Pacific region, according to Transparency International. Since 2015, India's world ranking in terms of corruption has been getting worse. India's corruption level in the public sector seems to be not getting better, in spite of the government's promise to provide clean governance, in spite of its promise of *sahi niyat*.

Secretive election funding by corporates (through electoral bonds), a policy that is promoted by BJP, is a major form of corruption made legal: a company will not give millions for nothing to a ruling party and/or provide material and ideological-social support to its vote-garnering forces masquerading as cultural organizations. A corporate, or a group of corporates, can buy *an entire policy package*, and not just this or that specific intervention on behalf of a company (e.g. buying a piece of government land for less than the market price by paying some politicians and officers a lot of money), and when an *entire policy* is bought, that is corruption but is not seen as that. It is quite likely that the total donations to BJP controlling the current government are several times the donations to all the other parties put together. One of the best ways to show that

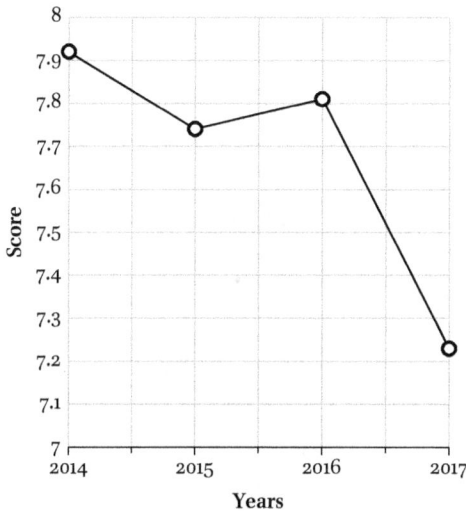

FIGURE 10.6    Democracy Index 2014–2017
Note: Score is out of 10; higher score =
greater freedom
SOURCE: DATA FROM HTTPS://WWW.SUDESTADA
.COM.UY/CONTENT/ARTICLES/421A313A-D58F-462E-
9B24-2504A37F6B56/DEMOCRACY-INDEX-2014.PDF;
HTTPS://WWW.YABILADI.COM/IMG/CONTENT/
EIU-DEMOCRACY-INDEX-2015.PDF;
HTTP://FELIPESAHAGUN.ES/WP-CONTENT/
UPLOADS/2017/01/DEMOCRACY-INDEX-2016.PDF

a party is non-corrupt is for it to tell the public who is funding it and how much. BJP will not do this. In fact, it has made it impossible for the donation for the 2014 elections to be investigated.

A society that does not respect the rights of women and children is a society with which there is something terribly wrong. In this context, it is important to note that, the number of crimes committed against women in big cities has been increasing under the BJP regime, from fewer than 38,500 to more than 41,500 between 2014 and 2016 (NCRB, 2016).

Similarly, as workers and as petty producers, Dalits (the communities occupying the lowest positions in the oppressive caste hierarchy in Hindu society) are most exploited, and as ordinary citizens, they are most oppressed. Instead of ensuring their democratic rights and dignity, there is increasing violence against them, because their views and practices do not conform to those of the upper-caste elite which supports the government. The number of crimes committed against Dalits in big cities has risen from 1,470 to more than 1,600 (NCRB,

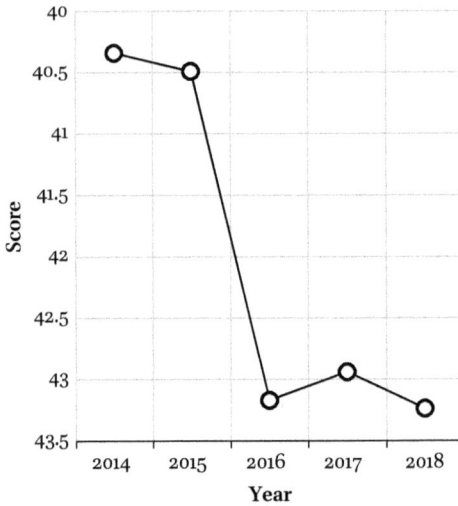

FIGURE 10.7     Press Freedom Index 2014–2018
                Note: Score out of 100. A smaller score on the report = greater
                freedom of the press as reported by the organization
                SOURCE: DATA FROM HTTPS://RSF.ORG/EN/RANKING/2018;
                HTTPS://TIMESOFINDIA.INDIATIMES.COM/WORLD/
                REST-OF-WORLD/IN-WORLD-PRESS-FREEDOM-INDEX-INDIA-
                RANKS-133RD/ARTICLESHOW/51941837.CMS; HTTPS://
                TIMESOFINDIA.INDIATIMES.COM/INDIA/PRESS-FREEDOM-
                IS-INDIA-IN-DECLINE/ARTICLESHOW/64009855.CMS

2016). According to NCRB, 40,801 cases of crime against scheduled castes were registered in the country as a whole in 2016, compared to 38,670 cases in 2015, an increase of 5.5%. Similarly, 6568 atrocities against Adivasis were recorded in 2016, compared to 6276 in 2015, a rise of 4.6% (Varma, 2018b).

> These two most oppressed sections of society together make up about 25% of India's population. The manuvadi and Brahmanical approach of the Sangh Parivar [the family of Hindu-communal groups] towards these sections is primarily responsible for their increasing marginalisation in the years against Modi rule.
> Ibid.

It is not surprising therefore to hear one BJP leader say this about Dalits:

> To us they are like a side dish, a pickle. You need a finger-lick (of the pickle) between mouthfuls to get your food down. But they can never be the

main course. It is ok to interact with them, in party offices. But our cultures are too different to sit down with them at home.

ANANDAN, 2018

Their *haath* (hand) is needed as workers and as voters, but their *saath* (their company) is shunned because they are perceived to be very low on the caste hierarchy. Uttering the name of Mr. Ambedkar, while having nothing to do with his ideas or practice in support of democratic rights of the oppressed, is one of the most hypocritical things a party and its leaders (and their paid-for savvy speech-writers) can do. That sort of strategy might result in some votes from some disillusioned Dalits (and aboriginal people), but it will do nothing to improve their economic and social conditions. Words do not fill a stomach. Empty words are worse at doing that job.

The incidents of communal violence have increased during the tenure of the BJP government (Figure 10.8). The victims generally receive little protection from police or other officials who must, generally, obey the party in power, and many of whom are themselves developing a communal attitude. Between 2014 and 2017, there was one communal incident, on an average, every 12 hours. In the communal incidents 389 people were killed (between 2014 and 2017) and 6,969 were injured (in 3 years from 2015). On the rise are incidents of violence by cow-vigilantes who illegally act against those who deal in and/or eat beef, and for whom cows' lives are, apparently, valued more than human lives. Targeting Muslims and *Dalits*, these incidents have increased from fewer than 5 in 2014 to more than 35 in 2017 (Figure 10.9). Varma (2018) reports that an 'estimated 700 attacks have taken place on churches, clergy, carol singers, Christmas and Easter events and missionaries across the country in the past 4 years' (2014–2018). Not surprisingly, India's record is getting worse in terms of what is called the Social Hostilities (religious unrest) Index:[14] In 2014, this was 7.9, which increased to 8.7 in 2015 (10 = worst). Even the sphere of personal life and love is not beyond communalization. A Muslim man having a Hindu partner is accused of engaging in 'love jihad': it is 'a supposed form of religious warfare by which Muslim men lure Hindu women away from their faith' (Bhatia, 2017). Even movies where such a relationship is shown are threatened with boycott.

---

14　The Social Hostilities Index looks at 13 indicators including crimes motivated by religious hatred, mob violence related to religion, communal violence, religion-related terrorist groups, using force to prevent religious groups from operating, the harassment of women for 'violating' religious dress codes and violence over conversion or proselytizing (Rukmini, 2017).

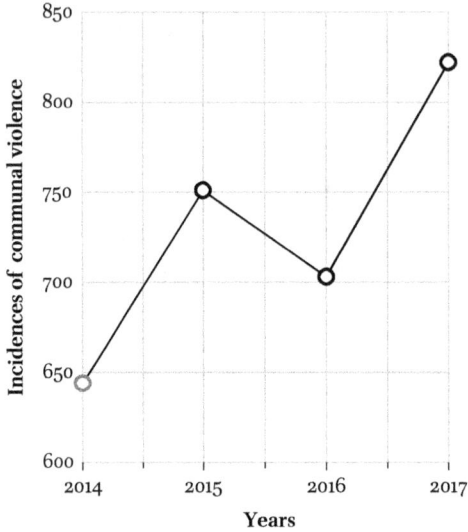

FIGURE 10.8    Incidences of communal violence, 2014–2017
               SOURCE: DATA FROM HTTPS://WWW.FIRSTPOST.COM/
               INDIA/INDIA-WITNESSED-822-COMMUNAL-INCI
               DENTS-IN-2017-SAYS-CENTRE-111-KILLED-2384-IN
               JURED-IN-VIOLENCE-4338217.HTML; HTTPS://WWW
               .FIRSTPOST.COM/INDIA/COMMUNAL-VIOLENCE-ROSE-
               BY-28-FROM-2014-TO-2017-BUT-2008-REMAINS-YEAR-OF-
               HIGHEST-INSTANCES-OF-RELIGIOUS-VIO
               LENCE-4342951.HTML

## 5    People's Response to False Promises

The Modi government has spent Rupees 4,806 crore on publicity of its achievements in its four years of rule, from 2014–15 to 2017–18. Writing in 2018, Varma
(2018) revealed that Modi's BJP government had indeed spent more than double
the amount on publicizing its achievements than was spent by *two* United Progressive Alliance (Congress-led) governments. Varma observed that this 'bar-
rage of publicity through all media platforms is meant to create the illusion that
the Modi government, which won the 2014 election promising *Achhe Din* [good
days] for Indians, has fulfilled its promises'. Taken from taxes and other imposts,
the money spent on publicity could have been spent on people's well-being.

The money is spent on illusions aimed at smudging the gap between what
the ruling class and its government actually do for the people on the one hand
and the life that people actually experience on the other. But the people's objective experience of life and government is registered in their consciousness.
There is a limit to how much and how long such propaganda can maintain the

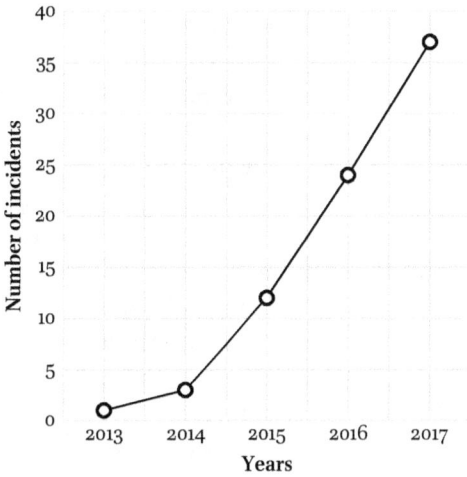

FIGURE 10.9     Hate crime: cow vigilante violence,
                2013–2017
                SOURCE: DATA FROM HTTP://DATA
                .INDIASPEND.COM/

falsehood. When not many jobs are created, when wage rises are stagnating, when the rich are getting obscenely richer, when farmers are not getting a fair price for their produce and hard work, there is likely to be disillusion with the government. Admittedly, this happens, however inadequately, unevenly, slowly and contradictorily. If a section of the population had supported the BJP which made lots of promises, the level of its support for the party and its government has begun declining. Of course, what might happen during the 2019 election, when BJP resorts to communally-charged emotional appeals to nationalism, is a different matter.

Given its failure to deliver on its big promises made just to garner votes, one way the BJP government has sought to maintain and bolster electoral support is religious hatred and hyper-nationalism. But the people are no longer so accepting of this zealotry, just as they are no longer accepting of the false economic promises. Many now understand that the issue of religious division between Hindus and non-Hindus is not the cause of their problems. Many now understand as well that as a nation India is not under attack from the forces that the BJP's so-called nationalist forces say it is; that is, religious minorities or indeed anyone who dissents from the party and its government. The evidence for this realization is seen in several areas. For example, since 2014, the BJP has been losing one election after another, and its vote share has been declining. In a by-election in Kairana, Uttar Pradesh, held on May 28 and May 30, 2018, the

BJP lost its own seat. Using its normal electoral engineering practice of raking up emotional issues concerned with religion or religion-based nationalism just before the election, the Hindu-nationalist party had attempted to consolidate Hindu voters by using the 'issue' of a photograph of Jinnah, the founder of the Islamic State of Pakistan, in Aligarh Muslim University in North India. However, this negative jingoism was countered by opponents who focused on real issues: 'What will be the poll agenda in Kairana by-election: Jinnah or *ganna* [sugarcane]?' This intervention on behalf of sugarcane farmers resonated with a perception that the BJP's invocation of the Jinnah photograph was by a party insensitive to the issues that really mattered in an area where sugarcane is the main cash crop and where delayed payment from sugar mills is the main issue. *Ganna* mattered: a coalition of Muslims, *Dalits*, Jat farmers and people from OBC background (Other Backward Class, a group of socially and educationally disadvantaged castes) highlighted livelihood issues, showing the BJP's divisive politics of religious identity was really a non-issue. Lies and false promises were trumped by the facts of real-life experience and hardship.

This also seems to be a message of the multi-round massive nation-wide survey referred to earlier, in which the decline of support for the BJP is highlighted: 'The survey found that there isn't a single major issue on which the Modi government is rated positively now' (Lokniti, 2018: 6). The BJP campaigned in 2014 declaring that it would promote development. Interestingly, 51% of those surveyed considered it had done little developmental work, while 64% felt it had not been able to address farmers' concerns and 61% felt it failed to control rising prices (see Figure 10.10). While the BJP consistently claims it believes in *sabka saath* (Together with all) and that it is not communal, its actions have been quite different, with 52% of those surveyed considering it had not maintained religious harmony. The BJP campaigned against the Congress Party in 2014, declaring it corrupt. Yet, 55% of those surveyed thought that the BJP government itself had been unable to curb corruption. In fact, three in five considered the Modi administration a corrupt government.

Given all these failures, one is not surprised to find the Lokniti survey (2018: 7) comment that: 'Overall, 44% of the voters thought that the country was headed in the wrong direction'. According to the survey, only '35% felt otherwise'.

Modi also promised *sabka vikas* or inclusive development but only 30% believe there has been *sabka vikas* in the government's time in office and the proportion of voters who do not believe development has benefitted everyone is increasing. The BJP-led government's claim of development of all is no longer convincing to people, as shown in the Lokniti (2018) survey. In May 2018, only 30% of voters believed development has been for all sections – the rich and the poor – a decline from 39% in January 2018. Meanwhile, a far greater percentage believed that the development promised by the BJP in 2014 had benefitted only the rich (up to 42% in May 2018 from 36% in January 2018), while about 22% believed there has been no development at all. This means that 64% of voters have a negative view of development under the BJP regime. This perception is in line with rising inequality between the rich and the poor and the failure of the government to address the unemployment problem, as mentioned above. It is hardly surprising that the level of support for the BJP-led government has been declining among middle and lower classes (see Figure 10.11).

In response to the government's failure to address caste oppression, in part due to the BJP's upper caste biases, the level of Dalit support has been falling (see Figure 10.12). In May 2018, only 22% of *Dalits* supported the BJP. This is 9% lower than in January 2018 and is down 2% on the 2014 Lok Sabha election. Three in five *Dalits* (60%) and over half the *Adivasis* (indigenous or aboriginal communities) (54%) said that they were dissatisfied with the concern shown by the Modi government towards growing crimes and atrocities against them. The BJP's pro-rich and pro-urban biases also mean that it has failed to address farmers' concerns, which is why their support for BJP is diminishing. This is reflected in the May 2018 Uttar Pradesh by-election and Lokniti survey results (see Figure 10.13). This is also reflected in the fact that in November 2018, thousands of farmers marched to Delhi protesting against the BJP government. Called the 'Farmers Liberation March', and organized by the All India Kisan Sangharsh Coordination Committee (AIKSCC), a joint front of 208 farmers organizations, including Left-led organizations, this is the fourth such rally in one year. Farmers are demanding a special Parliament Session to pass laws on debt waiver and higher prices for their produce.[15]

In the light of the various failures of the government, the percentage of people who are dissatisfied with it has been rising, and the difference between the percentage of people who are satisfied and the percentage of people who are not satisfied has now reached zero (Figure 10.14).

During the 2014 Lok Sabha election campaign, as widely known, Modi had promised to bring *achhe din* (good times). The proportion of voters who thought that he had failed in bringing *achhe din* has been increasing. In May 2018, more than half were still waiting for *achhe din* (see Figure 10.15).

---

15    This huge rally as a powerful political response to the real economic miseries of common people stands in marked contrast to ongoing attempts by communal forces to whip up support for a law to allow the construction of a Ram temple in Ayodhya.

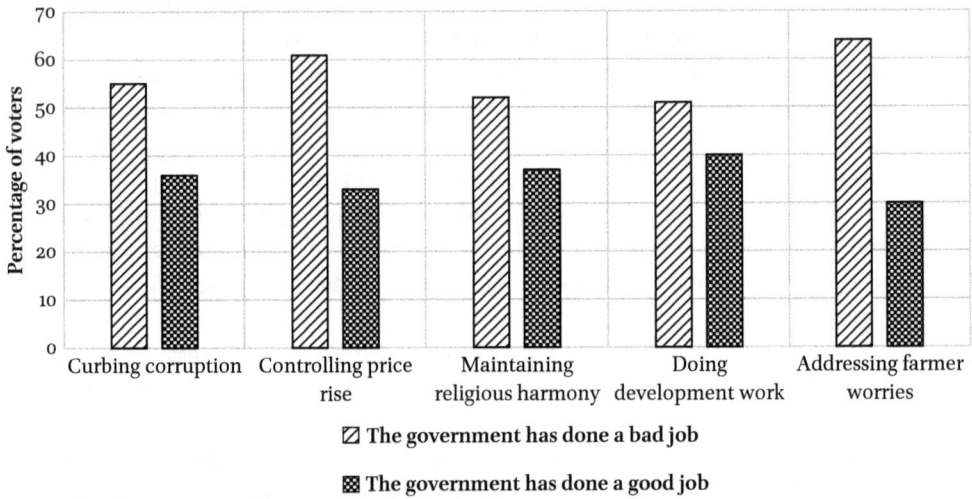

FIGURE 10.10    Voters' perception of the Modi Government's record (in 2018 May)
Note: Respondents were asked: 'Has the Narendra Modi-led Central government done a good job or a bad job with regard to the following?'
SOURCE: DATA FROM LOKNITI SURVEY, 2018

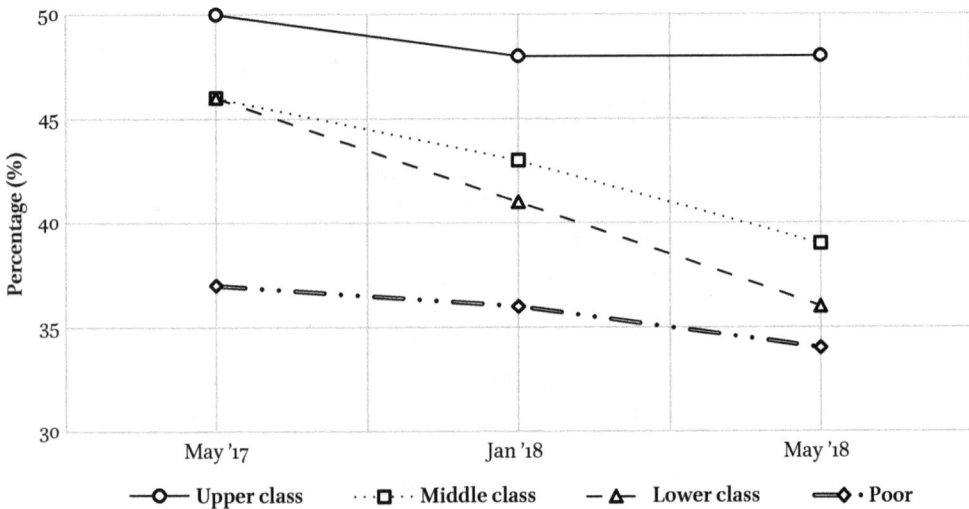

FIGURE 10.11    Percent of support for the BJP-led government
SOURCE: DATA FROM LOKNITI SURVEY, 2018

FIGURE 10.12    Percent of Dalits' supporters for BJP
            SOURCE: DATA FROM LOKNITI SURVEY, 2018

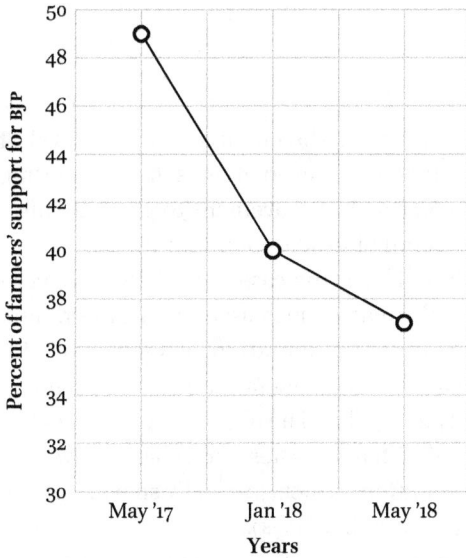

FIGURE 10.13    Percent of farmers' supporters for BJP
            SOURCE: DATA FROM LOKNITI SURVEY, 2018

In May 2017, 39% said they would vote for the BJP in the event of a snap national election. By January 2018, the figure dropped to 34%, although that was still an increase from the 31% who voted for BJP in 2014 election. By May 2018, there were more people in the country who did not want the Modi-led government to return to power after the next election than those who did. Nearly half (47%) of all respondents in the Lokniti's May 2018 survey said that the government did not merit another term in office. Only 39% thought it deserved another chance after the 2019 election.

The anti-government sentiment was found to be especially strong among religious minorities. About three-fourths of Muslims, three-fifths of Christians and well over half of Sikhs indicated that they did not wish to see the Modi government back in power in 2019. This is not surprising given the Hindu-nationalist government's dismal record on communal harmony.

Interestingly, the Lokniti survey found that a sizeable section of voters from the majority Hindu community also had an anti-government sentiment, with 42% of Hindu voters anti-government and 44% pro-government. Out of all Hindu communities, *Dalits* and *Adivasis*, who have been victims of violence and atrocities since 2014, were found to be strongest in their opposition to the government at 55% and 43% respectively. They were followed by dominant OBC communities (Upper OBC castes), with 42% opposed to the government (Lokniti, 2018: 13).

## 6      Conclusion

Under the Modi government, as we have seen, the country's average level of income has been high (by India's standards), even if it is not increasing particularly rapidly. There has also been some improvement to physical infrastructure since 2014. Yet, overall, the record of development during the BJP regime has been an epic of dismal failure. This is the case, especially if we consider the issues that affect the lives of the masses such as: unemployment and under-employment; low wages; increasing concentration of wealth and income; agrarian crisis; and increasing attack on democracy and secularism and attendant communalization of society and polity. The ultra-rich has had *achhe din*. But the vast majority of people of different castes and religions live and work under economic and political conditions which, generally speaking, have not been improving. They have had *bure din* (bad days).

According to the Prime Minister (or his erudite speech writer), *development* has become a vibrant *mass movement*. This is only in written or spoken words, however. One indirect indicator of the overall failure of the government is in

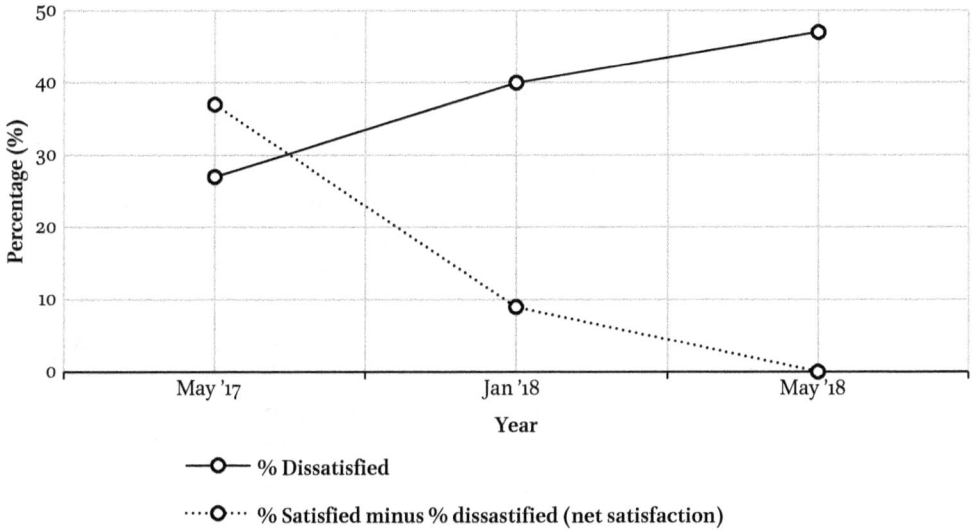

───○─── % Dissatisfied

····○···· % Satisfied minus % dissastified (net satisfaction)

FIGURE 10.14    Percentage of voters dissatisfied/net-satisfied with the BJP government
SOURCE: DATA FROM LOKNITI SURVEY, 2018

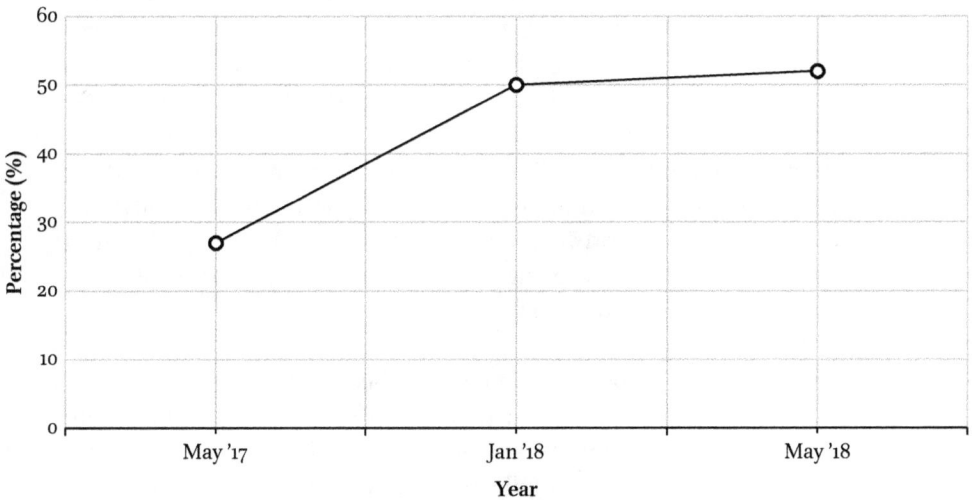

FIGURE 10.15    Percentage of voters who think Mr. Modi has failed in achieving *achhe din*
(good times)
SOURCE: LOKNITI SURVEY, 2018

fact the amount of money it spends on publicity. People are not experiencing development as much as BJP would like them to believe. So, it is spending millions on publicity on creating illusions.

Words *are* important. Yet, word ≠ world. There is development, but of the ultra-rich and not for the masses. Development as a mass movement is a beautiful idea. Development *should* become a mass movement. But it *will* become a mass movement when *masses*, democratically self-organized, *move* to take control over their lives. Development *will* become a mass movement when the masses (toiling workers and small-scale producers) control how nation's resources are used – i.e. when *they* are able to decide and say that nation's resources, which are, more or less, products of their *own* labor interacting with nature, are used to satisfy *their* needs, and *not* the needs of the business class for profit, *not* the needs of the political class for accumulating election funding, personal financial fortunes and power, and *not* the needs of the pliant bureaucratic and intellectual layers for their pecuniary and other privileges.

It might be argued that while the situation is not all that good, things can be better in the near future. There are no grounds for such an assumption, however. In fact, the BJP government's failure has a *necessary* character, because of its class and social (religious-sectarian and upper-caste) biases. Controlled by a right-wing party, the government is brazenly pro-big business and panders to a narrow, upper-middle class urban segment of highly educated technical personnel, who, in turn, churn out pro-BJP and communal propaganda and hyper-nationalism meant to dupe the masses, including by using social media. The overall economic orientation of the government is indicated by 'Modinomics'. Modinomics is India's version of 'Reaganomics', which is a product of right-wing economists representing the interests of the big business, both domestic and foreign, and given official approval by Modi, and his political advisors. Conservative American David B. Cohen, who served in the George W. Bush administration, praised Modi, saying that, like Reagan, he 'is an unabashed proponent of free market economics'. He added:

> As one who lived through Reaganomics, I believe that Modinomics can be the perfect antidote to the kleptocratic crony socialism that has kept India from realising her vast economic potential. If India's natural entrepreneurial dynamism is ever fully unleashed, the sky will be the limit.
>
> COHEN, 2014

Modinomics is, fundamentally, an anti-people package of pro-market, pro-business policies. It includes 'privatisation, cuts in food and fuel subsidies and a new sales tax [GST], a tax that is the most regressive way to get revenue as it hits the poor the most' (Roberts, 2017). Its aim, and its effect, are to create the conditions for enabling profits for the corporates through a combination of inter-connected processes: super-exploitation of the masses on the basis of flexible labor policies; extreme austerity, increasing people's vulnerability; reducing corporate tax liability; and surrendering society's natural and financial resources and state-owned enterprises to private business-owners. Modinomics is a vision of the most extreme form of neo-liberal capitalism that Indian state embarked on (see Das, 2015; also Chapter 4 of this book).

The multiple failures of the government can be tied to its blatantly right-wing nature. The government is *right*-wing for a reason: it is *right* for the business class, a class which is on the *wrong* side of history.[16] It is right-wing because its fundamental aim is to serve the business class. It therefore cannot be expected to do much that is right for wage-earners, farmers, the poor and small-scale entrepreneurs, in any systematic, logical and long-term manner, *even if* some in government may have good intentions and even if some crumbs may fall, and do fall, to the people in exchange for political support.

To judge a government's policy requires one to consider, for example, the extent to which the things (or use-values) it provides its common citizens have a commodified or de-commodified character (see Polanyi, 1944/2001; also Block and Polanyi, 2003). The more de-commodified the things are, the better it is for the majority, simply because the majority do not have a lot of money in their hands. One must ask: is water or education or healthcare of good quality provided to citizens in adequate amount by the government as a free use-value or, at least, at a minimal price, relative to the income of the people? From the standpoint of the majority, the purpose of a government is to provide an *antidote* to the ravages of the market, at least as far as the consumption of basic necessaries is concerned. However, true to its right-wing economic policies, what the BJP government, led by the party of the trading and business class, calls 'development' is a tradeable thing, a commodity. The so-called developmental benefits are market-mediated and even corporate-mediated and constitute the mechanisms for the creation or expansion of the market for commodities to be produced for a profit.[17] This is exactly what the neoliberal-capitalist state does. What use are electricity wires or LPG connections if people have no money to pay for electricity and LPG? What use are roads if these roads siphon off natural resources and the surplus of an area to other places,

---

16    The shelf-life of the business class is long over. The progressive character of the business
      class is a thing of the past. It is the proletariat that is objectively the rising class (see Das,
      2017; see Chapters 10–11 of this book on the relation between the proletarian struggle and
      the fascistic movement).

17    Consider the much-hyped insurance for farmers and how insurance companies are sali-
      vating over the profits available.

especially, big cities, the main seat of capital? What use are roads if these roads take one to the places where there is neither decent wage-work nor free or subsidized government-provided services? Something that is as simple as a road or electricity which everyone needs, comes to have 'metaphysical subtleties', when this 'very trivial thing' (Marx, 1977: 163) is seen in the context of the commodity-driven society that this right-wing government is intent on strengthening.

For the mathematically inclined, the impact of the BJP government can be rendered as: $I_{BJP} = I_{EP} + I_{CP} + (I_{EP})(I_{CP})$, where the impact of the BJP ($I_{BJP}$) on people is the sum of the impact of its right-wing economic policy ($I_{EP}$), its communal policy of authoritarian-communalism-hyper-Hindu-nationalism ($I_{CP}$), and the interaction between the two.

Common people are directly hurt by BJP's development policy and economic thinking, buttressed by right-wing economists, including some from the US, who had previously been marginalized. The communal-authoritarian policy that divides people and that crushes the right to dissent also directly affects the masses, in part by undermining their potential for resistance against the economic and the political elite. And given that BJP's economic policy is implemented in a context of communal-authoritarianism supported by vigilantism and mob violence, the adverse impact of the economic policy is magnified: its adverse impact is greater than what it would be if BJP was not *both* communal and economically right-wing.

If you are a Dalit or from a religious minority or indeed a woman who wants to live like an ordinary citizen with all the rights that men enjoy, then your life is one of fear. If you are someone who is against the regime of unreason, religious obscurantism, and on-going attacks on secular ideals, and who is courageous enough to speak the truth, then your life is one of fear as well. The world's largest democracy has been reduced to this. The question is why? Why is this turn to the extreme right-wing thinking and practices which are indeed characteristic of a fascis*tic* movement?

# Towards a Political Economy of Fascistic Tendencies

As we have seen in the last chapter, India is experiencing something like a national emergency. This is in the form of persistent attacks on the basic democratic rights of ordinary citizens, by hyper-nationalist Hindu-supremacist forces, which are supported by, and which support, a right-wing political party (Bharatiya Janata Party or BJP). Religious minorities, especially, Muslims, have become 'near-exact equivalent of the Jew' (Sarkar, 2016: 143). The right-wing forces are bent on creating a Hindu state, where religious minorities will remain subservient to the majority religion, and where Dalits (ex-untouchables) will continue to be oppressed by the higher castes in the Hindu social order. The Hindu-nationalist forces are targeting not only religious minorities and Dalits, but also Leftists as well as rationalists and secularists, who oppose their Hindtuva (Hindu-ness) ideology.

The rise of the BJP is a part of the world-wide right-wing bourgeois political trend moving on (or towards) a 'fascistic path'.[1] Fascistic forces are not a thing of the past as far as developed liberal-democratic countries are concerned, which is where they began in early parts of the 20th century. Their threat is very much present right now, including in the US. On April 6, 2018, a former Secretary of State of the US warns in *New York Times*: 'fascism – and the tendencies that lead toward fascism – pose a more serious threat now than at any time since the end of World War II' (Albright, 2018). And, there are fascistic forces in the less developed world as well. During the times of European fascism, there was 'a time when the entire bourgeois democracy in each country believed that fascism was possible only in the backward countries which had not yet graduated from the school of democracy' (Trotsky, 1940). And there are scholars (Vanaik, 2017) now who believe that fascism is not possible in less developed countries, as I will discuss later. I will argue that there *are* 'fascistic

---

1   This is reflected not only in anti-fascist movements happening in different places, but also in the growing attention being given to the topic in academic debates and discussions (e.g. Anievas et al., 2014; Baker, 2005; Banaji, 2016a; Chacko and Jayasuriya, 2018 and the special issue it introduces; Dobkowski, and Walliman, 2003; Kallis, 2003; Mann, 2004; Mason, 1995; Neiberg, 2018; Panitch and Albo, 2016; Patel and McMichael, 2008; Paxton, 2004; Rieman, 2018; Robinson and Barrera, 2012; Saull, 2015). There is also a large amount of discussion in newspapers, magazines, and blogs.

tendencies' – as a form of bourgeois politics or an extreme tendency toward the breakdown of bourgeois politics – in both richer and poorer countries. Just as the idea that private property is an eternal thing produces the view of capitalist class society as the natural order of things, similarly, the view that capitalism will always have a democratic system makes many people under-emphasize the danger of the collapse of the democratic set-up, which can lead to a fascistic threat. To the extent that such a danger exists, whether it is in rich countries or in poorer countries such as India, the question is how do we understand the threat as we face it, from the standpoint of removing it? This chapter and the next seek to explain fascistic tendencies.

The remainder of this chapter is divided into four sections. Section 1 deals with some definitional/conceptual issues concerning fascism. Section 2 introduces the topic of the fascistic threat in India and sheds light on its importance of the threat to India's Left and progressive culture. Section 3 deals with the political economy of fascism and fascistic tendencies, at a general theoretical level, but with an eye towards India. This section relates the fascistic tendencies to class society, to capitalist class-society and to India's capitalist society, in terms of *economic* as well as *cultural-political* processes, and in terms of society's *structural* conditions and class *agency* involved in the fascistic movement.[2] The focus of this chapter on the political economy aspects of the fascistic tendencies sets the context for the next chapter which discusses the bourgeois-political dynamics of the fascistic movement in India. The final section concludes the chapter.

## 1        Fascism and Fascistic Tendencies: Some Conceptual Issues

### 1.1      *Very Briefly, What Is Fascism?*
There are two forms of bourgeois rule. One is the democratic system. There is no doubt that bourgeois democracy is 'a great historical advance in comparison with medievalism' (Lenin, 1977c: 28). Marxists in fact 'demand the extension of ... bourgeois democracy' as a tool for working class organization, *in order to prepare the people for revolution* for the purpose of overthrowing ...the exploiters' (ibid.: 59; italics in original). Liberal democratic rights that have been won and sustained through mass struggles do provide *some* opportunities to the masses to express their interests and ideas, within limits, as compared to the opportunities available under feudalism or fascism. Yet, the bourgeois

---

2  In discussing the class agency aspect, I build on chapter 25 of Marx's *Capital 1* and Aijaz Ahmad's excellent work.

character of liberal-democracy should not be underestimated at all. It is, more or less, the case that:

> the exploiters inevitably transform the state (and we are speaking of de-mocracy, i.e., one of the forms of the state) into an instrument of the rule of their class, the exploiters, over the exploited. Hence, as long as there are exploiters who rule the majority, the exploited, the democratic state must inevitably be a democracy for the exploiters.
>
> LENIN, 1977C: 35

Liberal democracy, as a form of class rule, fully protects the interests of the tiny economic elite (say, top 1–5% or so) versus the masses (bottom 60–80% or so) who constitute the vast majority. Liberal democracy is much more useful for resolving conflicts between members of a given class (e.g. between two land-lords, two capitalists, two workers, etc.) than between two antagonistically-related classes. As Lenin (1918) says, 'the ruling party in a bourgeois democracy extends the protection of the minority only to another bourgeois party, while the proletariat, on all serious, profound and fundamental issues, gets martial law or pogroms, instead of the "protection of the minority"'. In a class society, there cannot be equality between classes, and without economic equality, de-mocracy as equal rights is of limited value. Liberal democracy – bourgeois de-mocracy – is, ultimately, sustained on the basis of the deployment of coercive measures and violence against the masses, or the threat of violence against them. There is indeed also always a threat to existing democratic rights of com-mon people. Just because a state currently tolerates democratic rights that does not mean it will always do so. In fact,

> whenever the proletariat comes forward as an independent force the bourgeoisie shifts over to the camp of the counterrevolution. The more audacious the mass struggle all the swifter is the reactionary degenera-tion of liberalism. No one has yet invented a means for paralyzing the ef-fects of the law of the class struggle.
>
> TROTSKY, 1939

This brings us to the second form of class rule: authoritarianism. Under certain conditions, authoritarianism can be transformed into a fascist/fascistic rule. Today no country has a fascist rule, if by fascism we mean the following:

> When a state turns fascist,… it means first of all for the most part that the workers' organizations are annihilated; that the proletariat is reduced to

an amorphous state; and that a system of administration is created which penetrates deeply into the masses and which serves to frustrate the independent crystallization of the proletariat. Therein precisely is the gist of fascism.

TROTSKY, 1944

The gist of fascism and its task consist in a complete suppression of all workers' organizations and in the prevention of their revival.

TROTSKY, 1932d

Some say that fascism is a political movement. 'Fascism ... is the ideology of nationalism upheld by an anti-democratic and totalitarian state', says Mackel (2010). But fascism is not an ordinary political movement. Fascism is authoritarianism. But it is different from Bonapartism, although fascism does have elements of Bonapartism.[3] 'Fascism is not merely a system of reprisals, of brutal force, and of police terror' (Trotsky, 1932i). It is a ruling-class-based intervention: it is class struggle from above, effected on the basis of threat and practice of violence against the masses, in order to protect capitalist class relations and to promote capitalist accumulation strategies. Trotsky continues:

Fascism is a particular governmental system based on the uprooting of all elements of proletarian democracy within bourgeois society.
In the course of many decades, the workers have built up within the bourgeois democracy, by utilizing it, by fighting against it, their own strongholds and bases of proletarian democracy: the trade unions, the political parties, the educational and sport clubs, the cooperatives, etc.
The task of fascism lies not only in destroying the Communist vanguard but in holding the entire class in a state of forced disunity. To this end the physical annihilation of the most revolutionary section of the workers does not suffice. It is also necessary to smash all independent and voluntary organizations, to demolish all the defensive bulwarks of the proletariat...For, in the last analysis, the Communist Party also bases itself on these achievements.

TROTSKY, 1932i

---

3    '[It is wrong to say that] fascism is simply a repetition of Bonapartism. There is an element of Bonapartism in fascism... Without this element, namely, without the raising of state power above society owing to an extreme sharpening of the class struggle, fascism would have been impossible' (Trotsky, 1940).

A political project such as fascism needs a class agency. Fascism's class agency is made up by: the petty bourgeoisie, old and new, and sections of the wage-earning class and the under- and unemployed, supported by sections of the propertied class (more on this later). Fascism is an authoritarian political movement against the masses, by the masses, on behalf of the ruling class.

## 1.2    *Fascism Not Possible Anymore?*

If fascism is, more or less, what we have just described it to be, it is clearly a dangerous thing. It is a serious threat to democratic rights. This means that it is also a serious threat to social-economic rights of the masses, as without access to democratic rights, they cannot demand social-economic rights. But some have argued that given strong liberal democracy in rich countries, and given capitalism's resilience, there is a very weak chance of fascism happening there (Vanaik, 2017: 297, 284). Vanaik (2017) says that Marxists have underestimated: 'the strength and durability of bourgeois democracy after 1945', and this under-estimation is the 'natural correlate of an obverse error – the overestimation of the 'structural crisis' of capitalism' (p. 299).[4] The idea that capitalism is in structural crisis is out of line with the fact of the 'remarkable productivity of late capitalism and its ability to learn from mistakes (preventing anything a repeat of anything approximating the Great Depression)' (p. 299).[5] The kind of social-economic dislocation that caused fascism in Europe is nowhere present now. 'Decades after the end of the long boom (itself never anticipated) the prospects of fascisms coming to power within remain dim', Vanaik says, al-though there are newer and stronger authoritarian pressures (p. 300). There is also little reason to expect fascism to come to the Global South. Firstly, 'Why should foreign capitals having controlling positions in the dominant class-coalitions or ruling-class alliances of specific developing world countries want to encourage, not just the authoritarian option, but the specifically fascist one?' (p. 302). Besides, crucial to the functioning of multinational companies is their control of knowhow and not so much of markets or of resources (p. 301). Secondly, the fascist option made sense in a context where there was a power-ful systemic threat to the rule of capital from the working class (especially where the possibility of its rapid mass radicalization existed) (p. 303). But in

---

4    This view is very close to Chibber's (2017) view that capitalism is not in crisis but neoliberal-ism is.

5    For Vanaik, because Marxism has under-emphasized capitalism – financial capital's – dyna-mism, it has over-emphasized inter-imperialist rivalry and war, which had triggered fascism in Europe in the 20th century. The most important feature of expanding capitalism has been technical innovation (Vanaik, 2017: 301). Political stability through democratic/semi-demo-cratic system and the preservation of capitalist relations are much more important to the imperialist project (Vanaik, 2017: 312, 300–302).

our times the tendency is towards de-radicalization of the working-class move-ment. Thirdly, while fascism is based on the squeezing of the middle classes in rural and urban areas (i.e. proletarianization), that is also not happening now in the less developed world: 'the assumptions of the classical Marxist theories of fascism have been shaken' (p. 305).[6] Fourthly, there is a discursive obstacle to fascism: the memory and awareness of what the historic experience of fas-cism has meant and the practical experience of prolonged bourgeois democ-racy are powerful vaccine within the working class (and even the petty bour-geois) against the fascist temptation' (Vanaik, 2017: 306). All in all, Vanaik says, 'In post-colonial societies, the political vehicles of religious fundamentalism or religious nationalism are not fascist formations but, at most, potential forma-tions' and that 'the conditions for the realization of that potential do not exist, and are not likely to surface' (p. 324). As far as India as a post-colonial country is concerned, 'there is no convincing economic rationale for emerging fascism, though there may be for emerging or deepening authoritarianism' (p. 302). Be-sides, the organized working class does not see communalism as representing fascism; only many of their communist leaders do (p. 334).[7] 'While the fascist state in India would necessarily be Hindu nationalist, the Hindu communal and nationalist state would not necessarily be fascist' (p. 324). There are, of course, several conceptual problems with the thesis that fascism, or something close to it, cannot come to the Global South, as suggested below; and that the-sis has to be counter-posed, *empirically*, to what is happening in Brazil under Bolsonaro in 2018.

### 1.3    *From Fascism to Fascistic Tendency/Tendencies*

Fascism must be seen as a historical process. This is in two inter-related senses. One is that it is a stage in the cycle of capitalism. It is a particular historical system of capitalist reaction. Bourgeois politics progresses through certain stages, and fascism is the last one (here no linearity is implied, however).

> we must differentiate three historical stages: at the dawn of capitalist de-velopment, when the bourgeoisie required revolutionary methods to

---

6  In most of the Global South, there is the fact of persistence of the peasantry. In the towns, the middle classes have usually had little pressure from below, from a working class. The relative size of this middle class is much larger in the South than in the early industrializing countries at a comparable stage (p. 305).

7  Note that the word communal is used in India not in its usual western sense, which is associ-ated with commons (e.g. communal property, communal living, etc.). 'Only in India does the word "communalism" refer to a malignant ideology and violence prone practice – even a form of "fascism" – which justifies itself in the name of religious difference' (Ahmad, 2013: 6).

resolve its tasks; in the period of bloom and maturation of the capitalist regime, when the bourgeoisie endowed its domination with orderly, pacific, conservative, democratic forms; finally, at the decline of capitalism, when the bourgeoisie is forced to resort to methods of civil war against the proletariat to protect its right of exploitation.

The political programs characteristic of these three stages: *Jacobinism*, reformist *democracy* (social democracy included) and *Fascism* are basically programs of petty bourgeois currents.

TROTSKY, 1932a

Thus fascism is, first of all, a stage in bourgeois politics representing the breakdown of the democratic system (see Figure 11.1 below).

There is another sense in which fascism is to be seen historically: it is that in any given society, traits of fascism and those of democracy can be combined in various proportions, however temporarily. This aspect of the historical character of fascism exists given the 'the law that governs the displacement of one social system by another, even though they are irreconcilably inimical to each other' (Trotsky, 1932d). Indicated here is a stage of potential transition to fascism proper:

during a given period, between the democratic and the fascist systems, a transitional regime is established, which combines the features of both... There are periods during which the bourgeoisie leans upon both the Social Democracy and fascism, that is, during which it simultaneously manipulates its electoral and terroristic agencies... But such a condition of the state and of the administration is temporary in character.

TROTSKY, 1932d

During the transition period: there cannot be further reforms of capitalism in the interests of masses, but 'neither Communism nor fascism is ready as yet to seize power' (Trotsky, 1932d). There is thus a tendency towards the crisis of bourgeois politics.

I approach the crisis of bourgeois politics as fascistic tendencies from two inter-related philosophical viewpoints. One concerns the distinction between tendencies and outcomes (and the related distinction between appearances and underlying reality): a mechanism – i.e. a way of acting or functioning of an object – exists necessarily by virtue of the nature of an object (i.e. the internal relations which constitute the object and its relation to other objects, within a system) and the effects of the mechanism (when it is active) may be mediated by – and even temporarily countered by – other mechanisms and by contingent

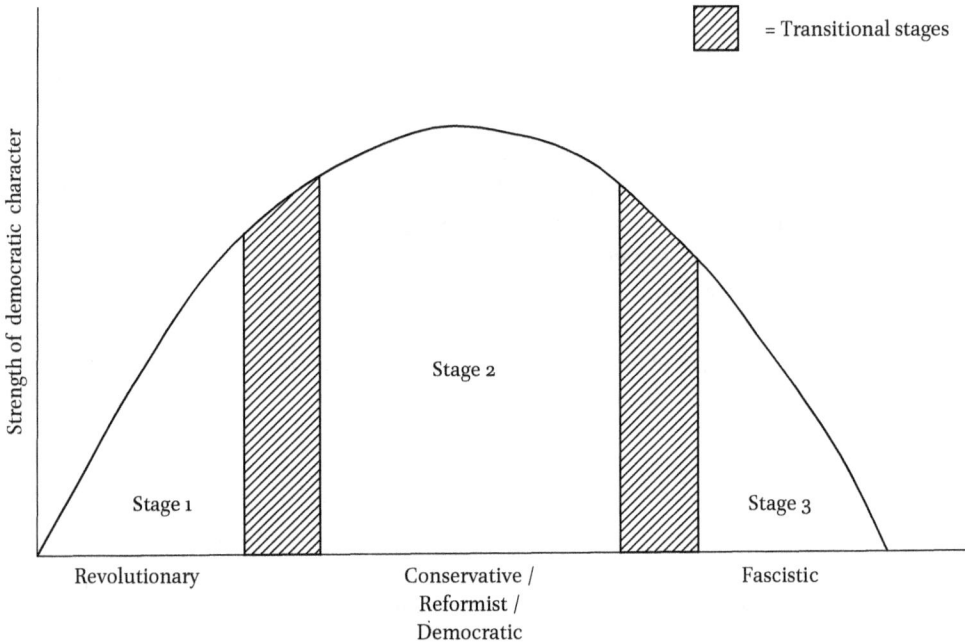

FIGURE 11.1  Curve of capitalist politics
            SOURCE: AUTHOR

conditions (see Sayer, 1992: 106), although what is called a tendency is ultimately more powerful than what is called a counter-tendency (Carchedi, 2010).
This philosophical view shaped Marx's theory of capitalist crisis caused by the
rate of profit to fall with the rising organic composition of capital. The second
perspective informing my view of fascism says that:

> understanding anything ... requires that we know something about how
> it arose and developed... our notion of anything [must] ... include, as as-
> pects of what it is, both the process by which it has become that and the
> broader interactive context in which it is found.
>
> OLLMAN, 2003: 13

This is the perspective of Marx, the dialectician, who studied capitalism of his
time not just from the standpoint of what it was but also from the standpoint
of where it was going (given its internal tendencies), what it was tending towards (e.g. development of monopolies; globalization; recurrent and intensify-
ing crises, etc.), even if many of the things he thought characterized capitalism
were going to be materialized to a greater extent in the 20th century than during the time when he was writing about it.

When I say fascistic tendency (tendencies), the term/concept refers to mechanisms (processes/relations), which exist by virtue of the capitalist-class society, and which, under certain conditions, can result in a fascist government/ state. There is a tendency towards the breakdown of bourgeois democracy, and 'The workers are aware that democracy is suffering shipwreck everywhere, and that they are threatened by fascism even in those countries where fascism is as yet non-existent' (Trotsky, 1940). While India or any other country does not have a fascist regime, there are fascistic movements and fascistic governments, as in the US of the late 1930s–1940s, and in many countries such as India and the US in contemporary times. There *are* fascistic *tendencies* (mechanisms/ forces/processes) which *can* produce a fascist outcome (i.e. fascist state) when favorable *conditions* are present. Fascistic tendencies can exist in a society which is not fascist. The transitional phase is obviously different from the stage where there is full-fledged fascism, but there are similarities: fascists aim 'at the domination of the traditional bourgeois parties in the name of the "strong state"; this is a fascist trait characteristic of the movement and of the regime' (Trotsky, 1934a). A party, an organization or a mob can be fascist – or almost fascist (fascistic) – without there being a fascist state. A mob or an organization can be fascist (almost fascist) within a broader movement that is fascistic, that shows fascistic tendencies. Fascism not only represents a stage in the history of capitalist politics. It itself develops in stages, like all processes do.

> [There] is no reason to argue that unsuccessful fascist parties are less fascist than successful ones. The German Nazi Party did not suddenly become fascist when it achieved success in the polls, it was already fascist before 1930. What made it fascist was its ambition to become a mass reactionary party.
>
> RENTON, 2007: 106

It is important that we call a thing by its right name.[8] 'Names are used to distinguish between concepts; concepts, in politics, in turn serve to distinguish among real forces' (Trotsky, 1932g). Fascism, fascistic tendencies, authoritarianism, Bonapartism, etc., need to be carefully used. I distinguish fascism from authoritarianism and fascistic tendencies (the mechanisms that can produce

---

8  Implied here is a tripartite relation: among (a) the real (what exists independent of the thinking mind), (b) what is reflected in our mind, as a mental image, which (c) is then given a name (a conventionally chosen sound). What is important is we get our concept right (Sayer, 2000).

fascism). Sometimes, I use the term fascistic tendencies to refer to the bearers – embodiments – of these processes and relations such as a given organization or a party. Of course, whether a group calls itself fascist or (Hindu-)nationalist is beside the matter, just as whether the bourgeoisie calls itself an entrepreneur class or the middle class cannot hide its class character. Whether the working class *sees* fascistic tendencies or mere communalism is really beside the point.

Even if the fascist movement today is not a mere replication of the fascism of the earlier times (say, 1930s), fascism – or strong tendencies towards fascism – has some common traits. According to Rieman (2018), the West is facing a threat of fascism which is the form of modern mass politics that actively cultivates people's worst irrational sentiments including resentment, hatred, xenophobia, and fear, and that mobilizes ignorance and prejudice by nurturing and flattering them.

A former Vice President of the US, Mr. Wallace, wrote an article in 1945, entitled 'The danger of American fascism'. In this article, several of its traits are described that are relevant to the contemporary fascistic tendencies including in India under the Modi regime:

a.  spouting populist themes but manipulating people and institutions to achieve the opposite;
b.  pretending to support ordinary working people, and paying lip service to their welfare;
c.  demanding free enterprise, but speaking for monopoly;
d.  putting money and power ahead of human beings;
e.  distrust of democracy because it stands for equal opportunity;
f.  claiming to be super-patriots, but wanting to destroy constitutionally-given liberty;
g.  super-nationalists' pursuit of power by deceiving citizens and playing to their fears;
h.  needing and using scapegoats;
i.  harboring an intensity of intolerance toward other races, parties, classes, religions, cultures, regions or nations than those fascists represent;
j.  using lies to promote civic division, which then justifies authoritarian crackdown;
k.  poisoning the channels of public information;
l.  never wanting to present the truth to the public but to use the news to deceive the public;
m.  giving currency to snide suspicions without factual foundation;
n.  directing all deceit towards the final goal of capturing political power and using state power and market power and thus keeping the ordinary people in eternal subjection. (Wallace, 2017)

The fascistic movement/project (fascistic tendency) is implemented differently in different countries and yet the fascist movement in one country (e.g. India) shares some traits with the fascist movement in other countries. Talking about India and the West, Patnaik (2017) writes that the fascist movement there has these attributes:

> the propagation of a "supremacism" ("white supremacism" in the West, "Hindu supremacism" here); an apotheosis of unreason (manifested in "supremacism" and the projection of a "messiah"); a grassroots movement (which distinguishes it from mere authoritarianism) and an alliance with big capital.
>
> PATNAIK, 2017b; see also DESAI, 2002

Fascism (in the sense of a fascist state or fascistic tendencies that can produce such a state) is a form of bourgeois class-politics. It is a political-ideological *mass movement* that seeks to rescue *capitalism* from its crisis (i.e. from its failure to develop productive forces and meet people's needs, and consequent economic slowdown) by employing *authoritarian* measures against ordinary people and against religious or ethnic minorities or indeed against any person/group/organization, and especially the Left, which seeks to protect the democratic and economic rights of ordinary people, including minorities (see Renton, 2007).

## 2     A Short Introduction to the Fascistic Movement in India

In India, BJP, which is the political head of the fascistic movement and whose current political leader is Modi, is a part of the Sangh Parivar ('family of organizations'), a collective of Hindu-nationalist groups/movements that propagate fascistic ideology and engage in fascistic political activities. The Sangh works under the ideological mentorship of RSS (Rashtriya Swayamsevak Sangh, or, National Volunteer Organization) established in 1925, the same year India's communist party came into being.[9] RSS is probably the world's largest voluntary organization. It is probably the world's largest cadre-based organization. Its own trade union federation is the largest in India. A fascist organization, RSS employs paramilitary uniforms and armed voluntary corps. It has borrowed the ideology of nation and race from Nazi Germany and adapted this to India (for a brief history of RSS, see Basu et al., 1993).

---

9   See Upadhyay (2018) on how the RSS builds its trade union organization.

BJP combines its forces with, and rides on the back of, its 'cousin', the communal-fascist RSS and other elements of the fascistic Parivar. BJP stands for, and is a part of, a *fascistic movement with Indian characteristics*. This is re-cruiting its cadres from middle class and semi/un-employed people and the wage-earning class, by making use of the discourse of the Hindu religion, of the idea of Hindutva (Hindu-ness).[10]

Given that I talk about *fascistic* tendencies, it is important that RSS's class character is emphasized. It is mistaken to believe that the RSS, the ideological guru/mentor of the BJP, the new national party of the Indian capitalist class, is merely a communal force with little respect for democratic rules, that it is mainly or merely a cultural-political force against bourgeois democracy. The RSS, the center of the fascistic movement in India, is, above all, an *anti-commu-nist* force. It is not only against bourgeois democracy, but it is also against pro-letarian democracy, i.e. against the organs of the proletarian democracy (e.g. proletarian parties, etc.). The RSS has been anti-communist historically, for its origin. It has been spreading its reactionary ideas through its own organiza-tions and through the friends/supporters in Congress and other non-left par-ties. In October 1949, when Mr. Nehru, the first Prime Minister of India, who was fundamentally a secular person (and far more secular than most in the Congress party he led), was away in the United States, senior Congress leaders said they would allow RSS members to join the party. Welcoming the move, the RSS said: 'It is the end of the Congress war on the Sangh. It is a right step in the direction of national consolidation', and that with 'Communists out to enslave Bharat to Russia and Socialists still trying to find their feet', commented the RSS in its journal, 'mutual goodwill and co-operation between the Congress and the Sangh is the surest guarantee of national unity in this hour of crisis' (quot-ed in Guha, 2018). In the early years of post-colonial India and in the aftermath of 1917, RSS leaders offered their services to Nehru's Congress, saying that RSS was 'the only way to meet the challenge of communism', and that it is RSS that provided the only ideology which can harmonize and integrate the interests of different groups and classes and thus successfully avoid any class war (ICL, 2014). RSS began building trade unions with the overt goal of fostering

---

10    There is much literature on the link between neoliberalism and Hindutva (Desai, 2011; De and Saha, 2002). It is being recognized that neoliberal capitalism is expanding the middle class, which, in turn, is the base for the fascistic movement. The hegemonic aspirations of the middle class, including its newly-created elements (such as those in the IT industry), have taken the form of a politics of reaction, blending market liberalism and political and social illiberalism (Heller and Fernandes, 2006). Chacko (2018) says that the BJP is not only pro-corporate but also pro-neo-middle class. It recreates the middle and 'neo-middle' classes as 'virtuous market citizens' who view themselves as entrepreneurs and consumers but whose behavior is regulated by the framework of Hindu nationalism.

harmony between capitalists and laborers. This fascistic organization also set up a party called Jan Sangh, which became in 1980 what is called BJP.[11]

With the elevation of Modi to the political leadership of the right-wing movement – Modi who used Gujarat under his Chief Ministership as a laboratory for communal and neoliberal capitalist interventions – RSS has got a shot in its arm: 'Modi's "achievement" in India consisted in effecting... an alliance between the RSS and Indian big capital' (Patnaik, 2017b). Not only has RSS openly associated itself with Hitler, it has also declared itself as openly anti-communist and a reactionary-*bourgeois* force.

Independent India's communal-fascistic movement has evolved over time. One can think of four stages.[12]

1947–mid-1970s: This was the time of Nehruvian socialism (read: state-directed peripheral capitalism), partly informed by the Bombay Plan referred to in Chapter 7. There was also a formal commitment to democracy and to secularism. Given weak material foundations, the basis for democracy, which always requires the state being able to provide material concessions in response to lower-class struggles, was weak. And for similar reasons, secularism as a part of democracy (in the sense of the respect for the rights for religious minorities) was also weak. Not only was it the case that 'Hindu nationalism was already an important stream in the wider flow of anti-colonial cultural nationalism', in that religious symbols were widely used in the anti-colonial struggle (Vanaik, 2017: 329). It was also the case that the fascistic movement, which had a very minor role in the anti-colonial struggle, had been against secularism, even if secularism, in India, means 'equal respect for all religions in the conduct of the affairs of the state' (Ahmad, 2013: 8).[13] Yet it is also true that RSS's attempt to collaborate with Congress is not successful, thanks to the presence of Nehru

---

11    For a short history of the BJP, see Basu (2013). On the BJP's post-2014 resurgence, see Palshikar et al. (2017). It should be stressed that, and as I have said, according to some (Vanaik), Indian communalism cannot be seen in terms of the concept of fascism. However, there is a literature that seeks to interpret communalism on the basis of that concept (Banaji, 2013; Harriss-White, 2003; Krishna, 2003). See also De Mello (2018): he relates the fascistic situation to what he calls Indian sub-imperialism (on the dangers of the countries of BRICS playing a sub-imperialist role, see Bond, 2014).

12    This brief historical discussion below is partly based in Ahmad, 2003.
       Also, it should be said that it is arbitrary to begin with 1947. There are distinct colonial roots of communalism. For example, in reaction to British imperialism during the 19th and 20th centuries, Indian Muslims and Hindus imagined and invented their separate and distinct religious communities and communal nationalisms. These were institutionalized in the subcontinent's political systems by the British government in collaboration with Indian politicians (Stern, 2000).

13    It should be noted that the word secularism has different meanings. Among many texts on secularism, see Thapar (2016). The original European meaning (the separation of the state from religion, which means that the state will not be influenced by religious beliefs

who was not only a major supporter of secularism and scientific temper, but who also commanded respect because he played a major role, with Gandhi, in the anti-colonial struggle.

Mid-1970s–late 1990s: This period coincides with the decay of the Nehruvian consensus on India's commitment to *state-directed* capitalism (called socialism by the Right), which included some control over capitalism.[14] This period also coincides with a weakening commitment to secularism and democracy.[15] In 1976, the Indian constitution was amended, officially making it a secular

---

of citizens or of those who conduct state affairs) is a different one from how secularism is used in India.

In India, secularism means 'equal respect for all religions'. This is the 'socialist approach to religion with Indian features'! However, how can believers treat each other as equal believers worthy of mutual respect? For Hindus, Islam is inferior, and for Muslims, Hinduism is inferior. In fact, 'equal respect for all religions in the conduct of the affairs of the state would necessarily lead, especially in the context of the corruptions of liberal democratic politics, to greater respect for the religion of the demographic majority whose votes count for more, whose privileged classes command much more money and power, and among whose middle classes new kinds of religiosity are now rampant. In India, the demographic majority of those defined as Hindus by the state itself is so overwhelming that the state must necessarily favour Hindus in its secularism regardless of which political party is in power; between the Congress and the BJP, there would necessarily be a difference of degree, thanks mainly not to different ideologies but to the differences in the constituency blocs that each wishes to address' (Ahmad, 2013: 8–9).

According to Chandra (2008: 2), the European definition of secularism as the separation of state from religion is a universal definition, and is held in India, and Mohandas Gandhi agreed with it. So 'to talk of any Indian definition of secularism which would deny this is to deny secularism' (ibid.).

'India is a land of religions', and from this arises 'another specific feature of secularism in India'. This is that: 'The state should have equal regard for all religions'. The two meanings are the same thing, Chandra says: 'the doctrine of the state neutrality towards religions takes the form of state extending equal opportunities to the followers of all religions and to atheists' (Chandra, 2008: 2–3).

14    On the topic of the shift from Nehruvian secular democracy to the recent right-wing, communal times, see: Frankel, 2005; Khilnani, 2017; Niclas-Tolle, 2015; and Corbridge and Harriss, 2013.

15    The commitment of the state to secularism has not been that strong from the beginning. For Aijaz Ahmad (2013) (and Perry Anderson): in India and for the Indian state, 'secularism [is used] as a legitimating ideology', or more specifically, 'the Indian state… is a Hindu communal state that uses secularism as its legitimating ideology'. Ahmad argues that: 'the Indian state is in large measure a communal state that can accommodate all sorts of communalisms, including notably the Muslim one, but it is predominantly a Hindu communal state simply because Hindu communalists are far more numerous and powerful than all the other communalists combined. … [The] Indian state can live with communalism perfectly happily so long as communal violence is minimized, because such violence, like any other violence in public affairs, creates a law & order problem [and is a threat to capitalist property]' (Ahmad, 2013: 8–9).

state, even though the constitution prohibits the slaughter of cows, an animal which many Hindus consider sacred. Yet, in the mid-1970s (1975–1977), a national emergency was declared suspending the democratic rights, and this was a response to, among other things, working class struggle (e.g. railways strike). There was a massive anti-emergency movement led by an alliance of non-Marxist (petty-bourgeois) socialists and some fascistic elements as well as Left forces. This movement against the attack on liberal democracy as well as post-emergency Janata government legitimized the fascistic elements (e.g. RSS) which actually represent a more dangerous attack on democracy than the Emergency. Jan Sangh, the right-wing political party that the RSS had set up in 1951 became what is now known as the BJP. Concurrently, the decline of the Congress Party, which had a formal commitment to secularism, began, but the non-Congress opposition, including the fascistic elements, were not able to provide a stable non-Congress alternative either, creating a space for a non-secular national-scale alternative. The demise of 'communist regimes' in the world also created an adverse climate for the Indian communist movement so whatever limited ability it had to fight the BJP did not materialize. The Indian ruling class turned to the imperialist US with the political support of all non-communist parties, nominally secular or not.

In 1991, the ruling class embarked on neoliberal capitalism in response to the crisis of state-directed capitalism which overlapped with the days of the Congress party's dominance. Institutionalization of politics of religion happened, with a tacit agreement between the Congress and some fascistic forces (laying the foundation stone for the temple in 1989; and destruction of the 16th-century Babri masjid (mosque) located in the city of Ayodhya, in 1992, which was not stopped by any part of the state, whether the Congress party or the coercive agencies, and this showed the non-secular character of the state as such, and not just as a party). *The Hindu*, a progressive newspaper, published an editorial on December 7, 1992, which it republished on December 7, 2918 (*The Hindu*, 2017). The following lines from the editorial are worth reading in today's context:

> It was religious fanaticism at its ugliest in Ayodhya yesterday, with the country's worst fears coming true in the nightmarish spectacle of the brutal destruction of the 450 year old Babri Masjid by thousands of frenzied kar sevaks [people who offer services for free to a religious cause]. The disputed mosque was razed to the ground with a barbaric savagery reminiscent of the crude traditions of settling scores in medieval history. The demolition of the Masjid has delivered a lethal blow to the image of a secular and democratic India.

The BJP and its militant allies, the RSS, the VHP and the Bajrang Dal stand exposed as having brought on this horrific denouement even *as the essentially destructive and fascist nature of its strategy and tactics* [italics added] cannot be in doubt any more. The BJP's claim to be a defender of the national interest lies in shreds today.

...what is vital is to recognise that this is a defining moment in India's history, a moment at which the country can be plunged into a dark abyss of primitive emotions threatening to erase four decades of a successful track record of a progressive secular democracy.[16]

The peaceful change of government from one fraction of the proprietary coalition to another fraction, through elections continues, and the vast majority of people continued to vote in national and provincial elections, showing that liberal-democracy continues to have much legitimacy in the minds of common men and women. Neoliberalism also creates a situation where all parties pander to business interests, so some have to play a politics of identity (including religious identity) to attract voters in a competitive electoral field (more on this in the next chapter).

Late 1990s–2014: A new and stable power bloc of the Indian Right arose with the BJP-led government at the national level elected. The Indian ruling class moved closer to an alliance with imperialism as a junior partner, a process which all non-Left parties support. The commitment to neoliberalism and globalization of economy also deepened. The capitalist class operating in India came to have a trans-nationalized segment, which, like the other segments, demanded a good business climate (de-regulation, austerity, wage repression, etc.). The Congress served as the formally secular face of the neoliberal capitalist class while BJP served as its communal face. All-non-Left parties have colluded with BJP. Evident was an increasing communalization of popular consciousness, on the basis of the mass work by RSS and its infiltration into state ideological and coercive institutions. India increasingly became a national security state, demonstrating fascistic tendencies.

---

16     The Hindu (2017) goes on to say: 'All the secular political forces must rally to the defence of the country and pull it back from the brink. A first step would be to rebuild the destroyed Babri Masjid as a gesture towards the minority community and as a reaffirmation of an unwavering commitment to the vision of a democratic India, free of any kind of bigotry'.

2014–present: With the BJP coming to power in 2014, the fascistic movement has experienced a boost. Led by the RSS, the fascist movement has indeed been making good use of electoral methods to mobilize the masses and to win support for their cause. In early 2019, the BJP is in power in a larger number of States on its own or with an alliance partner (Map 11.1). It is now the dominant party of the ruling class, and it supports, and is supported by, imperialist capital and its states. Many secular-minded leaders from Congress think that another election win by BJP in 2019 will produce irreversible damage to India's secularism.[17]

The fascistic movement continues to attack not only liberal-political forces that defend secularism but also the Left. The increasing political significance of the fascistic movement under BJP's political patronage is indicated by the fact that when for the first time in Indian electoral history, there was a direct electoral face-off between the Left and the BJP in March 2018, BJP won. This was in Tripura, a small State in North-East India. Even though the Left garnered 45% of the votes (down from 48.11% in 2013), the BJP, with its alliance partner, won the majority of seats with a vote-share of 50.5%. BJP did so by using money and muscle power, by swallowing up politicians of the Congress party, which is a traditional and non-fascistic party of the property-owning class, and by selling the dream of what it calls development. Within less than a month of the declaration of the Tripura election results, the violent attack on the communist movement in Tripura by the fascistic movement has taken the following forms: 'Nearly a thousand Left cadres have been physically targeted, 1699 houses have been ransacked and looted, over 450 shops burnt, over 800 Party offices have been attacked, looted and some burnt down and 134 offices of Left mass organisations have been captured and occupied by the BJP. Indiscriminate arrests and foisting of false cases against the Left cadre continue'. (CPI(M), 2018). In fact, soon after the results were declared, two statues of Vladimir Lenin were taken down by the fascistic mob.[18] The Governor of the State, who

---

17      A prominent Congress leader who is also an author of many books says: 'If they (BJP) win a repeat in the Lok Sabha [in 2019], our democratic constitution as we understand it, will not survive as they will have all the elements they need to tear apart the constitution of India and write a new one…That new one will be the one which will enshrine principles of Hindu Rashtra, that will remove equality for minorities, that'll create a Hindu Pakistan and that isn't what Mahatma Gandhi, Nehru, Sardar Patel, Maulana Azad and great heroes of freedom struggle fought for' (quoted in Times of India, 2018).

18      Interestingly, one of the most prominent statues of Lenin in India, at Esplanade in the center of Kolkata, remains in place even though the Left is no longer in power.

**INDIA**
STATE GOVERNMENT COMPOSITION
WITH A BJP PERSPECTIVE

| | |
|---|---|
| | BJP (Absolute Majority) |
| | NDA (BJP above 50%) |
| | NDA (BJP below 50%) |
| | INC Coalition |
| | Others |
| | UT (Governor's rule) |
| | Vacant (Governor's rule) |

Map not to Scale
Copyright © 2018 www.mapsofindia.com

MAP 11.1    The BJP in power in Indian States, early 2019
SOURCE: HTTPS://WWW.MAPSOFINDIA.COM/ASSEMBLYPOLLS/STATE
-ASSEMBLY-LEADING-PARTIES.HTML

should ordinarily be above party politics, justified this criminal vandalism by saying on Twitter: 'What one democratically elected government [the reference is to the communist government] can do another democratically elected government can undo. And vice versa'. All these and similar actions demonstrate the right-wing's deep disrespect for democratic values. Political violence against ideological opponents is one of the main means of acquiring influence and governmental power, for the BJP.

The election result in Tripura is being seen by the right-wing movement as its definitive victory over the Left, politically and ideologically, and this should be seen in the light of what I have said above about the anti-communist character of the RSS. Recall there was here, for the first time, a direct contest between the Right and the Left in which the Left lost. This election result will, no doubt, add to the obstacles to the communist movement (and not just to the cause of protection of democratic and secular values). The question is: what is to be done about the fascistic threat (the topic of the penultimate chapter)? Answering such a question presupposes an understanding of the nature of fascistic threat itself (the topic of this chapter and the next).

## 3          Political Economy of Fascistic Tendencies, Globally and in India

The fascistic movement involving discriminatory and violent attitude towards minorities, including religious minorities, cannot be seen merely as an ideological/cultural process. Cultural ideas exist under definite material conditions, even if these ideas cannot be simply reduced to the material conditions. So when one of the most prominent historians of India, Chandra (2008) says that 'Communalism is basically an ideology', that 'Communalism is ... a way of looking at politics and society ... around that ideology' and that the 'communal leaders and ideologues are primarily interested in spreading the communal belief system or ways of thought', he is only partly right (pp. 7–8).[19] When he says that

---

19    For an explanation of communalism in terms of ideas, but not ideas based in India but in the West, see Ranganathan (2018). According to him, the recent rise of the far right, communalism and nationalism in India are better understood as a continuation of Westernization. He says that India has long traditions of philosophies that take the job of reasonable living to be one of distinguishing our thoughts from our attitudes. Moreover, not only did Indian thinkers not endorse anything like the *logocentric* conflation of thought and language, they from the very earliest times treated disagreement and dissent as the proper mode of public interaction. Ranganathan argues that Hinduism is unique among religions in not being reducible to any core teachings or tradition. Rather, it constitutes the disagreements of philosophy with South Asian resources.

'Other aspects of communal activity are secondary and follow from the basic communal ideology', and that 'Communal ideology and not specific policies lie at the heart of a communal party', he is not even half right (pp. 7–8). Fascistic tendencies, including when the targets are religious minorities, are only partly ideological.

Similarly, when Simeon (1986) says that communalism is the Indian version of fascist populism and racist nationalism, the fascistic tendency appears to be mainly a political phenomenon. When one says that 'Fascism invades the public sphere with controlled mobs' and that it 'represents an assault on *politics*, a replacement of democratic dialogue by violent intimidation...' (Simeon, 2016: 154), one is un-dialectically (one-sidedly) stressing fascism as a merely *political* phenomenon.

Unlike Simeon, there are those scholars (e.g. Vanaik) who, as we have seen, deny that there is a fascist threat in India. They are 'much more likely to see the principal danger as residing not in something that lies *behind* Hindu communalism, or in some fascist core *contained within or hidden in* Hindu communalism, but as Hindu communalism *itself*, as the specific manifestation of the politics of cultural exclusivity and radical right-wing reaction' (Vanaik, 2017: 335; italics added). In other words, for these scholars, what appears on the surface is all that there is. There is nothing – or nothing much – *behind* it. In this alternative approach, the focus is on 'politicized Hindutva's deep roots and growth in civil society, well beyond the question of its capacity to appropriate the state' (ibid.: 335). Vanaik (2017) says: 'In a sense, the phenomenon is *more deep-rooted* than fascism, *more enduring* and *more difficult* completely or comprehensively to destroy' (p. 335).

Several problems with this denial of the fascistic threat approach should be noted. (1) What is being claimed is that India is experiencing merely a threat of communalism, an attack on the rights of religious minorities, but not a threat to liberal-democracy as such. (2) In this approach, as well, the threat of communalism is not because of any crisis of capitalism, so there is no material root for the on-going right-wing political activities. The latter exist because of such things as the decline of a specific kind of politics (e.g. Nehruvian project of socialism, secularism and democracy). It is 'the decay of the post-colonial project as originally defined that best explains the subsequent rise of reactionary authoritarian populism embodied in the Sangh combine' (ibid.: 329). In other words, the decline of Nehruvian *ideas and politics* – a centrist-populist ideological and political framework – has caused the rise of communal politics.[20]

---

20   In this vein, Nigam (2010) says that in times of crises, Nehruvian secular-nationalism has shown itself to be fundamentally Hindu in its latent assumptions. In its pursuit of a

All in all, whether the problem at hand is the threat of fascism (as in Simeon, etc.) or whether it is the threat of communalism, politics explains politics. Politics is the explanan, and politics is the explanandum.

Fascism or fascistic tendencies *are* ideological/cultural and political. But is there not a material reality *behind* their ideological and political character? In the middle ages, Catholicism might have appeared to be the dominant mode of life just like politics in ancient society did, but then 'the Middle Ages could not live on Catholicism, nor could the ancient world on politics', as Marx (1977:176) said in a famous footnote in Chapter 1 of *Capital*, vol. 1. In fact, it is the mode in which people gain their livelihood – i.e. the 'production and reproduction of life' and the class relations within which that happens – that, ultimately, determines, and that is, ultimately, indeed expressed in the form of, certain ideological and political practices, including, for example, how powerful religious ideas are to people's worldview, and how religious strife is made use of politically to gain material advantages. And, of course, ideological and political practices in turn influence their content: the production and reproduction of material conditions of life. Fascistic tendencies need to be seen in relation to the entire totality of capitalist class relation (including in terms of capitalist economic and political processes). Let us say that fascism is, at the minimum, a certain relation between the ruler and the ruled, a relation that is undemocratic in the extreme, that receives some political support from some sections of 'the ruled' (typically, politically backward sections of the lower classes) and that seeks to destroy the resistance of the politically advanced sections of the lower classes against class exploitation and domination, as well. Then that relation (fascism or tendencies towards it) has to be explained mainly in the relation of production (i.e. in the class relation), and its various necessary outcomes in terms of the accumulation of wealth. We may recall from Marx's point from Chapter 6 of his *Capital*, vol. 3 that: it is in 'the direct relationship of the owners of the conditions of production to the immediate producers', that we find 'the hidden basis of the ... the political form of the relationship of sovereignty and dependence' (Marx, 1991: 927). Marx's point is also that politics in class society is ultimately class politics. In *German Ideology*, Marx and Engels (1978) say:

---

national culture, it produced the dominant culture as the norm, marginalising minority cultures. Corbridge and Harriss (2013) make a potentially useful generalization when they say that Nehruvianism has been challenged by two revolts of the elites: economic liberalization and Hindu nationalism. These revolts have been challenged, in turn, by various movements, including those of India's lower and middle castes ('Backward Classes'). As it will be clear in this and the next chapter, economic liberalization and Hindu nationalism are deeply inter-connected. Once again, politics is understood, more or less, in terms of politics, and that too elite politics. Out of view is the operation of *capitalist* economy and *capitalist* politics.

all struggles within the state, the struggle between democratic, aristocrat-
ic and monarchy, the struggle for the franchise etc., etc. are merely the
illusory forms in which the real struggles of the different classes are
fought out among one another. (p. 54)

Marx also says that while politics is based on economic matters, politics also
reacts back on economic matters. In a letter, Engels clarifies the 'materialist
conception of history' that he and Marx had developed:

> the *ultimately* determining element in history is the production and re-
> production of real life. Other than this neither Marx nor I have ever as-
> serted. ...The economic situation is the basis, but the various elements of
> the superstructure – political forms of the class struggle and its results, to
> wit: constitutions established by the victorious class after a successful
> battle, etc., juridical forms, and even the reflexes of all these actual strug-
> gles in the brains of the participants, political, juristic, philosophical
> theories, *religious views and their further development into systems of
> dogmas* – also exercise their influence upon the course of the historical
> struggles and in many cases preponderate in determining their *form.*
> There is an interaction of all these elements in which, amid all the end-
> less host of accidents..., the economic movement finally asserts itself as
> necessary. Otherwise the application of the theory to any period of his-
> tory [or to any country] would be easier than the solution of a simple
> equation of the first degree.
>
> ENGELS, 1890; *italics* and parenthesis added

No political or ideological project hangs in the air. 'We must be able to discover
under the political form the economic and social content' (Trotksy, 1974: 34).
The right-wing project, including Hindu-supremacism, *is* an ideological-
political – cultural-political – phenomenon. But it is more than that. The Hindu
right-wing project is a class project, more than anything else. If bourgeois politics takes fascistic form as opposed to the democratic form, a major part of the
explanation must lie in the class relation of bourgeois production and exchange, in the miseries that the capitalist system produces for the common
people, and the resultant political struggles and defeats of the lower classes.
That is: the major explanation of the fascistic form of bourgeois politics must
lie in bourgeois political economy and bourgeois politics.[21] There are multiple
aspects of this.

---

21   The right-wing attack on rights is not merely an attack on one form of bourgeois political-
     ideological framework on another form of bourgeois-ideological framework. If it was
     merely so, it would be just an intra-family battle – a battle between those bourgeois forces

### 3.1  Capitalist Exploitation, Dispossession and Immiserization

Common people in all the countries of the world, whether India or the USA, face numerous pressing problems: low wages, un-/under-employment, insecure employment, forcible loss of access to land or other means of livelihood, crisis of rural economy, ecological degradation, lack of quality health care, education and shelter, etc.[22] These social problems, which are affecting common people like natural forces, are basically caused by the way the political-economic system works, by the totality of the relations between the basic classes. Supported by the capitalist state, nation's resources are controlled by a tiny minority (the ruling class). And actively aided by the state, the ruling class makes enormous profit by (a) exploiting workers (i.e. by paying them a very small part of the net product they produce, and often paying a wage that does not even cover the average cost of maintenance, and converting the surplus value thus produced into fresh installments of capitalist private property), and (b) using various methods of primitive accumulation in its modern forms (dispossessing small-scale producers, and by robbing society of its common financial resources whether these are in the form of un-returned loans from state-owned banks, or non-payment of taxes, etc.).[23] Income and wealth inequality is rising. The bottom 60–70% are living a precarious existence, given low wages, and insecure employment and growing unviability of small-scale producers in an increasingly competitive world with diminishing government support for them. Besides, millions are experiencing oppression and exclusion based on caste, race/ethnicity, gender, and religion. In short, there is an on-going attack on people's living standards, which is caused by the fundamental nature of capitalism and which is exacerbated by its neoliberal form.[24] Such an attack is reinforced by various mechanisms of social oppression.

In the less developed countries such as India, the normal effects of capitalism on the common people are more extreme than in more developed countries (even if this does not mean that the rate of exploitation – s/v, or the ratio

---

who are committed to democracy and secularism and those bourgeois forces who do not. The BJP is not just attacking secular and democratic values and practices of, say, the Congress party, the traditional party of the bourgeoisie. The BJP is also attacking social and democratic rights of the toiling masses. It is not only against liberal-democratic-secular bourgeois formations. It is also anti-communist.

22  Nearly half of the world's population – more than 3 billion people – live on less than $2.50 a day (any discussion based on the paltry $1.25 poverty line is absolutely meaningless), and more than 70% of the population live on $10 a day.

23  Chatterjee (2017) says that the most recent period of Indian history has seen marked by an attempt to create a new hegemonic bloc based on Hindu majoritarianism under conditions of rapid primitive accumulation and competitive populism.

24  The neoliberal form of capitalism drives the neoliberal policies of the state, irrespective of which party controls the governments.

of surplus value to value of labor power – in less developed countries is necessarily higher than in more developed countries). In the less developed countries, there is a backward form of capitalism. This form of capitalism potentially undermines the basis for democratic conduct. State officials and politicians 'oversee' a type of capitalist production which is not only based on a massive amount of dispossession of small-scale property owners (e.g. peasants) and privatization of state-owned enterprises and resources, but also on the regime of low wages and long hours.[25] It is not a capitalism where in the sphere of production the main method of surplus appropriation is based on systemic technological change aimed at increasing productivity of labor. The dominance of this form of capitalism has traditionally marked the more developed countries. When capitalism is based on formal subsumption of labor, it is hardly conducive to very democratic relations between state (officials) and citizens and between employers and employees. When profits come more or less from the naked exhaustion of the body of direct producers (or from their dispossession of property) rather than from increased productivity of their labor based on systemic logic of technological change in every sector and subsector, and when the very basic needs are not met by capital or the state, the relation between 'sovereignty and dependence', or the relation between the ruler and the ruled, tends to become a *coercive* relation, even if one is not tied to a given employer through extra-economic means.[26] One must also note that like in many other countries, India's capitalism has been experiencing a massive jobless growth and economic slowdown (especially, in manufacturing and farming). The relation between increase in GDP and an increase in employment has been becoming weaker and weaker: as Figure 11.2 below shows, the curves for GDP increase and employment increase are diverging more and more over time.[27] The unemployed people can be disruptive and need to be repressed, from the standpoint of the capitalist class and the state elite.

Similarly, when accumulation of money is based on the big business taking control over state-owned resources and over small-scale private property and collectively-owned property, what happens is a contradiction between two

---

25    Such a regime is called formal subsumption of labor as a form of capitalist class relation as we have discussed in Chapter 3.
26    This necessarily does not mean that economically advanced societies in the West are paragons of democracy. Democracy is a form of class rule, and class is the most important form of inequality. But between two class societies, the state in one can be a little more democratic than another.
27    In the 1970s and 80s, when GDP growth was around 3–4%, employment growth was about 2%, says Dr. Amit Basole, the lead author of a recent study. 'Currently, the ratio of GDP growth to employment growth is less than 0.1'. That means that a 10% increase in GDP results in a less than 1% increase in employment (reported in The Hindu, 2018b).

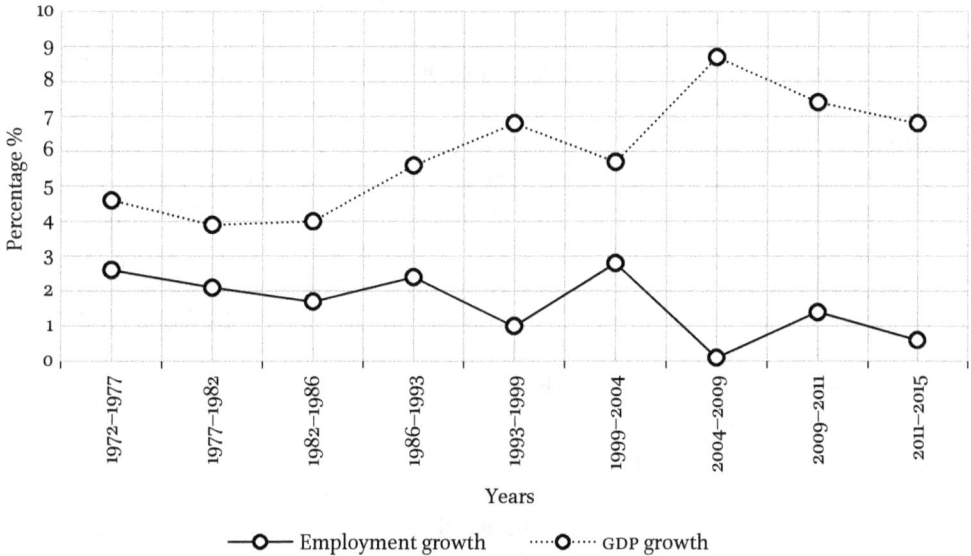

FIGURE 11.2 Employment growth and GDP growth in India, 1972–2015
SOURCE: DATA FROM *THE HINDU* (2018)

equal rights. This the contradiction between the right of the big business to take control over property which is not in the domain of private-sector capitalism on the one hand, and the right of the common people to use the small-scale or collectively-owned property and to enjoy the advantages of state-owned property on the other hand. Between two equal rights, it is the force of the big business, including its trans-nationalized segment, reinforced and supported by the state, that counts. Any opposition from peasants and ordinary citizens against privatization is met with repression. As well, the right of the common people to enjoy state-provided services and use-values contradicts the right of the big business – especially, the financialized segment – to see reduced fiscal deficit, a contradiction that triggers opposition. And as opposition grows, there is need for more repression. A fascist/fascistic state supplies those the means of repression.

Capitalism affects the layer of petty bourgeois families adversely, and not just workers. Whether in Germany after World War I or in the India of today, the capitalist system ruins 'some layers of the petty bourgeoisie' while it creates 'others anew: around the factories, artisans and shopkeepers; within the factories, technicians and executives' (Trotsky, 1933b). Economic crisis hits 'the artisans, the peddlers, and the civil employees' (ibid.). 'The economic crisis in agriculture' under capitalism is 'ruining the peasantry' (ibid.). 'The decay of the middle strata did not necessarily mean that they are made into proletarians, inasmuch as the proletariat itself ... [is] casting out a gigantic army of chronically unemployed' (ibid.).

Exploitation, oppression, dispossession of petty bourgeois producers and immiserization/inequality do not go un-challenged in any society. Ordinary people – workers, farmers, etc. and socially oppressed groups such as Dalits – are engaged in recurrent protests and struggles. There is a strike every week in one or another part of the world. It is true that people are reacting to the *effects* of the operation of the capitalist system rather than to the existence of the system itself. It is true that people are not class-conscious enough to adequately trace their problems to the root, i.e. the capitalist system operating through mechanisms of social oppression. Yet, people do engage in struggles. It is true that these strikes and struggles, which are often confined to specific workplaces or sectors or areas, have not been escalated to take on state power and the rule of capital as such, but that is not a reason to overlook the militant tradition of workers, peasants and oppressed groups, nor is there a basis for one to say that Left parties organize them to merely let off steam, i.e. to calm the anger of the people.[28] The intensity of strikes has increased (as indicated by increases in persons and person days lost per dispute) in India, even if the number of disputes has decreased, and strikes remain a major risk factor for the business world (Figures 11.3 and 11.4).

If a worker comes to work, there is a cost: she/he has to be fed and sheltered, which means they need a wage. If a worker stops work (as in a strike or a protest against low wages, unfair working conditions and casualization of work), there is also a cost to the employer, as his/her labor is withheld leading to the cessation of production.[29] There is a pressure on enterprise-owners to reduce *both* kinds of cost, which emanate from the economic and political logics of capitalism. To reduce these costs (by driving down wages and by making it difficult for people to strike), the enterprise owners need help from their political cousins (political party leaders). So, fascist/fascistic politics comes in handy.

### 3.2 *Ruling Class Counter Response to Lower Classes: Coercion and Consent*

The ruling class cannot exist without exploiting wage-labor and without maintaining the separation of common people from the means of production (the ruling class must continuously engage in dispossessing people of their access to commons and/or their individual property and/or state's resources). This

---

28   Saying so is resorting to functionalism: explaining an event merely in terms of its functions/effects.

29   The one-day strike in India in September 2016 reportedly caused a damage of more than $2.5 billion to its capitalist economy.

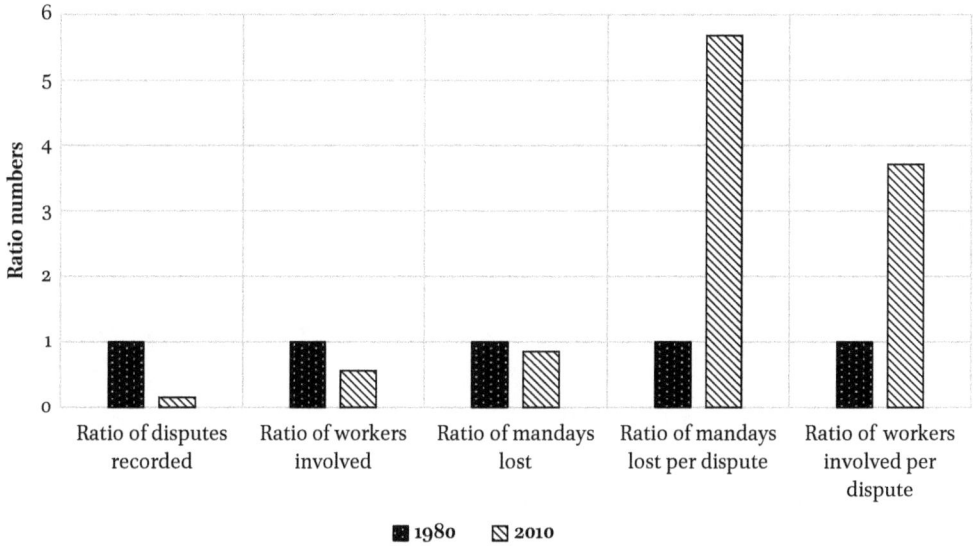

FIGURE 11.3  Increasing intensity of strikes in India
Notes: In the figure above, all the numbers (i.e. number of disputes, workers involved, mandays lost, and mandays lost per dispute and workers involved per dispute) for 1980 are taken as 1, and accordingly the numbers for 2010 are converted into a ratio, by dividing the 2010 numbers by the 1980 numbers. One can see this ratio has decreased for the incidents of disputes, workers involved and mandays lost, while the ratio of mandays lost *per* dispute and the ratio of workers involved *per* dispute (indicating intensity of disputes) has increased.
SOURCE: DATA FROM AIOE/FICCI (N.D.)

especially happens, if these resources are needed by the ruling class, and/or if these resources being in the hands of the common people significantly reduces their dependence on wage-labor. Exploitation and dispossession, however, prompt opposition from common people, (covert or overt), which, in turn, requires a ruling class response. One form of response is the use of coercion/repression, including an attack on democratic rights. This is from above (state agencies and policies). This coercive response occurs from below in the form of vigilante groups and lynch mobs organized/supported by fascistic forces, and private security forces and even criminals recruited by the members of the propertied class. Another response is making the lower classes consent to the system and thus weakening the lower-class opposition to the system. Note that it is not just the fact that the whole system of capitalism-in-crisis, that is increasingly failing to meet people's very basic needs, is justification on the basis of the production of consent and deception. It is also the case that to the extent that repression is used against lower-class opposition to the capitalist system, that repression also requires justification, which requires production of consent.

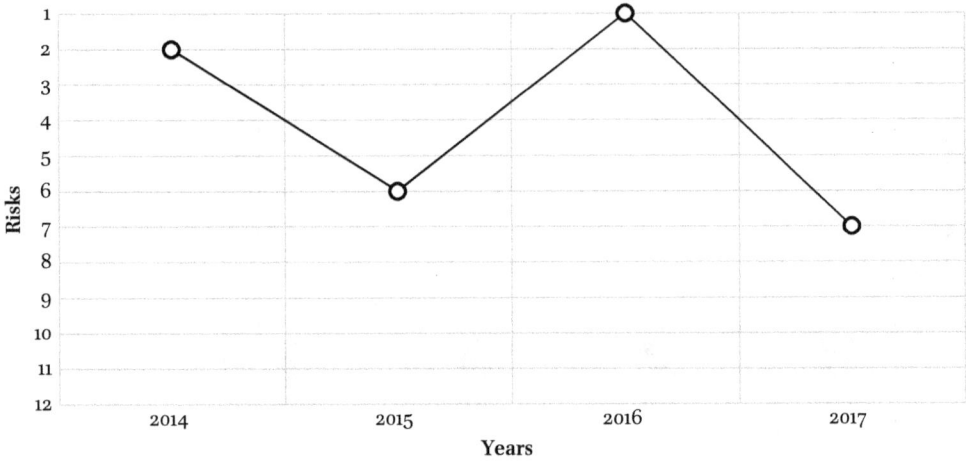

FIGURE 11.4 Corporate perception of risk from trikes, closures and unrest
Note: On a scale of 1 to 12 (there are 12 sources of risk), 1 = the most important source of risk
SOURCE: DATA FROM AIOE/FICCI (N.D.)

Consent is sought in many ways. It is sought on the basis of emotional appeals to various forms of identity politics including that based on nationality, religion, etc. (the pursuit of identity politics dominates over struggle against capitalism). These appeals also divide the opposition to capitalism and the state. Consent is also sought on the basis of giving limited material concessions as well as sheer deception. Deception involves the deployment of lies that can be religious/mythological lies. Deception also involves secular lies which include false promises of pro-poor policies which the government *knows* it will not be able to deliver. Both secular and religious/mythological lies are used in a capitalist society.

Developed bourgeois ideology is rationalistic and directed against mythology. The radical bourgeoisie tried to make do without religion and build a state based on reason rather than tradition. An expression of this was democracy with its principles of liberty, equality and fraternity. The capitalist economy, however, created a monstrous contradiction between everyday reality and democratic principles. A higher grade form of lying is required to fill up this contradiction. Nowhere do people lie more politically than in bourgeois democracies. And this is no longer the objective "lying" of mythology, but the consciously organized deception of the people, using combined methods of extraordinary complexity. The technology of the lie is cultivated no less than the technology of electricity.

The most "developed" democracies, France and the United States, possess the most deceitful press.

TROTSKY, 1927

As we see from the foregoing discussion, there is a chain of causal links and internal relations: these connect (a) exploitation and dispossession which characterize the capitalist society and which produce concrete adverse effects on lower classes, (b) opposition to exploitation and dispossession which then prompts (c) state's various responses on behalf of the ruling class such as the strategies of repression, consent-making and deception via lies and politics of identity based in religion, etc. (Figure 11.5 below).

I will elaborate on these ideas. The working people's fight-back, actual and potential, needs a counter-response from the economic and political elites who manage the capitalist economic-political system. The counter-response to people's fight-back comes in many forms. One is to allow some oppositional

```
                        Capitalist Class Society
                       (Including economic crisis)
                                 │
                                 ▼
                           Exploitation &
                           Dispossession
                                 │
                                 ▼
          Adverse Effects of exploitation and dispossession on lower classes
         (e.g. Low wages, un-and under-employment, farm crisis, and in equality)
                                 │
                                 ▼
                  Lower-class Opposition (actual/potential)
                                 │
                                 ▼
              Responses of the state on behalf of ruling classes
                                 │
      ┌───────────────┬──────────┴─────────┬───────────────┐
      ▼               ▼                    ▼               ▼
Attack on democratic   Allowing some      Appeal to religious   False promises and
rights of lower classes,  opposition & limited    etc. identities    lies (secular and
   & repression        material concession                          religious)
                           │                    │               │
                           ▼                    ▼               ▼
                      Produce consent      Division of lower   Deception of lower
                      from lower classes        classes            classes
```

FIGURE 11.5 Structural conditions for fascistic movement produced by capitalism

SOURCE: AUTHOR

activity to occur in order to stop people from being angrier, and to grant some concessions. From the 1950s for several decades, this was a strategy in many countries, including in India, and this produced a certain degree of consent to the system – to 'the reformed democracy'. Since the onset of neoliberal form of capitalism, such a strategy is less likely as income deflation for the majority is a necessary part of the neoliberal capitalism, which means that the states have reduced ability to provide economic concessions to the masses. States' inability to provide concessions contradicts the common people's democratic rights – especially, them having the right to organize and make demands. Of the many 'negative' forms of counter-response is an attack on democratic rights such as the right to form (independent) unions, the right to free speech, etc. as well as attack on the social rights (e.g. reduction in already-limited welfare benefits). These attacks weaken the bargaining power of the masses and make it difficult for people to exercise their democratic rights. This fact – and especially, the attack on labor rights – happens irrespective of which party – whether they are more democratic or more fascistic – is in power.

Another form of the counter-response from ruling-class forces is the use of identity politics. To distract attention from people's miseries, to weaken people's fight for equality and for a better life, bourgeois and petty-bourgeois class forces, their politicians and their organic intellectuals, divide the masses on the basis of social and geographical identity (e.g. caste; race; identity; location – migrants/refugees vs locals; regionalism expressed as demand for new provinces to be carved up from existing ones). Note that while the capitalist class can benefit from the politics of hatred, the latter can also be dis-functional if it creates too much of a law and order problem undermining the business climate, why is why: 'even influential layers of the bourgeoisie fear the fascist experiment, precisely because they want no convulsions, no long and severe civil war' (Trotsky, 1931a) (more on this in the next chapter).

### 3.3   *Special Role of Religion as a Mechanism of Deception*

Increasingly, religion as a basis of identity politics is used in such countries as India: when employers/owners and workers of a given religion are united in the name of religious loyalty, such an action is directly counter-posed to class politics which draws attention to, in theory and practice, the fundamental and irreconcilable interests between these classes.[30] Often religious identity is used in tandem with other identities such as those based on caste and aboriginality.

---

30    To the extent that the ideology of the politics of religion exists as a process in a way that is relatively autonomous from class relations and of capitalism, the bourgeoisie does not mind using such politics, where it exists, to manage any potential or actual opposition to its rule and to further its own economic interests.

Religion – like everything else – has to first exist for it to be used, although reasons for its existence (origin) may not exactly be the reasons for its continued use.[31] Its existence is deeply, if not reducibly, rooted in material conditions. Religion (e.g. Hinduism, Islam, Christianity, Buddhism, etc.) – in the forms of religious texts, sayings, myths, rituals, etc. – expresses, however imperfectly, the depth of human beings' suffering, whether it is caused by society or nature. Religion also expresses people's complaints/protests against their suffering. Religion popularly expresses – albeit in contradictory and inadequate ways – some aspects of the potential of humans, including their potential to have a degree of freedom from what neuro-scientists such as Davidson (2012) call afflictive emotions such as excessive anger against individuals, sadness, egoism and anxiety (from which Marxists and non-Marxists suffer) and to nurture wholesome qualities such as kindness, agreeableness, love and altruism. Both kinds of emotions arise in the brain, and positive emotions can be cultivated, including on the basis of some methods prescribed in world's major religions such as Buddhism and Hinduism (ibid.). Religion also expresses the humankind's eagerness for, a more humane world.[32] Religious texts/traditions may indeed contain important ideas, however, 'utopian', about what a good society might be. We can offer a couple of examples. From the Russian vantage point, here is Zetkin:

> Among the Russian small peasants, there are old and deeply felt traditions of indigenous village communism that have not entirely died away. They have been sustained and reinforced by primitive religious feelings

---

31    There has been a large amount of literature on religion from a Marxist perspective. A sample literature includes, apart from Marx and Engels (1964), the following: Avakian, 2008; Boer, 2009, 2011, 2012, 2013, 2014; Page, 1993; Saxton, 2007. Texts on religion in the Indian context include: Chattopadhyaya, 2013; and Habib, 2015.

32    This potential and this eagerness, as expressed in religious discourses and practices are products of objectively-existing relations: humans' relation with nature signifying their struggle to control it, and their relations with one another, including relations of conflict and harmony. Indeed, 'Man makes religion, religion does not make man. Religion is, indeed, the self-consciousness and self-esteem of man... Man is *the world of man* – state, society. This state and this society produce religion, which is an *inverted consciousness of the world*, because they are an *inverted world*. Religion is the general theory of this world, its encyclopaedic compendium, its logic in popular form, its spiritual *point d'honneur* [point of honour], its enthusiasm, its moral sanction, its solemn complement, and its universal basis of consolation and justification. It is the *fantastic realization* of the human essence since the *human essence* has not acquired any true reality. The struggle against religion is, therefore, indirectly the struggle *against that world* whose spiritual *aroma* is religion. *Religious* suffering is, at one and the same time, the *expression* of real suffering and a *protest* against real suffering. Religion is the sigh of the oppressed creature, the heart of a heartless world, and the soul of soulless conditions. It is the *opium* of the people' (Marx, 1843).

that view all property as ultimately from God, as God's property. These sentiments are nourished by the propaganda of Tolstoy's followers, Social Revolutionaries, Narodniks, and many religious sects. And these beginnings of communist understanding are systematically encouraged and promoted by the measures of the proletarian state.

ZETKIN, 1922[33]

Interestingly, similar religious feelings that view all property as God's property existed in India as well. Consider *Isa Upanishad*, a religious-philosophical text written by some insightful people who probably lived in a pastoral society 2500–3000 years ago (note that during those times, secular and religious ideas used to co-exist in a given text or in the minds of particular thinking persons). This text *begins* with what can be called a 'primitive'-communist type view of society, a society without private property. It says that: everything is owned by the supreme controller; one may enjoy what is allotted to one by that supreme controller but one should not encroach upon others' property.[34] Of course, such a view is not rooted in a scientific conception and is therefore utopian, but nonetheless it captures human beings' lofty aspirations for a better society. While the Hindutva people are proud of Hindu ideas *and* deeply worship private property, they should know that texts such as *Isa Upanishad* imagine a society without private property. It is human beings who create religion to help them cope with a world which is difficult and over which they have not much control. Indeed, objective conditions of alienation from one's own self, one's fellow human beings, from material conditions and access to resources, produce certain religious beliefs and practices (just as the same conditions of alienation and suffering, when scientifically thought through on the basis of the philosophy of materialist-dialectics, prompt production of socialist ideas). Religion as a set of ideas and practices can shape people's thinking, which in turn can, under certain conditions, prompt people to kill/hurt others in the name of religion. As long as objective conditions exist for the need for religion, religion will exist. So, freedom to satisfy that need, i.e. freedom to practice any religion, as long as it is more or less a private affair and does not affect state's actions, is an essential part of democracy, as are the need to protect the views and practices of religious minorities, the freedom to criticize religion from the

---

33    Commenting on this paragraph John Riddell (2009) says about Zetkin: 'she expresses a thought that I have not found elsewhere in world communist literature of the time'. On the idea that ancient Indian texts have atheistic and secular elements, see (Sen, 2005).

34    *Isavasyam idam sarvam yat kim ca jagatyam jagat, tena tyaktena bhunjitha, ma gridhah kasyasvid dhanam* is the first few lines of the Isavasya Upanishad. One might split the lines into parts like this: *isavasyam idam sarvam* – everything is owned by *isa*, the supreme controller. *Tena tyaktena bhunjitha* – you may enjoy what is allotted to you by Him. *Ma grdhah kasya svid dhanam:* but do not encroach upon others' property.

standpoint of science, and the freedom not to have any religion. Such freedom is under attack now, as a part of the attack on democratic rights.

Religion itself may not necessarily lead to politics of religious hatred any more than differences in skin color necessarily produce politics of racism. Yet, fascistic forces make use of people's need for religion (or indeed need for a similar sense of belongingness based on other identities), to divide a nation along the lines of religion, race, etc. and promote the political hegemony of given religious and ethnic groups.[35] This goes against the tradition of people of different religious beliefs and ethnicities generally having lived together peacefully in many countries, including India, the US, and many European countries.

As a form of class society which is a society of alienation and inequalities, bourgeois rule, at an abstract level, can exist without, say, religious (or racial) discrimination. But in reality, in many cases, that is not the case. The ruling class and its ideological and political representatives use religion (along with other similar tools) to divide people and to divert their attention from their own failure to meet people's needs.[36] Religious ideas, generally, do not represent, in any systematic way, the ruling class as being responsible for the miseries of the masses. Usually, problems that people face are said to be due to their own personal (moral) failings or acts of some unseen powerful agency (gods, etc.). Religious ideas make people rely not on their collective political action against their exploiters/oppressors and the state, but on supernatural forces and their own moral rectitude to fix their problems.[37] The ruling class makes use of many religious ideas to make people passive, in other words.

The 'need' of the ruling class to use identity politics whether it is based on religion or race (or indeed geography) for all these purposes is real. Trotsky (1933) wrote about the connection between fascism (national socialism) and race. By mainly replacing race with religion in his original lines, these lines

---

35    Not all religious belief leads to the politics of religious hatred but such politics where it exists 'is rooted in a sense of religious identity and in how these identities... are manipulated for political purpose, material advantage, violent competition and all the rest. Religion per se cannot be held responsible' [for the politics of religious hatred] (Ahmad, 2013: 7).

36    The poison ivy of communal politics can only thrive in a class society. It will not thrive in a class-less society or it will not have the force it has in a class society, as a class-less society is based on harmonious development of productive forces to allow for the inclusion of everyone in social progress, and on mutual solidarity rather than mutual alienation and competition.

37    Millions of Indians still take the help of religious ideas and practices to get cured of their physical and mental illnesses.

could be translated into a message to describe the fascistic tendencies in India to a large extent.

> In order to raise it above history, the Indian nation is given the support of the Hindu religion. History of India is viewed as the emanation of the Hindu religion. The qualities of the Hindu religion are construed without relation to changing social conditions. The theory of religion, specially created, it seems, for some pretentious self-educated individual seeking a universal key to all the secrets of life, appears particularly melancholy in the light of the history of ideas. On the plane of politics, communalism [i.e. political use of religious divide] is a vapid and bombastic variety of chauvinism. As the ruined landlord class sought solace in the gentility of its blood, so the mass of pauperized petty bourgeoisie and lumpen-proletariat and similar other sections befuddles itself with fairy tales concerning the special superiorities of Hindu religion and its symbols such as the holy cow. Worthy of attention is the fact that the leaders of the fascistic movement, like most Indians, are not native Indians but interlopers from other parts of Asia.

That the ruling class does have a need for the use of identity politics whether it is based on religion or race (or geography) is indeed real. What is also a fact is that it has the ability to do so. This is because the ruling class, more or less, controls the means of communication of ideas among the masses, which are now-a-days both electronic and non-electronic.[38]

### 3.4    *Lower Classes' Alienated Need for Identity Politics and Irrationalism*
The need of the ruling class for religion and other such identities to calm and control the masses coincides with the masses' own material and social-psychological need for religion and other forms of social identity. People resort

---

38    As is widely known, Marx and Engels (1978: 64–65) famously say: 'the class which is the ruling *material* force of society, is at the same time its ruling *intellectual* force. The class which has the means of material production at its disposal, has control at the same time over the means of mental production, so that thereby, generally speaking, the ideas of those who lack the means of mental production [such as workers and lumpen proletariat, etc.] are subject to it. The ruling ideas are nothing more than the ideal expression of the dominant material relationships, the dominant material relationships grasped as ideas.... The individuals composing the ruling class possess among other things consciousness, and therefore think. ...[They] rule also as thinkers, as producers of ideas, and regulate the production and distribution of the ideas of their age: thus their ideas are the ruling ideas of the epoch'. The ruling class ideas are produced not just by the ruling class intellectuals but also by elements of the ruling class itself, and these elements do disseminate reactionary ideas directly.

to such things as religion to cope with a hostile and difficult class-society that fails to meet their needs. If there is scarcity of resources in society, a common-sensical view is that a certain social-cultural group (e.g. a given religious group) is responsible for this, whether or not that view is backed by evidence and reason. People of a particular religion (or a caste or race) identify themselves with those from the same religion (or a caste or a race) in their daily lives. This has a material basis. For example, if a wage-earner is to get one of the few available jobs or if a small-scale producer is to sell some product in a highly competitive market, increasingly dominated by big business, a network based on a social identity (e.g. religion, caste, race, etc.) becomes helpful. Religion can be a powerful coping mechanism: belief in an all-powerful supreme being who will help in times of crisis or belief in the idea that life will be better after death, are comforting, and can obviate the need for political resistance. Besides, social identity can become a source of a psychological satisfaction which, for example, a rich Hindu shopkeeper and a poor Hindu wage-worker may enjoy by thinking that they belong to one religion. Such a sense of psychological satisfaction matters especially when people are experiencing material insecurity. Of course, such feeling of identity prompts supremacist ideas: 'my religion is the most natural religion, and yours is the most artificial', or 'my caste is superior to yours', or 'this is my country in which you have no place'. And such feelings cause political friction among followers of different religions or castes, etc. In the process, the real friction – the conflict between common people on the one hand and big business and its state on the other – is replaced by friction among common people themselves, a friction that is more or less illusory.

The task of using religion (or a similar such thing) by the ruling class to weaken potential and actual lower-class opposition to the social order becomes easier in societies (e.g. those in the global periphery) where pre-modern, pre-capitalist ideas and practices have not been eliminated due to an incomplete bourgeois-democratic revolution, and where therefore these ideas and practices are 'combined' with those of advanced capitalism, a process of 'combined development' that means, as suggested in Chapter 3, 'an amalgam of archaic with more contemporary forms' (Trotsky, 2008: 5).

As mentioned, not everything in what are called religious texts is about religion, as there are philosophical ideas about human beings and nature, etc. in these texts. But a lot of what goes on in the name of religion represents irrational thinking, the thinking that is not, and that cannot be, backed by scientific evidence. Capitalism creates a need and an opportunity for irrational thinking, and thus for the use of religion and similar things (e.g. race) to weaken lower-class opposition to the existing social order, and thus feeds into the ideological basis for fascistic tendencies which thrive on irrational and anti-scientific thinking. This happens both in rich countries and in poor countries such as India. The following lines, even if they talk about a very developed stage of the fascist movement in the 1930s, can be interpreted as *something* that reflects the contemporary reality in India and elsewhere very well:

> Fascism has opened up the depths of society for politics. Today, not only in peasant homes but also in city skyscrapers, there lives alongside of the twentieth century the tenth or the thirteenth. A hundred million people use electricity and still believe in the magic power of signs and exorcisms [and one might add, going to miracle-making gurus; cow urine and the fact that plastic surgery existed in ancient India as proven by the elephant-headed god, Ganesh].[39] ...What inexhaustible reserves they possess of darkness, ignorance, and savagery! Despair has raised them to their feet fascism has given them a banner. Everything that should have been eliminated from the national organism in the form of cultural excrement in the course of the normal development of society has now come gushing out from the throat; capitalist society is puking up the undigested barbarism. Such is the physiology of... [fascism or strong fascistic tendencies].
>
> TROTSKY, 1933b; parentheses added

As mentioned, the dominant condition for fascistic tendencies is capitalism. This is the case especially when capitalism experiences economic crisis, as indicated by a slow economic growth leading to un-and under-employment and a government inability to provide welfare. By creating extreme inequality and by failing to satisfy the needs of the masses, the system (or, those who manage the system) makes some people believe in, and act on, their illusory needs such as the need for pride based in religious identity, which trump real needs (e.g. need for decent employment, etc.). This, in turn, creates a situation where a section of the population is mobilized to pursue the illusory needs. As well, for the same reasons (economic crisis, inequality, etc.), the state becomes increasingly authoritarian, and its liberal-democratic foundation begins to shake, because the system cannot meet the political demands from a large section of the population

---

39    It is possible that cow urine or any other animal's urine or some such thing has medicinal properties. And just because it might have been mentioned in some ancient texts that have religious content, that itself does not necessarily mean that such things have no usefulness. *However*, before their usefulness is *scientifically proven*, this cannot be taken as true on the basis of religious belief. From the vantage point of a class society, which creates condition for religion, there is also nothing inherently wrong with a group of people treating an animal as sacred, in the sense of being worthy of special admiration and worship, but it is deeply problematic when that belief is used to create political antagonism between (a) people who hold such a belief and (b) people who do not hold such a belief, and to hurt the latter group which poses no material threat to the former, when that belief shapes the affairs of the state and when that belief is given the same epistemological significance as evidence-based ideas based on reason.

for a better life. Under certain conditions (e.g. relative weakness of resistance), political authoritarianism can take an extreme form. This, when supported by a segment of lower-class population, can produce fascistic tendencies.

### 3.5    Agents – Foot Soldiers – of Fascistic Movement

Capitalism indeed does not only create the *structural* condition for fascistic tendencies by producing economic problems for the masses, who then blame their conditions on an enemy (e.g. religious minority; refugees). Capitalism also creates the *agencies* through which the fascistic project, including its violence aspect, is carried out. Here the role of petty bourgeois elements is important as fascistic movement's storm troopers or foot soldiers. This is because they are crushed by big capital so much so that they are only owners in a nominal sense, with their debts often outstripping the current monetary value of their property:

> The main army of fascism ... consists of the petty bourgeoisie and the new middle class: the small artisans and shopkeepers of the cities, the petty officials, the employees, the technical personnel, the intelligentsia, the impoverished [and pauperized] peasantry.
>
> TROTSKY, 1931a

It is true that what is called the petty bourgeoisie 'is characterized by the extreme heterogeneity of its social nature' (Trotsky, 1932c), and that 'ideologically it scintillates with all the colors of the rainbow' (Trotsky, 1932c). While 'At the bottom it fuses with the proletariat and extends into the lumpenproletariat', whose ranks expand thanks to capitalist crisis, 'on top it passes over into the capitalist bourgeoisie' (Trotsky, 1932j). The petty bourgeoisie 'may lean upon old forms of production but it may rapidly develop on the basis of most modern industry (the new "middle class")' (Trotsky, 1932j), including in what is now called information technology where workers are so alienated in the workplace that they resort to such things as religion (as a mechanism to cope with mental stress), a fact that, in turn, makes many of these people directly or indirectly support the agenda of soft Hindutva and some may even support the strident political movements based on religion. Research conducted by the social anthropologist Carol Upadhya of the National Institute of Advanced Studies, Bangalore, conducted among IT professionals in Bengaluru in the early 2000s, finds that:

> the price of their new-found wealth is the inability to maintain social and family relationships or even to have a meaningful existence outside of work... [this] lack of a sense of social connection or community may

account for the fact that a large number of IT professionals attend courses offering 'fast food' packaged spirituality....

Quoted in DESHMANE, 2017

Capitalism stokes the anger of the petty bourgeoise, including small scale producers, leading them to demand an authoritarian rule, falsely believing that
that is the solution to their problems. 'The sharp grievances of small proprietors never out of bankruptcy, of their university sons without posts and clients, of their daughters without dowries and suitors, [demand] ... order and an
iron hand' (Trotsky, 1933b).

Fascism penetrates the proletariat from below and from above. Many class-
strata such as 'Salaried employees, the technical and administrative personnel,
and certain strata of the functionaries [government officials]' (Trotsky, 1932h)
which were democratic can go into the fascist camp and 'are capable of drawing in their wake... a stratum of the labor aristocracy' (Trotsky, 1932h), and all
this is indicative of the fact that fascism is 'penetrating into the proletariat
from above' (Trotsky, 1932k). Then there is penetration of fascism into the proletariat from below:

> Considerably more dangerous, however, is... [fascism's or fascistic move-
> ment's] possible penetration from below, through the unemployed: No
> class can long exist without prospects and hopes. The unemployed do not
> represent a class, but they already compose a very compact and substan-
> tial layer, which is vainly striving to tear itself away from intolerable
> conditions.
>
> TROTSKY, 1932k

Important to the fascistic mass-movement are certain layers of the reserve
army that Marx (1977) talks about in *Capital* volume 1.

One category of 'the relative surplus population is the stagnant population.
This forms a part of the active labour army, but with extremely irregular employment. Hence it offers to capital an inexhaustible reservoir of disposable
labour-power. Its conditions of life sink below the average normal level of the
working class...It is characterised by maximum of working time, and minimum of wages' (p. 796). Another relevant layer is 'the lowest sediment of the
relative surplus population' which 'dwells in the sphere of pauperism'. This
layer includes 'vagabonds, criminals' etc.; in other words, 'the actual lumpenproletariat'. The lowest sediment is filled with those who are: 'the demoralised
and ragged' and many other layers of the unemployed population (p. 797).
When the reserve army expands (in part thanks to on-going primitive accumulation, privatization of state-owned companies, and migration of the poor

from the villages), it puts pressure on wages of those who are employed. This has a series of cultural implications that Marx does not consider, and which should be considered in order to shed light on the relation between capitalism and fascistic tendencies.

Thanks to the reserve army,

> the wage is so depressed that a proper proletarian culture is hard to sustain and many from inside the proletariat itself tend to get lumpenized: living partly by labour and wage within the capitalist system, but also supplementing it often with earnings generated by wit and, at times, even crime.
>
> AHMAD, 2013: 19–20

Not just that:

> the army of the unemployed is so vast, so permanent, that an innumerable number of them just stop seeking that kind of work, fall out of the capitalist system properly speaking, partaking of no labour that creates surplus value, falling into the underbelly of a pseudo-economy that runs parallel to the real economy and is governed by no rules, not even of exploitation, and where one can earn anything from a daily living to a fortune to a sudden death simply by going from one wager to another, often taking wit and/or crime in one's stride.
>
> AHMAD, 2013: 20

This sort of material processes has real effects on consciousness.[40] 'A stable life of productive labour gives one pride, or at least a grounding, in what one does' (ibid.: 20); besides, 'The life of value-producing labour is lived in a community of others who do the same' (ibid.: 20). This is not the case with the un-and under-employed. With them:

> lack of [their]... productivity, that sense of who one is, robs one of pride in oneself [and] that pride must somehow be regained, even if it is by

---

40  Breman (2016) talks about how pauperism is produced under Indian capitalism: the non-laboring poor who never had, or have lost, their ability to take care of themselves; the footloose labor driven away from the village for lack of work but also driven back 'home' again when they are thrown out of their casual employment; and, finally, an urban underclass redundant to demand, experienced by the better-off as a nuisance and brutally evicted from their slum habitat. These elements are a potential basis for the fascistic movement.

harming others, be it by way of crime or by that purported non-crime that is communalism itself, with all its violences.

Ibid.: 20

As well:

the life of the lumpenproletariat is by its nature one that creates no community out of any shared conditions of labour but must always work within collectivities that are tentative, transitional and forever in need of getting re-invented out of the emergencies that individuals in this quasi-class face all the time. Bereft of class belonging, they are prone to temptations of community-belonging to caste, religion or whatever – a kind of belonging far more abstract than the concrete belonging to a community of labour.

Ibid.: 20

So a chance to be recruited into communal politics and similar endeavors often gives them the much-needed purpose of life, which is reinforced by a sense of religious belongingness, though it is a fictive sense of 'belonging to a real community'. And, 'In the process, the aggressivity of posture that is so important for sheer survival in lumpen life can get easily transferred to communal/fascist kinds of organized violence' (Ahmad, 2013: 18–19).[41]

There is indeed a direct relation between communal and fascistic mobilization on the one hand and criminality on the other, and especially, a criminality which not only satisfies a social psychological need (for a feeling that one is doing something in life) but which also can generate material reward (e.g. some income; some loot from sectarian riots; even a post in the fascistic party organization or its Ministry).

The culture of the lumpen (and similar other) elements that is conducive to the politics of hate is not entirely governed by its economic conditions of capitalism, however. Relevant here are also political processes in capitalism, which mediate in the relation between the economic conditions and culture. Firstly, the class of people which has nothing but its labor power to sell – the working class, including those who are currently not employed – needs democratic rights to be able to put organized pressure on the capitalist class and its state

---

41    It is not surprising that, as Ahmad (2013: 3) says: 'Bulk of the storm troopers for any fascism or any religious inflamed violent conflict, and in ethnic cleansing always come from among those' who are victims of (a predatory) capitalism and 'who have been spiritually destroyed and morally disoriented by the cruelties they suffer in their everyday life'.

for an increased private wage and increased social wage (government benefits), so it can have an adequate access to food, shelter, etc. that it needs. However, to be able to avoid having to give any concession, the capitalist system must curtail working class' democratic rights. This is why the force of identity politics is a measure of the fact that people's level of progressive consciousness – that they are members of a democratic secular republic, with certain rights irrespective of their religion or any other identity, that they, as workers and peasants, have some rights and can demand certain things based on their collective strength – is extremely low. The content of such a politics of identity (religious identity) can take authoritarian and then fascistic forms. Secondly, when there are vast segments of the working class who have no hope of regular employment and which have indeed no experience of employment, they have no *need* for democratic rights to put pressure on the employer: they *have* no employer. They have no taste *of* democracy. They have no taste *for* democracy. When millions of people in a society have no need for, and experience of, democracy, this potentially creates a condition for fascistic tendencies. They can easily become pre-disposed towards becoming storm troopers for fascistic tendencies. This shows that sheer criminality and undemocratic attacks on others who, generally, are like them in class terms (e.g. people belonging to religious, etc. minorities) can indeed be a source of some reward. So ultimately, the politics of religious and other forms of identity, including in its fascistic forms, are rooted in material conditions and their class form (and especially, the capitalist class form).

Indeed, when millions live in poverty and misery in an increasingly unequal society, then:

> Extreme religious faith and ethnic nationalism are often all that gives their lives purpose and dignity. Many, with good reason, believe that colonialism, capitalism, multi-national corporations and their own indigenous leaders have all harmed them. Thus, they return to fundamentalist beliefs of their ancestors or are susceptible to political manipulation....
>
> DOBKOWSKI and WALLIMAN, 2003: 13

It is simply wrong to say that the actually-existing proletariat are not or cannot be conservative in their political attitudes. Workers as a class are progressive, but only potentially. In their daily lives, individual workers and groups of workers can have reactionary attitude, partly thanks to worsening economic conditions and partly thanks to the absence of political education from the communist and progressive movements. Even if some of them have the memory of Nazism, that memory is no vaccine against their belief in fascism or fascistic ideas at all (pace Vanaik). Marx knew this. Trotsky said:

The workers are by no means immunized once for all against the influence of fascism. The proletariat and the petty bourgeoisie interpenetrate, especially under the present conditions, when the reserve army of workers cannot but produce petty traders and hawkers, etc., while the bankrupt petty bourgeoisie effuses proletarians and lumpenproletarians.

TROTSKY, 1932k

There is one more dimension of capitalism that potentially connects it to fascistic tendencies. Capitalism is driven by the logic of accumulation for its sake, by the incessant pursuit of wealth in its abstract form (money). Such a regime of production will not survive without incessant consumption. Thus capitalism creates cultural attitudes whereby people see themselves as consumers of commodities chasing their own 'well-being', and they do so partly to counter their alienation-from-one-another in the workplace and in the labor-market. But in the process, they lose their ability to empathize with fellow-human beings' suffering, signifying their alienation from other people. If, as the neuroscientist, Richard Davidson says (2016; also 2012), generosity (altruism) is one of the four aspects of human mental well-being, a trait that many religions, including Hinduism and Buddhism, emphasize, clearly people are losing their ability to be generous. Among many contingent manifestations of such lack of empathy and of such a high degree of alienation is the fact that not only does a large segment of the population engage in sectarian-fascistic violence that kills thousands of innocent people but also is such violence tolerated by others in their everyday lives.[42]

## 4        Conclusion

In understanding the rise of fascistic forces, one has to keep in mind Marx's theory of politics in class society. It is in 'the direct relationship of the owners of the conditions of production to the immediate producers', in which we find the hidden basis of 'the political form of the relationship of sovereignty and dependence' (Marx, 1991: 927). He also says that: 'all struggles within the state' – for example, struggles over democracy, etc. – 'are merely the illusory forms in

---

42    It is also interesting that such sectarian violence is condoned/supported by some politicians as reaction-to-an-action, an idea that mistakenly physicalizes the human being. Such physicalization of human beings actually contradicts the religious belief in the name of which people engage in sectarian violence: a part of the religious belief is that there is more to the human being than their physical body.

which the real struggles of the different classes are fought out among one another' (Marx and Engels, 1978: 54). Avoiding economic reductionism, Marx
asserts that while politics is based on economic matters, politics also reacts
back on economic matters.

The rise of the BJP is a manifestation of a global phenomenon that is expressed in India: the global phenomenon is the fact that the big business facing
an economic and social crisis is resorting to social reaction, politics of hatred,
and authoritarianism (both authoritarianism from above – the state; and authoritarianism from below – rightwing forces). The increasing strength of
right-wing forces, including the rise of the BJP as the political head of these
forces in India, has been engendered by four mechanisms, three of which –
and these are mainly political-economic mechanisms, are discussed in this
chapter.

a.    The first is the crisis of global capitalism, the crisis that is manifested
      in India. Associated with this is the crisis of post-colonial bourgeois-
      nationalist-developmental-statism (i.e. crisis of post-colonial national
      capitalism), and the attendant crisis of livelihood of common people.
      The bourgeois system of the world and India's backward capitalism oper-
      ating within the influence of imperialism and imperialist institutions,
      have been simply incapable of meeting the basic needs of the toiling
      classes. Masses are subjected to exploitation (and indeed, super-exploita-
      tion) and dispossession and immiserization. To the extent that imperial-
      ism shapes the lives of common people in India (and similar other coun-
      tries in the South), one can say that fascistic tendencies are 'the expression
      of the most slavish dependence on foreign imperialism' (Trotsky, 1974:
      34).

b.    The combination of exploitation, dispossession, and immiserization re-
      quires legitimization/justification in the minds of the masses. As well,
      that combination prompts potential and actual opposition. A ruling class
      response is authoritarianism, that also requires justification. There is
      thus a need for double justification (or consent from the masses): the
      system of exploitation/dispossession/immiserization needs justification,
      and the coercive response to the lower-class struggle against the system
      also requires a justification. There is a need for the weakening of the low-
      er-class opposition too. The ideology of religion – religious divide be-
      tween Hindus and religious minorities – and associated Hindu-national-
      ism, provides such justification. It also divides the masses along the lines
      of religion and fake view of nationalism that considers vast sections of
      the population anti-national. Deployment of religion and religion-based
      politics is supplemented with lies and false promises, to obtain consent

to the system, and this, in a liberal-democracy, includes obtaining votes for fascistic political outfits. All in all, a structural space is created for increasing strength of fascistic forces, which have been existing in India since 1920s.

c.  Capitalism not only creates the space for fascistic forces, but also a need for these forces. Capitalism also produces a class-agency for the fascistic project. It produces a reserve army of labor and pauperized small-scale producers (who are on their way to becoming completely propertyless), the elements of which, in a poor economy without social benefits (or with very limited benefits) from the government, are vulnerable to lumpenization and criminality. Having been 'spiritually destroyed and morally disoriented by the cruelties they suffer in their everyday life', these victims of (neoliberal) capitalism, not surprisingly, form the bulk of the fascist storm troopers (Ahmad, 2013: 4). There are vast sections of the population whose needs are not met by capital or the state, and they blame their situation on, for example, minorities.

Just because capitalism creates a need for fascistic forces and just because capitalism creates lumpen elements that can be used by the fascistic project, that does not necessarily mean there will be fascistic forces in *active operation*. The bourgeois-*political* dynamics of the rise of fascistic tendencies will be discussed in the next chapter.

# Bourgeois-Political Dynamics of Fascistic Tendencies

A fuller understanding of fascistic tendencies must take us beyond the sphere of the political-*economic*, which was more or less the focus of the last chapter. We must pay attention to the sphere of politics in a bourgeois society. The political dynamics of the fascistic tendency have been different in different countries. Focusing on the Congress and the BJP as two faces of bourgeois politics, I will now deal with the fascistic tendencies as they are manifested in the *concrete political situation* in India, in the light of the *general* discussion of the political economic dynamics of the fascistic tendencies, in the last chapter.

The Congress Party, and the Communist parties (which are social-democratic *in practice*) constitute the combined forces of the 'Center' and the Left, and can be called, with *some* justification, 'reformist democracy'. I will begin, in Section 1, with the Congress Party as the traditional party of the bourgeoisie. I will, as well, briefly mention the failure of the Left which has supported the Congress against the BJP. I will discuss how it is that the various failures of 'reformist democracy' – the failures on the economic front and the failures to protect democracy and secularism – have produced a situation for the right-wing forces to become stronger, electorally and otherwise. In Section 2, I relate the rise of the BJP as a part of the fascistic movement, to the logic of capital, including in its neoliberal form, and to the capitalist class. The relation between the capitalist class and the fascistic movement is not straightforward, as communal tensions can affect the business climate. The BJP has intelligently responded to the mild business concerns about political tensions. In Section 3, I will deal with the multiple ways in which the BJP as a part of the fascistic movement has been garnering support, electorally and extra-electorally. In Section 4, I show how the BJP – and the fascistic movement – is a contradictory process. The final section concludes the chapter and sets the context for a discussion on how to fight the fascistic movement.

## 1 The Failure of 'Reformist Democracy' to Weaken Fascistic Tendencies

Coming out of the anti-colonial movement which it led, the Congress party has hitherto been the traditional party of the post-colonial bourgeoisie. It 'was built by a multi-ethnic coalition of middle [Congress party] class elites in alliance with small rural landholders', and the coherence of these groups' class interests 'facilitated the emergence of a strong party espousing an inclusive and programmatic nationalist ideology' (Tudor, 2013, discussed in Clarke, 2017: 581; see also Chibber, 2010). Such an ideology 'allowed it to downplay and depoliticize other potentially relevant lines of difference in India, including those dividing regions, linguistic groups, and castes. The combination of its inclusive, nonsectarian version of nationalism and its coherent distributive coalition gave it a stable base on which to build a postcolonial democratic nation' (p. 585).

But the influence of the party within its own lower-class and socially oppressed base has been in decline (as has that of the Left) in part because of the fact that neo-liberal capitalism has forced it to pander to ruling class interests at the expense of those of lower classes (Figure 12.1). Demagogically presenting itself as a champion of the lower-classes (and Hindus), the BJP has now (almost) displaced the Congress as the new dominant party of the capitalist class, a process that has slowly happened over time. In fact, the BJP's electoral acceptability – in terms of vote share – has been increasing over time even if unevenly (Figure 12.1).

One might ask: how different and similar are these two political 'arms' of the capitalist class (i.e. the Congress and the BJP)? The Congress plays the religion card to win elections.[1] More specifically, it often deploys soft Hindutva.[2] It has failed to protect secularism. For example, it has failed to hold accountable those responsible for: the carnage of Sikhs in 1984, in Delhi, and of Muslims in 2002, in Gujarat. It has failed to stop the demolition of the Babri mosque in

---

1   The Congress party has 'nurtured and supported' the Shiv Sena, BJP's right-wing cousin, 'for over two decades from the mid-sixties to the mid-eighties. In the early phase, this support was given to break the Communist hold over the trade union movement in Mumbai; in the later phase, it was to settle factional scores within the Congress itself' (Dhawale, 2000: 1–2). Congress and RSS also do not belong to two different planets: 'The RSS ... has often come out in appreciation of the [Congress party] when it feels the tactical interests of Hindu communalism demands it. The RSS would ideally want the major national party to become Hindu oriented. In 1987, a powerful RSS leader said: 'We are not anti-Congress. Our founder leader was a Congressman. Our organisation is opposed only to the Congress policy of appeasing the minorities' (Karat, 1992; parenthesis added).

2   In its election campaigns in Madhya Pradesh to be held in December 2018, the Congress is planning Ram yatra. Its politicians, including its national President, openly and publicly display their religiosity and show that there are devotees of this or that Hindu god (Ghose, 2018). As well, 'the Congress Party is busy trying to showcase its 'soft Hindutva' ideology. Days before the Election Commission's poll bugle, Congress president Rahul Gandhi went on a temple, mosque, gurudwara run across MP. ...In its manifesto too, Congress played the soft Hindutva card to woo Hindu voters, traditionally seen as the BJP's vote bank. The manifesto promised to build *gaushalas* (cowsheds) in every gram panchayat, set up new *adhyatmik vibhag* (department for spirituality) and open new Sanskrit schools across the state' (Dutta, 2018).

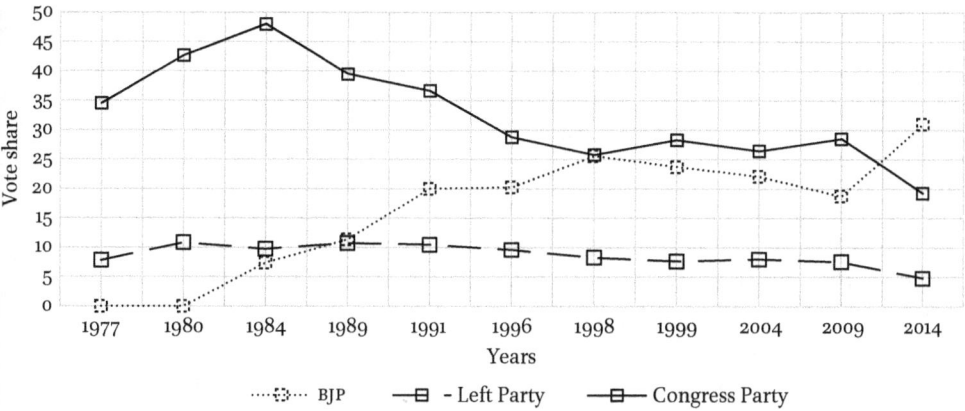

FIGURE 12.1 BJP, Left Party, and Congress Party's vote share, 1977–2014

1992 in Uttar Pradesh by the Hindu-communal forces. It has also failed to stop the forced migration of hundreds of thousands of Hindus from the Jammu valley, and deaths of hundreds of them in the hands of Muslims. It has failed to stop the deaths of civilians, many Hindus, during the Khalistani movement in the Punjab. During the Congress rule, in 1976, Indian constitution was amended, officially making it a secular state, and yet the constitution prohibits, on religious grounds, the slaughter of cows, an animal which many Hindus consider sacred. However, the Congress will *generally* not go against the principle of secularism *to the extent that* the BJP will and does. Its politics is not dominantly based on the politics of sectarian hatred. Besides, within the Congress, there *are* intellectual forces of liberal democracy and secularism (e.g. Shashi Tharoor, Mani S. Aiyar), and some of its senior leaders even think that a stronger electoral Left, even if it is their political rival, is good for democracy.

As far as economic policies – the policies concerning capitalist development – are concerned, there is relatively little difference between the BJP and the Congress, although the Congress can be slightly more pro-poor than the BJP can ever be as a matter of principle. Both are enthusiastic supporters of bourgeois class relations. Both support neoliberal forms of capitalist accumulation. The BJP and the Congress are two factions of the dominant bourgeois political formation. If anything, the BJP is 'the right-wing of the Congress'. The Congress has failed to significantly raise people's living standards, including of minorities. There have also been corruption scandals involving the leaders of the Congress and the members of the business class. The Congress has also not protected liberal democracy always: it declared national emergency suspending democratic rights in the mid-1970s.

If the Congress has failed to protect social and political rights, the Left has not succeeded much either. Like other regional off-shoots of the Congress in power (regional parties), the Left has, more or less, implemented the same neoliberal capitalist economic policies in the States where it has been in power (this is not to deny that the Left has invested in the social sector in its States and has tried to act as Left-Congress to some extent). Focused more on electoral battles than on extra-electoral mobilization, the Left has not organized its basic class forces (workers and small-scale producers) on a large enough scale to enable them to challenge communal thinking and practice and the on-going attack on their democratic rights. Indeed, failing to develop common people's class consciousness is one of the most important failures of the Left. It has tried its best to keep the BJP out of power several times, but it has not used the breathing space thus achieved to adequately mobilize its class forces against both capitalism, including in its neoliberal form, and communalism.

To repeat, the Left has been undeniably committed to secularism and protection of minority rights. Yet, before, during, and after the 1992 mosque demolition (the latter definitely signaled an attack on democracy and secularism, from the fascistic forces and which enabled the political rise of these forces), 'at this decisive moment in modern Indian history, the parliamentary left could not even carry out a counter-mobilization against the onslaught of communalism' (Vanaik, 2011: 102).

## 2 The BJP, the Fascistic Movement, and (Neoliberal-Peripheral) Capitalism

In this section, I will discuss the symbiotic relation between the capitalist class and the fascistic movement. I will then discuss the various ways in which the entire family of fascistic forces has pursued an agenda that is pro-capitalist as well as a communal, in the extreme.

The capitalist economic logic includes the fact that capitalist property relations need to be protected and that conditions for capitalist profit need to be ensured. Any political party – from the Right, Center and the Left – that manages the collective affairs of capital and of its state must reproduce the economic logic of capitalism. Given the economic logic of capitalism, the Congress and the BJP, the two main parties of the capitalist class, are very similar in terms of economic policies. They must support – they must be embodiments of – the capitalist economic logic. The BJP as a capitalist party has to pursue capitalist development like the Congress does. While in power, like the Congress, the BJP has indeed implemented neoliberal capitalist policies, and while in opposition, it has also supported such policies. This is the political effect of the economic logic of capitalism.

Thanks to the *neoliberal* capitalist strategy reflecting the demands of the capitalist class, the strategy that the Congress Party ushered in and that all parties including the Left have supported, capitalist economic growth has caused a greater un/under-employment, income-deflation for the masses, and rising inequality, with a top tiny class massively benefitting from economic growth and the vast section living in misery (see Figure 12.2 below). The miserable situation of the masses, aggravated by the inability of the state to provide for them in a less developed economy, has created a support-base for the BJP's agenda over the last 4 decades or so: this has allowed the BJP to lie that it can do things differently. The situation has also enabled the BJP and its family to produce their storm-troopers who come from angry petty bourgeois people and from un/under-employed people.

It should be noted that the economic failure of the Congress is not just a political failure, the failure of a political party. It is a part of the failure of the entire bourgeois system of politics which is subordinated to the crisis-ridden bourgeois political economy operating within the capitalist world market. Given the pressure of the world market and imperialist institutions, maintaining a protected economy for long was going to be difficult anyway, especially given the balance of power between the capitalists and the masses in a peripheral-capitalist country being heavily tilted towards the former. It should also be noted that while capitalism constrains political parties, the constraints are never absolute. Capitalism sets limits within which political parties can autonomously act. Depending on the balance of power between classes that is reflected in their programs, they can be more or less pro-people, once again within limits. Under the political pressure of the Left and progressive forces, the Congress was able to introduce, for example, a rural employment program, which the BJP has not been keen on implementing as strongly as the Congress as we have seen in Chapter 10. That fact reflects their slight differences in relation to the welfare of the masses (and slight differences between them and Left parties). These are differences in degree, however.

As far as common people are concerned, and considering the Congress' overall character (including on the economic front and in relation to secularism and democracy), the perception is that there is little economic difference between these two parties. This is partly signified by the fact that perhaps there is not

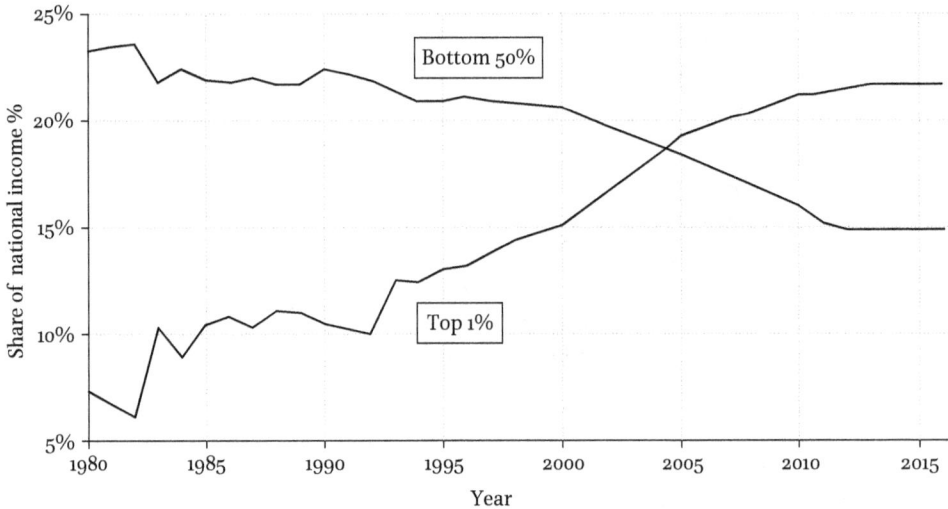

FIGURE 12.2 Income inequality in India, 1980–2015
SOURCE: HTTP://WIR2018.WID.WORLD/FILES/DOWNLOAD/WIR
-PRESENTATION.PDF

much qualitative difference in the nature of electoral support for either of the parties: people who support for Congress today may support the BJP tomorrow, and vice versa (Figure 12.3 below). There are States where both the BJP and the Congress have received high vote shares (Gujarat, Rajasthan, Madhya Pradesh, Chhattisgarh, Himachal Pradesh, Uttarakhand and to some extent, Karnataka as well – the States in the upper right corner of Figure 12.3). There are States where both parties have received limited amount of electoral support in the form of vote shares (e.g. Tamil Nadu, Bengal, Andhra, Telangana, Maharashtra, Bihar – the States in the lower left corner of Figure 12.3). In fact, the vast majority of States (i.e. taking into account what are known as major States), fall in either of these categories (and this has political implications, as we will see).

There is no doubt that the BJP, as a part of the fascistic movement, is funda-mentally a capitalist party. The fascistic forces are not just based in certain re-actionary *ideas*. They have a deeply material character. There is no doubt that RSS, the ideological guru and mentor of the BJP, is not just an anti-democratic and communal force, but also it is a deeply *anti-communist* force. Anti-communism animates the entire fascistic movement, and that is an attraction for the capitalist class. In contrast, the Congress can be slightly conciliatory towards the Left.

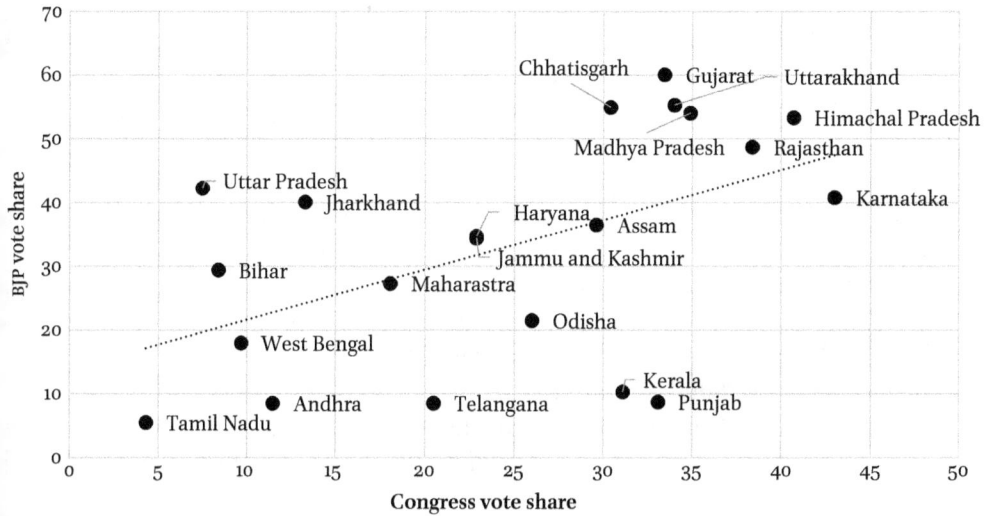

FIGURE 12.3 Congress vote share vs BJP vote share in India's general election, 2014

RSS is not only the motor force behind fascistic ideology that justifies a reactionary political project of the Hindu state as well as anti-people and pro-business economic policy (in spite of fruitless references to such empty terms as Gandhian socialism, Swedishi, etc.). It seems that much like the Christian missionaries who laid the groundwork in the past for the European colonial-capitalists and their political representatives, to colonize countries, the Hindu-tva missionaries (e.g. the RSS cadre) are helping the BJP now to colonize the space of India's secular-democratic fabric and to inflict a fascistic agenda on the country, in the interest of the capitalist class and to appease some politi-cally backward obscurantist elements in the population.[3] RSS's groundwork that gets the BJP votes includes coercion and consent: brutal attacks on minorities, secularists, democrats and communists, as well as ideological brainwashing and charity work. Often the charity work has a direct ideological function promoting fascistic ideas.[4]

---

3   For the BJP, the secularism of non-BJP parties is 'Pseudo-secularism' which it basically de-fines as 'the practice by all parties which denies the essentially Hindu character of the coun-try and therefore pampers the minorities and appeases minority communalism for garnering votes'. So what the BJP calls pseudo-secularism is equal to minorytism. For it, 'Genuine secularism requires recognition that Hinduism is the cultural essence of Indian society and its binding force', and therefore, 'only acceptance of Hindutva could make one a genuine secularist – what it calls positive secularism. Any defence of legitimate minority rights be-comes minorityism' (Karat, 1991: 4).

4   Consider the RSS-funded network of schools in rural areas, that takes advantage of the com-plete collapse of state-funded education. That the RSS has infected the minds of millions of

Underlying the different factors behind the BJP's post-1980s popularity, is the fact that sections of the ruling class itself (the bourgeois and big landlords), have shifted their moral, intellectual, financial and political loyalty to the BJP from the Congress, often willingly, and sometimes unwillingly.[5] The reason is that it does not matter whether the BJP and its foot-soldiers kill Muslims and secularists and communists; if the ruling class elements can benefit from the BJP's authoritarianism that helps its implement neoliberal capitalist policies and that curtails the freedom to criticize pro-capitalist policies, why not support it? It is not surprising that: in 2009, Anil Ambani said that 'Narendrabhai has done good for Gujarat and imagine what will happen if he leads the nation. A person like him should be the next leader of the country' (quoted in Karat, 2014: 7). Similarly, Sunil Mittal, head of the Bharti group, echoed Ambani: 'Chief Minister Modi is known as CEO, but he is actually not a CEO because he is not running a company or a sector. He is running a State and can also run the nation' (ibid.). These words from the ruling class proved to be prophetic, as Mr. Modi indeed became the Prime minister in 2014.

Indeed, what use-value is the facade of secularism Hindu fundamentalist forces allow the moneybags to amass a lot of money? We have seen that the business class economically profits from the labor of workers and small-scale producers and politically 'profits' from a right-wing government unleashing 'the reserve army' of the forces of reaction that divide and intimidate any potential anti-capitalist force (and thus playing a role that is complimentary to that of police, etc.).

However, the relation between capitalist economy and the right-wing character of capitalist politics may not always work in favor of the capitalist class in a straightforward way, and indeed, under some circumstances, the capitalist class can present some limited counter-vailing mechanisms to right-wing-ism. As mentioned earlier, communal violence can destroy property, including capitalist property. It can also create a law and order issue that can undermine the business climate (in a communal riot, people may not go to work, and they may reduce/stop the purchase of commodities, and both of these facts will

---

children is clear. In 2004, reports surfaced of high-school textbooks in Gujarat, which was led by Mr. Modi for years, that admired Nazism and fascism. In a section called 'Ideology of Nazism', the textbook said Hitler had 'lent dignity and prestige to the German government', that he 'made untiring efforts to make Germany self-reliant' and that he 'instilled the spirit of adventure in the common people' (Schultz, 2017). To cite another example: when 25 mostly upper-middle-class students at a private French school in Mumbai, a city that is home to fascistic tendencies, were asked to name the historical figure they most admired, nine of them picked Hitler. That India's cultural atmosphere is demonstrating fascistic traits is clear.

5  Writing just before the 2014 general election, Karat (2014) said: 'Whatever the outcome of the election, there is no doubt that Hindutva is witnessing a second coming, and that there is a shift among the big bourgeoisie in favour of the right-wing communal party, the BJP' (p. 3).

adversely affect business profit). And the law and order situation is already getting worse, as shown in the recent killing of a police officer by Hindutva forces.
This is the logic here: when a *culture* of mob lynching is encouraged within,
and by, the fascistic movement, this culture can easily spread. It can hurt and
discipline not only its usual targets (e.g. Muslims), but also the security personnel if they dare to do their duty by investigating lynchings or other such atrocities by the fascistic forces.[6] So domestic capital and global capital can put *some*
restraints on the right-wing party by using such mechanisms as words of warn-
ing, and threat of producing a bad image about the investment climate.

Domestically, certain members of the ruling classes (e.g. Godrez or Bajaj)
have been concerned about communalism, and it is possible that some of
them – as individuals and not as bearers of the economic logic of capital – do
care about secularism as a value (see Gurcharan Das, 2012). The global capital
is also concerned about the law and order situation that communalism can
create. In November 2015, Moody's Analytics asked Modi to keep the BJP members 'in check or risk losing domestic and global credibility' (quoted in Kumar
and Jones, 2015). The reason is not that the global business cares about the
protection of democratic rights as such; in fact, Modi, who was an international pariah because of his role in Gujarat riots, was warmly and widely em-
braced, by imperialist capital and politicians and was accorded high status at
global capital's family gathering at Davos.[7] Much rather, the reason is pecuniary. Moody Analytics warned that 'the belligerent provocation of various Indian minorities has raised ethnic tensions' and that an increase in communal
violence and increased opposition in parliament to such violence mean that
'debate turns away from economic policy' (quoted in Kumar and Jones, 2015).
Moody criticized Modi for not implementing economic reforms fast enough.
Spending time on fomenting communal tension against minorities is not en-
dorsed by global capital because it draws attention away from policy-making in
favor of capital. So the right-wing dispensation responded positively at the
time, however temporary or muted the response was.[8]

When sections of the domestic capital have showed their uneasiness with
communalism, Hindu supremacists arm-twist them into supporting them: in
one case, they put pressure on a major national trade organization of the capitalists (Confederation of Indian Industry) to retract their statements of concern

---

6   The growing mob culture is threatening the constitution and putting the life of police inspec-
    tor at a greater risk of losing life while performing professional duty. The inspector was the
    Investigating Officer in a 2015 lynching case that killed a Muslim person.
7   Modi has wanted to refurbish his image by making numerous foreign trips.
8   The BJP's chief and Modi's right-hand man, Amit Shah, asked Haryana Chief Minister Khat-
    tar and a few other politicians to temper their communal appeals so as not to impede the
    implementation of the BJP's economic 'reform' agenda (Kumar and Jones, 2015).

about communalism. It is possible that the BJP will listen to capitalists' 'warnings' and positively respond to the uneasiness about communalism. But there is a limit to the extent to which the BJP can keep its forces in check. This is because to serve capitalists, the Party has to win, and to win the party depends on these reactionary forces during election time and at other times. And, as long as the law and order situation can be maintained through the *intensification* of state- and vigilante-violence, killing of minorities and anti-reaction dissenters might be just fine, from the standpoint of capital. Besides, not all communal-fascistic action is in the form of coercion or killing. A large part of this is in the form of spreading communal and hyper-nationalistic ideas on the basis of the fascistic capture of cultural-educational institutions (e.g. universities and research centers), and that does not concern the business class as that does not create communal tension on the street as yet. Money wins. Capitalists are in competition with one another, and a special relation with a ruling party can enhance one's competitive advantage. Which capitalist would want to be on the wrong side of a party, given that the party can benefit him/her in a big way? Besides, many of the capitalists involved in the $40-billion-dollar Hindu-spiritual market and promoting soft Hindutva are directly and indirectly supportive of the fascistic tendencies.[9] For global capital, India is a low-wage platform for making money (especially, given that the average wage is much lower than in China where living standards double every 13 years, as Roberts, 2018 reports, while India is obsessed with trivial cultural identity issues), and with its cheap labor and cheap natural resources and its state-owned companies for sale, global capital might not be too critical of the forces of capitalist reaction in India (unless there is another India-like territory in terms of profit-making opportunities but one where the political-sectarian tension does not exist).

---

9   'While keeping the business of spirituality centre stage and claiming to retain a non-political and ideological stand, these spiritual entrepreneurs and their outfits [selling spiritual advice, herbal health products mentioned in religious scriptures, etc.] have actually been effective in becoming platforms to promote "soft Hindutva" to a large and influential captive audience. The rise in religiosity and conservative tendencies within Indian society appears to have only aided the efforts these platforms have made to push forward soft Hindutva' (quoted in Deshmane, 2017). Also: 'Ramdev's admirers and followers get more than medical advice: they also get a lesson in Hindu traditionalism and Hindu pride. Interspersed with yogic postures and medical virtues of herbs and food items, Ramdev offers a steady harangue against Western culture, Western medicine, and Western corporations. He equates the promotion of the physical health and well-being of Indians with the promotion of *desh ka swabhiman* (national self-pride) through a revival of its ancient sciences. He has made no secret of his association with the Sangh Parivar: a picture of him doing the RSS ... salute at a convention of the women's wing of the RSS is available in the RSS weekly, *The Organiser*. But Ramdev's open embrace of Hindu right-wing ideas has not diminished the enthusiasm of the masses, which is a strong indication of how normal and ordinary the world view of Hindu supremacy and revival has become' (Meera Nanda quoted in Deshmane, 2017).

But we have seen that capitalist reaction is everywhere. There is a race to the bottom here as well. Given that there is capitalist reaction in all major countries, India will not lose out easily in the eye of global capital for unleashing the forces of reaction. Capital, ultimately, does not care about democracy or secularism. Ultimately, it cares about money, about profit and interest, and about the preservation of capitalist social relations. In this, different fractions of capital are the same, except that while foreign money capital and the trans-nationalized segment of Indian capital are more mobile, capital invested in mining, manufacturing and large-scale agribusiness is a little less so, which means that the law and order situation created by communal tension might affect these relatively-immobile fractions a little more than it would other fractions of capital.

Thus the right-wing forces, led by the BJP, like the Congress itself, deliver the business class what it wants, and in the process, have garnered the support of this class. And where/when this class has murmured a bit about the religious tensions that are created by these forces, the concerns of the business class have been temporarily heeded in a subdued manner or more or less ignored.

## 3 Political Techniques of the Fascistic Movement

It is to be reiterated that the political character of the right-wing forces including the BJP must be seen from the standpoint of capitalism's logic and from the standpoint of similarities and differences between the BJP and the Congress as two political parties of the bourgeoisie. There are two inter-related points to be made. (1) Capitalism has not only an economic logic but also a political logic to support the economic logic: there is a need to weaken any potential/actual opposition to the rule of capital. And as we have seen, this is where specific political techniques are important in reproducing capitalist rule. (2) It is the case that the economic problems created by capitalism and the failure of the Congress Party to help people to cope with these problems, have created a structural space for fascistic forces to rise. But to assert this is not enough. The structural space for fascistic forces has to be actively made use of. And these forces *have made use of* the opportunities by employing specific political – cultural-political – techniques. These techniques include demagogy (lies; false promises). These also include, and importantly, violent measures, suppression of dissent, and making emotional appeals to people on the basis of religion, and nation. I will discuss these techniques below.

### 3.1 *Demagogy*

The extreme form of demagogy – associated with the populist character of fascistic tendencies, defines the BJP. It comes to power by appealing to the masses, by exploiting their resentment against existing economic and political elite and by promising lots of good things, including millions of job and assistance for farmers and unearthing of unearned income (black money as it is called in India) and distributing it among common people. But the party delivers little because it has to satisfy its real boss: big business. To some extent this resonates with German fascism.

> Fascism in power is least of all the rule of the petty bourgeoisie. On the contrary, it is the most ruthless dictatorship of monopoly capital... Fascism succeeded in putting them [the middle classes] at the service of capital. Such slogans as ... the elimination of unearned income were thrown overboard immediately upon the assumption of power.
>
> TROTSKY, 1933b; parentheses and ellipses added

As just mentioned, it is the economic failure of the Congress to significantly raise people's living standards, including of minorities (Muslims are among the poorest among the different communities in India after decades of 'reformist democracy'), and to ensure that benefits of capitalist economic growth are distributed in a reasonably fair way, that has allowed the BJP to practice demagogy to attract voters: the demagogic BJP chants the mantra of development (read: free market capitalist development). It seeks to garner votes by making promises that it knows it can never deliver.

It should be stressed that whether during the election time or during another time, the promise of development is more ideological than material. Its main aim is to obtain consent (in the form of votes) so that the government can implement a twin agenda: (a) pro-market, pro-business, neo-liberal, economic policies that are buttressed by (b) an unashamedly communal strategy of dividing the masses along religious lines, ensuring that any significant opposition to (neoliberal-)capitalism is blunted. Of course, some minor developmental (redistributive) concessions (e.g. social services from the RSS; toilets or cooking gas cylinders from the government) that can hardly improve people's living conditions significantly and on a sustainable basis, *are* made to certain sections of the population. Demagogy cannot work in thin air.

The Congress has also been vulnerable to corruption scandals involving its leaders and the members of the business class that the party is keen to serve. This has prompted the BJP to practice demagogy on a different front: the BJP chants its other mantra – good 'governance'. It wants people to believe that it is a cleaner variant of the corruption-ridden Congress, even if it is not (as we have seen in Chapter 10). In reality, that term (good governance) means that the BJP can make the decisions concerning capitalist involvement – and this includes giving away people's land and public money, etc. to the business class (domestic or not) – without being much worried about the due process and the impacts of such decisions on the people and the environment. More broadly, for the BJP: good governance means the centralization of power in the hands of Prime Minister's Office and at the federal level at the expenses of the provinces; pro-business governmental interventions including transfer of society's resources and public loans to private businesses at below-market rates; and close relation between businesses and political leaders/officials so investment clearances are made with inadequate screening of the impacts of investment on society and environment, or without proper public input. The BJP's 'governance talk' complements its 'development talk' very well.

### 3.2     Sectarian Appeal to Religious Identities

The RSS and other elements of the fascist parivar recruit their cadres from middle class and semi/un-employed/under-employed people and from some wage-earners, by making use of the discourse of the Hindu religion and the idea of Hindutva (Hindu-ness).[10] Hindutva is euphemistically called a way of life to make it appear non-religious.

Resorting to politics of religious identity helps the BJP to *distinguish* itself from the Congress, in order to sell itself in the voter market as a different and a unique political commodity. The Congress, once again, is not immune to the politics of sectarian hatred. But playing the politics of difference based in religious identity is the *differentia specificia* of the BJP, or of the entire right-wing movement of which the BJP is a part.[11]

It *is* a fact that people have a need for religion and religious consciousness, given conditions of suffering, as we have seen. The BJP takes advantage of this

---

10    Plausibly, 'an urban, upper caste, middle class, socially conservative Hindu' might be 'spontaneously oriented toward accepting the Hindutva proposition that what is unique about India, and therefore its defining feature among nations, is that the great majority of its citizens are Hindu, and Hindu culture must therefore be accepted as national culture; those who do not accept this culture as the normative culture of India are really not Indian in the deeper sense' (Ahmad, 2013: 11). Underlying such a conservative belief is another belief: that religion is the defining trait of a culture. 'And this belief can go together with ideas of Religious Tolerance, Sarva Dharma Sambhav, the belief that Hindus are tolerant, liberal, peace-loving by nature, and that national disunity comes from others who are much too narrow-minded, fundamentalist, socially backward etc. So, when we ask ourselves whether or not communalism could ever become not just a majoritarian ideology but in fact something of a common sense for millions upon millions of people – possibly the majority of Indians – the answer would probably depend on which version of communalism we have in mind' (ibid.: 12).

11    In fact, the BJP's project is based on the coalescence of three kinds of hatred against or distaste for: religious minorities, a progressive economic policy benefitting the working masses, and democratic conduct/values. On the topic of the oppression of Muslims in India, see Jamil (2017).

fact. People are being 'encouraged' and forced by the right-wing forces to subscribe to a communal ideology, which purports to describe and explain society's major problems in terms of a combination of two things. (a) One is a
(bodily/mental/spiritual/economic) individualism: the idea of a strong, hard-
working, nation-loving, individual with the right morals and with a sense of
economic entrepreneurship based in private property. Individuals with these
traits are said to be necessary to solve society's problems. (b) Another is religious identity: every aspect of society is seen from the standpoint of the Hindus versus non-Hindus divide.[12] India's problems are because of what non-
Hindus do now or did in the past, and implicitly, because of what the
Muslim-dominated Pakistan did or does. If one puts (a) and (b) together, the
right-wing manifesto for national development points to the importance of
cultural-nationalistic and economic individualism: love your Hindu nation,
hate non-Hindus unless they do/think exactly as Hindus want, and have the
right morals as sanctioned by Hindu scriptures, and be a hard-working entrepreneur (even if that means selling tea and pakoras). With respect to the
Hindu – Muslim divide, it should be added that, according to the right-wing
forces, all things associated with living Muslims or with the India ruled by the
kings who practiced Muslim religion are inherently bad, and all things associated with those who are Hindus or with ancient India are inherently good,
even if it is the case that both Muslims and Hindus came from what is now
called India or even pre-1947 India and that *all* the epochs of the Indian society, like all societies, have had both progressive and regressive features in
terms of economic development, class relations, cultural changes, and so on
and therefore should be both celebrated and critiqued. Concomitantly, the
BJP also seeks to change people's way of thinking from one that is based on
empirical-historical evidence and on reason, to a way of thinking that does
not care (much) about evidence and reason, and that treats beliefs and myths
as empirical evidence.[13] If in Hindu mythology, a god G was born in place P,

---

12    This means that: society's problems are mainly seen as those that are created by the di-
      vide between religious groups and by the lack of Hindu-nationalist pride and unity, by the
      wrong things that minority-alien religions have apparently done to the majority group,
      and that solutions to the problems are claimed to lie in the supreme cultural-political
      dominance of a united majority religion (Hinduism). The majority religion is considered
      to be the only original religion of the nation, as compared to all other smaller religious
      groups which are alien religions having come from outside. It is also believed by majority-
      communalists that India's past is like no other country's and is always superior to other
      nations, and that major scientific achievements of the West, including plastic surgery, can
      all be traced to India's history.

13    What is true in the world is, more or less, independent of what is made out to be true, on
      the basis of power relations one has. It is true that the earth revolves around the sun, that

then that god is a real person, and that place is a real place which must be defended against its use by non-Hindus. It also seeks to encourage a way of thinking that is un-critical and conformist, and that seeks to assert, at all cost, the supremacy of Hinduism. Any historical or contemporary event that glorifies Hinduism, as the Sangh Parivar sees it, and that respects Hindu *sentiments* as the Parivar sees them, is both real and good, and needs to be defended. To the extent that fascistic supporters of the BJP have any critical attitude, it is mainly directed at the critics of their own conservative and un-scientific views about society, economy, and history.

### 3.3    The Fascistic Idea of the Nation

The nation is seen by fascistic forces, ultimately, as the territory of the majority-religion (Hinduism). The aim of these forces is to seek to establish a Hindu *rastra* (state), a state where Hindus will have rights and non-Hindus will have no rights or very limited rights. As Golwalkar, a Hindutva ideologue and a former head of the RSS, expressed it, "in this land, Hindus have been the owners, Parsis and Jews the guests, and Muslims and Christians the dacoits [bandits]". It provocatively asked: "... do all these have the same right over the country?" (cited in Guha, 2006). Non-Hindus can only live in a way that is subservient to Hindus, culturally and politically.[14] It is not anti-national in the eyes of the BJP or of the fascistic movement as a whole, when its government gives away to big business-owners, *nation*'s land, or nation's state-owned companies that have been built on the contributions of the ordinary *working people of the nation*, or indeed money from *nationalized* banks to rich investors who do not return the money, and who indeed flee the country with their un-earned money, while the government is watching. It is also not anti-national in the eyes of the fascistic movement when the government prostrates before the American imperialist military strategy, making Indian soil available for refueling US

---

Madhya Pradesh is to the south of the Himalaya mountains, and that Aryans came from outside of what is currently called India. All this is true even if political control over scholars and over their professional organizations, and violent means may be used to make people believe otherwise. There is a difference between what is true and what people *think* is true, and between what people normally believe to be true and what people are forced to believe as being true. Resorting to unreason and making people accept unreason as reasonable is a hallmark of fascistic tendencies.

14    Following the Godhra riots in which hundreds of Muslims were killed by Hindutva-fascistic mobs, at a meeting in Bangalore in mid-March, 2002, the RSS adopted a controversial resolution titled 'Godhra and After' in which Muslims were cautioned that they would only be safe in India if they won the 'goodwill' of Hindus. By 'Hindus', the resolution, of course, meant the RSS. 'Let Muslims realise that their real safety lies in the goodwill of the majority', the resolution stated (Varadarajan, 2009).

warplanes.[15] This is because all this is done to serve the interests of the nation as the right-wing Hindutva brigade *sees it*.[16]

### 3.4    *Violence/Intimidation and Intolerance towards Dissent*

Slowly creating a consent to the fascistic agenda is not enough. Resorting to intimidation and violence is necessary. RSS cadres are adept at making *ad hominem* and physical attacks on those who challenge them intellectually or politically.[17] Intense (religious) passion and higher decibels of one's speaking, with a touch of masculine aggressiveness, decide the truth status of the words spoken by these people. The idea of Hindutva is used by fascist forces to criticize any person, whether a Hindu or non-Hindu, who does not favor the use of religion for politics and who may be critical of certain ideas and practices sanctioned by Hindu religion. Ominously, violence is often justified on religious grounds: in one case, after killing a Muslim man by accusing him of cow slaughter, the fascistic RSS justified this by saying that: 'Vedas [Hinduism's oldest scriptures] order killing of the sinner who kills a cow. It is a matter of life and death for many of us' (quoted in Bhardwaj, 2015). The fascistic movement makes use of violence to force conformity on people to Hindu morals and practices, the morals and practices of what is defined as the majority group that forms the nation.

In communal violence, organized by the fascistic leaders, various communalist vigilante groups are involved.[18] These foot-soldiers of Sangh Parivar

---

15    'Under Modi, India has emerged as a veritable frontline state in Washington's drive to encircle, strategically isolate, and prepare for war against China. The Modi government has parroted the US line on the South China Sea, where the US has repeatedly conducted provocative "freedom of navigation" exercises, supported Trump's war-mongering against North Korea, and expanded cooperation with the leading US allies in the Asia-Pacific region, Australia and Japan' (Kumara, 2018b). As well: 'India has opened its military ports and airports to US battleships and warplanes, and taken advantage of the Trump administration's support to recklessly escalate tensions with its regional nuclear-armed rival, [Muslim-dominated] Pakistan' (Kumara, 2018b).

16    Fascistic tendencies know only one form of nationalism and bulldoze over all different kinds of nationalism and are deliberately oblivious of the fact that: 'There can be the fascist nationalism of Nazi Germany [which is similar to Indian fascistic nationalism], the imperialist nationalism of the United States, the revolutionary nationalism of communists who led wars of liberation in such diverse countries as Vietnam or Angola; there can be secular Arab nationalism, and there can be clerical nationalism of contemporary Iran'. (Ahmad, 2013: 11).

17    A student activist from JNU said to me: 'RSS people will give us blankets in the night and beat us up in the day', meaning they can be very nice but when you argue with them, they will beat you up. A major human rights activist and former professor in a major Central University said this to me: 'RSS people, when they join a public debate, always make personal attacks on, and shout at, those who challenge them, because that is their overall strategy, but in private they might apologize'.

18    This is, of course, happening in a context where Hindutva has infected everyday life (Berti et al., 2011).

who conduct the lynchings and killings of minorities, communists and people who do not follow their communal ideology or practices, are administratively and politically protected – and are indeed aided by – the BJP-in-power.[19] Once in power, one's words speak the truth: what one says becomes true. One's blatant lies can be words of absolute truth. After ordering the police not to protect the Muslims against a Hindu mob or encouraging a Hindu mob to kill innocent Muslims, one can tell naked lies that one has nothing to do with Muslims being killed. It is not surprising that as fascistic-communal forces are gaining ground, communal incidents – incidents involving conflicts between different religious groups – are on the rise (see Figure 12.4 below). An extreme form of violence that is resorted to is burning people of minorities background alive, as it happened in Gujarat where, for example, a Congress Member of Parliament from the Muslim community was burnt alive.[20] Another is rape, including of children.

Violence is used not only against religious minorities. It is also used against lower castes who are oppressed by, and who therefore resent, Hindu ideas and practices, and against women who may wish to not obey traditional Hindu morals. Despite its rhetoric and active work to woo scheduled castes, tribals and other socially oppressed groups. The BJP is a party, which aims to defend all aspects of the moribund in-egalitarian Hindu society. It is profoundly hostile to the social emancipation of oppressed groups such as women and Dalits, whose oppression has been justified by a set of ideas, if not all ideas, within Hinduism (Karat, 2004: 13). Of course, the BJP seeks to increase its level of acceptance by giving limited concessions to some oppressed groups, including religious minorities. The BJP as a political party *has* had some adherents from religious minorities. This is due to a strategic reason: to broaden its mass base. As long as Hindus' supremacy is recognized, the BJP does not mind granting minor concessions, in part to gain wider consent to its reactionary rule. This strategy includes selective co-optation of leaders of religious minorities and

---

19      '[The] pogroms that engulfed Gujarat in 2002 [included] a spate of "spontaneous" violence that was calculated to generate mass support through communal mobilization'; it was characterized by the complicity of state institutions (Banaji, 2016d: 224). I should say, however, that the idea of complicity of state institutions is becoming hard to justify, given that the boundary between the state and the fascistic Sangh Parivar is being terrifyingly blurred.

20      'Burning people alive has sinister advantages and a macabre logic not available to the usual forms of killing. It can be easily executed by organized groups with tacit support or acquiescence of their community, used to wipe out large numbers indiscriminately, poses no danger to the perpetrators and helps to create an internal climate of terror...' (Ansari, 2011: 135–136).

```
┌─────────────────────────────────────────────┐
│                                             │
│    Engineer attacks on religious minorities  │
│                                             │
└─────────────────────────────────────────────┘
                      ▼
┌─────────────────────────────────────────────┐
│                                             │
│     Polarize votes and get Hindu votes       │
│                                             │
└─────────────────────────────────────────────┘
                      ▼
┌─────────────────────────────────────────────┐
│                                             │
│              Win elections                   │
│                                             │
└─────────────────────────────────────────────┘
                      ▼
┌─────────────────────────────────────────────┐
│   Use state power to lunch further attacks on │
│     religious minorities and to attack        │
│     democrats, securalists and  the Left      │
└─────────────────────────────────────────────┘
```

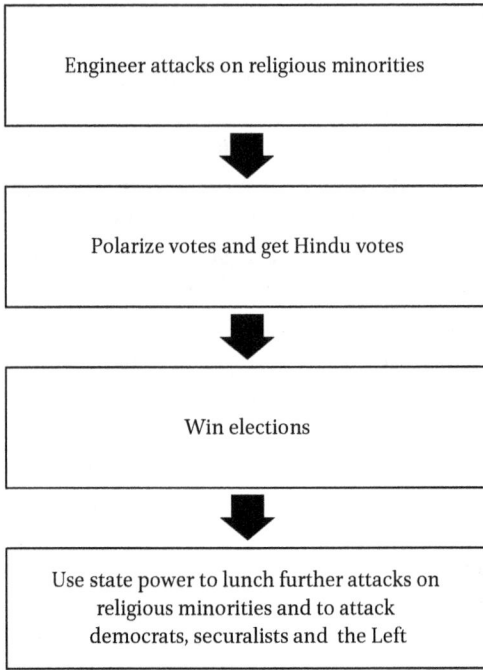

FIGURE 12.4
The fascistic logic of
religious-sectarian riots during
election season
SOURCE: AUTHOR

lower castes.[21] It has included some minority leaders within its umbrella by offering some political and material rewards. And some minority people may have been forced by circumstances (e.g. threat of majority communalism) to accept the BJP.[22]

Resorting to communal violence (including the use of lynching mobs) becomes a means of dividing and intimidating the toiling masses and of diverting attention from the BJP's failure to improve people's economic conditions, a failure that is a given because of its utterly pro-business character.[23] So the

---

21    'The BJP manifesto promises to look after the welfare of the Muslims, their educational and economic status and promote Urdu. All this is possible, if the Muslim minority recognizes that Hindutva is a way of life which they must come to terms with' (Karat, 2004: 6).

22    Karat (2004) writes that a section of the Muslim community 'is now veering around to some sort of accommodation with the BJP. Though a small section, it is a portent of things to come. One motivation is simply the search for the crumbs of office and the opportunist quest for minor concessions which is seen in persons like Arif Mohd. Khan joining the BJP, or, the Delhi Jama Masjid' Imam's new-found softness for the BJP. The other is a resigned acceptance of living under conditions of majority dominance – what the RSS chief Sudarshan graphically described as living on the goodwill of the majority' (p. 6).

23    'The more the regime's failure in the economy and social welfare sector manifests itself, the more it resorts to open communalism, encouraging violence against Muslims and

business class is happy with the BJP, even if its hands are colored red by the murders of minorities, democrats, secularists and communists. Money has no color or religion.

Intolerance towards those who share different views is a hallmark of fascism and of fascistic tendencies. Fascistic forces in India and elsewhere have an antipathy towards intellectuals (of Marxists and other progressive varieties).[24] Within limits, and in certain respects, the fascistic movement shares a space with identity politics, and its attendant idealistic, irrational thinking has taken a religious and nationalist form in India. Fascism also targets many of the promoters of identity-based, social-constructionist academic thinking, who may be somewhat championing the rights of the socially oppressed groups, or at least, of the more privileged layers in these groups.[25] A major object of fascism's ideological hatred is Marxism, however, even if the movement hardly has the intellectual tools with which to critically engage with such a powerful body of thinking as Marxism. Important to note is the fact that India has one of the biggest communist movements in the world (even though it is weak, relative to the task at hand). Marxism – in terms of Marxist theory and Marxist movement – is the most consistent supporter of the democratic and secular discourse, of scientific attitude, and of the objective interests of the toiling masses. Fascism – or fascistic tendency – comes to exist as the most strident and complete opposite of Marxism. When Marxism is fought against and marginalized,[26] then what one gets is its polar opposite (fascism). Marxism is for socialism and against capitalism. It is internationalist, and against parochial inward-looking nationalism, while it celebrates the accomplishments of a nation as a part of the family of nations, and criticizes everything that happens in a nation that is against social and democratic rights of common people of that nation and of

---

Dalits (Arun Jaitley, the finance minister, can in parliament hold beef-eating a worse crime than the lynching and murder of Muslims)' (Habib, 2017).

24    About the fascist movement of his time, Trotsky said: 'The leaders of the movement are liquidating "intellectualism" because they themselves possess second- and third-rate intellects, and above all because their historic role does not permit them to pursue a single thought to its conclusion. The petty bourgeois needs a higher authority, which stands above matter and above history, and which is safeguarded from competition, inflation, crisis, and the auction block. To evolution, materialist thought, and rationalism – of the twentieth, nineteenth, and eighteenth centuries – is counterposed in his mind national idealism as the source of heroic inspiration' (Trotsky, 1933b).

25    This sort of thinking has been promoted by certain academic trends since the 1980s mainly to counter Marxism theory and politics. On the relation between the attack on secularism and certain styles of academic thinking (e.g. post-modernism), see: Baber (2006), and Nanda (2007).

26    Marxism is marginalized in academic circles, media, political movements, and popular (online and offline) conversations. It is fought against by people who give in to idealism and politics of identity.

other nations. And Marxism is for popular democracy, and against authoritarianism. Fascism could not be more different from Marxism in all these respects.[27] It is not surprising that 'Hitler gave himself the ambition to be the 'destroyer of Marxism', and that it was this goal which made him and his movement fascist, even before the party had achieved significant size' (Renton, 2007: 106). It should be stressed that Hitler, the rabid anti-Marxist and anti-communist, continues to inspire the fascist movement in India as elsewhere.

### 3.5    Mobilization of Foot-Soldiers and Supporters

The fascistic movement is not ordinary Bonapartist authoritarianism. It includes violent grassroots organizations of certain class-fractions or class-strata: urban petty bourgeois people; un-employed and semi-employed people; some sections of the working class and of upper-caste landowning class. Their material interests are not met by the capitalist system. Steeped in hyper-nationalistic ideas, they angrily turn themselves against their socially constructed or perceived enemies (minorities; and Marxists and even liberals, who reject their identity politics and who reject their undemocratic intolerance). These forces are engaged in what Gramsci would call a war of attrition (see Roberts, 2011). The fascistic movement is a cadre-based movement from which the BJP benefits electorally.[28]

The task of mobilizing the foot-soldiers gets easier given that for many people (who are of petty bourgeois background and who are un/under-employed), being a part of the fascistic movement is a source of material reward including from criminal activities that we have talked about earlier. For many, being a part of such a movement is also a source of social-psychological satisfaction (emanating from a sense of belongingness to a religious community).[29] Participating

---

27    Perhaps one common ground between Marxism and fascism is that both are rooted in mass movements but with completely opposite purposes.

28    As Vanaik (2018) writes: 'the BJP's biggest asset remains its massive cadre base, which includes foot soldiers willing to wreak violence on command. The rise of the far right is a worldwide phenomenon, but nowhere else is there a force like the Sangh, which has had an unbroken existence of over ninety years and a width and depth of implantation in civil society unmatched in any other country. The BJP and the Sangh, the broader family to which it belongs, represent a far-right force with undeniable neo-fascist characteristics. Apart from the BJP and RSS, the VHP (World Hindu Council) is the other main pan-Indian body. It is the 'overlord' for cultural-religious activities, with mutually beneficial links to the leaders of numerous Hindu sects. VHP muscle and money help these sects to grow, thereby enhancing the aura of their leaders, who duly call on their devotees to support Sangh campaigns, programmes and electoral candidates'.

29    Whether such a belongingness actually exists across a large country such as India, and how strongly it does, is a different question. The fictional character of such community feeling, of such belongingness, should be stressed. Ahmad (2013) brilliantly writes: 'the

in communal riots might give the economically desperate lumpen elements a sense of satisfaction that they are capable of doing something in life. The BJP takes advantage of people's need for religious beliefs in an alienating world and of the fact that for some people their economic insecurity appears to be alleviated by a sense of agency and empowerment. This sense is created when what one does/thinks has some palpable effect: killing fellow-citizens, destroying monuments, aggressively lobbying to change Muslim place names to Hindu names, and so on.[30] Besides, 'Hatred against the Muslim minority has been systematically inculcated in such a manner that violence of barbaric proportions against them is not only widely condoned but also even enjoyed by certain sections of the Hindu communities' (Ansari, 2011: 135–136).

But the foot-soldiers of the fascistic movement fail to understand that they are putting an axe on their own feet, and that are merely pawns in the larger a communal-corporate game that is ultimately against their own economic and democratic interests as citizens. Mistakenly called *fringe* elements, these forces are *central* to the whole communalist-fascist enterprise: they help the BJP garner electoral support by polarizing votes along religious lines. So the BJP government cannot but support them. The BJP forces incite the right-wing mob and then justify the criminal violence committed by describing it as spontaneous reaction to the alleged action of a perceived enemy (e.g. religious minority, or communists or rationalists), a justification that is based in the physicalization of human beings that I have referred to earlier.[31]

---

way we frequently speak of 'Hindu community', 'Muslim community' etc. strikes me as purely fictional; it is very doubtful that Muslims of Kashmir and Muslims of Kerala share very much more than some religious rituals, a handful of founding texts of Islam, and a common fear of Hindu communalism. And, it is equally hard to believe that Christians of Nagaland and of Kerala are all members of a Pan-Indian Christian community. The idea of there being a Hindu 'community' across regions, castes, occupations etc. is ... absurd. ... And yet, in all our discourses of politics and policymaking the existence of such homogeneous, pan-Indian religious communities is simply taken for granted as if this was a self-evident fact. This fictive identity has been superimposed upon real society by self-serving politicians, mullahs and mahants, self-serving and cynical politicians, and the state itself which, like the colonial state, much prefers dealing with 'community representatives' than with class politics' (p. 7).

30    'It is perfectly plausible that a Kar Sevak [an RSS worker], pulled out of the miseries of the lumpenproletariat and brainwashed with glorious ideas of Hindu heroic duty to liberate Lord Ram's Janmbhoomi, may indeed fancy himself a hanuman in the army of Ram as he climbs up to a dome of the babri masjid in order to pull it down. Religion is not responsible but it is not entirely innocent either. The less religion there is in society at large and the more strictly it is separated from all forms of political life, the less violent and persistent communalism would be' (Ahmad, 2013: 7–8).

31    'The reaction of this murderous incident [in which Hindutva forces killed Muslims in a riot in 2002] in Gujarat was natural and spontaneous. The entire Hindu society cutting across all divisions of party, caste and social status reacted....' (quoted in Varadarajan,

Apart from on-the-ground foot-soldiers (e.g. various vigilante groups), the BJP, the political vanguard of the fascistic movement, receives help from a variety of inter-connected sources: the *babas* (spiritual masters) selling/offering tips, based in religious texts, for mental and spiritual peace and sound physique; the so-called intellectuals with dubious academic credentials but with loyalty to the Hindutva-fascistic movement, who have suddenly come out of nowhere, some of whom having been made the managers of educational institutions,[32] and RSS cadres (who are highly disciplined and austere and who truly think what they are doing is in the interest of the nation as they see it). There are also a few party spokes-persons who regularly show up on TV channels, who seem to know everything about everything and who forcefully champion the views of the right-wing forces, trying to make up for their intellectual deficiency by using emotionally charged words about the nation and Hinduism and facts from mythology treated as historical evidence. The BJP uses all these resources, apart from the media and secretive funding from the business class, to shape the manner in which people think about society and history and act in their daily lives. The ideas of the ruling class and of those who manage its affairs politically gradually become ruling ideas.

In appealing to majoritarian-sectarian identity (Hindutva) and in mobilizing its foot-soldiers, the BJP, in pursuit of a reactionary-bourgeois project, has little regard, however, for bourgeois institutions, including institutions of law and order.[33] This is evident from the following words of the then Prime

---

2009). 'The first use of this morally perverse 'Newtonian' logic of action and reaction to justify the killing of Muslims after Godhra was made by Modi in an interview to Zee Television on 1 March, even as the violence was at its peak. And ironically, it wasn't so much a reference to the burning of the Sabarmati Express as to press reports that former Congress MP Ehsan Jafri – who was lynched by a Sangh Parivar-led mob at his residence in Chamanpura, Ahmedabad on 28 February – had fired at the mob in order to try and disperse them. Modi said that Jafri's 'action' of firing had infuriated the mob and that the massacre which followed was a 'reaction'. Since his remark generated a huge controversy and led the Gujarat information department to deny that he had said any such thing, it is worth reproducing his exact quote: 'What is happening is a chain of action and reaction. What I want is that there should be no action and no reaction'. Asked about the violence which erupted throughout Gujarat on the day of the VHP-sponsored bandh, he said: 'It is natural that what happened in Godhra day before yesterday, where forty women and children were burnt alive, has shocked the country and the world. The people in that part of Godhra have had criminal tendencies. Earlier, these people had murdered women teachers. And now they have done this terrible crime for which a reaction is going on' (quoted in Varadarajan, 2009).

32   This is just like the Moghul tax collectors who were made land owners by British colonialists.

33   Jaffrelot (2011) says that in the post-Nehurvian period, the simultaneous and related rise of Hindu nationalism has put the minorities and secularism on the defensive, and in many ways the rule of law is at risk too.

Minister of India, Mr. Narasimha Rao (of the Congress), during the time the fascistic forces demolished a 16th century place of worship for Muslims. Upon hearing the news on 6 December that the mosque has been destroyed by Hindu activists, Mr. Rao expressed himself thus in a speech:[34] 'While this [demolition] was going on, the local authorities and the police appeared to be standing as mute spectators'.[35] Mr. Rao continues:

> This dismal picture of inaction and dereliction of duty was because of orders from the Chief Minister of U.P. [who was of the BJP] not to use force...
> In the context the Supreme Court held that 'the demolition of Babri Masjid in brazen defiance of the order of this Court is indeed a challenge to the majesty of law and the Constitution. ... The Demolition is an unprecedent attack on the secular foundation of democracy, the authority and dignity of this Court. The Court thus stands betrayed as never before'

The kind of foot-soldiers that the fascistic movement mobilizes can be indirectly garnered from Table 12.1 below. It shows partisan response to the demolition of the mosque on December 6, 1992, an event that is definitely a watershed in the history of post-colonial bourgeois India's record on secularism: the table shows that a very high percentage of supporters of BJP and its allied parties thought that the demolition of the mosque was actually justified, relative to supporters of Congress and the Left. While 40.7% of the BJP supporters thought the act was justified, only 22% of all voters thought so (the numbers were much lower at 9.1% for Left supporters and 16.5% for Congress supporters).

It should be said that while Mr. Rao, the then Prime Minister, appears to lament the demolition of the mosque and seems to be helpless, the same Mr. Rao mobilized all the energies of the state to change India's economic regime from dirigisme to de-regulation, against opposition from below. Why was he

---

34　His speech is reproduced in Singer (2012: 173).

35　The direct and indirect effect of the communal mobilization on the security apparatus is clear from the following lines from Vanaik (2018): 'In the late eighties and early nineties, during the 'Rama's Birthplace' campaign – the Ram Janmabhoomi, in which right-wing Hindu groups fought to build a temple on the site of the old Babri Masjid in Ayodhya, Uttar Pradesh, claiming the mosque was located where the god had been born – Indian Army chiefs made clear they would not take responsibility for protecting the mosque because Army *jawans* were overwhelmingly Hindus whose battle cries were invocations of Lord Ram. (The Indian Army exhibited no such qualms when it came to military assaults on the Sikhs' Golden Temple in 1984 or the Muslim shrine of Charar-e-Sharif in Kashmir in 1995.)'.

TABLE 12.1   Partisan response to the demolition of Babri mosque in 1992 (in %)

|  | Congress | BJP+ | Left | Total |
|---|---|---|---|---|
| **Response** | | | | |
| Unjustified | 42.9 | 25.7 | 54.9 | 38.1 |
| Justified | 16.5 | 40.7 | 9.1 | 22.7 |
| Not heard about it | 32.6 | 22.2 | 26.9 | 29 |

SOURCE: NATIONAL ELECTION STUDIES, CSDS, DELHI 1996, QUOTED IN MITRA, 2011: 128

powerless in one instance and powerful in another is a question to ask.[36] Besides, while the fascistic forces disregarded the courts, army, police, etc., the following question should be asked: would the same courts, army and police, etc. allow 'a mob' of workers take over a factory to manage it by themselves in order to meet their daily needs, or a multi-story residence of a member of the super-rich for their own use? The demolition of the mosque and similar other fascistic actions such as lynchings of non-Hindus suggest that it is not just the BJP but the entire bourgeois political system that is thoroughly compromised when it comes to the defense of secularism and democratic rights.

## 3.6   *The Tactical Constructions of the Individual Icons, from the Past and the Present*

From time to time, within the fascistic movement, certain lesser-known individuals are elevated to a status of wider acceptability, and this is done in the same process which deliberately downgrades other individuals. The process involves making some people acceptable who are otherwise not acceptable, and making some people unacceptable who are otherwise acceptable. The fascistic movement has made an ideological use of those who are dead and who might have had nothing (much) to do with communal ideology, as their own. Individuals from Sardar Patel, to Bhagat Singh to Bhimrao Ambedkar and Subhas Bose, all freedom fighters, are shamelessly and hypocritically constructed as the BJP's own. Doing this is necessary in part because the fascistic movement which hardly had a record of fight against the British, has had no

---

36    It is clear that 'Congress Prime Minister Narasimha Rao did nothing to stop the campaign that would defy the Constitution, with impunity, by demolishing the Babri Masjid in Ayodhya in 1992 – demonstrating the de facto sovereignty of the forces of Hindutva in defying the law' and he did this for a simple fact: 'fear of offending "Hindu sentiment"' (Vanaik, 2018).

widely-accepted and legitimate icon from the anti-colonial movement. On the other hand, blatantly communal leaders, whom most Indians cared little about, have been resurrected as leaders of the (Hinduized) nation. To repeat, individuals who have nothing to do with communalism but who are widely respected are made a part of the ideological family of the fascistic project while the deeply communal leaders – both Indians as well as non-Indians such as Hitler – are elevated to a high status in the minds of the people and/or made more acceptable than they normally are. As a part of the same process, certain individuals – from the center and the left – are deliberately denigrated or ignored: Nehru and Gandhi as well as Lenin and Marx (note: Marx and Lenin are bad in part because they are aliens, but Hitler of Germany, who continues to shape the Indian fascistic thinking, is not considered to be an alien).

Then, at one time, Mr. Vajpayee (a BJP leader who became a Prime Minister) was constructed as a moderate face of Hindutva, so he could make appeal to the masses based on his (poetic) charisma. Currently, Mr. Modi has been elevated to the position of the supreme leader. A small-time RSS person a few decades ago, he has been constructed as someone who is a strong leader, with oratory skills and mass appeal. This is an illusion that has also fed into the so-called Modi wave, which is created by the media and disseminated by it among an accepting section of the public.[37] Both Mr. Vajpayee and Mr. Modi are even seen as statesmen, even if, for example, a massive carnage of Muslims occurred under their tenure.

Individual personalities *are* important in any political project. It is very difficult to implement a fascistic movement without individuals with fascistic or deeply authoritarian traits. Modi is effectively the current leader of the fascistic movement. Nandy (2002) says that Modi has a fascistic personality:

> More than a decade ago, when Narendra Modi was a nobody, a small-time RSS *pracharak* trying to make it as a small-time BJP functionary, I had the privilege of interviewing him ...It was a long, rambling interview, but it left me in no doubt that here was a classic, clinical case of a fascist.

---

37    'The announcement of Modi as the leader of the BJP's [2014] election campaign saw a massive and sustained campaign in the corporate media, both television and print, to project Modi on a development and good governance platform. This unprecedented campaign is a result of the total backing of the corporate sector, which owns the bulk of the mass media in the country. At the same time, the corporate media have blacked out the communal aspects of the BJP campaign and the big role the RSS is playing in the campaign. ...This campaign explains the genesis of the "Modi wave", which is then repropagated by the very corporate media that created it. The impact and the appeal that Modi has among educated youth and sections of the middle classes in various parts of the country is a result of this media campaign' (Karat, 2014: 8–9).

I never use the term 'fascist' as a term of abuse; to me it is a diagnostic category comprising not only one's ideological posture but also the personality traits and motivational patterns contextualising the ideology.

Modi, it gives me no pleasure to tell the readers, met virtually all the criteria that psychiatrists, psycho-analysts and psychologists had set up after years of empirical work on the authoritarian personality. He had the same mix of puritanical rigidity, narrowing of emotional life, massive use of the ego defence of projection, denial and fear of his own passions combined with fantasies of violence – all set within the matrix of clear paranoid and obsessive personality traits. I still remember the cool, measured tone in which he elaborated a theory of cosmic conspiracy against India that painted every Muslim as a suspected traitor and a potential terrorist. I came out of the interview shaken [thinking that] ...for the first time, I had met a textbook case of a fascist and a prospective killer, perhaps even a future mass murderer.

While individuals *are* important in any political project, it is important that individuals be seen as always operating within social relations which are manifested through the individuals.

The king is king only because the interests and prejudices of millions of people are refracted through his person... [The] leader is always a relation between people, the individual supply to meet the collective demand...Not every exasperated petty bourgeois could have become Hitler [or Modi], but a particle of Hitler [Modi] is lodged in every exasperated petty bourgeois.
>
> TROTSKY, 1933b; parentheses added

Following Marx, I assume that ultimately, 'individuals ... are the personifications of economic categories, embodiments of particular class-relations and class-interests'. One should not 'make the individual responsible for relations whose creature he socially remains, however much he [or she] may subjectively raise himself above them' (Marx, 1977). There are objective political economic processes and class relations that underlie the fascistic movement, as discussed earlier, within which certain individuals' authoritarian personality plays an important role.

## 3.7 *Normalization of the Fascistic Movement*

Interestingly, it is the ideological success of the RSS–BJP forces that many have forgotten that the Indian state had banned the RSS several times (in 1948, 1975 and 1992). RSS is now taken to be a normal organization, like any other, with which one can have exchanges. Some people might believe that 'I voted for the BJP because the Congress did not do anything'. This statement mistakenly assumes that the BJP, hitched to the fascistic RSS, is a normal party in a democratic set-up, that it can be one of the choices for voters.

In spite of its reactionary traits, the BJP is indeed seen by millions of ordinary citizens (even if still a minority of the country, though a large minority) as well as by sections of the economic-political elite in India (and in imperialist countries), as a political party like any other. This is indicative of the weakness of Left-democratic culture, and of the strength of communal-political thinking of which the fascistic movement is to be credited for. This kind of thinking – that the BJP and RSS are normal organizations in a liberal-democratic system – is actually infecting all-non-Left parties, so much so that they are happy to accept former BJP- and RSS-leaders in their fold.[38] In a sense, non-BJP, bourgeois parties have contributed to the acceptability of the discourse and the political practice that the BJP stands for. Bannerji (2006) says that RSS has made use of media, including transmission of TV serials (e.g. Hindu epics such as Ramayan and Mahabharat) to promote Hindutva. The idea that the BJP is a party like any other is an illusion that has been accepted by many voters. This illusion has been helped by the media, which is, more or less, the propaganda channel of the different fractions of the ruling class, and which is increasingly communalized.[39] The fact that leaders/spokespersons of the BJP, RSS and

---

38   Indeed, many non-BJP parties, including even Congress, welcome 'middle-level leaders and activists of the BJP when they leave their parent party due to some disgruntlement, mainly of not getting tickets, by the Congress and other bourgeois parties' such as the Samajwadi party and the RJD (Karat, 2004: 1). Karat goes on to make this insightful comment: 'This approach indicates a serious misreading of the BJP and the game plan of the RSS. In class terms, the BJP has been the rising force getting increasing support from significant sections of the ruling classes. For such a party which is bent upon legitimizing the Hindutva agenda, it is actually beneficial if there is greater political promiscuity. Politicians from the non-BJP stream joining the BJP gives its respectability and those from the sangh combine joining other parties helps to make its politics less untouchable' (ibid.). Karat continues: 'the spectacle of Kalyan Singh joining hands with Mulayam Singh and then returning to the BJP fold in the space of three years; Laloo Prasad Yadav nominating a known VHP man in Muzafarpur and a Babri Masjid demolitionist in Gaya; or the Congress leadership beaming at the arrival of a defector from the BJP are not symptoms of the weakening of the BJP but the facile acceptance of the BJP as another bourgeois party, though fortunate enough to be in power at the Centre'. What all this shows clearly is that with respect to secularism, the bourgeois-secular parties are only vacillating allies of the Left.

39   One may remind oneself of Bhagat Singh, the non-sectarian freedom fighter, here: 'The real duty of the newspapers is to educate, to cleanse the minds of people, to save them from narrow sectarian divisiveness, and to eradicate communal feelings to promote the idea of common nationalism. Instead, their main objective seems to be spreading ignorance, preaching and propagating sectarianism and chauvinism, communalising people's

other members of the family propagating Hindutva, have gained a place on TV channels and academic platforms (including in Science congresses) demonstrates how normalized the fascistic tendencies have been, especially, in the minds of urban middle 'classy' people and other strata.[40] Such a process of normalization was achieved partly by the BJP hiring a PR firm (Washington-based, APCO) to obliterate the bad things that it does and to hype up its false promises to make them appear more real than they are (Banaji, 2016b: x). The fascistic cause has also obtained support from the diaspora elements who seem to be more 'communal-patriotic' outside of the country than when they were inside. The Hindu-diasporic elements, like the new middle class elements in new sectors such as the IT industry, seek to fill their 'cultural vacuum', their lack of connection to society from which they have come from, by turning to 'godmen' and religious teachers, as Chris Fuller and John Harriss suggest (quoted in Deshmane, 2017), and this has contributed to the BJP's cause.[41]

### 3.8    *Electoral Tactic*

The fascistic movement is not just interested in remaining a movement. It is interested in using elections to capture state power, and use state power to further the fascistic agenda. Now, how does its electoral strategy works?

It has become a common electoral practice to incite the sentiments of the religious minorities and act against their interests, engineer a communal riot (especially where its base is weak or its acceptability is in decline), polarize votes and win elections, so several months prior to a major election, communal riots happen or conditions for these riots are deliberately created by the fascistic elements (see Fig. 12.4).[42] Such a strategy, the aim of which is to garner

---

minds leading to the destruction of our composite culture and shared heritage' (quoted in Habib, 2018).

40    A retired professor of political science once told me that there was a need for leftists to engage with and inform the Right-wing people about the leftist views. Such an approach to fascists is different from the non-platform approach (Renton, 2007): fascistic people who have no respect for democratic values, cannot be allowed a platform for discussion.

41    'Indians settled abroad, clinging to obscurantist versions of their religion in an effort to salvage their identity in an alien context, have thrown their weight – and funds – on the side of reaction in their home country' (S. Gopal quoted in Singh, 2010: 86). Interestingly, many of these people are highly educated Indians living in modern cosmopolitan and multi-cultural and multi-religion cities like Toronto, New York, Dallas, etc.

42    'The Godhra train incident in March 2002 provided Narendra Modi with the perfect opportunity to sponsor massive "retaliation" against Muslims' (Ahmad, 2013: 10), and such a retaliation by galvanizing conservatives Hindus boosted BJP's electoral strength. The latter was used to attack the interests of the ordinary people, whether Hindus or Muslims, through the BJP's 'neoliberal-predatory' capitalist policies originally in Gujarat, and later, at the national level, following the 2014 general election. There is a parallel here with US imperialism: the US used the 9/11 as a pretext, as an opportunity to launch a new round of

Hindu votes, may be combined with some demagogic promise of economic help, which hardly comes.[43]

And when the party comes to power, two things happen. First, RSS and other elements of the Sangh Parivar get support from the BJP being in power, to expand its (i.e. RSS's) tentacles inside the apparatuses of the state, including educational and coercive institutions, which is why any illegal and undemocratic activity by the *Parivar* can go unpunished. Second, violence against the minorities continues as a means of the expansion of the communal-fascistic influence (and in opposition to secular forces including of the Left),[44] and this is possible because the attackers know they will be, more or less, protected by the government (Figure 12.5).

By deploying all these techniques, the fascistic movement led by the BJP has been growing in strength. This has had a palpable material effect of the communal-fascistic-bourgeois movement that is also blatantly anti-communist. This can be seen from the standpoint of the fascistic forces' relation to the business class and to the masses. In India's contemporary conservative climate – which has been in the making since at least the late 1980s and which is characterized by the emergence of the BJP, as a party of the Right (a blatantly pro-business party) – what is good for the business class is seen by this authoritarian party as being good for the nation (all one needs to do is hide the interests of the business class by such talk as 'development'). Indeed, seven things have come together as different elements of the deadly fascistic tendency which have made the BJP such a strong bourgeois party with a communal agenda: *nation*, interests of the *business class*, *development*, *governance*, *Hindu religion*, and an *authoritarian political party*, that is rooted in a *mass movement*. Several conflations exist. The interest of the nation is the interest of the business class. And the territory of Hindu religion is the nation's territory, as Hinduism defines the soul of the nation. This means that: the interests of the *business class* are the interests of the nation, which is defined as the nation of Hindus (all those subordinated to Hindus), and the interests of the Hindu nation are the interests of the business class. Business interests are also hidden behind the screen of *development* and *governance*, both of which the government is apparently pursuing in a manner it sees fit. If one says anything against the government's pro-business policies (or any other policies that adversely impact ordinary people and minorities), or against the undemocratic

---

imperialist-military attack. On the connection between electoral competition and communal riots, see Jairath (2014).

43    The BJP does treat Hindus – and especially those who subscribe to Hindutva – as a vote bank, even if it has criticized Congress for engaging in vote bank politics.

44    Fascistic violence is justified on the basis of hurt sentiments: perceived insults, including to tradition, religion, nation, etc. is used as a pretext for mob violence (Simeon, 2016: 161).

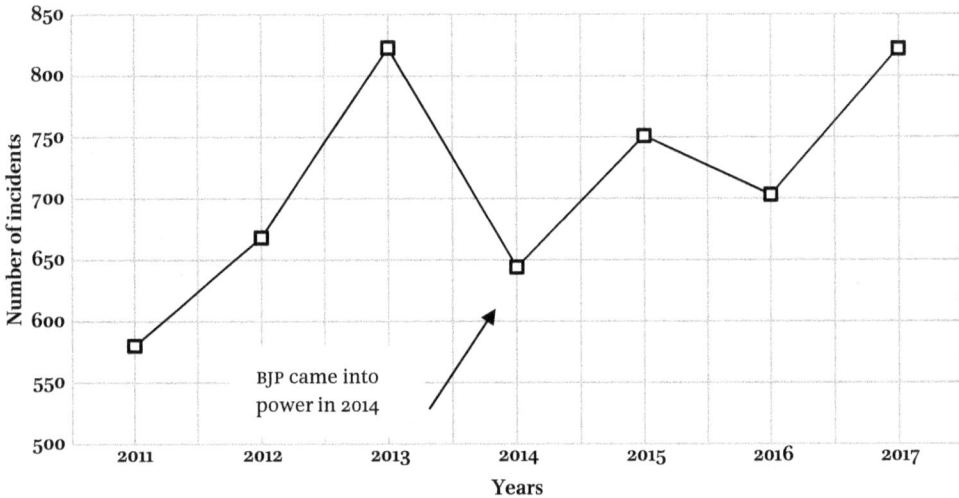

FIGURE 12.5 Incidents involving conflicts between different religious groups in India

aspects of the majority religion or against the empirically false claims of Hindutva ideologues, one is considered anti-national. One has to accept, it seems, that whatever the right-wing authoritarian Hindu-nationalist government does is for the nation.[45]

The *ideology* of the homogenous nation is used to support pro-business policies and thus has a *material* effect: for the ruling class, fascistic tendencies are a blessing (even if not in an entirely unproblematic way). The nationalist ideology has a material consequence for the masses as well, but in a diametrically opposite way. For the masses, it means material sacrifice at the altar of *vikas*. The BJP asks for sacrifices from masses for the nation, which, for it, stands above the masses and their exploiters. In concrete terms, the fascistic notion of the nation means this: 'in the interest of the nation, give your hand and land for industrialists', and 'do not ask for higher wages or better working conditions from your employers'. The notion of nationalism held by the fascistic brigade is a religion-driven mental state (a Hindu nation) rather than one that signifies the nation as the nation of the toilers of different religions, genders, and castes, so the BJP's notion of nationalism is such that it cannot be used as a tool in the fight against the capitalists who exploit the toilers, whether they are Hindus or Muslims or Christians. The BJP's notion of the nation is

---

45    When Arun Jaitley, a prominent leader of the BJP and the current finance minister, says that 'freedom of expression cannot be at the expense of the nation', he is demanding in effect that people should "sacrifice" their freedom of expression, which is their fundamental right, for the sake of this metaphysical concept of a "nation" (Patnaik, 2016: 6).

also not the nation as a people oppressed by imperialism, so such a notion of the nation cannot be mobilized against imperialism either; and yet the Hindu-tva movement hypocritically calls itself nationalist.[46] The fascistic-nationalist movement is not only palpably pro-capitalist but also is it shamelessly subordinating the interests of toiling masses living in India to imperialism.[47] This is the real treachery, and this is the real treason, as far as the toiling tormented majority are concerned.

## 4      The Contradictory Character of the BJP

What one thing, or what one process is, is because of its relations to many other things and processes. The world is the world of internal relations. In dialectics, of all the different types of relations, contradiction is the most important relation (Ollman, 2003). Lenin (1914b) says: 'The splitting of a single whole and the cognition of its contradictory parts... is the *essence*... of dialectics'. And contradiction permeates the body of internal relations. The current situation in India and the world is one of major contradictions.

a.    The contradiction between productive forces and production relations is ultimately behind the economic crisis of capitalism, which is expressed in the fact that the economic growth rate, rise in productivity and the rate of increase in the creation of jobs, etc., all suffer. Productive forces are being fettered by capitalist social relations of competition, profit-making, and exploitation.

---

46    When anti-imperialist nationalism is undermined, this opens an opportunity for communalist-fascistic nationalism: 'In its relations with the global economy', the Indian state 'no longer represents the Indian people and their interests to the world; the principal task that the neoliberal state in India has assigned to itself is that of transmitting the interests and orders of international finance capital to the Indian people. And this is so despite the surviving but utterly hollowed out institutions of representative electoral democracy. In this situation, the state must in practice abandon the kind of secular nationalism that had been the basis of our anti-colonial movements, and a powerful Right-wing gets into high gear to redefine Indian nationalism in religious, obscurantist, High Brahminical terms which offer no resistance to imperialism' (Ahmad, 2013: 21).

47    The Hindutva brigade, actually, had no/little role in the anti-colonial struggle itself that created the nation that we see now; in fact, the fascistic movement offered to cooperate with the colonial powers, treating the Muslims as the real enemy. According to Vanaik (2017), RSS is not fascist because it supported colonial power or did not fight against it. He says: 'That the 'ultra-nationalism' of the RSS and Hindu Mahasabha never led it to participate in the National movement for independence from British colonial rule, or even openly to espouse anti-imperialism, has always been an embarrassment of sorts for those labelling them as fascists' (p. 312).

b.    The economic crisis becomes the social crisis (or social and ecological crisis) in that capitalism simply fails to create enough opportunities to meet the social-ecological needs of the masses (there are hunger and malnutrition and rising inequalities; and there is massive environmental degradation).

c.    In capitalism, there is a contradiction between economic inequality (property owners and property-less) and political equality (all citizens are equal before law).

d.    The latter contradiction now comes to coexist with another contradiction. This is within the sphere of bourgeois politics. When economic and social crisis creates a condition for authoritarianism, the formal political equality – the formally democratic character of relations between the rulers and the ruled – is undermined: some citizens (a religious majority; people with right-wing views) are politically privileged relative to other citizens (religious minorities; people who dissent from the system). The right-wing party makes use of grass-roots right-wing forces to intimidate, repress and divide the masses, and makes use of state's repressive forces (e.g. police; investigative agencies such as Central Bureau of Investigation in India, etc.) against minorities and progressive forces and indeed against even opposition bourgeois parties. This means that there is a contradiction between formal political equality and actual political *inequality*.

e.    Further, when a right-wing party comes to power promising to address people's problems and thus respond to the economic and social crisis of capitalism, but fails to do anything (much), a further political contradiction is created. This is a contradiction between policy-promise and policy-outcome, and thus between words and reality, which will potentially fuel the resentment of the toiling masses. Resolving this *political* contradiction further reinforces the tendency towards the use of authoritarian methods, in the absence of a sufficiently strong Left movement, an absence that reflects a contradiction of its own (contradiction between the severity of economic-political problems of the masses and the weakness of the Left movement relative to the task at hand).

The rise of the BJP represents the crisis not only of bourgeois economics but also of bourgeois politics: the bourgeois system, and therefore, the bourgeois ruling class, has, simply, failed to secure not only social rights but also democratic rights, including rights of religious minorities. So the blame for the current situation – attack on democratic rights and the growing strength of fascistic forces – must be at the door not only of the BJP and its supporting forces, but also the bourgeois class itself. That is why the fascistic threat is a class project, and not merely a political-cultural project. The contradictory aspect of that class project is this: while the ruling class is increasingly losing its right to be the ruling class, the masses are not yet ready to say 'we cannot take it anymore'.

In other words, what all this signifies, and points to, is a strong tendency towards the breakdown of the liberal-democratic shell of India's (peripheral) capitalism. The current situation is one of a series of contradictions in the economic, social, and political spheres. And because the contradictions are those that are of the bourgeois system as a whole, they cannot be resolved by capitalism and its political system, even if it is managed by a party such as India's BJP, which is seen as, and which claims to be, a strong party, led by a strong leader.

## 5    Conclusion

The increasing strength of right-wing forces, including the rise of the BJP as the political head of these forces in India, has been engendered by four mechanisms. Three of these mechanisms are discussed in the previous chapter. These are mainly political-economic mechanisms.

The first is the crisis of global capitalism, the crisis that is manifested in India. The second is the combination of exploitation, dispossession, and immiserization requires legitimization/justification in the minds of the masses as well as an authoritarian response. And then there is the fact that capitalism produces a vast reserve army of labor and pauperized small-scale producers, the elements of which, in a poor economy without social benefits (or with very limited benefits) from the government, are vulnerable to lumpenization and criminality.

However, just because capitalism creates a need for fascistic forces and just because capitalism creates lumpen elements that can be used by the fascistic project, that does not necessarily mean there will be fascistic forces in *active operation*. The political has a relative autonomy. The bourgeois-political dynamics of the rise of fascistic tendencies are discussed in this chapter.

The failure of bourgeois politics as well as Left politics – indeed, the failure of the entire bourgeois political system – to defend democracy and secularism is a crucial process contributing to the rise of the BJP. The whole determines the parts and the parts influence the whole. The Congress and the BJP are two faces of Indian bourgeois politics, both promoting neoliberal capitalism, and the BJP using the religious divide to distinguish itself in the election market. There has indeed been the decline of the relatively secular bourgeois national party (the Congress) and attendant 'capital flight' from the Congress to the BJP. It is as if the following has happened: as Nehruvianism (semi-statist developmental model with very muted elements of social democracy), in part influenced by the Bombay plan, saved the Indian bourgeoisie from the any threat of struggle from below (any communist threat, potential and actual) in the post-1917 period, the fascistic threat came in its turn to liberate the bourgeoisie from Nehruvianism, in a condition where a strong Left movement is absent.

Much of what we see in India and elsewhere in terms of fascistic tendencies can be captured by these lines except that we are not talking about fascism but fascistic tendencies: 'Fascism is a product of two conditions: a sharp social crisis on the one hand; the revolutionary weakness of the ... proletariat on the other' (Trotsky, 1931a).[48] The proletarian has been kept weak due to bourgeois-reformist organizations of every type and by the communist parties which have failed 'to unite the workers under the banner of the revolution' as well as by the far left tendencies to do much to organize the workers (Trotsky, 1931a).

The 'turn of the fascist regime arrives' when 'the "normal" police and military resources of the bourgeois dictatorship, together with their parliamentary screens, no longer suffice to hold society in a state of equilibrium' (Trotsky, 1944). Then 'Through the fascist agency, capitalism sets in motion the masses of the crazed petty bourgeoisie, and bands of the declassed and demoralized lumpenproletariat – all the countless human beings whom finance capital itself has brought to desperation and frenzy' (Trotsky, 1944). But during a transitional stage, such extreme measures are not yet necessary. Normal resources play the dominant role, supplemented by fascistic forces. But the latter forces play a consent-generating role: deploying lies and brainwashing about what a nation means, about the Hindutva, etc., to make people believe in the fascistic vision. The petty bourgeois fascist forces also seek to undermine ideas about labor and proletarian movement.[49] The proportion of assistance that capital mobilizes from the normal resources (e.g. state's police forces) as opposed to fascist sources can also change depending on the severity of crisis and strength of the anti-capitalist forces. But (already) the division between the normal forces and the fascistic forces is getting blurred because of the increasing penetration of fascistic ideas and practices inside the state. This means that

---

48    'Fascism is ... the final link of a specific political cycle composed of the following: the gravest crisis of capitalist society; the growth of the radicalization of the working class; the growth of sympathy toward the working class and a yearning for change on the part of the rural and urban petty bourgeoisie; the extreme confusion of the big bourgeoisie; its cowardly and treacherous maneuvers aimed at avoiding the revolutionary climax; the exhaustion of the proletariat, growing confusion and indifference; the aggravation of the social crisis; the despair of the petty bourgeoisie, its yearning for change, the collective neurosis of the petty bourgeoisie, its readiness to believe in miracles; its readiness for violent measures; the growth of hostility towards the proletariat which has deceived its expectations. These are the premises for a swift formation of a fascist party and its victory' (Trotsky, 1944).

49    'The passage to fascism, on the contrary, is inconceivable without the preceding permeation of the petty bourgeoisie with hatred of the proletariat' (Trotsky, 1934a).

elements inside the state' normal coercive forces are sympathizing with, and even supporting, the fascistic forces, who, in turn, protect these elements from any potential threat of punitive action from what is left of bourgeois democracy and its constitutional rules.

The increasing strength of right-wing forces represents a most extreme form of the latent tendency towards an attack on democracy, the tendency that exists in capitalist societies when there is massive inequality and where the most basic needs of the masses remain unmet while a tiny class basks in obscene amount of wealth and income, under conditions of capitalist economic crisis. The tendency is expressed when capitalism is no longer a progressive force, when it is constantly in crisis, when the working class poses a threat to its class rule, while it fails to transcend the capitalist class relation.[50]

The ruling class comes up with a solution to its crisis-ridden life by resorting to fascism or fascistic tendencies. Fundamental to the worldview of the forces playing the politics of hatred against religious and other types of minorities, is the idolization of *free market economics* in the interest of the business class, and of *authoritarian politics*. Authoritarian politics is necessary to implement free market economics in the interest of property-owning classes. This is especially so in an unequal, poverty-stricken, relatively backward society like India where millions of people are not only subjected to economic miseries caused

---

50   What this means is that when capitalism is due for overthrow but is not overthrown morbid symptoms appear. In his last article, Trotsky said this in response to those who say that 'contrary to Marx's prognosis fascism came instead of socialism'. 'Nothing is more stupid and vulgar than this criticism. Marx demonstrated and proved that when capitalism reaches a certain level the only way out for society lies in the socialization of the means of production, i.e., socialism. He also demonstrated that in view of the class structure of society the proletariat alone is capable of solving this task in an irreconcilable revolutionary struggle against the bourgeoisie. He further demonstrated that for the fulfillment of this task the proletariat needs a revolutionary party. ... [The] opportunism of the summits of the working class, subject to the bourgeoisie's influence, could obstruct, slow down, make more difficult, postpone the fulfillment of the revolutionary task of the proletariat. It is precisely this condition of society that we are now observing. Fascism did not at all come "instead" of socialism. Fascism is the continuation of capitalism, an attempt to perpetuate its existence by means of the most bestial and monstrous measures. Capitalism obtained an opportunity to resort to fascism only because the proletariat did not accomplish the socialist revolution in time. The proletariat was paralyzed in the fulfillment of its task by the opportunist parties. '[There] turned out to be more obstacles, more difficulties, more stages on the road of the revolutionary development of the proletariat than was foreseen by the founders of scientific socialism. Fascism and the series of imperialist wars constitute the terrible school in which the proletariat has to free itself of petty bourgeois traditions and superstitions, has to rid itself of opportunist, democratic and adventurist parties, has to hammer out and train the revolutionary vanguard and in this way prepare for the solving of the task apart from which there is not, and cannot be, any salvation for the development of mankind' (Trotsky, 1940).

by capitalism but are also fighting against their miseries, and who therefore have to be suppressed/managed through authoritarian means, if the business class has to be kept happy. The ideology and practices of free market economics and authoritarian politics are dressed up by right-wing demagogic leaders, as, for example, development and good governance, respectively, and sold to voters in the election market. These two catchwords – development and good governance (or similar terms) – resonate with common people who are economically poor and who are also subjected to bureaucratic apathy. These terms are used, along with hyper-nationalism based in the idea of the supremacy of an ethnic group or a religion (e.g. Hinduism), to help produce/spark a *mass movement*. In short: blatant free market economic ideas and policies,[51] rabid religious nationalism, and authoritarian intolerance towards rational dissent: all these come together, support each other, and produce a grassroots movement. This is the best way to describe it all: fascist/fascistic tendency (see Figure 12.6). I describe the Indian situation as one which has fascistic tendencies but which is not yet fascist.[52]

Make no mistake: the BJP is not an ordinary political party. Yet, the fact that it is an ordinary party is the perception among wide layers of the population. This is a perception that has been slowly produced, over decades, by the corporate media, sections of the middle class and of the business world, so much so that the views of this party and its fascistic supporters including RSS ideologues on a given topic have become a part of polite, civilized and public discussions on television channels, in classrooms, conferences, and elsewhere. This shows how far to the right public life has moved in India.

The BJP's goal is to see an India that is not only 'Congress-free' ('Congress-mukt') (because the Congress has generally tried to 'defend' secular values) but also 'Left-free' ('Left-mukt') or indeed 'communist-mukt'.[53] This shows that the right-wing forces are much more than mere Hindutva-nationalist forces. Their threat is much more than the threat to secularism and bourgeois democracy. They are fundamentally capitalist, anti-proletarian, anti-communist forces whose fascistic aim is to destroy not only the democratic-secular ethos of the nation but also those militant organizations of the class-conscious masses, of

---

51  In the advanced country, free market economics inside a country can co-exist with protectionism; in poorer economies, free market economics is appealed to both inside a country and globally (liberalization of import and export, for example).

52  Fascistic tendencies in terms of mechanisms that *can* produce a fascist or a fascist type state, and in terms of fascistic organizations.

53  'In their victory speeches made at the BJP headquarters in New Delhi after the results of the Tripura elections were announced, Prime Minister Modi and the President of the ruling party promised to free India of communists...a "Communist-*mukt Bharat*". Modi declared that it was an "ideological victory" over the communists'.

workers and peasants of India that do not preach class unity between the exploiter and the exploited (to the extent that the fascistic movement wants).

The BJP makes use of whatever elements of the democratic system it can use to subvert the values of the democratic system itself in the service of a communal-bourgeois agenda and to establish a system where political power is always in the hands of the majority-religion. It acknowledges the existence of minority religions as long as the latter lie low and do not assert their rights or challenge members of the majority religion.[54] It is worth repeating that the BJP is at the center of, and political head of, an ideologically-driven mass movement that is rooted in small-scale producers and un- and under-employed people and politically backward elements in the working class, a movement that attacks democratic and social rights of workers and peasants. This fascistic movement is like an auto-immune disease in which the body's own immune system kills the cells of the body by mistakenly treating them as foreign and harmful. It is a movement *by* common people *against* common people.[55] While the working class is the strongest defenders of the democratic rights (in part because it needs these rights to mobilize itself), some elements of this class turn themselves against other elements, mistakenly treating the latter as anti-national and harmful. And such divisions within the working class and indeed among the small-scale producers, benefit the bourgeoisie and the parties representing its interests. True to its right-wing nature, the BJP pursues neoliberal policies to create opportunities for national and imperialist capital. It subordinates India to US or any other form of imperialism, in spite of its demagogic, hypocritical discourse about nationalism; it would indeed justify such subordination to imperialism on the ground that that makes the nation stronger militarily. The BJP along with the fascistic movement is a threat to everyone who is committed to the culture of decency and civility in public discourse, to democracy, secularism and to the principle of rational dissent.[56] It is against the basic class interests of the majority of the population.[57] There

---

54    It is true that the 'majority of Muslims have punctually sought a secular electoral alternative' but then this fact is 'not because they are particularly secular in their own outlook', but 'because they expect greater security for themselves in a secular dispensation.'; indeed, Muslims can be as communal as Hindus (Ahmad, 2013: 16).

55    The foot-soldiers of the fascistic movement as a mass movement are ordinary people and that movement by supporting capitalism works against the ordinary people.

56    In fact, in a typical fascistic style, prominent members of the Sangh Parivar, including the BJP, represent any criticism of their statements and practices as illiberal and as intolerant; they paint themselves as victims.

57    Interestingly, when the Shiv Sena, the Right-wing organization as a part of the communalist-fascist family, campaigns against Biharis coming into Maharastra for wage-work, it does not distinguish between Hindu Biharis and non-Hindu Biharis (Ahmad, 2013: 18).

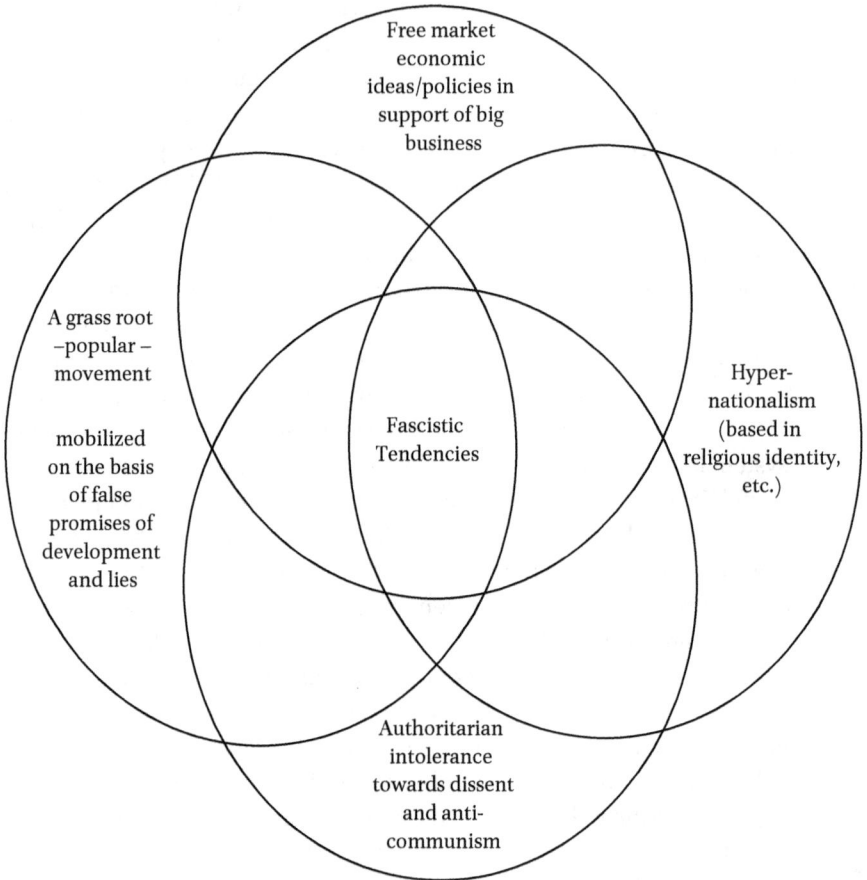

FIGURE 12.6 Anatomy of the fascistic movement
SOURCE: AUTHOR

is no doubt that the bourgeois political rule in India – as in many other countries of the world – is taking an increasingly fascistic form, even if India does
not as yet have a fascist state, the 'finished product' that has finished elements
of democracy. When a robber with a weapon is running towards us from a distance, we may not see him fully and we may see his silhouette only, but that

And this 'illustrates how easily a communalism can move back and forth between the
religio-fascist form of Hindutva and the sub-national, ethno-regional posture of Marathi
exclusivity' (pp. 18–19). So, the problems of Maharashtra are seen as being caused by migrants and not because of capitalism and the uneven development it produces.

does not mean that he is not running towards us and that we are not in imminent danger.

It is less true to say that the BJP is a communal party that just happens to support the business class. It is truer to say that the BJP is fundamentally a bourgeois party that makes use of communal hatred to attain political influence and in the process serves bourgeois interests (as well as some reactionary interests of a bigoted section of the citizenry). Communalism (religious-sectarian hatred), or antagonism based in religious difference, may have a degree of autonomy with respect to capitalism or with respect to capitalism as it exists at a given point in time. But once it exists, capitalism makes full use of it and feeds into it.

The BJP, like similar parties elsewhere, is a party with a mission: to destroy the deeply-cherished values of a civilized society. When all parties more or less aspire to satisfy the demands of the business class, then in the competitive market for votes, it helps if a party can make use of dangerous gimmicks such as religious pride and hyper-nationalism to package itself as a unique commodity in the electoral market. The BJP is a national party that is not only pro-business but also communally divisive, a party that crushes not only economic rights but also democratic rights of toiling masses. While the BJP government defends the interests of the top 1–10% by not restricting the greedy pursuit of profit, it hurts the economic interests of the masses *and* undermines their power to fight back. While all recent governments have, more or less, done the same, the BJP's method is much more dangerous: it makes use of religion, hyper-nationalism and historical distortions in order to divide the masses. It resorts to authoritarianism to weaken those who oppose it and its policies, bypassing parliament and harassing critics. It now seems a common BJP strategy to engineer a communal riot, polarize voters and win elections based on hatred and fear.[58] And once this communal party is in power, there are further communal attacks as the perpetrators know that they will be directly or indirectly protected by the BJP. Communal riots often give a sense of satisfaction to the economically desperate lumpen elements created by capitalism, making

---

58    In fact, it is widely known that the BJP came to prominence from obscurity on the basis of
      demolishing a centuries-old mosque in Uttar Pradesh by mobilizing its right-wing Hindu-
      fundamentalist forces in mid-1990s. In more recent times, in the recently concluded
      Karnataka elections in May 2018, a major reason it garnered votes was that it created
      Hindu-Muslim tensions and communal violence, in coastal Karnataka. It is also mobiliz-
      ing its forces to build a temple for Lord Ram in the place (where there was a mosque
      which the communal right-wing forces demolished in 1992) in order to stoke communal
      tension in the run-up to the 2019 federal election.

them believe that they can do something in life. But many of them are, more or less, unaware pawns in the larger communal-corporate 'game'.

A part of the blame for this tragic situation must be on the Left itself. The Left defines the current stage of Indian revolution as a democratic revolution, a stage at which an important task of the Left is to protect the democratic rights of minorities. Yet, what we see is the fiercest attack on democratic rights from communal-fascistic forces. At the same time, it is also the case that the fascistic forces have come to constitute a very powerful obstacle to the Left movement, including in the bastions of Left influence.[59] And, the relative weakness of the Left is partly responsible for the increasing strength of the fascistic forces. These forces are a clear threat to the communist movement on the ground, as we have been seeing in Tripura and Kerala (and also in West Bengal), where communists and their offices are being physically attacked. So, the fascistic forces will have to be stopped, and stopped right now. The question is how?

---

59   Note that the appearance of communal politics has split Left's political energy between the fight against neoliberal policies and the fight against communalism.

# Forward March of the Right and the Relative Weakness of the Left: What Is to Be Done?

The bourgeois political rule in India – as in many other countries – is taking an increasingly fascistic form, even if India does *not* have a full-fledged fascist state. The rise of the BJP, the political 'head' of the fascistic movement in India, has been engendered by a multiplicity of mechanisms, which are, more or less, rooted in bourgeois economy and bourgeois politics. The fascistic forces constitute a very powerful obstacle to, and reflects relative weakness of, the progressive and the Left movement. In several parts of India, communists and their offices are being physically attacked, and communists are being killed or harmed by the fascistic forces. So, the fascistic forces will have to be stopped immediately. These forces must be the target of an all-out fight, a fight on economic, political and ideological fronts.[1] The question is how, and what role the Marxist Left has in this?

This penultimate chapter begins with the Marxist theory of Left politics (Section 1). It argues that the Marxist Left must mobilize its *basic classes* (skilled and unskilled workers, self-employed small-scale producers, and unemployed people) with help from politically progressive ('de-classed') intellectuals, against the fascistic brigade, in the *extra-electoral* sphere, as a part of the struggle to transcend the capitalist class relations that are at the origin of the fascistic tendencies. This should be *the dominant approach* to fighting the fascistic movement. On the basis of their large numbers as well as rallies and general strikes, and local-level people's committees, Marxist forces must take the lead, where possible, in countering the fascistic movement and stop it from physically intimidating people.[2] It must be stressed that the Marxist movement is the most principled opponent of fascism. This was understood by Hitler.[3]

---

1  In some ways, the BJP is to the Indian communist movement what the Tsar rule was to the Russian communist movement, and must be treated accordingly.

2  Actually, the BJP has done one good thing: by putting the Left in the same category as Muslims and Christians, as the threat to the nation, it has treated the Left as a friend of minorities. That strategy is  potentially making the fight against fascistic tendency a part of the fight against capitalism.

3  Hitler said: 'Only one thing could have stopped our movement – if our adversaries had understood its principle and, from the first day, had smashed with the utmost brutality the nucleus of our new movement' (quoted in Renton, 2007: 113).

In the light of the basic Marxist principles, the relative strength and weakness of *actually-existing* Left politics in India are discussed in Section 2. It deals with the question of what is to be done *now* to undermine the fascistic threat? If the fascistic forces return to power in 2019, a huge amount of irreparable damage will be done both to the democratic movement and to the communist movement. The Indian Left – all the Left parties from the right to the left – must mobilize its forces extra-electorally against the fascistic movement at local, regional and national scales. But to the extent that the electoral arena is also an important area of struggle in a liberal democracy, some might argue that the Left, given its relative electoral weakness, will have to have some temporary 'understanding' with 'reasonably secular' non-left political parties (*without* being a part of any governmental front and with its full organizational autonomy). Such a proposal potentially contradicts the principle that the Left politics must be independent of bourgeois forces. Section 3 then turns to what I will call *Lenin's theory of temporary revolutionary compromise,* hoping that this will help us critically assess the possibility of, and necessity for, a temporary compromise between Left forces and secular non-Left forces, in order to thwart fascistic tendencies *now* and thus *advance* class struggle. The last section concludes the chapter. It returns to Marx to remind the Left that the fight for democracy (including the fight for the rights of religious and other minorities) is only a beginning on a long march towards a socialist society, one that is democratic in the political sphere as well as the economic sphere. Whether the Indian Left's theory and practice are in line with Marx's principles is a different matter.

## 1      A General Theory of Left Politics in an Age of Fascistic Threats/Tendencies[4]

Capitalism is the root cause of the attack on democracy and on the living standards of the masses. Capitalism does not grant democratic rights and economic concessions without a fight for these by the masses, and no matter how contradiction-ridden capitalism is, it will not fall without class struggle. Whether it is state-directed capitalism or neoliberal capitalism, workers and small-scale producers will have to engage in a united battle to defend and deepen democratic rights, including the rights of religious minorities, and to get some concessions for an improvement in their living conditions, as a part

---

4   This section is informed by Das (2017: Chapters 11–12), and Das (2019).

of the fight for a new society beyond capitalism. There is no other way out of
their problems:

> The revolutionary dialectic has long since pointed the way out and has
> demonstrated it by countless examples in the most diverse spheres: by
> correlating the struggle for power with the struggle for reforms; by main-
> taining complete independence of the party while preserving the unity of
> the trade unions; by fighting against the bourgeois regime and at the same
> time utilizing its institutions; by relentlessly criticizing parliamentarism –
> from the parliamentary tribunal; by waging war mercilessly against
> reformism, and at the same time making practical agreements with
> the reformists in partial struggles.
>
> TROTSKY, 1932b

One might even entertain the possibility of entering into a compromise with
the hangman. Not always, but under certain conditions:

> To support the hangman in every action directed against the workers is a
> crime, if not treachery: that is just what the alliance of Stalin with Chiang
> Kai-shek consisted of. But if this same Chinese hangman were to find
> himself engaged tomorrow in a war with the Japanese imperialists, then
> practical fighting agreements of the Chinese workers with the hangman
> Chiang Kai-shek would be quite permissible and even – a duty.
>
> TROTSKY, 1932l

Of course:

> The possibility of betrayal is always contained in reformism. But this does
> not mean to say that reformism and betrayal are one and the same thing
> at every moment. Not quite. Temporary agreements may be made with
> the reformists whenever they take a step forward.
>
> TROTSKY, 1929

Workers should fight for concessions to improve their conditions within capitalism. The struggle for reforms can – and must – include the struggle for the
conditions of struggle, i.e. the 'political freedoms, the right of assembly and
association, and the freedom of the press', etc. (Marx, 1871a). The fight against
capitalism does require a fight for the conditions for that fight. And in our
times, the Right-wing, fascistic, hyper-nationalist forces are the most potent
conjunctural obstacle right now to the fight against capitalism.

The struggle for reforms is necessary because without this struggle, workers' conditions will be worse: 'capital, if not checked, will recklessly and ruthlessly work to cast down the whole working class to ... the utmost state of degradation ...' (Marx, 1976: 54). The struggle for economic and political reforms can create: 'elbow-room for development and movement' (Marx's letter to Kugelmann in Marx, 1868a). It is problematic to say that one should not struggle for a rise in wages on the ground that 'to struggle to increase one's wages or to prevent their decrease is like recognizing *wages*' (Marx, 2010: 327; italics in original).

The struggle for reforms, in economic and political spheres, can not only cause some improvement of people's conditions. This can also contribute to the development of their consciousness, as they learn about economy and polity on the basis of their agitational experience.[5] As '*the tribune of the people*', a Marxist party/movement must: 'react to every manifestation of tyranny and oppression, no matter where it appears, no matter what stratum or class of the people it affects; who is able to generalise all these manifestations and produce a single picture of police violence and capitalist exploitation' (Lenin, 1901). Lenin elaborates the idea of the tribune of the people thus: '*Any and every* manifestation of police tyranny and autocratic outrage' [is] a means of "drawing in" the masses' into political struggle' (ibid.). The cases of tyranny and oppression include:

> *the flogging of peasants, the corruption of the officials* and *the police treatment of the "common people"* in the cities, the fight against the famine-stricken and the suppression of the popular striving towards enlightenment and knowledge, the extortion of taxes and *the persecution of the religious sects*, the humiliating treatment of soldiers and *the barrack methods in the treatment of the students and liberal intellectuals*.
>     Ibid.; italics added

In the Marxist theoretical perspective pursued here, Marxist parties, retaining their organizational independence vis-à-vis bourgeois forces, must mobilize workers and small-scale producers (e.g. poor peasants) for a multi-pronged struggle. Firstly, it is a struggle against the curtailment of democratic rights. These rights include: the right to free speech (online and offline) and public assembly and to form a trade union and to engage in political resistance,

---

5   Marx at times appeared to be more sanguine than necessary about his view of the role of the struggle for reforms in generating anti-capitalist political consciousness.

without intimidation from the state or private forces.[6] The democratic rights also include the rights to: practice any religion one wishes; eat whatever food one chooses (beef or not); love and marry whoever one wants to; and be free from caste, gender, linguistic, ethnic, and geographical discrimination, and from remnants of feudal oppression. An important democratic right to struggle for is the right to receive an education that not only respects scientific temper, secularism,[7] and international solidarity with peoples of other nations and respect for their culture, but also encourages students and the wider citizenry to (a) celebrate the scientific successes of a nation, including those that might be recorded in its ancient and modern non-fiction and literary texts, as well as its literary and mythological accomplishments,[8] and (b) to develop an evidence-based, critical attitude towards one's history, culture, and the political-economic system.[9] Democratic rights cannot be respected where certain groups defined on the basis of religion or caste or race or gender, have inferior rights than other such groups.[10] The fascistic forces are crushing or curtailing all these democratic rights, so a lower-class mobilization is necessary against such curtailment, on the basis of the strength of communist workers.[11]

---

6    These include: moral police of the Right; private armies or goons of landlords/capitalists and politicians; and Hindutva vigilante groups.

7    The Left's demand must be: no one – no religious leader – should be allowed to use religion and religious places for political activity.

8    All social groups, including indigenous communities, who happen to practice different religions, have made contributions to society. These contributions are recorded in their religious and secular texts and which exist in their oral traditions. In earlier times, when society had a rather limited amount of control over natural forces, religious ideas (including deification of nature) had a special significance which is why some secular ideas about society, nature and the mind were embedded in what are dominantly religious (and mythological) texts. One can always examine these ideas, based on modern science and modern theory of society, to look for scientific and proto-scientific insights in those ancient texts, distinguish them from mythological and purely religious ideas, and where possible further develop them, and reject the unscientific ideas that exist.

9    It is interesting to note that Buddhist ideas about meditation, embedded in what are religious texts, have now been, more or less, corroborated by neuro-scientific investigation (Davidson, 2012). It is also important that a text which is mythological (in which it might be written that god x and goddess y were born in place $p_1$ or place $p_2$) should not be treated as one that is historical.

10   One's own religious preference must be, more or less, a private affair, and the state must not show any preference, or loyalty, for any specific religious group. The state must ensure that minority religions are protected against discrimination from the majority religion. The state must not also tolerate violent attack on majority religious groups from minority religious group.

11   One can say that the number of people supporting fascism or fascistic groups electorally (and otherwise) is increasing or large, relative of those who support communists. But this is a mistaken comparison. 'Yes, they have received many votes. But in the social struggle, votes are not decisive. On the scales of election statistics, a thousand fascist votes weigh

Secondly, workers and small-scale independent producers led by the Left must fight against the attack on their living standards, expressed in the form of government austerity, deplorable working conditions, repression of wages, and growing economic inequalities. The masses must make not only immediate demands but also transitional demands.[12] And the concept of the transitional demands must be suitably expanded to include both economic (and political) concessions and ecological sustainability.[13] In the process of organizing such struggles over democracy – these include struggles against fascistic threat to democracy – and over economy, and through imparting ideological education and mobilizing people on the basis of immediate and transitional demands, the Marxist parties must, gradually, help the basic classes transform the reformist (trade unionist) consciousness into class consciousness proper, which means this: given that wealth and income (profit, rent and interest) come, ultimately, from the fruits of labor of workers (and from dispossession of petty-producers), the fundamental interests of these classes and those of the ruling class cannot be reconciled, and therefore capitalism has to go; it also has to go because capitalism is incompatible with long-term ecological sustainability.

This process of development of consciousness will prepare the basic classes to fight for a state, controlled by proletarians/semi-proletariat, in an alliance with small-scale independent producers, for new society. This is a society: where all remnants of feudal/'semi-feudal' relations are destroyed and bonded labor relations completely annihilated, and land[14] is equitably distributed

---

as much as a thousand Communist votes. But on the scales of the revolutionary struggle, a thousand workers in one big factory represent a force a hundred times greater than a thousand petty officials, clerks, their wives, and their mothers-in-law. The great bulk of the fascists consists of human dust' (Trotsky, 1931a).

12  *Transitional demands* stem 'from today's conditions and from today's consciousness of wide layers of the working class and unalterably leading to one final conclusion: the conquest of power by the proletariat' (Trotsky, 1938). These are the demands that are much more radical and progressive than immediate and partial demands (e.g. a little rise in wages; demand for democratic rights) reflect masses' needs (e.g. employment and decent living conditions for all; workers' control over businesses) which, if met, will undermine capitalism. The transitional demands aim to raise the level of class consciousness to revolutionary consciousness.

13  In fact, the fight for ecological sustainability can be seen as a fight for a form of social wage, an ecological social wage (Das, 2018b).

14  This includes land held by non-toiling large-scale landowners. This also includes land and other natural resources (water bodies; forests) that are now held by industrialists in excess of their need and which were taken away from peasants or from control of the state or the village community, with inadequate compensation and with the help of force and/ or cronyism.

among actual toilers who are also provided financial help from the state and many of whom may be organized into cooperatives voluntarily. As well, this is a society which is democratic in economic, political and cultural spheres, one where, among other things:

a)   the process of democratic change, under the proletarian leadership, is uninterruptedly[15] extended to gradually socialize (democratize the control over) major means of production and private finance and means of transportation and communication that are owned by domestic and imperialist capital;

b)   markets that may exist in certain limited spheres initially are state-controlled, and ecologically sustainability is promoted;

c)   exploitation of wage-labor and forcible dispossession of small-scale producers are dis-allowed, with the latter receiving assistance from the state;

d)   all able-bodied people engage in productive work with a decent wage and job security for all irrespective of gender, racial, religious, etc. backgrounds;

e)   surplus labor that is performed by toilers, and land and other natural resources, does not exist in their capitalist form; and

f)   the development process focuses on the satisfaction of material and cultural *needs* of men, women and children, rather than on the pursuit of *profit* for a few (top 1% or so).[16]

---

15   'Uninterruptedly' does not necessarily mean 'all at once' or 'suddenly'. It means minimization of the period during which a proletarian state has to supervise a society dominated by capitalist class relations, because such a state of affairs would signify the contradiction between political power of proletarians over the state on the one hand and economic power of capitalist over means of production on the other. 'Uninterruptedly' and 'gradualism' are not necessarily mutually contradictory. 'Non-gradualism' does not mean 'more revolutionary'. Here are some relevant lines from Engels's (1848) 'Principles of communism'. 'Do you intend to replace the existing social order by community of Property at one stroke? Answer: We have no such intention. The development of the masses cannot he ordered by decree. It is determined by the development of the conditions in which these masses live, and therefore proceeds gradually'. 'Will it be possible for private property to be abolished at one stroke? No, no more than existing forces of production can at one stroke be multiplied to the extent necessary for the creation of a communal society. In all probability, the proletarian revolution will transform existing society gradually and will be able to abolish private property only when the means of production are available in sufficient quantity'.
Engels continues to say that communist action will involve:
'Gradual expropriation of landowners, industrialists, railroad magnates and shipowners, partly through competition by state industry, partly directly through compensation in the form of bonds'.

16   All societies must perform surplus labor (labor that is more than necessary to meet the current needs) and must produce a surplus product. Surplus product will be necessary in a non-capitalist society not only to build future productive forces (e.g. new bridges and

When even the limited forms of democracy that capitalism allows are being increasingly questioned in words and in practice in a process that is extending into fascistic tendencies, and when the limited form of assistance from the state that is available (in the form of meagre pro-poor intervention) is being withdrawn/shrunk by fascistic (and other) forces, and when the very small amount of the asset-base that petty producers have is being taken away, there should be class-based mobilization by organizations of workers and small-scale producers, under the leadership of Left parties. I am abstracting from the question of what kind of Left parties can achieve such a task.[17] An important aim of such Left-led mobilization must be to confront, as non-violently as possible, the fascistic/communal forces, including on the street, as a part of the fight against capitalism. Masses must be made aware of the three levels of their struggle, i.e. the struggle against the attack on democratic rights, including from fascistic forces, the struggle against the attack on living conditions, and the struggle against capitalist class relation itself.

The fight against fascistic tendencies is a defensive fight, so it has to be a part of a fight for more. Even if this fight succeeds, its success will be inevitably transient just as success in obtaining economic concessions will be temporary. This is because the ugly head of fascistic tendencies will rise (and the attack on living standards will continue) as long as there is capitalism, along with its eternal tendency towards crisis and uneven development, and the attendant need to deceive and divide the lower-class opposition. So, the fight against fascistic tendencies must gradually develop into and be a part of, a fight, by Left-led workers and small-scale producers, for a socialist state and socialist society. The Left has to help the masses understand that genuine long-term success in achieving democratic rights and qualitative improvements in living conditions cannot be achieved within capitalism, that concessions received today can be

---

new roads, etc.) but also to make sure that those who are not able to work (children and pregnant women, retired workers) can satisfy their needs and can meet new needs that enrich the quality of life, spiritually and in other ways. When the major part of surplus labor takes the form of surplus value (roughly, capitalist profit, capitalist interest and capitalist rent, apart from taxes paid to capitalist state, much of which returns to property owners through various policies), we live in a capitalist society. Capitalist surplus labor is thus a surplus product in a 'quantitative' sense *that has a class character*: it is the surplus product produced by direct producers, made possible by development of productive forces, that is appropriated by the ruling class.

17    On many occasions, they, while maintaining their organizational independence, will have to combine their forces with non-communist workers and non-communist small-scale producers to fight for democratic rights and economic concessions (as, for example, in a nation-wide general strike) and against fascistic tendencies.

taken away tomorrow and that significant reforms in a country are produced generally as byproducts of revolutionary struggles in that country and/or in other countries from which they can spread.

## 2   Left Forces in India: Their Strength and Weakness

India's social-economic and political situation is dangerous for the toiling masses. What is urgently needed therefore is the political mobilization of the multi-caste, multi-religion, multi-regional working class and poor peasants of the vast diverse country against all factions of the capitalist-landlord propertied classes and their political formations. Such a mobilization must defend secularism, democracy, against the attack on these from fascistic forces, and national sovereignty vis-à-vis imperialism. And such a mobilization must be not for a democratic capitalist society whatever that bourgeois-democracy is euphemistically called, but for a workers' and poor peasants' government. It is only such a government that can root out the seeds of the on-going attack on secularism and democracy, and that can help the masses gradually construct socialism. Masses must be conscious of the fact that it is only such a government that can guarantee that the toiling masses enjoy a decent standard of living and practice proletarian (bottom-up) democracy, and that people live in harmony with one another and with nature. Needless to say that such a mobilization in India must be a part of the mobilization at greater geographical scales for socialism in one country is a reactionary and fake idea.[18] These principles must be always kept in mind. They constitute the lighthouse during the long and tortuous journey towards socialism.

We must also bear in mind that:

> the class war takes place on the soil of history, and not in the stratosphere of sociology [or 'bald sociological abstraction']. The point of departure in the struggle against fascism is not the abstraction of the democratic state, but the living organizations of the proletariat, in which is concentrated all its past experience and which prepare it for the future.
>
> TROTSKY, 1932e[19]

---

18   The fight against capitalism in India, to succeed and to deepen, can only be a part of a world-regional (e.g. South Asian) and an international fight, because capitalism is an international system.

19   We must also not forget that: 'in politics, as in all other serious fields, one must know well: what; when, where, and how. Also, it cannot hurt to understand: why' (Trotsky, 1932l).

Fascistic attacks are happening in India, and the BJP is expanding its influence, not only because of (a) the failure of the ruling class to satisfy the needs of the masses, whose living standards are under attack while ruling class is accumulating a massive amount of wealth, and (b) the 'secular' political representatives of the ruling class to defend democracy and secularism (as indicated by the decline of the Congress). Fascistic tendencies are progressing also because of the weakness of Left forces[20] (manifested partly in their geographical confinement to specific parts of the country), relative to what is necessary to conduct the democratic, trade unionist, and socialist movements.

If fascistic forces, that are always the handmaiden of capital (or its hegemonic fractions), are not stronger than they are, and therefore, if India does not yet have a *fascist state*, this is also partly because of the relative weakness of the Left movement, so perhaps there is, ironically, an advantage of political backwardness. This is because: The Left (the bloc of communist parties), does not yet present the spectre of communism/socialism as a serious threat. Instead given their overall political vision, they are merely fighting against the remnants of landlordism, for a more equal distribution of farm-land, and against the attack on living standards of workers and peasants from a specific form of capitalism (neoliberal capitalism and/or a capitalism dominated by specific fractions of capital). These fights *are* absolutely relevant. Yet, it can be seen that the Left is fighting for a particular progressive form of democracy, which also means that it will be the political shell for a particular form of capitalism (a more egalitarian and a more economically developed capitalism) for an indefinite period, under the supervision of a new class-alliance than what exists now. So, in a sense, communists are not really a big threat to the principle of capitalist class relation itself in India now or in the future, as they were in certain advanced capitalist countries in the 1930s, in the aftermath of 1917. Unlike in Germany on the eve of fascist ascendancy, as the CPI(M) General Secretary himself acknowledges:

> In India today, the ruling classes as a whole have not yet come to the conclusion of abandoning the present form of parliamentary democracy, notwithstanding the severe stress and strain that it is under. On the other hand, the threat of the immediate seizure of power by the proletariat is not on the agenda today. Finally, this is also because the stage of the

---

20      From now on (and unless indicated otherwise), I use the term Left to mainly refer to the various formally organized streams of the Marxist Left in India. When I am not talking about India I sometimes use the word 'Left' to indicate the Left that is necessary to mobilize the exploited classes and oppressed people against capitalism and for socialism.

revolution in India [according to all communist parties which have any real presence] is democratic, while in Germany it was Socialist.

YECHURI, 1993: 5; parenthesis added

In fact, *in practice*, and not just in theory, the Left is also not a serious threat to capital*ists* in India, whether big or not, given that when in power at the provincial level, it woos capitalists for investment and to create jobs. And therefore fascistic forces are not yet confronted with the task of having to defend capitalist *property relations* and *fundamental class interests of capitalists* against any significant organized proletarian political opposition. Nonetheless, the fascistic forces, given their inherently pro-business character, are responding to the need to sustain capitalist accumulation at a high rate, and counter the declining rate of profit.[21] Such a need can be met in part by thwarting any potential or actual mass and class struggle against the employers-financiers-traders-landowners combine, including against the super-exploitation of labor and mindless dispossession of small-scale producers. And, such a need of the ruling class is expressed in the form of attempts by extreme Right-wing elements within the bourgeois class to turn to several methods. Resorting to the fascistic movement is a major one. The conjunctural co-existence of the 'relative weakness' of the fascistic movement (i.e. the fact that the fascistic tendencies have not yet captured *state* power fully) and the relative weakness of the Left, can make the Left oblivious of an important ontological fact: that the existence of a thing and its higher levels of development are different *and* are united by a *common* underlying characteristic. And ignoring such an ontological fact can create the illusion about the non-seriousness of the threat from fascistic forces to democracy and to the communist movement.

We should recapitulate two facts here. Firstly, fascistic forces do exist mainly because of a potential and actual ideological and political struggle against certain effects of capitalist accumulation and crisis, a struggle much of which is led by the Left. Established in the same year as the Communist party of India, the RSS, as mentioned earlier, is anti-communist from its origin. Secondly, because the threat to capital is not strong enough from the Left (in a global climate of relative decline of the Left), the need for a fully-fledged fascistic state has not yet arisen on capitalist-economic grounds.[22] If the Left was so strong

---

21   According to Roberts (2016), like many other BRICS countries and advanced countries, Indian capitalism has been experiencing a declining rate of profit.

22   Such a state of affairs is also because the fascistic forces themselves are not yet strong enough, even electorally, *relative to* the challenge from the totality of secular-democratic forces. This is partly evidenced by the fact that they can be electorally defeated, or heavily weakened, by the unity of the forces that are reasonably secular.

that it would pose a threat to capitalist property but not strong enough to take power, the existing fascistic movement could turn into a fascist regime, or to something very close. These two facts are because of a common factor: the relative weakness of the Left movement, a fact that has received much attention recently, including in popular circles.[23] And this concrete situation of the weakness of the Left needs to be briefly explained.[24]

One may start with mainstream communist parties [e.g. CPI and CPI(M)]. Along with their partners within the Left Front, they have launched many struggles for reforms and have remained an important part of India's progressive political culture.[25] This is reflected in the fact that among the lower-income people ('very poor') and among unskilled workers and agricultural workers, a proportionately higher percentage of them votes for the Left parties than for other parties (Table 13.1). For example: if 7.5% of all voters voted for

---

23  The recent literature on the Left which discusses its weaknesses, among other aspects of its history, includes: Banerjee, 2012; Bidwai, 2016; Chakrabarty, 2015, 2014; Crowley, 2014; Das and Mahmood, 2015; Josh, 2011; Kersell, 2018; Maitra, 2011; Prashad, 2015; Vanaik, 2011; and Vidyasagar, 2005. See Suniraj and Heath (2017) and Williams, 2009 on how the CPM has received support from disadvantaged groups. On the actual workings of left governments, there is a large amount of literature including: Heller, 1999; Kohli, 1987; Oktem, 2012; Lofgren, 2016; and Mallick, 1994. The criticisms of the communist Left have come from various theoretical and political strands even within what can be broadly called Leftist. For example, there are differences between a Bidwai and a Vanaik on the one hand and an Anjan Chakrabarti on the other. Anjan Chakrabarti (2012) says that: the problem with the communist movement lies in their commitment to state-centric politics and a vanguardist party structure that comes at the expense of advancing the Marxian project of nonexploitation, fair distribution, and democracy. While one criticism is that communist parties are less communistic and more social-democratic, others say that they are probably not even social democratic (for example, Herring (2013) says that it is increasingly unclear that platforms of left parties coincide with the interests of subordinate classes).

24  In this discussion, I include three streams, abstracting from a fourth group: individuals and non-party organizations who are Marxist (although this group has some overlap with my third stream). There are also many individuals and groups who are sympathetic to Marxism and who are involved in grass-roots mobilization of the exploited and oppressed groups and of those who are adversely affected by the massive environmental damage caused by capitalism.

25  They include not only Forward Bloc and Revolutionary Socialist Party (and sometimes, Socialist Unit Center of India), but also, and more recently, CPI(ML)-Liberation. The latter is a (militant) party with roots in the Maoist/Naxalite movement that began in 1967, and combines electoral and extra-electoral work mainly focussing on rural areas. See Kotovsky (1992) and Tharamangalam (1992) on the role of communist parties in organizing workers and peasants (see also Mannathukkaren, 2011; and Heller, 1999).

TABLE 13.1    Percentage of voters who voted for various parties/alliances (in national elections in 1996 and 2004)

**1996 Election**

|  | Congress+ | BJP+ | Left Front |
|---|---|---|---|
| All India average | 27.5 | 24.9 | 7.5 |
| Very poor | 29.6 | 16 | 11.3 |
| Unskilled worker | 30.6 | 17.0 | 10.8 |
| Agri- and allied worker | 28.4 | 17.8 | 8.9 |
| Scheduled caste | 31.6 | 14.4 | 11.0 |

**2004 Election**

|  | Congress+ | BJP+ | Left Front |
|---|---|---|---|
| All India average | 39.5 | 37.9 | 6.4 |
| Very poor | 42.9 | 32.8 | 7.5 |
| Unskilled worker | 42.6 | 27.4 | 8.0 |
| Agri- and allied worker | 43.4 | 36.6 | 6.8 |
| Scheduled caste | 39.7 | 25.9 | 8.8 |

SOURCE: ORIGINAL DATA FROM CSDS (CENTRE FOR THE STUDY OF DEVELOPING SOCIETIES) AND ELECTION COMMISSION OF INDIA, QUOTED IN MITRA, 2011: 118–119

the Left in 1996, among the sections that are defined as 'very poor', a much higher percentage (11.3%) voted for the Left. This is in stark contrast to the Right: if 24.9% of all voters voted for the BJP and allied parties in 1994, from the 'very poor' category, only 16% voted for them. The Left's support base is indeed disproportionately among the very poor, agricultural workers, unskilled workers and scheduled castes.

Based on the above numbers, one can calculate what I will call the relative popularity quotient (RPQ) of a party/alliance, relative to specific groups of voters, by using this formula: Percentage of voters from a social group which votes for a party/alliance divided by the percentage of all voters who voted for that party/alliance. If the ratio for a party/alliance is greater than 1, that means that a disproportionately higher percentage of a given social group supports that party/alliance. If the ratio for a party/alliance is less than 1, that means that a disproportionately lower percentage of a specific group supports that party/alliance. The higher the ratio, the higher the RPQ. One can see that the RPQ for the Left is not only very high as compared to the Right (BJP+); it is also

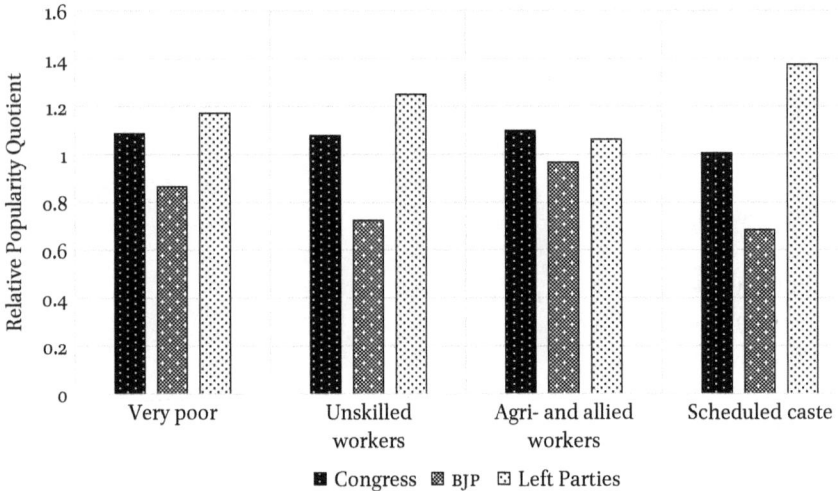

FIGURE 13.1 Relative popularity quotient among lower classes and Dalits (2004 national election)

(generally) high as compared to the Congress as well. The RPQ for the Left for, for example, 'very poor' and for 'unskilled workers' was 2.34 and 2.11 times the RPQ for the Right for these categories, in 1996, although the RPQ for the Left for some of these groups did come down in 2004 (Figures 13.1–13.2).

India's Left and progressive culture would be poorer without the main-stream Left. Yet, they have spent far too much time on elections and on managing the bourgeois-state apparatuses at local and provincial levels. As a result they have failed to transform what are merely democratic consciousness and trade union consciousness of workers and small-scale producers to what is called class consciousness proper, or socialist consciousness. The idea of the struggle for socialism – with which development of class consciousness is associated – is hardly raised in the Left discourse and Left political work.[26] The ideological and political work of the Left is, more or less, shaped by the assumption that, as mentioned earlier, the goal of communists is merely to have a more democratic and more egalitarian capitalism for an indefinite period.[27] The language of socialist vision and the struggle for socialism is as scarce as

---

26   A former veteran communist, Mr. Jyoti Basu, had said in 2008: 'Socialism is a far cry. Socialism is our political agenda and it was mentioned in our party document but capitalism will continue to be the compulsion for the future' (The Economic Times, 2008).

27   Once a well-known communist leader said this to me about West Bengal before the fall of the Left front from power: the Left Front needed to establish capitalist industries first to create a working class, and it would then fight against capitalism.

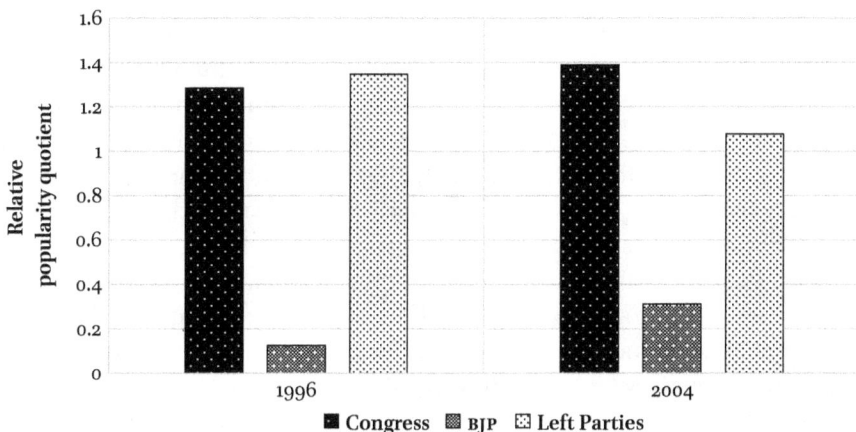

FIGURE 13.2 Relative popularity quotient for Muslims (2004 national election)

water in the Rajasthan desert.[28] What is plenty in evidence is the combination of electoralism and trade unionist consciousness, like water in Cherrapunji. It is being forgotten that the effect of the fight for democratic rights and economic concessions is greater when these take place within the framework of a struggle against capitalist property relations as such, and when a large section of those who engage in these fights has what is called class consciousness proper. The level of ideological education of members and followers of major communist parties is not very high. Obsession with the desire to win many seats in the elections is associated with reformism: a communist party can win many seats to manage a bourgeois apparatus only by making too many compromises with the system and thus by sacrificing the goal of class struggle. Besides where it has been electorally successful and managed to control state power at the provincial and sub-provincial scales, it has pursued capitalist, even neoliberal capitalist policies, so the objective of developing cadres' class consciousness through electoral battle is further undermined. Electoral success and attendant electoral consciousness (= political form of trade union consciousness) has thus come at the expense of class-consciousness which is what the Left should be promoting.

What about the Maoist-inspired Left which is seen as existing to the left of mainstream Left parties? As discussed in two earlier chapters, this segment of

---

28    This applies to even to the class-conscious workers, and perhaps, to most of the communist leaders.

the Left involving many self-sacrificing people who are passionate about the defense of the right of the poor, has also launched many valiant struggles, especially in rural areas and in areas dominated by the culturally rich but economically exploited and politically oppressed indigenous communities living in what can be called, with some justification, 'internal colonies' (see Das, 2019b). But much of this Left – especially, the more militant part of it – is, more or less, isolated from the political mobilization of urban workers, given their belief in the peasants as being the most revolutionary class.

Then there are little groups to the Left of mainstream and Maoist communist parties. They provide excellent analyses of the current situation that actually emphasize the need for the struggle for socialism, by employing insights from revolutionary Marxism.[29] However, the actual influence of these groups on the politics and consciousness of people has been almost non-existent thus far. In other words, the high quality of their intellectual analysis is not matched by their actual political interventions on the ground. This unfortunate state of affairs is in part because right from their origin [consider the history of the Bolshevik Leninist Party of India (BLPI)], this stream of Marxist movement in India (as in many other countries) has shown a tendency towards extreme fragmentation (and indeed unprincipled entrysm) and towards also sectarianism. There are little groups, some of them based in India and others being branches of international organizations. In many instances, when some of them seek to intervene ideologically in the Indian communist movement, they have a tendency to see no distinction between the Left movement and what is plain bourgeois politics, so much so that every instance of electoral (or nonelectoral) defeat of the Left becomes an occasion for a small 'celebration' on their part. Some of their criticisms of the Indian Left, including the fact that it

---

29    Their Marxism, includes, and rightly so, the ideas not only from Lenin (including the Lenin of *April Theses*) but also ideas of Luxemburg and Trotsky (and all those who have tried to develop the ideas of these classical thinkers in the more recent times). It should be noted that the last two figures, Luxemburg and Trotsky, and especially, Trotsky, are consistently and systematically ignored – and indeed, blacklisted – by theoreticians and leaders of mainstream communist parties as well as by Maoists, indicating their own version of sectarianism. When a progressive publisher sent to one of the major communist parties a few books on Trotsky, a party representative complained about this, citing political differences between the party and Trotskyism. When the person was requested later to return the books, the publisher was promptly informed that the books had been bought already by some people from the party's book-shop! A communist movement must pay careful, honest and critical attention to the entire Marxist tradition. To do so would be a more holistic view of Marxism than what is often practiced by major parties/movements and Marxist scholars. Such a holistic and non-sectarian view, by reducing some of the (avoidable/non-basic) differences, will contribute to the success of any communist movement (see Das, 2019 on the need for a non-sectarian approach to class struggle).

is not militant enough, are legitimate. Some are not. Consider the following. If there is no Left-led movement in an area or a sector or a work-place, the Left is criticized by some of these Far Left groups, and rightly so. But these groups do not say why *they themselves* do not organize the workers and peasants or why they have not been able to be in a position to organize these classes, despite the fact that these groups or their predecessors have existed for 70 years or so. Further, when workers go on a strike, they are praised for their militancy by these small groups, while forgetting that the strikes are organized by the Left. And, in fact, when the Left does organize strikes and protests, and the Left does this numerous times, it is accused of merely containing the anger of the masses and is thus supportive of the bourgeois system. The Left is also criticized on the ground that it is intentionally confining the strike in one workplace to that place and that it is not mobilizing workers from across workplaces. Of courses, left-led strikes have often been confined to particular places, and that is a problem. But if doing so was the necessary part of Left's strategy, how has it been organizing nation-wide strikes and region-wise farmer movements, and so on? Often the word 'Stalinist' is used by many of these small groups to describe the Indian Left movement. 'Stalinism' is an analytical-political category (Das, 2018c). Is using 'Stalinism' mainly as an abusive-descriptive term, like the abusive use of 'sectarianism' by the Left movement for the Far Left groups, not potentially harmful to the socialist political and trade union movement? The Indian Left movement is Stalinist in its origin and in terms of its dubious theory of revolution (and I have presented my criticisms of its theory of revolution in Chapter 3 and elsewhere). But one must ask: how does the incessant and automatic invocation of 'Stalinism' and spontaneous hatred for and fear of anything to do with the existing Left movement, benefit the Marxist cause, including in the trade union sphere, to be promoted by socialists, who 'have no interests separate and apart from those of the proletariat as a whole' and who 'do not set up any sectarian principles of their own, by which to shape and mold the proletarian movement' (Marx and Engels, 1848)?

Some of the 'negativist' criticisms of the Indian Left's 'reformist' struggles by small Far Left groups, which are mainly propaganda groups, are almost akin to the type of criticisms of working class actions that is indicative of what Marx called 'political indifferentism'. It says that, for example, a struggle against a wage strike is bad because it supports wage-slavery under capitalism or that the struggle for state funding of primary education is bad because primary education is inadequate, or that getting concessions through struggle is bad because it means compromise with the system. Marx himself countered this sort of criticisms (Marx, 1873; see Das, 2019 for a longer discussion on this matter).

The center of gravity (the organizational basis) of some of these groups is also not deeply and extensively immersed in Indian politics and history, so what they say about the Indian society is not rooted in their *active struggles* on the ground.[30] This isolation from active struggles partly explains the sectarian tendency of these groups, which feeds into their isolation from active struggles. Nonetheless, it is important to reiterate that many of the criticisms of the bourgeois society and of Left politics from this Marxist stream, however inadequate, are examples of serious Marxist work and unflinching committment to socialist revolution. And India's Left culture would be also impoverished without these criticisms. India's Left culture will be impoverished in the absence of comradely and critical dialogues between this stream and other streams, which might, in the future, create the possibility of a tactical united front of separately existing Left parties to fight against fascism and other aspects of capitalism and against capitalism itself. But ultimately, the existing Left parties must transcend their limiting view of society and revolution whereby they are wedded to the idea of a democratic revolution and not a socialist revolution as a part of South Asia-wide and global process. This is a most fundamental obstacle to a serious communist movement.

The totality of the Left political landscape is therefore one that is politically rich. It is probably richer than in many western-advanced capitalist countries, which is why an average western intellectual would not even believe that India has such a fertile panoply of leftism. Of course, it has all sorts of problems including those that concern the determination of Indian society's class character, and the determination of the stage of revolution, the nature of the united front strategy. One need not go into these issues here.

Given the over-all left-political situation as briefly described above (i.e. the relative weakness of the Left, given the low level of class consciousness among the masses), it is difficult to see how the struggle for a workers and poor peasants' state can begin *at this very moment*, without being idealistic, voluntaristic and adventurist,[31] especially given that fascistic forces are literally out there to

---

30    Some of these groups lack a dialectical approach to the relation between class exploitation and non-class oppression, including caste and religion, etc. They agree that class relations and struggle against class relations have primacy. From this right premise, they draw the wrong conclusion that non-class relations are effectively not important in the struggle against class.

31    It is adventuristic when one raises the slogan of revolution without prior ideological and political preparations and without the majority of the workers saying yes to a call for revolution (as Lenin says). Marx was called a traitor by some of his contemporaries for cautioning against adventurists. 'Marx, Engels, and Willich worked together on a league and refugee matters through the summer of 1850, but a rift began developing over strategy... Although Marx had put aside all theoretical work since 1848 in favor of political agitation and opposition journalism, it was becoming apparent to him that a revolution was *not*

physically destroy the Left and progressive movements. But it is also not clear how it is that outside of a framework of the struggle for socialism, there can be a fight to completely and permanently eliminate the fascistic tendencies – a fight which is much more than electorally getting rid of the BJP from power: as long as there is capitalist class relation, there *is* an underlying tendency towards the society both shunning its democratic shell, turning towards fascism, and attacking the living standards of the masses. The fascistic tendency is one that may not always manifest itself, and when it is manifested, it may not always be strong enough to take state power. But this is a tendency that is inherent to capitalist class relation, which produces crisis and misery for the majority. The preparation that is necessary to make a demand for a socialist state must be made sooner than later, and an enormous conjunctural obstacle has to be cleared for that to happen: the clearing of that obstacle must be seen as a part of the tortuous, non-linear, process of the fight for socialism.

3      The Indian Left and the Two Forms of the Fight
       against Fascist Tendencies

The fight against fascist tendencies, once again, cannot merely seen as a fight to replace the BJP with a more secular government nor can the fight against fascistic tendencies be merely confined near-permanently to be a fight for a capitalist society that has no trace of feudalism, that is more democratic, and less unequal and where the state intervenes on behalf of the poor and regulates private businesses. In fact, the fight against fascism and against neoliberal attack on living standards can only be seen as twin inter-connected steps towards, and as a part of, the protracted fight for socialism. Clearly, capitalists do not mind doing business with, and actively supporting, undemocratic and authoritarian forces and even *fascistic* political forces, whether these forces have slaughtered religious minorities or crushed democratic rights or are striking at the root of national unity. This fact is a reason enough to assert, and to tell the masses now, that capitalism itself has to go. Capitalism will go only when the Left – class-conscious toiling masses organized by the communists – overthrows it.

---

imminent. Willich, however, ... believed the [communist] league, despite its small numbers, could through sheer force of will trigger an uprising, and he disagreed with Marx's dawning conclusion that massive social change was more than likely years away. For his part Marx argued that certain things were necessary for a successful revolution... According to Wilhelm Leibknecht, ...Willich and Barthélemy began plotting against Marx: "They called Marx a traitor and said traitors must be killed"(Gabriel, 2011).

Such a class politics requires a much stronger Left, which in turn requires greater organizational strength, attempts at expanding its political hegemony, and the struggles in the legal and extra-parliamentary spheres (Chakrabarty, 2015). It also requires principled Left unity [note that there is effectively very little substantive difference between CPI and CPI(M)]. Such unity must produce a gradually expanding united front of Left forces as representatives of workers, semi-proletarians and peasants, the forces which may remain separate organizationally and which may engage in polemical battles for theoretical and political clarity as long as they need to, but they must strike together in action. It must deploy the full spectrum of parliamentary and extra-parliamentary methods, with the primacy given to the latter. In the fight against fascistic forces, what should be targeted are not only the political and cultural views of these forces (their attack on democratic rights and secularism, their hyper-nationalism, etc.) but also, and this is very important, their pro-business economic and pro-imperialist, policies. Once again, two aspects of fascist movement, communal authoritarianism with fascistic tendencies and idolization of free market economics, serve national and imperialist capital, and go together. Both of these must be fought together. It is idealist and politicist to say that merely an educational attempt to make people's way of thinking less communal, and a mere fight for secular politics, can succeed in fighting fascistic tendencies, without there being a simultaneous fight against policies that the fascistic government implements in the interest of capital.

The electoral sphere is indeed one of the spheres in which class struggle – and indeed struggle for 'social justice' – happens. There are many dimensions to the struggle within the electoral sphere. The latter is important given that liberal democracy is a shell of Indian capitalism and that it has also deep roots in people's consciousness thus contributing to the legitimacy of the system. Unlike in advanced capitalism, the vast majority of voters vote in India. Winning a few seats in the parliaments/assemblies, etc. gives the Left a chance to make its voice of reason heard against fascistic tendencies and against an attack on people's livelihood. An important part of the protracted process of class struggle in the current conjuncture is an attempt to stop a fascistic party from coming to, and/or from retaining, power and from making use of state's resources to attack social and democratic rights of ordinary people and to destroy – or at least severely weaken – the communist movement. Among various forms of bourgeois government, some forms are more conducive to class-mobilizational work by the Left than other forms, so the Left cannot be neutral to which forms of bourgeois government exist, just as it cannot be neutral towards whether capitalism is peasant capitalism or landlord capitalism or whether in a capitalist society wages are lower or higher or whether school education for children is state-funded or not. A government that is run by fascistic, communal and hyper-nationalistic elements, a government that attacks democratic rights *as well as* living standards of people, is the least conducive to class-based movements. One can see this when communists are killed or hurt, statues of communist icons are demolished, when communist offices are ransacked. It is worth repeating this: the process of fighting for a new society must include the fight for the conditions for that fight itself. The Left must fight for these conditions. And only the Left can fight for these conditions in a consistent way. So, it is necessary to fight electorally even if the priority has to be given to the extra-electoral fight to be conducted in opposition to all bourgeois forces. However, electoral success has to be seen dialectically, from the standpoint of the law of transformation of quantity into quality and vice versa.[32]

One might ask (and people do ask this question): why will the voters vote for the Left, given (a) that Left leaders do not generally engage in corrupt behavior which means that they cannot help people make money,[33] and (b) the Left does not get enough votes to be able to run the government so they do not control the purse to provide material help.[34] They have no money themselves to give away in support for votes. These arguments must be listened to and countered. In my view, it is not necessary for the Left to be in government in order for it to be with the masses, to speak on their behalf, to be relevant to their lives (in fact, the more the Left is embedded in governing bourgeois state

---

32    Too little of electoral success would deny the Left access to the parliament and assemblies to represent its views, and it would also deny the Left the chance to feel the pulse of the masses. But if the level of electoral success becomes too much, it can lead to the Left capturing power at, say, the provincial level (or being a part of a national government). This can also be politically problematic, even if the Left is able to alleviate some of the economic miseries of the masses. It can, generally speaking, come to power in a bourgeois system only by making too many compromises with the system, and this fact can blunt the edge of class struggle of its basic classes, because their fighting instincts must somehow be kept in check in a capitalist system, in order to allow a certain level of accumulation of money in the hands of capitalists who are free to move across provinces. This will be the case whether the Left is a partner of a popular front (a bloc of capitalist parties and left parties) or comes to power on its own. And such a control over class struggle would lead to the loss of popularity of the Left among its basic classes. And if the Left, while in power, does engage in too much struggle against employers and traders, then capital will leave (and/or will invest less), leading to unemployment and low wages, which, in turn, will lead to the loss of its popularity among its basic classes.

33    Note that even common people do not mind making a little money from the government sources through corrupt means.

34    A vote for a left party in Kerala is effective but it is wasted in Gujarat, Herring (2013) says.

apparatuses, the less relevant it becomes to the masses).[35] The Left mediates between the masses and the resources of society as a whole that are controlled by the government, the resources that constitute the commons. They include natural commons such as land, forests and water bodies, as well as state-owned resources built on the basis of contributions from ordinary people (state-owned companies providing secure jobs and state benefits in the form of de-commodified use-values). The Left must fight against the commons being given away to capitalists. It must fight for greater access of ordinary people to the existing commons and for an expansion of the existing commons (e.g. expansion of the public sector enterprises and subjecting them to increase democratic control by manual and mental workers; and public provision of services such as education and health-care, sports facilities, theatres, parks, museums, and libraries). Besides, the Left must mobilize people to (a) have a better share of their own product that is taken away by the capitalists in the form of high profit, interest and rent, a process that the state supports, and (b) reduce taxes on them and increase taxes on the super-rich. And the Left must mobilize people around transitional demands that connect immediate demands to the struggle for a socialist society, the demands which include such things as employment for all for a living wage. More specifically, the Left must show its practical relevance to the masses in at least four ways:

1. by mobilizing the masses to win concessions from employers, traders, bankers and landowners on the basis of strikes and protests;

2. by mobilizing the masses to win concessions from the government at all levels (center and State), in the form of progressive policies to meet people's needs, including the policies which reflect the needs of the masses *whether or not the system says it can meet them;*[36]

3. by making sure that the policies introduced under the pressure of the Left are actually implemented, and reach the masses in a transparent, non-divisive, and non-corrupt way, including at the city and village level

---

35    Given the venality of the bourgeois electoral process, in which votes are bought by many parties and sold by many voters, the Left *is* at a disadvantage. But then it is better that the Left should not obtain votes from such voters. In fact, the use of money power in elections must be an issue that the Left should campaign as a part of its fight to deepen democracy.

36    These include: food security, secure employment for all, inflation-adjusted living wages for men and women, increase in the relative wage, or the reduction in inequality between what masses get and what property owners take from the fruits of the labor of the masses, better prices for petty producers and protection from unfair dispossession from their small-scale property, freedom-from debt; free time (reduction in working hours); pension; socialized and universal access to publicly provided quality health-care, education, housing, transportation and culture.

(this would make sure that the policies announced by a government do not serve as an ideological tool as false promises);[37] and

4. by being able to impart education to the masses to develop solidarity among them – education against practices of discrimination based on religion, gender, caste, etc. – and to protect the democratic rights of the socially oppressed groups.

There are thus objective reasons why the Left can have political relevance by winning concessions for the masses, as a part of its struggle for socialism, to the daily lives of the masses and why it can obtain some level of electoral support, even in areas where its presence is not traditionally very strong. [38] But it is clear that merely implementing, or advocating for, progressive policies is no recipe for undermining the fascistic forces.[39] The spread of communalist-fascistic

---

37   False promises amount to lies, the aim of which is to merely calm and deceive the masses (who have also been deceived by non-fascistic bourgeois governments). Fascistic tendencies specialize in promising to deliver good things for the poor people, better than any other alternative political movement (bourgeois-democratic or leftist), without meaning to do anything or much, and in the process, they recruit sections of the masses into, and gain support for, their mass reactionary movement. They cannot deliver what they promise because doing so will hurt the basic interests of capital which they are servile supporters of.

38   Of course, one might say that if the Left is able to do all these to obtain concessions for the masses, why would they be interested in the fight for more (socialism)? The answer is: through struggle for reforms on the basis of immediate and transitional demands and on the basis of ideological education, the Left will help the masses to get more than what the masses would get without any struggle, but no matter how strong the fight for concessions is, the system will never meet the masses' need to any significant extent and on a long-term basis (concessions are also reversible). The fight for concessions, including for things that the system will never agree to (e.g. secure work for all with a living wage and with access to socialized and free quality health care and quality education), will reveal, to some extent, the true nature of the system (i.e. its structural 'bias' against the needs of the ordinary people), and such a fight for concessions, combined with Marxist education in theory and history, will radicalize the masses and prompt them to demand a (stadial) transcendence of the system. It is not enough that Marxist leaders and intellectuals know that there are limits to what the system can deliver. Masses must realize that these limits exist, based on their practice (and some theoretical reflection). Of course, to this one can counter-argue by saying that if the Marxists know that there are limits to reforms, would common people not be demoralized by fighting for these reforms? That counter-argument holds only if the fight for reforms happens without an ideological education which says explicitly to the people that there are such limits and that one should not expect much from the capitalist society.

39   In Tripura, the Left has tried to implement pro-poor policies, within the class and institutional constraints, but this was not enough to stop BJP from winning in the 2018 assembly election. In spite of progressive policies (progressive, that is, relative to blatantly bourgeois regimes in other States such as Gujarat, a laboratory for communal-fascistic-neoliberal-capitalist policies) implemented by the Left Front in Kerala, Kerala has seen a growth of right-wing fascistic forces.

ideology can counter the effects of progressive policies, so an ideological struggle against communalism and fascistic ideas *is* important. Of course, merely fighting against the attack on such ideology is not enough – especially in a country where almost 3 out of 4 people do not have access to an adequate amount of food. Besides the communal-fascistic ideology is rooted in material concerns of the ruling class, which are incompatible, ultimately, with those of the masses. The fight against the fascistic tendencies must be linked to the fight for economic concession, and both of these fights must be a part of the fight against the capitalist class relation itself. In fact, the arrival of fascistic tendency as a part of, and as a response to, capitalist crisis and reaction, and the resultant miseries for common people, is a great opportunity for the Left to say this to the masses (at least, to relatively politically advanced workers and peasants, in the first instance): the ruling class and its political parties are failing not only to meet economic needs but also they are failing to support basic democratic values, and therefore must be overthrown.

Once again: the Left must mobilize its basic classes (workers and small-scale producers) in extra-electoral activities, to fight for democratic rights and secularism and to fight for economic concessions, as a part of, and as steps towards, the fight for socialism. It must also engage in electoral struggle but that must be seen as *only a small part* of its overall political work, a prime aim of which must be the development of democratic-secular consciousness, and of trade union consciousness, and then the transformation of these forms of consciousness into communist consciousness or class consciousness proper. It is this Marxist perspective that must shape Left's approach to the electoral fight against fascism. In the remainder of this section (Section 3), I am going to present a less revolutionary approach as a thought experiment, only for readers' critical reflection, but this is an approach which, in my view, is utterly inadequate and problematic.

As mentioned earlier: unity of Left forces – all forces that are basically guided by Marxist theory of class society and of what is to be done – is fundamental to the task of fighting the fascistic forces electorally (and also extra-electorally). What is also needed is the unity among all secular, non-fascistic forces, including bourgeois forces: in as many constituencies as possible, as many secular-minded parties/movements as possible must be united against the BJP and its allies, before, during, and after the elections, and inside the parliaments/assemblies and outside. There should be as wide a secular front against communalism as possible, a front that is at the same time, to the left of the BJP and the pre-BJP governmental regime, in terms of economic policies. How this can be done is a different matter. One way to think about this is as follows.

There are at least a dozen regional parties in India that are relatively 'secular' in the sense that they do not employ the communal card as consistently

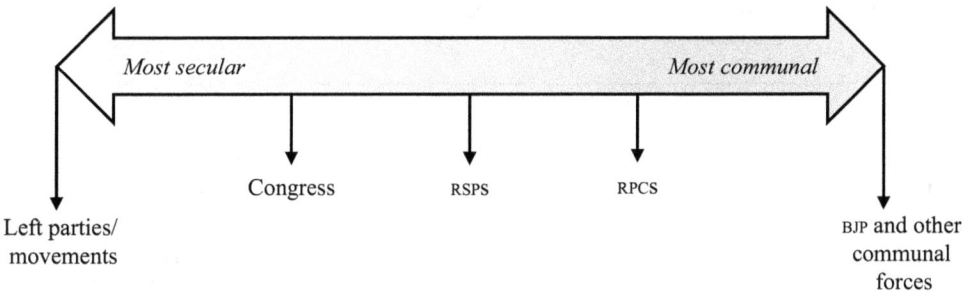

FIGURE 13.3 Scale of secularism
Notes: Where, RSPs: Regional parties, which are relatively, if not unwaveringly, secular. RPCs: Regional parties, which are currently a part of the electoral front dominated by the Hindu-communalist, BJP but which are formally not a part of the Sangh Parivar
SOURCE: AUTHOR

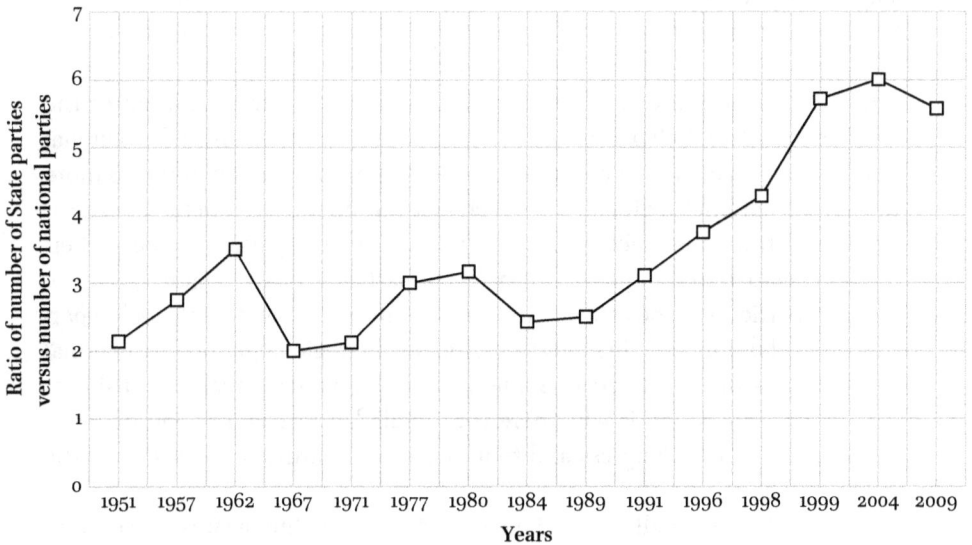

FIGURE 13.4 Ratio of number of State parties versus number of national parties as listed by ECI, 1951–2009

and as forcefully as the way the BJP does, and they are not fascistic as the BJP and the saffron family are: BJD, RJD, BSP, SP, JMM, DMK, AAP, TMC, PJC, etc.[40] (see Figure 13.3 above). Regional parties are basically parties that represent the

---

40   BJD = Biju Janata Dal (from Odisha); RJD = Rashtriya Janata Dal (from Bihar); BSP = Bahujan Samaj Party (mainly from Uttar Pradesh); SP = Samajwadi Party (mainly from Uttar Pradesh); JMM = Jharkhand Mukti Morcha (from Jharkhand); DMK = Dravida Munnetra

TABLE 13.2   Percentage of voters voting for a parties/alliances (in 1996 and 2004 national
            elections)

**1996**

|            | Congress+ | BJP+ | Left Front |
|------------|-----------|------|------------|
| All voters | 27.5      | 24.9 | 7.5        |
| Muslims    | 35.3      | 30.1 | 10.1       |

**2004**

|            | Congress+ | BJP+ | Left Front |
|------------|-----------|------|------------|
| All voters | 39.5      | 37.9 | 6.4        |
| Muslims    | 54.8      | 11.8 | 6.9        |

SOURCE: ORIGINAL DATA FROM CSDS (CENTRE FOR THE STUDY OF DEVELOPING
SOCIETIES) AND ELECTION COMMISSION OF INDIA, QUOTED IN MITRA, 2011: 118–119

interests of land owners, better-paid sections of the salaried stratum or the
'professional class' living/working in a province; and, importantly, the regional
bourgeoisie – the fraction of the bourgeoisie whose scale of operation is more
or less sub-national/regional and which faces competition from big bourgeoisie.[41] Over time, the electoral importance of regional parties is rising: their
number relative to the number of national parties is rising (Figure 13.4). The
regional parties, *may* be called, with *some* justification, what Lenin called parties of small proprietors. In many ways, the secular regional parties are regional
counter-parts of the Congress. Some of them are actually regional offshoots
of the Congress, which is why there is generally an inverse relation between
the strength of the Congress and that of regional parties, irrespective of the
strength of the Left.

The Left has, generally, been the most principled fighter against the curtailment of democratic rights and against the attack on secularism. It is perhaps not
an accident that in 1996, while 7.5% of all voters voted for the Left, 10.1% of all
Muslim voters voted for the Left (in 2004: the corresponding figures were 6.4

---

Kazhagam (from Tamil Nadu); AAP = Aam Aadmi Party (mainly from Delhi); TMC = All
*India* Trinamool Congress (mainly from West Bengal); PJC = People's Justice Centre (in
Tamil Nadu).

41   Note that the distinction between the two is not necessarily clear-cut, as regionally oper-
     ating smaller firms are connected to nationally-operating larger firms, as suppliers and in
     other ways.

and 6.9). As a contrast, while 24.9% of voters voted for the BJP and allied parties, only 3.1% of Muslim voters voted for them (in 2004: the corresponding figures were 37.9 and 11.8) (see Table 13.2).

Based on the above numbers, one can calculate the relative popularity quotient (RPQ) of a party/alliance, relative to Muslims, by using this formula: Percentage of Muslim voters who vote for a party/alliance divided by the percentage of all voters who voted for that party/alliance. If the ratio for a party/alliance is greater than 1, that means that a disproportionately higher percentage of Muslims supports that party/alliance. If the ratio for a party/alliance is less than 1, that means that a disproportionately lower percentage of Muslims supports that party/alliance. The higher the ratio, the higher the RPQ. One can see that the RPW for the Left is not only very high as compared to the Right (BJP+); it is also high as compared to the Congress. The RPQ for the Left was about 11 times the RPQ for the Right in 1996, although the RPQ for the Left did come down a bit in 2004 (Fig 13.1).

In so far the Left is committed to secularism, one that is partly expressed in the support of Muslims for the Left, and in so far as it is a great reservoir of democratic-secular consciousness, the Left, acting as *the tribune of the people in the Lenin sense*, and maintaining its organizational independence via a vis bourgeois parties, must help establish a national-level coordination committee (a political discussion platform, or some such thing) for the fight against communalism and fascistic tendencies. A part of this process, from an electoral angle, should be an attempt to establish a federation of regional parties, to which the Left should provide any intellectual and other forms of help as required. From the Left standpoint, the unity among regional parties must be based on at least three commitments. One is the commitment to secular politics: the regional parties must be opposed to conducting politics in the name of religion, and they must be opposed to discrimination against any group based on religion, whether it is majority religion or minority religion. Where these parties (e.g. the BJP, BJD, BSP, TMC) were in an alliance with the BJP in the past and have opposed the BJP since, they must critically review their past practice, draw the lessons, and publicly re-forge their commitment to secularism and to non-cooperation and non-alliance with the BJP. Second, millions of people are attracted to the Right-wing BJP because of the failure of economic policies of the Congress, so the regional parties, if they wish not to be eaten up by the BJP (and the BJP does, and can, eat into regional parties' support base), must be committed to people's welfare, which would also require a commitment to place *some* political restriction on the power of capitalists and landowners to amass limitless wealth, including at the expense of peasants and aboriginal people's access to land and natural resources. Enduring opposition to secularism, in the short and medium terms, cannot be possible unless it is based on the opposition to Right-wing economic policies hurting the masses, i.e. unless such opposition is based on progressive economic policies.[42] Once again, free market economics and authoritarian communalism rooted in a mass movement, are two sides of the same coin, whether or not some free marketers oppose communalism and whether or not some communalists support some amount of state control and state support for the poor. Third, regional parties must be committed to a *supra*-regional, i.e. a national vision. They cannot operate at the center (federal level) *merely* as a motley of regional parties. The collectivity of *regional* parties must have a *national*-scale vision of how to make sure that: (a) India remains a secular-democratic nation with a reasonably independent foreign policy until recently (especially in relation to imperialist countries) and a policy of good relations with neighbors, and (b) it remains a country where federalism – equitable, democratic, relations between the Center and the States – matters. If voted to power, the regional parties must think and act *as if* they are parts of a national party – i.e. as a *federation* of regional parties, which, collectively, will seek to improve conditions of people of India as a whole (its workers and peasants, and various oppressed groups such as indigenous communities, women, Dalits, religious minorities, etc.) and not just in their particular States where these parties rule or have an influence, although they will maintain their own regional identities. In fact, such a *regio-national* approach of regional parties is increasingly necessary given that development of one State is linked to, and dependent on, development in another State, because of the flow or movement of people, investment, water, polluted air, etc. *across* State boundaries.

So, all in all, the national federation of *regional* parties must be based on their *common* commitments to the people of India, the commitments, which have only *regional* manifestations.[43] The three commitments of regional parties

---

42    Regional parties' election manifestos actually do contain some welfare measures for ordinary people, and this is made possible partly because agriculture, education and health are State subjects, over which State governments have much control. Yet, it is also true that regional governments have been active in taking away the land of peasants and aboriginal people to give it to big business (to their regional branches) for a tiny amount of money, and often the money spent on welfare is a small part of the very little amount of money that companies pay in return for the vast amount of wealth they receive. This is a part of the process that links provincial capital and global capital: as Parthasarathy (2015) says: 'Provincial capital and peasant politics ally with global capital, and take advantage of the opening up of new regional and global trade routes which account for urban practices in metropolitan cities, and the processes of urbanization in the countryside' (p. 835).

43    Without those commitments, even if these parties defeat the BJP once, the latter will come back with a vengeance, citing the fact that the regional parties are not (much) better for the masses than the BJP, economically.

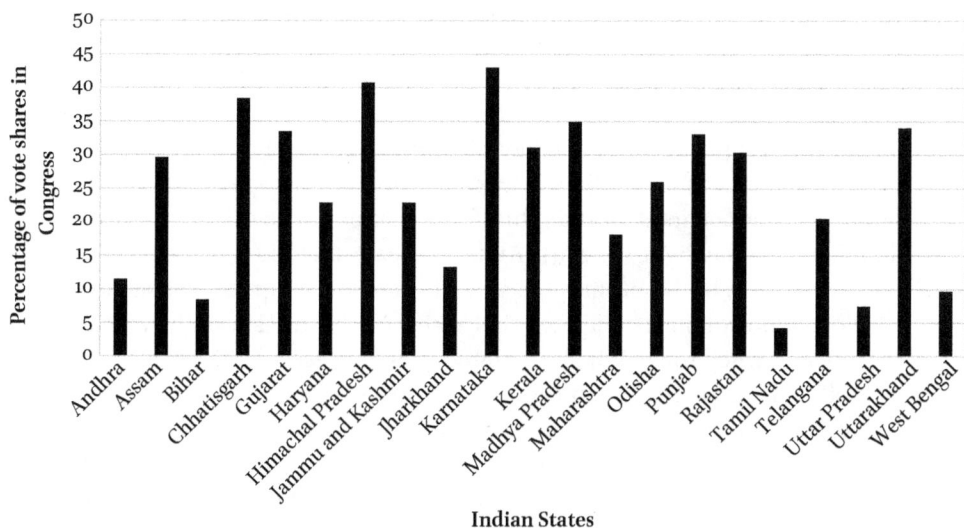

**FIGURE 13.5** Congress Party's percentage of vote shares in the 2014 general election in India
SOURCE: AUTHOR

that are just mentioned indeed overlap with Left's own values: secularism, pro-poor policies, and a multi-scalar approach.[44] So they may create a condition for some amount of tactical and short/medium term – not strategic and long-term – cooperation between the regional parties and the Left.

What about the approach of the Left to the Congress, which has been a topic of debate within and outside of the Left? The Congress is not a paragon of secular values.[45] But it cannot go to the extent that the BJP goes to, in attacking secularism. Like most regional parties, the Congress does not have a fascistic agenda. And it is the only non-BJP party, which has a modicum of *pan-Indian* presence; this is in terms of its vote share if not in terms of its actual presence in the Parliament (i.e. seats won) (see Figure 13.5 above).

The Congress could be the main anti-BJP national force and must receive support from all secular forces, both from the Left and outside, in those States where a major regional party is not contending for power, and where the Left is also weak. However, for this to happen, i.e. for the Congress to avoid competition from non-BJP secular parties and to enhance its electoral success

---

44    The latter (i.e. a multi-scalar approach) includes going beyond the narrow confines of a region.

45    Yet, 'it would be a mistake to write off the Congress … as one irredeemably compromised by its failure to uphold secularism' (Banaji, 2016c: 237).

against the BJP, it must change its hyper-neoliberal approach to development (which it, more or less, shares with the BJP). It must adopt an approach that gives much more emphasis to the bottom 70% of the population than it normally has; it must be publicly committed to significantly addressing the issues of: growing inequality and the billionaire raj, the agrarian crisis, employment security and a decent standard of living in cities and villages, and ecological problems. The Congress must do this if it wishes not to be eaten up and/or be dominated by the Right-wing BJP. And this means that: the Congress must be less subservient to the business class, and it must give up its obsession with trickle-down economics, the idea that when the business class increases its income and when the national economic growth rises, conditions of the less-well-off will automatically improve. To get support from other parties, including Left parties, any tactical support from the Congress cannot be based on the following: the Congress shares with the BJP its Right-wing economic policy, and it fights against the BJP merely on the ground that the BJP is communalist. To adequately fight the BJP and to be a partner in the fight against the attack on secularism, the Congress cannot be merely a more or less secular BJP.[46] The extent to which and the durability with which the BJP's electoral support can be dented, and thus the wings of the fascistic movement's political ambition can be trimmed, depends crucially on how economically progressive the anti-BJP front is (whether this front is called a secular-democratic front or a movement against the fascistic movement). The extent and the durability of the fight against the reactionary capitalist politics as fascistic tendencies, presenting themselves partly in the form of the authoritarian repression of democratic rights of religious minorities, depends on how *anti-capitalist* – and how pro-people – the fight is, and *how united* the Left is, and *how independent* it is organizationally vis-à-vis bourgeois forces.

Whether it is the Congress or the federation of regional parties, all parties must be willing to have a vision of development that counters the BJP's model of free-market-based development, which hurts the ordinary people, including those who are foot-soldiers of the fascistic movement itself. The Left must advocate for this, only to unite anti-BJP forces (i.e. the forces of the fascistic movement) in order to stop them from taking control over governmental power, even if these parties will not go beyond a limit in pursuing a non-neoliberal, pro-people developmental path and even if these parties will not support any

---

46    Note that the Congress, already, is no paragon of secularism; it practices, for tactical reasons (for electoral exigencies), a version of Hindutva, and many people supporting the Congress have a soft corner for Hindutva's followers, and/or are erstwhile the BJP supporters/leaders.

serious attack on capitalist private property. The degree of Left's reliance in these bourgeois forces to fight fascistic tendencies is not a constant phenomenon. It happens on the soil of class struggle: the more the Left gets stronger in the process of mobilizing people, the less reliant it will be on some bourgeois forces in order to fight the bourgeois-fascistic forces. Mere talk of secularism is not enough. It is not enough for people to be protected against attacks on their political freedom, including religious freedom. They need to experience freedom from hunger, from farm debt, from job-insecurity, etc. The business class must be *politically forced* by all secular forces, by the masses from below, to grant significant economic concessions (such a process will potentially show the real limit of the liberal-democracy to the masses). And the apparatuses of the Sangh parivar must be actively weakened, with popular support on the ground, aided by the secular-democratic government.

The Left must not be a part of a national governmental front, which is inevitably a *bourgeois*-democratic front, no matter how secular it may become. It must be outside of the front and provide only temporary tactical support (critical support), in its fight against the fascistic tendencies. The Left must demand pro-poor policies from the secular-democratic front and insist on their implementation when introduced. And it must carry on its extra-electoral, mobilization against capitalists and large-scale landowners, maintaining its organizational independence. This means that beyond a point, the secular bourgeois parties will not be the friends of the Left; they are only its temporary allies. Being a part of the national popular front would be an enormous barrier to Left's extra-parliamentary class politics which should be the main form of Left politics. And all these aspects of the struggle against the fascistic movement, including the need to work with some bourgeois forces, must be transparently and publicly explained to the ordinary members of the working class and the class of small-scale producers.

India is a large and geographically diverse country where social and political conditions vary enormously. The fight, within the electoral sphere, against fascistic forces will therefore have to be somewhat different in different States. Basically, the aim should be to minimize divisions among the non-BJP voters (the 69% or so of voters who did not vote for it in 2014). Where the Left is weak and has little chance of winning a seat it may consider giving tactical support to the party or bloc of parties that are anti-BJP. In the constituencies, where the Left is relatively strong (in its traditional areas of support), publicly acknowledging its past mistakes and recommitting itself to the basic interests of the masses including non-dispossession of their property, the Left must campaign against neo-liberal capitalism and communalism, against all contending parties, on the basis of its mass and class movements, to retain and regain its electoral base.

There is an objective condition for a front that is reasonably secular-democratic, with a progressive economic policy. On the one hand, only 31 per cent votes were cast for the BJP at the 2014 general election. This means that merely 20 per cent of the eligible voters, or, 14 per cent of India's population, supported it. In other words: potentially, 86% of India, 80% of eligible voters, and 69% of the people who voted *did not* support the BJP. Note that even in Tripura 57% of voters did not vote for the BJP. This massive subjective force can produce the conditions for the struggle for democracy, secularism and progressive economic agenda. This is the struggle of the 69% versus 31%, or indeed 86% versus 14%. And the 31% (or 14%) includes many people who voted for the BJP not because they accepted the BJP's vision, and especially its Hindutva politics, but because the Congress, the BJP's economic other, disappointingly failed to meet their needs; there was no credible secular and economically progressive national alternative on offer.

On the other hand, there are millions of ordinary people who vote for Left parties (at least 25 million people voted for Left parties at the last election). The CPM and CPI together have 1.7 million Party members, and mass and class organizations of CPM only have a total membership of 70–80 million men and women. In a large majority of Left-oriented constituencies, Left parties are major forces (in terms of electoral support); they have lost partly because of the faulty electoral system (the first-past-the-post system). The Left parties' vote share in West Bengal is nearly as much as the BJP's vote share at the Center.[47] Apart from Left-oriented unions, there are progressive civil society organizations, including those of artists and writers, associated with the Left. There are secular-minded people inside smaller non-Left parties including the parties that came out of the non-Marxist 'socialist' movement. There are secular-minded people in AAP which is a middle class party, with support from poor people, a party that came out of the grassroots movement against corruption within the government. The class-conscious workers in those parties may provide some support to the secular-democratic front.

Any political project requires intellectual ideas. In spite of a recent Right-wing turn in academia, partly due to the pressure from the Sangh Parivar, India has one of the largest concentrations of progressive intellectuals in the world.

---

47      Even in Tripura where the Left lost (in March 2018) after being in power for decades, 45% of voters voted for the Left.

They are committed to scientific and secular values. They think from the stand-point of the masses. The intellectual power of the Sangh Parivar is nowhere close to the intellectual might of the Left (and, indeed, of the Left and demo-cratic forces). The community of Left scholars based in India, without whom fascistic-communal culture would be stronger than it is, has a point of view on important topics confronting India. The Left's viewpoint on different topics far outshines any comparable point of view of the fascistic movement, which has an anti-intellectual trait.[48] The Right-wing movement simply has no counter-parts of the Left luminaries in India, living or deceased.[49] The force of the Left will be stronger if one includes Left scholars working on India but liv-ing outside of India. Left scholars working on India have produced important analysis of a wide array of issues.[50] There is indeed an intellectual deficit in the Right-wing movement, one it seeks to fill by non-intellectual means: capturing power and forcing their regressive ideas which defy reason and evidence, on people through political and violent means.[51] But the intellectual might of the Left and progressive forces is not enough to fight the fascistic movement, in-cluding its attack on progressive intellectuals and secular education.

## 4      Such a Big Compromise?: Return to Vladimir Lenin

The 'thought experiment' presented in the last few pages, i.e. the idea that the Left should help establish an economically progressive front of secular

---

48    The Italian dictator, Mussolini, in 1934, called for an end to 'intellectualising' and he thought that the 'sterile intellectuals ...are a threat to the nation'; Hitler as well, a year af-ter, exalted the inner voice, heart and faith etc. of the German people over 'hair-splitting intelligence' (quoted in Sarkar, 2016).

49    They include: Aijaz Ahmad (who until recently worked in India), Javeed Alam, Venkatesh Athreya, Amiya Bagchi, Amit Bhaduri, Sumanta Bannerjee, Dipankar Bhattacharya, An-jan Chakrabarti, Neera Chandhoke, Bipan Chandra, C.P. Chandrasekhar, Kunal Chatto-padhyay, A.R. Desai, Jayati Ghosh, A.K. Gopalan, Dipankar Gupta, Irfan Habib, Rohini Hensman, Murzban Jal, P.C. Joshi, K.P. Kannan, Brinda Karat, Prakash Karat, D.D. Kosam-bi, Ashok Mitra, Manoranjan Mohanty, EMS Namboodiripad, K.M. Pannikkar, Prabhat Patnaik, Utsa Patnaik, Archana Prasad, Pradhan Prasad, V.K. Ramachandran, Ashok Rudra, Ranabir Samaddar; Kalyan Sanyal, Sumit Sarkar, Mohit Sen, K.M. Shrimali, R.S. Sharma, Dilip Simeon, Randhir Singh, Romila Thapar, Sitaram Yechuri, Achin Vana-ik, and so on.

50    These include: colonial oppression; colonial resistance; pre-modern history; economic, regional and class inequality; imperialism; economic under-development; agrarian crisis; poverty; technological change; unemployment; gender oppression; caste oppression; eco-logical change; nature of democracy; growing authoritarianism in politics and culture; and nationalism.

51    This is why the Right-wing is relishing the Tripura election result. But an election victory will itself not necessarily deliver an intellectual victory.

bourgeois parties and/or provide tactical (critical) support to it, in order to fight fascistic tendencies, is clearly in contradiction with the principle that the Left should mobilize its own forces, independent of bourgeois forces. After all, if the Left's fight is against capitalism and for socialism, how can it be with any *bourgeois* force? Such a contradiction, potentially, exists even if Left's electoral-political work must be subordinated to its extra-electoral work aimed at raising class consciousness through education and political organization and struggles. Besides, various regional parties have been with the BJP from time to time and have not been consistently secular, and as we have seen non-BJP, non-Left parties have had no problem accepting into their arms leaders from the BJP camp. They are also *bourgeois* parties, pursuing capitalist and neoliberal policies. In fact, regional-bourgeois parties have converging interests with larger-scale bourgeoisie and with the BJP. This is partly because the regional bourgeoisie wishes to benefit from the neo-liberalization that the BJP promotes, including by directly entering into competitive deals with national and global capital. The latter also opens branches in the States, to which regionally-based small-scale capitalists are linked through the supply chains.[52] Also how can the Left have any relation with the Congress, which is a blatantly neoliberal capitalist party, like the BJP is?[53] In the name of protecting secularism and fighting fascism, if the Left fails to defend social-economic rights which are under attack by both BJP and non-BJP parties with near-equal severity, then what would be left of the Left? Has the Left not supported bourgeois coalitions since the 1970s in order to keep the BJP at bay, and in spite of that how has the BJP come to power with an absolute majority? There is also indeed a real danger that workers and peasants affiliated to the Left parties will be politically subordinated to the bourgeois parties who will hold power and with whom the Left will be cooperating, however tactically. If the Left is in an electoral understanding with bourgeois parties to fight communalism, and when these parties pursue policies that attack people's living standards, how and to what extent can the Left counter-attack these policies/parties?

---

52   'It is this changed position of the regional bourgeoisie which has led to the convergence of interests between the BJP, a representative of the big bourgeoisie, and the parties representing the regional bourgeoisie. At the political level, in many states, the regional party is the main rival of the Congress and therefore the alliance with the BJP is expedient as it provides additional support against the Congress in electoral terms and secondly it enables its entry into a coalition government at the Centre which can be utilized to consolidate its position in the state. Secularism is a barrier which can be breached when class and political interests converge' (Karat, 2004: 3).

53   This question is a little problematic on the ground that the Left itself has acted like the neoliberal Congress in the provinces where it has been in power. Geographical scale cannot be an excuse for inconsistency: one cannot advocate for more progressive policies at the national scale and less progressive policies at the provincial scale. Luckily, the Left is rethinking its land acquisition policy.

These and similar questions and their underlying theoretical standpoint cannot be evaded at all in order to fight an imminent danger, the danger of fascistic tendencies. The aim of a theoretical principle is to unpack what is happening and why, and to guide political action. A fight to abolish landlordism must be conducted in such a way that the masses (workers and poor peasants) are mobilized independent of the capitalist class as it has lost its anti-landlord fighting qualities, given its fear of the working class. As a general principle, the fight against the capitalist class relation must be conducted in a way that is independent of any fraction of the capitalist class (e.g. progressive or national, etc.). The fight against fascistic tendencies must obey the same principle. But given the serious threat that the fascistic movement poses to the communist movement against capitalism and to common people's democratic rights and living standards, could one argue that the fight against the fascistic movement must be a part of the fight to create the conditions for the fight against capitalism and therefore must be a part of the fight against capitalism. I do think that in a long and winding journey towards socialism, if the Left is not to remain mainly an abstentionist political propaganda machine or an organization with only negligible ability to influence national political affairs, one cannot automatically reject all possibilities of conditional and revolutionary temporary compromise with non-Left non-fascistic forces. This is so especially when the subjective forces of the Left have lagged behind the progress of bourgeois reactionary forces and when one enemy is holding a gun and another is holding several dosages of poison, both of which can kill the toiling masses and their political movement. But what does such compromise as a political practice really mean? To answer this question, one must ask another question: what 'alternative' *theoretical* standpoint does that *practice* presuppose? More specifically, is a temporary compromise with some secular-democratic bourgeois forces justifiable? And to answer this question, we need to read about that practice of temporary revolutionary compromise from someone who is, arguably, the Marxist theoretician and Marxist politician *par excellence* of the 20th century. This is Vladimir Lenin whose statues, as mentioned earlier, fascistic forces brought down immediately the BJP's first-time win in Tripura, dislodging the Left and this shows what is going to come. Let's briefly consider what I will call *Lenin's theory of temporary revolutionary compromise*.

### 4.1    Definition and Typology of Compromise

In an article entitled, 'On Compromises', Lenin (1917) says this: 'The term compromise in politics implies the surrender of certain demands, the renunciation of part of one's demands, by agreement with another party'. In thinking about any compromise, Lenin (1920) says in *"Left-wing" communism: an infantile disorder*, 'the greatest efforts are necessary for a proper assessment of the actual

Temporary revolutionary compromise

Forced        Voluntary                          Trade union      Political (including,
                                                 or economic      electoral) struggle
                                                 struggle

                    With the main        With petty-bourgeois-
                    class enemy          democratic parties
                    (the bourgeoisie)

FIGURE 13.6 Types of temporary revolutionary compromise
          SOURCE: AUTHOR (BASED ON LENIN'S TEXTS)

character of this or that "compromise". Such an assessment will be helped by
the acknowledgment that compromises are of different types (Figure 13.6
above). From one vantage point, compromises are forced or they can be voluntary. The first type – forced compromise – is a compromise that is caused by
objective conditions but that does not minimize devotion to carry on class
struggle: 'compromises are often unavoidably forced upon a fighting party by
circumstances' (ibid.). The voluntary type of compromise is one that is caused
by the action of traitors to the working class. Lenin eloquently explains the difference between objective and voluntary compromises:

> Every proletarian – as a result of the conditions of the mass struggle and
> the acute intensification of class antagonisms he lives among – sees the
> difference between a compromise enforced by objective conditions (such
> as lack of strike funds, no outside support, starvation and exhaustion) – a
> compromise which in no way minimises the revolutionary devotion and
> readiness to carry on the struggle on the part of the workers who have
> agreed to such a compromise – and, on the other hand, a compromise by
> traitors who try to ascribe to objective causes their self-interest ... their
> cowardice, desire to toady to the capitalists, and readiness to yield to
> intimidation, sometimes to persuasion, sometimes to sops, and some-
> times to flattery from the capitalists.
>
> LENIN, 1920

Voluntary compromises cannot be allowed by the Left but compromises that are imposed by objective conditions such as lack of funds or outside support (for a local struggle) or the relative weakness of the subjective force relative to the enemy's strength, can be, *under certain conditions*.[54] From the second vantage point, the compromise may be with the main class enemy, i.e. the bourgeoisie, and or with 'nearest adversaries', the petty-bourgeois-democratic parties. And, from the third vantage point, compromises can be in trade union struggle (economic struggle) or in politics (political struggle) (more on this below). Compromises in economic struggle can be objective or voluntary, so can compromises in political struggle. Explaining compromise in politics, Lenin (1920) says:

> In politics, where it is sometimes a matter of extremely complex relations ... between classes and parties, very many cases will arise that will be much more difficult than the question of a legitimate "compromise" in a strike or a treacherous "compromise" by a strike-breaker, treacherous leader, etc.

### 4.2    *Nature of Temporary Revolutionary Compromise in Politics*

We will focus on compromise in politics. In the course of the struggle to transcend the capitalist society and establish a new, genuinely democratic society, circumstances force the Left to make compromises in the political sphere. Therefore, it is important to bear in mind that: 'The task of a truly revolutionary party is not to declare that it is impossible to renounce all compromises' (ibid.). Engels says against the Blanquist communards, it is mistaken to believe that 'we want to attain our goal without stopping at intermediate stations, without any compromises, which only postpone the day of victory and prolong the period of slavery' (quoted in Lenin, 1920).[55]

Lenin was scathing in his criticisms of some German communists who thought that 'All compromise with other parties ... any policy of manoeuvring and compromise must be emphatically rejected' (ibid.). To launch class struggle, which is protracted and complex, against the bourgeoisie, nationally and globally, 'to renounce in advance any change of tack, or any utilisation of a

---

54   Further, as Lenin (1920) explains in *Leftwing communism*: 'In the practical questions that arise in the politics of any particular or specific historical moment, it is important to single out those which display the principal type of intolerable and treacherous compromises, such as embody an opportunism that is fatal to the revolutionary class, and to exert all efforts to explain them and combat them'.

55   So, 'It would be absurd to formulate a recipe or general rule to suit all cases. One must use one's own brains and be able to find one's bearings in each particular instance' (ibid.).

conflict of interests (even if temporary) among one's enemies, or any conciliation or compromise with possible allies (even if they are temporary, unstable, vacillating or conditional allies) – is that not ridiculous in the extreme?'
(ibid.).

Echoing Lenin's point that the fight against capitalism requires some temporary agreements and a degree of principled unity among proletarian groups,
Trotsky (1933a), whose views on the topic we began the chapter with, says:

> No successes would be possible without temporary agreements, for the
> sake of fulfilling immediate tasks, among various sections, organizations,
> and groups of the proletariat. Strikes, trade unions, journals, parliamen-
> tary elections, street demonstrations, demand that the split be bridged in
> practice from time to time as the need arises; that is, they demand an *ad
> hoc* united front, even if it does not always take on the form of one. In the
> first stages of a movement, unity arises episodically and spontaneously
> from below, but when the masses are accustomed to fighting through
> their organizations, unity must also be established at the top.[56]

---

56    Here are some examples of compromise Trotsky gives: 'The Jewish bourgeoisie in Czarist
      Russia represented an extremely frightened and demoralized part of the entire Russian
      bourgeoisie. And yet, insofar as the pogroms of the Black Hundreds, which were in the
      main directed against the Jewish poor, also hit the bourgeoisie, the latter was forced to
      defend itself. To be sure, it did not show any remarkable bravery on this field either. But
      due to the danger hanging over their heads, the liberal Jewish bourgeoisie, for example,
      collected considerable sums for the arming of revolutionary workers and students. In this
      manner, a temporary practical agreement was arrived at between the most revolutionary
      workers, who were prepared to fight with guns in hand, and the most frightened group of
      the bourgeoisie, which had got into a scrape' (Trotsky, 1932f).
         The Bolsheviks more than once proposed to the Mensheviks and Social Revolutionar-
      ies in 1917: 'Take the power, we will support you against the bourgeoisie if it should resist'
      (Trotsky, 1932g). During July and August 1917, Kerensky, then head of the government,
      was in fact fulfilling the program of Kornilov, the commander-in-chief of the army. ...On
      August 26, Kornilov broke with Kerensky because of the latter's vacillation, and threw his
      army against Petrograd. The status of the Bolshevik Party was semi-legal. Its leaders from
      Lenin down were either hiding underground or committed to prison...These persecu-
      tions emanated from Kerensky's government... What course did the Bolshevik Party take?
      Not for an instant did it hesitate to conclude a practical alliance to fight against Kornilov
      with its jailers – Kerensky, ... etc. Everywhere committees for revolutionary defense were
      organized, into which the Bolsheviks entered as a minority. This did not hinder the Bol-
      sheviks from assuming the leading role: in agreements projected for revolutionary mass
      action, the most thoroughgoing and the boldest revolutionary party stands to gain always.
      The Bolsheviks were in the front ranks; they smashed down the barriers blocking them
      from the Menshevik workers and especially from the Social Revolutionary soldiers, and
      carried them along in their wake (Trotsky, 1932j).

### 4.3    Why Is Temporary Revolutionary Compromise Necessary and Possible?

Let us consider the matter of temporary compromise from the standpoint of: nature of the class enemy and nature of the working class.

The matter of class has many aspects, which exist at different levels (Das, 2017). Class interests exist at one level. Their political representation by parties exists at another. What happens at the level of the political representation of objective class interests has some autonomy relative to, and therefore, cannot be reduced to, the level at which objective class interests exist. The class enemy of the working class, and indeed every class, is both unitary and fragmented in terms of its interests and consciousness, etc.

In so far as all bourgeois parties support capitalists and landlords, they are the same class enemy for the Left. But these parties support the ruling classes in *different* ways. Some parties – like some sections of ruling class – may be more secular-minded than others.[57] Some may be *slightly* more pro-poor or pro-worker, pro-peasant, than others. In terms of the political representation of ruling class interests, there are two facts. First, different interests of the ruling class (with its multiple fractions) are represented by different parties.[58] Second, these parties, to remain in electoral competition, which is their self-interest, if not for any basic *principle*, will represent the given interests of the ruling class differently, and in ways that are conflictual, within limits.[59] Some of these ways may partially overlap with the Left's agenda (e.g. an increase in the wage) than other ways. These two facts concerning the political representation of the ruling class constitute an objective reason why temporary compromise by Left is *possible*:

> The more powerful enemy can be vanquished only by exerting the utmost effort, and by the most thorough, careful, attentive, skilful and *obligatory* use of any, even the smallest, *rift between the enemies..., any conflict of interests among ....* the various groups or types of bourgeoisie ..., and

---

57    Consider how Gurucharan Das, an organic intellectual of the capitalist class, is wanting that a blatantly pro-capitalist party which is secular be established.

58    More generally, every class is represented by a party, or, more commonly, by a set of parties, because of internal subjective and objective differences within a class. A given class has different class-strata: while at one level their interests are common, at another, they have conflicts, which are reflected at the level of political representation of class interests by parties.

59    These limits mean the following: all parties must support capitalism and private property, and within these limits, specific political parties can pursue their interests that may be relatively autonomous of ruling class interests, and sometimes may even slightly deviate from ruling class interests (in profit-making, etc.) in the short term.

also by taking advantage of any, even the smallest, opportunity of winning a mass ally, even though this ally is *temporary, vacillating, unstable,
unreliable and conditional.*

LENIN, 1920; italics added

Lenin (1920) warns: 'Those who do not understand this reveal a failure to understand even the smallest grain of Marxism, of modern scientific socialism *in
general*' (ibid.; italics added). Once again we must remind ourselves about
Marx's point about the need to prove truth in practice.[60] And in line with Marx,
Lenin (1920) says this:

> Those who have not proved *in practice*, over a fairly considerable period
> of time and in fairly varied political situations, their ability to apply this
> truth [i.e. the truth about the need for temporary revolutionary political
> compromise] in practice have not yet learned to help the revolutionary
> class in its struggle to emancipate all toiling humanity from the exploit-
> ers. And this applies equally to the period *before* and *after* the proletariat
> has won political power. (Parenthesis added)

Let's turn to the nature of the working class in relation to the need for compromise. The working class is potentially the most revolutionary agent. There is no
Marxist party/movement without this class. No anti-capitalist revolution is
possible without this class, apart from this class, over the head of this class, or
with a substitute for this class and its organization. Yet, although it is an objective reality, the working class does fall short, ideologically and politically. This
class is deeply politically divided, in part because of the uneven level of consciousness within this class. The level of class consciousness and political pre-
paredness of the working class has to be much improved; that the largest trade
union is the one led by the fascist organization (RSS) indicates this. The working class's consciousness is shaped by the ways in which capitalism operates on
the basis of competition, individualism, commodity fetishism, etc. It is also
shaped by the ideas and interests of non-proletarian classes within capitalism.
As Lenin (1920) says:

> Capitalism would not be capitalism if the proletariat *pur sang* were not
> surrounded by a large number of exceedingly motley types...'. [These

---

60      'The question whether objective truth can be attributed to human thinking is not a ques-
        tion of theory but is a practical question. Man must [ultimately] prove the truth – i.e. the
        reality and power, the this-sidedness of his thinking in practice' (Marx, 1845; parenthesis
        added).

types exist] intermediate between the proletarian and the semi-proletarian (who earns his livelihood in part by the sale of his labour-power), between the semi-proletarian and the small peasant (and petty artisan, handicraft worker and small master in general), between the small peasant and the middle peasant, and so on, and if the proletariat itself were not divided into more developed and less developed strata, if it were not divided according to *territorial origin, trade, sometimes according to religion*, and so on. (Italics added)

This is especially true in countries such as India experiencing belated capitalist development.

Fascism – the fascistic tendency – operates not in the abstract two-class mode of capitalist society, but in a society where there are different classes and class-strata between capitalists and workers. As Trotsky says: fascism – or in our times, the fascistic movement – penetrates the proletariat from below (through the unemployed) and from above (through the middle class people such as salaried employees, etc.). The political implication, as Lenin says, is this:

From all this follows the necessity, the absolute necessity, for the Communist Party, the vanguard of the proletariat, its class-conscious section, to resort to changes of tack, to *conciliation and compromises with the various groups of proletarians, with the various parties of the workers and small masters.*

Ibid.; italics added

So: temporary compromises *in the electoral sphere* are objectively *necessary* because the working masses are divided and not class conscious (enough) and concomitantly, the Left is relatively weak, at a given juncture. Compromises are *possible* because there are conflicts of interests within the economic elite and within the political elite (i.e. among various parties).

In line with Lenin's theory, I would argue that compromises in the electoral sphere, which do pose ideological and political risks (of subordinating workers and peasants to bourgeois forces), are justified *only when* the following criteria are met (making the temporary agreement as a part of the revolutionary struggle highly conditional).

First, compromises are unavoidable or forced by conditions (e.g. Left is weak relative to, say, fascistic forces, so it needs allies in some cases). The compromises that the Left can allow cannot be because of Left leaders' 'cowardice, desire to toady to the capitalists, and readiness to yield to intimidation, sometimes to persuasion, sometimes to sops, and sometimes to flattery from the capitalists' (Lenin, 1920). Second: compromises, ultimately, contribute to the political project of raising the level of consciousness of the masses and advancing the goal of the communist struggle against (a) capitalism's adverse consequences for the masses, and against (b) the capitalist class relation as such. As Lenin says, tactics of temporary compromises are applied only 'to *raise* – not lower – the *general* level of proletarian class-consciousness, revolutionary spirit, and ability to fight and win' (Lenin, 1920). Third, Left forces maintain their organizational and ideological independence versus non-left parties and movements. The principle of independence must permeate the spirit of united front action:

> [Y]ou must never dare to merge, mix, or combine your own party organization with an alien one, even though the latter be most 'sympathetic' today. Undertake no such steps as lead directly or indirectly, openly or maskedly, to the subordination of your party to other parties, or to organizations of other classes, or constrict the freedom of your own agitation, or your responsibility, even if only in part, for the political line of other parties.
>
> TROTSKY, 1928

The Left will always have the right to criticize, and to politically go against (mobilize its classes against) its temporary allies when their policies attack living conditions of ordinary people.

Fourth, the Left's *dominant* focus is on extra-parliamentary mobilization, including for economic concessions, of workers and peasants, and *not* electoral battles. The point of temporary agreement is not to resort to confine class struggle only to the parliamentary/electoral sphere. 'A parliamentary agreement against fascist predominance in the ... [parliaments] etc., would constitute merely one component part of' the fight against fascism or fascistic tendencies. 'Naturally the Communist Party would prefer to resolve the whole question at one blow outside of parliament. But preferences alone are not sufficient where the forces are lacking' (Trotsky, 1932g). So:

> Compromises are admissible and, under certain conditions, obligatory. The whole question lies in what aim the compromise shall serve; how it looks to the masses; what its limits are. To confine the compromise to the [parliamentary fora], ... means to sink completely into parliamentary cretinism.
>
> TROTSKY, 1932g[61]

---

61    Trotsky continues: 'The situation is completely different when the [communist] party sets itself the task of the systematic and planned struggle for the Social Democratic workers on the basis of the united-front policy' (Trotsky, 1932g).

Once again, 'The task of a truly revolutionary party is not to declare that it is impossible to renounce all compromises, but to be able, *through all compromises*, when they are unavoidable, to remain true to its principles, to its class, to its revolutionary purpose, to its task of paving the way for revolution and educating the mass of the people for victory in the revolution' (Lenin, 1917).[62] The point of political compromise is not to arrive at, and settle for, a capitalist society that is slightly tolerable and that just needs to be managed by the Left forces forever. The compromise in question here is revolutionary compromise (compromise as a part of, and with the purpose of, advancing long-term goals of class struggle), like Luxemburg's revolutionary reforms or reforms as the 'means of the class struggle', whose goal is revolution (Luxemburg, 2009: 129), the compromise that is *temporarily* necessitated by the force of *circumstances* relative to the strength of the Left forces, in order to advance the long-term *revolutionary* goal, the goal of transcending capitalism and not to help sustain capitalism *sans* fascistic tendencies. Therefore: 'Naïve and quite inexperienced people imagine that the permissibility of compromise *in general* is sufficient to obliterate any distinction between opportunism...and revolutionary Marxism, or communism'. In fact, 'the entire history of Bolshevism, both before and after the October Revolution, is *full* of instances of changes of tack, conciliatory tactics and compromises with other parties, including bourgeois parties!' (Lenin, 1920). Lenin says that

> It is entirely a matter of *knowing how* to apply these tactics in order to *raise* – not lower – the *general* level of proletarian class-consciousness, revolutionary spirit, and ability to fight and win.
>
> LENIN, 1920

Fifth, any temporary compromise with less revolutionary forces must be mindful of the usefulness of the united front tactic. Here is Trotsky on this point:

> Assuming a defensive position means a policy of closing ranks with the majority of the ... working class and forming a united front with the Social Democratic and nonparty workers against the fascist threat.
>
> TROTSKY, 1930

---

62   'To agree, for instance, to participate in the Third and Fourth Dumas was a compromise, a temporary renunciation of revolutionary demands. But this was a compromise absolutely forced upon us, for the balance of forces made it impossible for us for the time being to conduct a mass revolutionary struggle, and in order to prepare this struggle over a long period we *had* to be able to work even from *inside* such a "pigsty"' (Lenin, 1917).

And the task of such a united front is to fight fascism and it is also 'the task of the systematic and planned struggle for the Social Democratic workers on the basis of the united-front policy' (Trotsky, 1932g).

However, there should not be a united front fetishism.

> we in no way advocate lapsing into a united-front fetishism. An agreement ... remains in effect so long as it serves the practical goal for which it was concluded. If the reformists begin to curb or to sabotage the movement the Communists must always put to themselves the question: is it not time to tear up the agreement and to lead the masses further under our own banner?
>
> TROTSKY, 1932g

So, a temporary compromise may be struck by the Marxist Left only when these conditions are met. Of course, what form that compromise will take is a different matter. Now, one might assess the relevance of Lenin's theory of temporary compromise for the Indian conjuncture where there is *right now* a fascistic mortal threat *to the very existence* of the actually-existing Left movement: note the BJP's aim is to see a 'Left-free India', 'Communist-free India'. Note also that the largest trade union belongs to the fascistic RSS.

The idea of United Front applies, originally, to the idea of the unity of masses, of workers. 'The united front is to unite the Communist and Social Democratic working masses [and non-party workers] and not to patch up an agreement with political groups that are without the masses' (Trotsky, 1932j).

India does *not* have this conjuncture. The equivalents of Germany's social democratic party, or of the communist party (which almost led a revolution in Germany), do not exist in India, thanks to the weakness of the various Marxist streams, including the Far Left. The existing communist parties are effectively social-democratic parties (see Heller, 1995; Chakrabarty, 2015). And, there is no social democratic party, although there may be elements of social democratic *policy* in multiple bourgeois parties that are primarily driven by bourgeois-political formations' need to obtain votes, which, in turn, provide them access to the state to be used in the interests of the bourgeois strata and in the interests of the bourgeois political elite. Workers are not concentrated in working class parties. The working class parties – the communist parties – are not strong enough to meet the challenge of fascistic tendencies on their own. The majority of working class men and women of different castes and religions, do not belong to a communist party or to a non-existing social democratic party, but are members and supporters of bourgeois parties, including bourgeois-fascistic parties. The bourgeois parties all have workers as their members but that does not make them workers' – social-democratic – parties. This explains why it is that in pursuit of a short-term goal (i.e. electoral defeat of fascistic forces), a united front of communist parties and groups and of non-Party-affiliated Marxist groups and individuals, on a tactial basis, is needed. These parties may enter into some understanding with the parties of small scale producers (or, in Lenin's words 'small masters'). Any agreement with the Congress, the traditional party of Indian capitalist class, should be avoided in the fight against fascistic forces, except perhaps in an extremely exceptional case. It must be immediately said, however, that whether it is the Congress or the parties of small masters, they are thoroughly compromised as far as the fight for secularism and democratic rights is concerned, and therefore any agreement with them by the Left must be a rare occasion.

One might argue that there are some objective conditions for some electoral cooperation among Left and non-Left secular forces representing small-scale masters not only because of an imminent existential threat from fascistic forces to the Left, but also because of potential and actual conflicts between the BJP and the non-Left forces. In liberal democracy, there is electoral competition among bourgeois parties, representing interests of bigger capitalists and regional capitalists, and landowners. A non-BJP party may not necessarily be genuinely interested in protecting secularism. To merely exist as a party,[63] it must compete with the BJP. To compete with the BJP and to represent the bourgeois interests almost like the way the BJP does because it is also a bourgeois party, it must politically differentiate itself from the BJP. If secularism is not the basis – or not the sole basis – for differentiation, then what (else) might it be? The answer is: to the extent that regional parties seek to represent peasants and small-scale property owners ('small masters' in Lenin's words), the BJP's neoliberal policies – like such policies of the Congress – are adversely affecting these strata, creating, among other things, agrarian crisis and farmers' suicide. The BJP's major weakness is this: it can satisfy the need for a religion and for a sense of belonging to a Hindu rastra, but it cannot feed people with Hinduism, temple-building and mosque-destroying. Even to go to a temple, one needs to have eaten or one needs to eat soon after the visit! One needs shelter, education, healthcare, affordable transportation, leisure, a good environment, and freedom from fear of being killed or hurt for one's religious and other view. With its blatantly free market pro-business policies, the BJP cannot

---

63    Note that in spite of all the talk about neoliberalism, it is the case that being in the government and being able to use governmental power is a source of immense amount of income and wealth, earned by helping the business class make money at the expense of the masses and indeed the nation as a whole.

satisfy these needs. The BJP's policies are, and will be, depriving ordinary people of what they need to live. And it is the conflict between what the BJP is and what people need, and therefore, the conflict between the BJP and other parties that are reasonably secular and that may seek to somewhat address people's issues in part to distinguish themselves from the BJP, that can be, and should be made use of, by the Left.[64] One should also consider the fact that there is some potential conflict within the big bourgeoisie in relation to the fascistic threat. Through fascistic forces such as the BJP, the ruling class keeps the masses *divided* against its class rule. The BJP's right-wing economic policies help the big business. But the ruling class's support for the BJP beyond a point can potentially backfire. The BJP's majoritarian communalism can lead to minority communalism of Sikhs, Muslims, etc. This can then undermine the territorial unity of the nation (e.g. a large national market, etc.) and thus go against the economic interest of the ruling class.[65] Besides, communal-fascistic violence can lead to an enormous loss of property, including capitalist property. A proper business environment requires a politically calm situation. So potential adverse implications of the BJP's communalism, in a situation where there is not yet a fascistic state that can completely destroy any protest against fascistic tendencies, can lead to some support from the ruling class, for its traditional party (the Congress). Growing disenchantment against communal strife and attack on living standards caused by the fascistic tendencies led and aided by the BJP is also causing a part of the 'molecular' anger of the masses to be channelized towards the Congress already (as seen in the by-elections in 2018 and in

---

64   Support from the Left may include: not contesting against the non-BJP secular parties in areas of Left's electoral weakness, and outside support in the parliament to keep the BJP outs. Yet, the Left parties must tell the workers and peasants that such support is highly conditional and that all parties, BJP or not, are their targets, when it comes to the livelihood issues, because all these parties, more or less, pursue (neoliberal-)capitalist policies and that even with respect to democratic rights and secularism, the so-called non-BJP parties are vacillating allies.

65   'The ruling class…realises that to keep India, with its enormous size and diversity, united, such a communal agenda would not serve the purpose. The geographical unity of India needs to be maintained for the ruling classes in order to consolidate and strengthen its class rule. A communal divide like what the BJP is mounting today, also justifies the ideological foundations of separatist movements like Khalisthan etc. This can only act contrary to the interests of the leadership of the Indian ruling classes in their effort to maintain the geographical unity of the country…. Thus, we find representatives of the big business-like Tatas coming out openly against such communal violence'. It is also the case that 'the ruling classes exercise their class rule through agents, which are political parties. When an avowedly communal party makes a concerted bid for state power sections of the bourgeoisie themselves will vacillate and some will extend support to it' (Yechuri, 1993: 14–15).

the Gujarat elections in late 2017), sharpening its conflict with the BJP. In other words, a certain amount of conflict within the ruling class and within the sphere of bourgeois politics where its interests are represented, can create a limited potential for a *temporary* and *conditional* Left compromise with bourgeois forces, in order to fight fascistic tendencies and remove a major obstacle to the Left movement. But whether that potential will be realized by the Left and in what form depends. I will repeat that the Left's main approach to the fight against the fascistic tendencies cannot be the electoral approach, including making temporary electoral compromises with non-BJP bourgeois parties.

Note that the secular-bourgeois forces' aim is less to protect capitalism against the proletarian struggle at this juncture, and more to preserve a democratic form of the state of the capitalist class, thus there is a contradiction between the fascistic sections of the bourgeois political formation and the bourgeois political parties that are a little more democratic and secular, a contradiction that can be exploited by the Left. It is true that the smaller bourgeois parties, and the big bourgeois parties (the Congress) and the BJP are not united now but they will be united when there is a revolutionary situation (and in fact, they were all – including the BJP – united when it came to supporting the legislation to approve of India's subordination to imperialism). But that does not mean that they always and under all conditions share the same ideas and engage in same practices. They are all similar (because they are all bourgeois) and there are differences among them because they are different in terms of how to implement the bourgeois economic-political and cultural agenda. The situation resonates, to some extent, with the one Trotsky describes:

> Just now their interests [political parties'] diverge. At the *given* moment the question that is posed before the [democratic parties] ... is not so much one of defending the foundations of capitalist society against proletarian revolution as of defending the semi-parliamentarian bourgeois, system against Fascism [or fascistic tendencies]. The refusal to make use of this antagonism would be an act of gross stupidity.
>
> TROTSKY, 1932i; parentheses added

But how exactly to make use of that antagonism is a different matter.

## 5    Conclusion

The fascistic-nationalist movement is not only profoundly pro-capitalist but also is it shamelessly subordinating the interests of toiling masses to imperialism. This is the real treachery, and this is the real treason, as far as the toiling majority are concerned. The common people who really love their country as a part of the family of nations and who are mistakenly listening to their communal-fascistic misleaders must reflect on this cruel fact. As the most consistent supporters of principles of democracy and secularism and with its unique commitment to the welfare of the toiling masses, the Left must mobilize the basic classes (workers, and small-scale, non-exploiting, produc-ers) to (a) fight for democratic rights and against fascistic tendencies, (b) fight for significant improvements in conditions of living, on the basis of immediate and transitional demands, *as a part of* – and *within the overall framework* of – the fight for a socialist society.[66]

The rise of the BJP represents the crisis not only of bourgeois economics but also of bourgeois politics: the bourgeois political-economic system, and there-fore, the bourgeois ruling class, has, simply, failed to secure not only social rights but also democratic rights, including rights of religious minorities. So the blame for the current situation must be at the door not only of the BJP and these forces, but also the bourgeoisie itself, or the bourgeois system as a whole. That is why the fascistic threat is a class project, and not merely a political-cultural project. The threat exists in the following context: while the ruling class is losing its right to be the ruling class, the masses are not yet ready to say 'we cannot take it anymore', although some stirring in their consciousness is apparent. This contradiction is causing the BJP itself to be contradictory. The BJP's major contradictions are structural in that they are inter-related and are parts of the capitalist class system in India.

First, there is a contradiction between its promises (which are secular lies) and what it can deliver to the people, given its blatantly right-wing character. Politics of dividing and deceiving the masses is the DNA of class society.[67] And, fascism – or fascistic tendency – as the most extreme form of this politics – is

---

66    This framework is opposed to the framework within which the fight for a socialist society
      is postponed indefinitely, a framework that contradicts the idea that the humanity's fun-
      damental problems are caused by capitalist *class relations* and cannot be significantly
      resolved as long as these relations exist.

67    Class society is a society that is defined by this: 'Wherever a part of society possesses the
      monopoly of the means of production' and therefore 'the worker, free or not free, must
      add to the labour-time necessary for his [her] own maintenance an extra quantity of
      labour-time in order to produce the means of subsistence for the owners of the means
      of production' (Marx, 1977: 344), and (partly) as a result of this, the needs of the majority
      remain unmet, which is why one social group (Hindus) mistakenly blames another social
      group (Muslims) for its miseries.

in the DNA of capitalism as a class society.[68] To hide its right-wing character, the BJP has to make promises which objectively contradict what it can deliver. Common people should critically reflect on the false promises of the party-in-power supported by fascistic forces, and on the dismal record of its government on development, democracy and governance. This failure is not coincidental. It is a *necessary* product given the right-wing, pro-business, pro-market, government which has been implanted on the poisonous soil of putrid communalism. Both the soil and the plant are bad for the nation and for the world at large.

Second, given rising economic inequality, and given the failure of all forms of the government to meet people's needs, the contradiction between political equality among all citizens, and economic inequality, is becoming more and more stark, a contradiction that is signified by the BJP embodying the fascistic movement. The contradiction is being sought to be resolved not by reducing economic inequality but by undermining the nominal political equality (i.e. by not treating citizens from different religious and other backgrounds as equal).

The nature of the BJP's fascistic tendencies highlights the vulnerability of bourgeois democracy. India's democratic character can no longer be taken for granted. Therefore, the rise of the BJP can potentially create fertile ground for more radical struggle against the bourgeois system itself: there is not only a contradiction between the BJP and the masses but also between the system as a whole and the masses. The genuine and long-term resolution of these contradictions requires the removal of the system. The situation points to the need to fight not only against the fascistic and anti-secular character of bourgeois politics in India and elsewhere. It also points to the following fact: on the basis of the fight against the right-wing politics/political economy, a fight has to be launched against the very logics of capitalist society, which are behind such right-wing politics and political economy. This is as true for India as it is for all the countries where fascistic forces are rising.

Democratic politics and fascistic politics in societies dominated by bourgeois mode of production and exchange are both forms of bourgeois class rule. If ultra-right politics, like its more-democratic variant, is the political intervention of the ruling class to cope with its own crisis, then arriving at a different politics requires the political intervention of the masses of workers and petty producers, and their organic intellectuals. It is only their struggle, launched on

---

68   If politics of division and deception of the masses is the DNA of the capitalist class society, then fascism is the nucleotides, the molecules that constitute the DNA.

the basis of sound theory and with the assistance of democratically-organized, multi-scalar, anti-capitalist, socialist, revolutionary organizations, that can ensure that every country will meet the basic needs of every man, woman and child of all religions, castes, races and locations, where a culture of democracy and of mutual love and compassion among the ordinary toiling people prevails.

Controlled by a Right-wing party, the BJP government, whether now or in the future, is not, and will not be, in sync with the political culture of a country, where the vast majority of its men and women of different religions and castes do not have the means to satisfy their basic needs and where there is a deeply-felt desire for democracy and secularism. The majority of Indians are religious. But they do not necessarily favor the political-sectarian use of religion to make one group hate another. They do not necessarily favor politicians who spread religious hatred for political gain. However contradictory and utopian religious ideas are, all religions propagate 'spiritually' uplifting ideas, even if it is the case that many religious ideas do contribute to the reproduction of unjust social arrangements. Religious ideas express, among other things, people's desire to be much better than what they normally are and what they can be. Religious ideas teach people to be 'spiritual', generous, loving and kind-hearted, so even if people are religious, they can oppose the misuse of religion for narrow, divisive political gains undermining the secular-democratic character of the country.[69] Arguably, this is why there is a high level of resentment against the BJP among a large proportion of Hindu voters. This suggests that there is opposition to the Hindu nationalist party's attempt to *unite* all Hindus to garner their votes on the basis of religion and on the basis of the utterly false notion that Hindus are under threat from Muslims.

Common people must ask, and the Left and progressive forces must encourage them to ask: who is it that fears the citizens united to fight for their rights against the economic elite? Is it not the case that what is under attack is

---

69    Calling for secularization the social sphere is important but it is limited. As long as there are reasons to be religious, people will be religious and when that happens, political use of religion is few steps away. 'The abolition of religion as the *illusory* happiness of the people is the demand for their *real* happiness. To call on them to give up their illusions about their condition is to call on them to *give up a condition that requires illusions*. The criticism of religion is, therefore, *in embryo, the criticism of that vale of tears* of which religion is the *halo*. ...Religion is only the illusory Sun which revolves around man as long as he does not revolve around himself' (Marx, 1843).

neither Hinduism from Islam, nor India as a nation from neighboring countries, but 'the nation of ordinary people' who work for a living as wage-earners and/or as petty-producers, and whose most basic needs are not met? Are those elements attacking this nation of common people not the economic elite, which controls society's resources using them for their own profit, and which is supported by the BJP's politicians and the pliant officers, and by their propagandists in academia and the media? Is there not more common ground among them (wage-earners and among small-scale producers of different religions and castes) than there are differences among them?

People must ask: whose interests are the politicians who spread religious hatred serving? How will religious hatred solve the country's major problems? How does religious hatred or a feeling of hyper-nationalism based on Hindu identity, help a society address problems of unemployment, poverty, inequality, caste- and gender-based oppression, environmental pollution, natural resources depletion, the country's subjugation to powerful foreign powers, localised semi-feudal oppression, agrarian distress, lack of affordable healthcare, housing and education? How can these problems be caused by the fact that some people are Hindus and others are not? Is it or is it not the case that: when political leaders and big business fail to solve people's major problems, they seek to divert people's attention *from* such failure *towards* non-issues by using religion, myths, false nationalism and so on, to divide the people? Is it not true that weakening the unity of common people diverts them from their fight against the business elite and the government such as the one led by BJP? Why is it that the right-wing government feels threatened by any attempt to forge a unity of secular political forces, prompting it to use undemocratic measures against opposition forces? Those in the business world cannot also be allowed to maintain their 'silence': they must be asked by the masses this question: do they or do they not support the forces which are communal and which spread sectarian hatred and which repress any force of dissent?

Not only must one ask questions, and ordinary people *are* already asking questions, such as the ones posed above. They must also *fight* to deepen and defend their democratic rights, including the right to practice any religion, to eat any food, to engage in any occupation or to love anyone. They must also fight for economic security. And in fighting for their democratic rights and economic security, they must be conscious of what *binds* them: what binds them, irrespective of their different religions, is the fact that their democratic rights (*including* secularism) and their right to a decent livelihood, *are* under attack by this government, while the rich elite in control of big business and their right-wing lackeys (hangers-on) in academia and media are having *achhe din*

(good times). The BJP and its authoritarian government, and all the reactionary forces on the ground supporting them, must continue to face the collective
and democratic might of the toiling masses and progressive intellectuals.
There is, and there can be, no force that is more powerful than the united force
of the organized and class-conscious workers and small-scale producers. If
they withdraw their labor from the farms, factories, offices, laboratories,
schools and universities, or if they do not bring the products of their labor to
the market, or if the unemployed, demanding decent jobs, start a non-cooperation movement by not only boycotting elections but also stopping the movement of commodities on roads and railway lines, then the system is in big
trouble. It is time that the masses of India (and of South Asia) begin to ask
fundamental questions about what kind of society they are living in, what kind
of society they wish to live in, and how to get there. If the Hindutva-nationalistic
forces are pitting the Hindu-dominated India against the Muslim-dominated
Pakistan and treat Indian Muslims as de facto Pakistanis and consider Muslim
immigrants from other countries as second-class citizens, then the workers
and peasants of India and Pakistan and Bangladesh must fight together against
the fascistic forces and against their ruling classes and not allow themselves to
be divided along the lines of religion and nation.

In struggling against the regime and in the *current conjuncture*, what is
clearly needed, and what needs to be demanded by common people, *as a
minimum*, therefore, is a government that (a) respects the rights of religious
minorities, low castes, women, and children, and that respects the general
democratic rights of the ordinary citizen, both in words, speeches, and in actual practice, and (b) *simultaneously* prioritizes meeting the basic needs of the
bottom 60–80% in a sustainable and long-term manner *over* ensuring achhe
din for the class (the business class) which already has *achhe din*. But the current right-wing government is *not* the government that can do what the masses
need. It cannot do what the nation – the nation of workers and peasants and
small-scale entrepreneurs – needs. The type of the government that there is
can give neither political democracy and social peace nor can it ensure that
people have *daal* (lentils) and *chawal* (rice), and health-care and education
and housing, etc. It must face the widest possible united opposition from political parties and people's movements that value principles of reason, democracy, secularism and welfare.

A struggle of the masses can start spontaneously. But to have some success,
it needs political guidance. This is what the party of workers provides. In the
fight against fascistic tendencies, which represent the extreme form of
capitalist tyranny, the Left must play a leading role. It must dominantly focus

on non-electoral activities aimed at class-based mobilization of workers and small-scale producers, much more than electoral activities, against fascistic forces. The Left should have its own mobilizational work: apart from mobilizing people against fascism, the Left must mobilize people (a) against curtailment of democratic rights more generally, and (b) against the on-going attack on living standards. Keeping its organizational independence, the Left must engage in these two forms of struggle, on the basis of concrete immediate and transitional demands, *as a part of* and *within the framework of,* the fight for socialism, a fight that is local, regional, national and global.[70] By being involved in struggles inside and outside the workplaces (farms, factories, offices), in the struggles that are economic, political and ecological, in the struggles for economic concessions and that are against social oppression of religious and caste minorities and women, the Left can truly be the tribune of the people in the Lenin sense. Such Left action is necessary to alleviate the suffering of the oppressed groups and to unite those members of its basic classes who are social oppressed (e.g. Dalits) with those who traditionally are not. In the process of such struggles, the lower classes can aspire for the ideological-political hegemony, and ultimately, for the status of 'the new ruling class'. One can imagine the economic and political struggles of workers and small-scale producers as three concentric circles, beginning, first, with the struggle around immediate economic and political demands, and then struggle around transitional economic and political demands, and finally, moving on to the struggle for a workers' and small-scale producers' government.

Within the extra-electoral struggles in all these different spheres, the Left must support the various progressive movements led by non-party Marxists and by non-Marxist radicals such as people's science movements, movements against obscurantism, and ecological movements.[71] The Left must also support the mass movements against social oppression and for economic concessions (e.g. higher wages) that are led by non-party Marxists and by non-Marxist radicals, including those involved in the literacy campaigns, temple entry movements on behalf of Dalits, right to information campaign, and so on. Within the extra-electoral struggles in all these different spheres, the Left, keeping its organizational independence, must build, and must not shy away from, principled *alliances* with non-communists (e.g. non communist progressive scientists and

---

70    'We have known for a long time that only a revolutionary tactic engenders, as a by-product, "reforms" or concessions from the government' (Trotsky, 1934).

71    It is important that the Left be involved in the science movement (to popularize science) and ecological movement because communal-fascist forces are trying to communalize both science and ecological movements on the basis of their espousal of 'vedic science' and 'dharmic ecology', respectively (see Nanda, 2005).

artists), on the ground of liquidationism, or on any other ground. The Left in India (and elsewhere) must pay serious attention to Lenin's advice on the need for alliance between communists and non-communists and to the idea that revolution cannot be made by revolutionaries alone.

> One of the biggest and most dangerous mistakes made by Communists (as generally by revolutionaries who have successfully accomplished the beginning of a great revolution) is the idea that a revolution can be made by revolutionaries alone. On the contrary, to be successful, all serious revolutionary work requires that the idea that revolutionaries are capable of playing the part only of the vanguard of the truly virile and advanced class must be understood and translated into action. A vanguard performs its task as vanguard only when it is able to avoid being isolated from the mass of the people it leads and is able really to lead the whole mass forward. Without an alliance with non-Communists in the most diverse spheres of activity there can be no question of any successful communist construction.
>
> LENIN, 1922

As far as the fight against the fascistic movement is concerned, the Left must make sure that: workers, self-employed non-capitalist producers, their political parties/movements, class-conscious trade union members, their progressive organic intellectuals and independent activists participating in class-based social movements, come together, at local, regional and national levels, starting from a city-neighborhood and a village. These elements must form multi-religion, multi-caste working class, and anti-fascism/anti-communalism action committees (or defense guards), with the aim of struggling against the attack on democratic and social rights of these basic classes and class-fractions, in the first instance. What is needed, in India (as elsewhere in similar contexts), is a *class*-based extra-electoral 'coalition' (i.e. a 'united front') of proletarian political forces that are organizationally independent of the big-business parties, in order to struggle for secularism and democracy (and more). Such extra-electoral struggle should be a vehicle for the development of democratic consciousness[72] and win the masses to the cause of a large-scale political project

---

72    Prejudice against religious minorities and Dalits *is* widespread among ordinary people, thanks to their own alienated living and working conditions requiring scapegoating and externalizing the source of their problems, and thanks to the ideological intervention of bourgeois-fascistic forces. The Left must fight this prejudice.

of defending and deepening democratic rights and to the cause of socialism/communism. Apart from the extra-electoral struggle, the Left must fight the fascistic tendencies within the electoral arena, on the basis of the idea that the former struggle is to subordinate it to the electoral struggle.

It is to be stressed that the defeat of fascistic tendencies should not be equated to the electoral defeat of the BJP: the BJP may be defeated and yet fascistic tendencies will be involved in their usual ground-work, covertly and overtly, although without formal access to state power through the BJP they will lose some of their force. So the fight against fascistic tendencies must be a much greater fight than the electoral fight to defeat the BJP. And no other political movement can engage in that fight more strongly than the Left can. It is also clear that when fascistic tendencies are weakened/eliminated and when the focus of Left's attention is more on class struggle against capital as such than on fascistic movements, the so-called secular parties which are competing with one another are most likely to be united with those which are not, in order to fight the Left. That is all the more reason why the fight against fascistic tendencies must be seen as a part of the fight for establishing a socialist government.

The struggle against fascism or fascistic tendencies must ultimately be to cut its roots in capitalism. In the process of mobilizing the masses for concessions (including economic concessions within capitalism), the Left must develop their class consciousness and gradually prepare them to demand a workers' state, supported mainly by non-exploiting small-scale producers. The fight against fascistic tendencies, initially a *defensive* fight, should be seen positively as opening a door towards socialist struggle.

Any temporary and tactical agreement with non-fascistic bourgeois forces that might be made objectively necessary because of the relative weakness of the Left can, once again, be justified only if the genuine aim of the Left is to prepare the masses to fight for socialism, and not to just fight for a capitalism that is more democratic, more egalitarian and less neoliberal. The masses and the leaders and the Left intellectuals must breathe, live, and fall in love with, the very idea of a more humane society that is democratic in every possible manner, a society which goes by this name: socialism. Any temporary compromise on the socialist principle in order to fight fascistic tendencies is not worth it, if it is not consciously *seen as a part of* the project to advance the socialist cause, the masses' struggle for socialism:

> If communalism is not just an ideological, superstructural, epiphenomenal force and if the totality of the communal forces are structurally rooted in this predatory capitalism, then it necessarily follows that the

struggle against communalism is not only a matter of an ideological struggle on behalf of secularism but part of a struggle against capitalism itself. That is, ... the real, enduring alternative to communalism is communism as such. [In] India, secularism is no longer a bourgeois virtue, as it once was for the Enlightenment bourgeoisie in Europe and among many during our anti-colonial struggle.

AHMAD, 2013: 22

The threat from the fascistic movement and the massive crisis of livelihood of the masses are reason enough for a thorough rethinking of what kind of Left is needed. This rethinking involves rethinking the stage of revolution itself: must the Left not fight to abolish capitalism rather than to fight for a better form of capitalism? Is it really the case that capitalism is not ripe, for a struggle to begin to overthrow it? As we have seen in Chapter 3, India is dominantly a capitalist society: the most general form of capitalism does exist as the dominant form of class relation in India, and the transition to a more developed form of capitalism is blocked by capitalism itself, operating in a world of imperialism. Let the Indian Left read and reflect on Lenin's *April Theses*. And let leaders of the communist movement, advanced workers and Marxist intellectuals reflect honestly and seriously in a way that is non-sectarian, the following lines from Vladimir Lenin's most trusted comrade and his co-architect of 1917:

All talk to the effect that historical conditions have not yet "ripened" for socialism is the product of ignorance or conscious deception. The objective prerequisites for the proletarian revolution have not only "ripened"; they have begun to get somewhat rotten. Without a socialist revolution, in the next historical period at that, a catastrophe threatens the whole culture of mankind. The turn is now to the proletariat, i.e., chiefly to its revolutionary vanguard. The historical crisis of mankind is reduced to the crisis of the revolutionary leadership.

TROTSKY, 1938

Indeed, 'Without a socialist revolution, ... a catastrophe threatens the whole culture of mankind', and fascism *is* a part of that catastrophe.

Philosophically speaking, capitalism exists at the level of fundamental class *relation*, which has three aspects (relation of exchange, relation of property, and relation of value and surplus value) (Das, 2017a: Chapter 7), and at the level of mechanisms and the *effects* of the *mechanisms* of capitalist accumulation on the masses. And, capitalist society can be (more/less) fascistic and (more/less) democratic. It is important for the Left to fight against the adverse effects

of capitalist accumulation for short-term progressive policies and against fascistic tendencies, on the basis of immediate and transitional demands. Now,
given the danger that fascistic tendencies pose to them, the secular-
democratic bourgeois and petty bourgeois forces may at best want to confine
their political activity to the creation of a polity that merely weakens such tendencies making the society more democratic, leaving intact the capitalist class
relation. And that political aim, however limited from the Left vantage-point,
does overlap with the Left's aim to undermine – to revolt against– fascistic
tendencies. But such a revolt has to be also a revolt against fascists' pro-business policies and against the attack on workers and small-scale producers' living standards. And there is still more to do: fighting for democracy and against
fascistic tendencies, and for some economic concessions is not enough. These
fights must grow over into the fight for socialism.

The question is: does the Indian Left agree with this perspective?

# Conclusions and Reflections

In this concluding chapter, I will summarize the main points made in each chapter and draw out their implications for political practice. A major challenge in social analysis of a country is to arrive at a general perspective. This perspective, I have argued, must be the class perspective.

Class analysis must stress the relation of exploitation between classes on the basis of control over the productive resources on the part of the minority class (the exploiters). And in terms of capitalism as a class relation, it must see capitalism as a series of inter-connected relations: of exchange, property, production, value and surplus value. Class relations promote and fetter the development of productive forces, which impact class relations, which have ultimate primacy over productive forces. So, class defines the character of its economy, which in turn sets limits within which the state generally functions.[1] The state is fundamentally a class state. It is the class character of economy and of the state that must be the crucial explanation of forms of economic development, technological change, dynamics of poverty, and the political activity in which the exploiting and exploited classes and their agents engage in.

To be dialectical, class analysis must take seriously that which is not class: it must take seriously mechanisms of *non-class* oppression (or relations and practices of social-cultural *difference*). In India, caste and gender have been emphasized, and rightly so. In addition to women (and children) and low castes (especially, Dalits), it is very important to stress the oppression of religious minorities, and especially, Muslims, in contemporary India. Oppression of religious minorities is deeply connected to class exploitation, and both are aspects of what I call the fascistic tendency in India.

Class absolutely matters. One can agree with Herring (2013: 139) when he says that: 'economic class determines not only who gets what, but how: what must be done, can be done, to alter life chances?' And because that is the case, 'some obfuscation of class universally serves political interests' (p. 131), i.e. the interests of those who benefit from the class system. Such an obfuscation might be intellectually justified by saying that the Marxist notion of class is a Western notion, and that it cannot be applied to India because Indian society is too complex, because caste is the backbone of Indian society and that

---

1 Over a long period of time, class relations generally influence politics (see Moore, 1993), which, in turn, have a certain influence on class relations.

India has many other social divisions, and so on. To quote, once again, Andre Beteille, who is not a Marxist and who is one of foremost Indian thinkers, again: 'Marxism occupies a central place among the intellectual resources of the modern world, and we can neglect or reject it only at our own cost' (Beteille, 2000: 46–47). And in more recent times, Jal (2014: 77) has said this from a Marxist perspective: 'Give up the essence of Marxism, give up the masses, humanism and internationalism; and the spectres of fascism, neo-conservatism and Stalinism will strike back'.

In this book, apart from outlining what a class analysis should look like at a general level (Chapter 2), I use the class perspective to examine a variety of issues that concern contemporary India, including: the Maoist movement considered to be the largest threat to the state's security, and the fascistic tendencies as a threat not only to democracy and secularism but also to the economic rights and political organizations of workers and peasants.

## 1 Class Character of Indian Economy/Society

In thinking about the class character of Indian society/economy, one has to bear in mind a set of key points. These include the following. Class is a relation/process which is objectively expressed in the form of large groups of people in terms of their relation to social economy, in both rural and urban areas. This relationship is produced by the fact that a minority class controls the means of production, production process, and the surplus product, while the majority class does not. Class exists at multiple levels: history of class society, capitalism, capitalism at a specific stage of development, capitalism, and neoliberal capitalism, in India, etc. Capitalism is to be seen, above all, as a class relation (more below), and as such capitalism in India has similarities to, and differences from, the capitalism from advanced countries. In examining Indian class society, one may begin with the two class model. But one has to bear in mind the fact that class polarization including proletarianization, occurs through certain mechanisms which can be countered, to some extent, by other mechanisms, which is why one finds intermediate classes between capitalists and workers. Indian capitalist society is characterized by a system of class relations of: accumulation by class differentiation, accumulation by dispossession, and accumulation by exploitation (which in turn comes in two forms of subsumption of labor, as explained below). Classes and class-fractions (intra-class divisions) have common and different interests. Classes undergo changes over time, and conditions of class can vary over space, especially, in a large country such as India. At a concrete level, there are non-class relations within class relations, such that we have not only a worker as a category but also a Dalit worker. It is very important to understand how class relations of exploitation feed into and are supported by non-class relations of oppression/domination/exclusion such as those based in not only caste and gender but also, and increasingly, religion. Ideas about class and objective conditions of existence of class inter-connect, while the objective conditions have a degree of primacy over ideas. Similarly, class politics and objective conditions of existence of class set limits within which class politics – and indeed non-class politics – are played out, with a degree of autonomy. Just as class polarization is subjected to mechanisms and counter-mechanisms, similarly, class politics, especially, lower-class struggle, which comes in different forms (e.g. trade union struggle, political struggles by the Indian communist movement), is subjected to processes that are conducive to, and those that impede, the lower-class struggle. The lower-class struggle exists along with what I call class struggle from above (i.e. what urban capitalists and rural large-scale landowners do against the lower classes). Actions of the property-owning class and its state, including the fascistic attack on lower classes and their organic intellectuals, can be seen as class struggle from above.

## 2        Capitalism as Class Relations of Subsumption of Labor

Like everything, class as an objective reality comes in many forms. Capitalism is a form of class. How to conceptually think about capitalism in India, and not just class in India, is a big intellectual challenge. By deploying Marx's notion of subsumption of labor, I have critiqued a restrictive concept of capitalism that many Indian Marxist political economists subscribe to. This is a concept in which the development of capitalist class relations is conflated with the development of productive forces *under* such relations. In the restrictive concept, capitalism as such is equated with advanced capitalism, rather than the latter being seen as a higher *form* of capitalism. Therefore, in this restrictive concept, where there is a lower level of economic development, it is assumed that capitalism does not exist or that it exists only partially.

In advancing a subsumption of labor perspective, I claim that formal subsumption of labor is the most abstract – general – form of capitalism. For Marx, real subsumption of labor entails the formal subsumption, but the converse is not necessarily true (Marx, 1977: 1019). Contrary to what Marx might (sometimes) have believed (perhaps, this was one of Marx's Eurocentric moments), the transition to real subsumption – the transition to a form of capitalism associated with system-wide productivity-raising technological change – is not automatic. I accept that there *is* a long-term tendency towards the real subsumption of labor, associated with a rise in the ratio of constant to variable capital, that follows formal subsumption in which lots of workers are hired to work for long hours on an enormous amount of raw materials with little labor-shedding technological change used. This long-term tendency, under certain conditions, is countered by the possibilities for a prolonged process of formal subsumption. The transition to real subsumption is mediated by the balance of power between capital and labor, including more overt struggle against formal subsumption of labor, within a context where the national economy is shaped by imperialism and the world market.

In India, there *are* the necessary conditions for capitalist relations (e.g. a class of legally 'free' laborers; commodity production; investment of money in production and exchange to make more money). Therefore, as capitalists else-where, property owners hiring these nominally free laborers possess the same sorts of causal powers (e.g. they can earn profits) and suffer from the same sorts of causal liabilities (e.g. they can lose their means of production if they do not produce commodities efficiently, i.e. at the value). They are capitalists whether or not they use, for example, the Green Revolution type technology or biotechnology or any other form of technology. In some areas, property owners may be formally subsuming labor, and in other areas there may exist real subsumption. The ways in which capitalists' powers and liabilities are ex-pressed in actual patterns of investment, and the effects of the exercise of these powers and liabilities on the development of productive forces (i.e. whether the transition from formal to real subsumption of labor under capital happens), other things constant, depend on the balance of power, or strug-gle, between property owners and workers. The forms and outcomes of the struggle – which are affected by the overall capitalist development and developmental activities of the capitalist state at the national and provincial scales – condition the extent to which competing capitalists cut costs of pro-duction through the use of technology aimed at increasing labor productivity per hour or through, for example, the formal subsumption of labor. The formal subsumption may benefit specific capitals in specific places but opportunities for formal subsumption, along with imperialist exploitation, may counter the long-term and system-wide tendency towards the development of productive forces that Marx associates with real subsumption of labor. Real subsumption does happen but there are serious limits to it. From the perspective of many participants in the celebrated Indian Mode of Production debate, it is the so-cial relations of usury or rental extraction from direct producers that fetter the development of productive forces under capitalism. While this may be true in specific cases, a larger nation-wide obstacle is formal subsumption of labor itself: being able to appropriate surplus value in its absolute form on the basis of formal subsumption alleviates the pressure to have to resort to real subsumption in a systemic way. In other words, a nation-wide obstacle to the development of productive forces is capitalism itself, in its most general form (i.e. formal subsumption of labor).

This conclusion has a general theoretical implication, i.e. an implication for the debate on fettering, for example.[2] The idea is that existing class relations block possible *further* development of productive forces (leading to a slow or slower growth rate, for example), a situation I will call 'development-fettering'. Use-fettering means that the rational use of *existing* resources is blocked by the current set of class relations. That is, productive capacities that have already been *developed* are at present un-*used* or under-*used* due to existing class relations. The discrepancy between capacity and use is not to be seen in an absolute sense, however. As Cohen (2000) says, the question is not under-deployment (or use) of resources, but 'grotesque over-deployment in some directions and injurious under-deployment in others', indicating an irrational deployment of resources.[3]

The mode of production in India is decidedly and near-exclusively capitalist. This is capitalist at least in the sense of formal subsumption of labor under capital. And it is decidedly not semi-feudal. Of course, the semi-feudal thesis continues to be subscribed to by many (see Kar, 2018; Sugden, 2017).

The view of capitalism and capitalist (uneven) development offered here is different from that of many Indian Marxists. For them, to the extent that the development of productive forces has taken place, it has taken place due to capitalist reinvestment of surplus in specific areas. Patnaik, like Bhaduri, thinks that only when technological change happens is there capitalism. What follows from this is that, for her, uneven *development of productive forces* is a function of the spatially limited amount of *development of capitalist social relations*. This is a mistaken view. The development of capitalist relations in India, including in rural areas, is much more widespread than the theory advanced by these scholars would allow for. As I have said before, this is in the sense that (and to the extent that) property owners (including landowners), as bearers of the capitalist social structure, are subject to the same sorts of profit-making opportunities as well as constraints in capitalist societies as elsewhere. But in

---

2  That social relations fetter the development productive forces is a common Marxist argument. For a discussion on the topic, see Sitton, 1996; also Das, 2001c on the importance of the 'fettering argument' in the less developed country context.

3  One can also examine what I will call use-fettering. Use-fettering is the *irrational* use of existing resources located, caused by class relations domestically and internationally. Consider the fact that while millions are starving, vast amount of resources are being used to produce high value luxury goods such as shrimps for the world market, within an international division of labor created by imperialism.

what ways they do so (for example, whether they use labor-saving technology) is a different matter. Like most large countries, India is highly diverse, both ecologically and in terms of other factors (e.g. the degree of concentration of means of production, etc.). There is geographical variation in the factors that shape the potential/actual balance of power between capital and labor. So one will expect that in some areas or sub-sectors of economic activity, property owners, including those who must cut costs under the pressure of the world market, are unable to rely mainly on the use of labor that works for low wages and for long hours, and are therefore economically compelled to use productivity-raising technological change, thus manifesting capitalism's long-term tendency towards real subsumption. This mechanism causes productive forces to be developed in some areas or sub-sectors to a greater extent and more systematically than in other areas, causing uneven development *under* capitalism. In other words, a more *general* tendency under the capitalist mode of production (i.e. the pressure on competing capitalists to make a profit, the pressure coming from the capitalist class relations) interacts with *locally* existing contingent conditions (e.g. balance of power between the basic classes) to produce geographically uneven development (Das, 2017c), the concrete forms of which must be subjected to empirical analysis at the local scale.[4]

All political economists agree that there is uneven development in India. Most of them think that uneven development exists because of the existence of 'non-capitalist' relation (e.g. pre-capitalist type relations) in some areas, associated with low level of economic development, and capitalist relations in other areas, associated with higher level of development. My argument, however, is that, uneven development is mainly taking place because of, and in the framework of, social relations that are predominantly *capitalist* in terms of *class relations*. At the level of mechanisms (and not surface 'appearances'), uneven development is partly a product of uneven transition to the real subsumption of labor under capital. Uneven development is a *capitalist* matter.

Further, there is a relatively ignored fact that uneven development is happening within the framework of varied class relations in a backward country (backward in terms of the lower level of labor productivity per hour), one where technological change is partly happening under the influence of the world market, and where, therefore, uneven development is *uneven and combined* development. But what is the *combined* character of uneven development? This concept refers to 'a peculiar combination of different stages' in the

---

4 Note that this does not mean that the local scale is autonomous of the functioning of the capitalist class relation. Uneven development at time $T_1$ creates different areas with their specificities, which, in turn, interact with the general dynamics of capitalist class relation at $T_2$ to produce another round of uneven development, and so on.

history of economic development of less-developed countries. It means that, for example, in a less developed country, technologically backward 'peasant land-cultivation' can co-exist with an industry which 'in its technique and capitalist structure' is 'at the level of the advanced countries', and in certain respects it can even surpass industry in advanced countries (Trotsky, 2008: 8)., In India, robots, tractors, threshers coexist with technologically-backward production processes, mass scientific ignorance, massive functional illiteracy, and superstitious beliefs.

It is not just that capitalist development is *uneven* but also that capitalist relations are *combined* with pre-capitalist relations (e.g. serfdom). This is an advance over the perspective (for example, that of Harvey, Myrdal, etc.) that focusses only on the unevenness of capitalist development. Trotsky's perspective, like that of Harvey (1982), however, does not distinguish between different forms of capitalist class relation itself. It thus abstracts from the ways in which the balance of power between capital and labor intervenes in the transition from one form of capitalist class relation (formal subsumption) to another form (real subsumption) and thus limits the extent to which and the pace at which a higher level of capitalist development (indicated by higher per hour labor productivity) can happen, whether in farming or industry, and irrespective of what the state policies are. It thus abstracts from the obstacles to the transition *within* capitalism, and therefore obstacles to economic development. His perspective of uneven and combined development needs to be broadened a little in the light of the class theory of capitalism around subsumption of labor, as presented here. In India and similar other backward countries, it is not just that capitalism is combined with pre-capitalist relations existing in specific areas. The matter is more complex than that.

Firstly, what is happening is that class relations of formal subsumption of labor, hybrid subsumption, and localized pre-capitalist relations, including relations of commons, as in aboriginal areas, co-exist with class relations of real subsumption, the latter being, in part, driven by an external influence (i.e. imperialism as indicated by the operation of the capitalist world market backed by militarily powerful states of advanced countries). Secondly, there are not straightforward ways in which India (and other similar countries), operating under the impact of the world market, can move to the stage of real subsumption of labor quickly, and exhibit a systemic tendency towards a rise in productivity of labor per hour. The introduction of advanced techniques could strengthen not only the use of unfreedom and extra-economic relations, but also relations of formal subsumption of labor. We may recall that: formal subsumption of labor can exist 'alongside the *specifically capitalist* mode of production in its developed form' i.e. the real subsumption (Marx, 1977: 1019). In other words, enterprises using advanced technology can – and do – resort to a regime of long hours and low wages, just as they can use unfree labor.[5] Besides, while the imperialist world market can contribute to economic development based on a degree of technological change (through such processes as the relocation of enterprises to take advantage of cheap skilled and unskilled labor; the need to sell new technologies as commodities), imperialism can also inhibit long-term systemic economic development, given its exploitative character causing, for example, transfer of surplus to advanced countries in various forms. As long as there is the class relation of capitalism, there will be imperialism, which is a relation of exploitation of direct producers of India and other poorer countries by the big business of advanced countries. And as long as there is imperialism, its main tendential effect is to limit development in the periphery rather than to promote it, a tendency that reflects the mechanisms of uneven development at the global scale. The long-term tendency for the average rate of profit to fall in imperialist countries, thus causing periodic economic crises there, also impacts India and other low-income countries, in part by reducing their exports and by increasing the need to raise the rate of exploitation of labor in, and to acquire cheaper natural resources from, these countries. Besides, India itself is experiencing its 'own' profitability crisis, as Michael Roberts suggests, and this crisis further limits India's development prospects, including in the industrial sector. Given all these traits of global capitalism and of capitalism in India (and other low-income countries), good or bad state policies and stronger or weaker state capacities can make only marginal difference and only for a short time period. Quite simply, capitalism has become a barrier to the development of productive forces – a barrier to economic development – under the rule of capitalist class relations.

The second major implication of my discussion of the class character of capitalism in India is this: associated with the uneven and combined development of capitalism is the topic of capital switch. Once we assume that there is a class with money (property owners, more generally) intending to make money by investing it in production and exchange, the concept of switching capital comes to be an important one. There are three forms of capital-switch. (1) When the rate of profit is low in the production sphere, capital switches to financial, etc. services (Smith, 2010). (2) And, according to Harvey, when there is overaccumulation in the sector that produces commodities that are produced and consumed within a given time period (primary circuit),

---

5   Note that unfree labor is definitely not a necessary indicator of non-capitalist relation (e.g. semi-feudalism) (Brass, 2012) and that it can be made use of by capitalists who resort to both formal and real subsumption of labor, although the possibility of relative surplus value can, to some extent, reduce the pressure to resort to formal subsumption (see Das, 2013c).

capital is switched to the sectors that specialize in the built environment for production and for consumption (e.g. durables) and into science and education as well as social welfare and repressive and consent-generating activities (Harvey, 1978). (3) Within economically less developed capitalist social formations, capital switch takes different forms. (3a) One form is one that Utsa Patnaik (1986) and others have dealt with: when property owners can make more money by investing it in production, they will switch capital from rental and usurious activities to production. Patnaik says: the person renting out her land to peasants will switch to what she calls *capitalist* production if she can make more profit in production than by leasing out land (i.e. the rental income) and by lending money-capital at a higher rate of interest (usury). But a rate of profit that can prompt switching capital to production is very high (because rental income and usurious interest are very high), and is difficult to obtain, unless there is a quantum jump in productivity caused by technological change. In other words, the obstacle to the switch to capitalist production comes from *outside* of capitalist production. (3b) Further, there is the switch of capital from formal subsumption (or indeed from hybrid subsumption) to real subsumption of labor in capitalist production, as I have discussed. This switch is not yet complete. This leads us to the topic of the specificity of capitalism in India, and this is the third implication of my discussion of the class character of capitalism in India.

How different is Indian capitalism from the capitalism of the European core? For Subir Sinha (2017: 540), capitalism, or what he calls mature capitalism, exists with 'capitalists and workers responding to "the dull compulsion of economic force"'. It is characterized by 'generalized commodity production, in which the imperative of accumulation drives capitalists' behaviour, and where labour [sic] becomes a commodity'. India does not have capitalism in this sense, for Sinha. The incomplete transition to generalized commodity production 'is the central point of difference between capitalism in India and in the original trajectories of the European core' (Sinha, 2017: 540). And, this incompleteness is signified by the fact that non-capitalist ways of life 'are kept alive by development interventions [of the state] to benefit those who are excluded from capitalist relations but have some political power in the form of laws and justice and solidarity discourses that ... put limits to the violence of the universalization process on extra-economic grounds' (p. 541). Interestingly, according to 'more traditional' political economists of the 1970s mode of production debate genre, it is the non-capitalist, or pre-capitalist, relations that act as a fetter on the development of capitalist class relations (as in the work of Patnaik and others), while according to such recent writers as Sinha (and Sanyal, 2013), influenced by the cultural turn and post-modernism, 'non-capitalist forms of subjectivity ... put limits' on the universalization of capitalism. So, what limits capitalism is not an agent within capitalism (i.e. the working class) but an agent that is outside of capitalism ('non-capitalist forms of subjectivity'). While the recent writers wish to distinguish their thinking from that of the more traditional political economists, they end up in the camp of the latter. As well, politically, it is easy to see how close their thinking is to some of the discourse that informs class struggle in India (e.g. Naxalism, discussed in Chapters 8–9).

It is true that wage-labor co-exists with other forms of labor, although this does not license resorting to the descriptive concept of 'classes of labor' of Henry Bernstein (2007), that many others make use of. This concept is problematic not least because it conflates class-fractions with class. But to the extent that wage-labor co-exists with other forms of labor, India's capitalism cannot be credited with any uniqueness relative to advanced countries. In all capitalist countries, wage-labor exists along with other forms of labor, to varying degrees, with wage-labor as the dominant form of labor. But that does not mean that the imperative of *capitalist* accumulation does not exist where wage-labor as the dominant form of labor coexists with other forms of labor, as in India. Capitalism does not require that *all* labor power become a commodity. As long as a sufficient amount of labor power is in the commodity-form, capitalism's fundamental mechanisms (e.g. competition, appropriation of surplus value, etc.) can be set in motion. In fact, the existence of a semi-commodified labor power is no barrier to capital's pursuit of surplus. Capital can benefit at the expense of petty producers in multiple ways, including by getting raw materials at below-market price from these producers and benefit from their wage-labor when offered for sale. The *main* difference between India and the European core is *not* what the likes of Sinha and Sanyal say. The main difference is that India is characterized by the dominance of formal subsumption of wage-labor under capital (i.e. capitalism in its more general form), which co-exists with real subsumption of labor (as well as relations of hybrid subsumption and remnants of pre-capitalist exploitation based on extra-economic coercion and natural economy), in a context of the operation of the world market and imperialist subjugation. There *is* an incompleteness, but one that is indicative of combined development in capitalist society. But this is not in the sense of the incomplete transition to capitalism, for India is decidedly a capitalist country already. Much rather, the incompleteness exists in the sense that there is an incomplete – ongoing – transition to real subsumption of labor, within the landscape of uneven and combined development of *capitalist* social formation.

To view that Indian or any other social formation is decidedly capitalist has a different political implication than the contrary view which has a much less progressive implication. This contrary view is that (a) the social formation is not dominantly capitalist or is capitalist in limited ways, and (b) obstacles to capitalist development are in pre- or non-capitalist relations. There are two implications of this view. One is that capitalist class relation is everywhere and all times associated with higher level of development of productive forces, and therefore, capitalism must be promoted/protected always and everywhere. Another is that: the obstacles to capitalist development are not in capitalism as such and can be removed by forces other than those that seek to abolish capitalism. That is, a democratic government still operating within the logic of capitalist relations can remove these barriers and promote a nicer form of capitalism, a capitalism without non-capitalist barriers.

If a country such as India is dominantly semi-feudal or not capitalist enough, then the political energy is to be directed against semi-feudal landlords or at the creation of advanced capitalism somehow. This is a strategy that licenses a long and indefinite wait for the fight for socialism (= abolition of class relations) to start and requires collaboration with some good (progressive) capitalists. In reality, the time for that strategy never comes, in part because the political work that happens now has little connection to the socialist project. But if what is present is already capitalism, albeit one that is not very progressive, and one that is not going to be very progressive for a long period of time because of all the constraints on the transition to real subsumption of labor within the contemporary imperialist world market, then the nature of class politics must be seen in an entirely different manner: this means that revolution as the highest point of class struggle against capitalism must be on the agenda right now. The core of this agenda must be the anti-capitalist struggle of the working class which is the object of capitalist exploitation including in its most general form (i.e. formal subsumption of labor). This class must be politically allied with small-scale producers which are adversely impacted, in so many ways, by the capitalist class (and by its class partner, i.e. rent-receiving landlords). The combined and common goal of these two toiling classes must be a socialist state, a state of workers and self-employed small-scale producers who constitute the majority of the population. By driving all propertied classes (pre-capitalist or capitalist) from their ruling positions, such a state can create conditions for a higher level of development of productive forces and for a society without exploitation and oppression.

## 3      Capitalist Class Relation in a Neoliberal Form

Like everything, capitalism comes in many forms. It comes in the forms of formal and real subsumption of labor, from one vantage point. It also comes in the form of, for example, social-democratic or state-interventionist and neoliberal forms, from another vantage point. Neoliberalism *is* a specific form of capitalism, whether in advanced countries or in countries such as India, although the critical analysis of capitalism has been replaced by that of neoliberalism as such. Neoliberalism is not to be seen primarily as a set of government policies which can be replaced by another. Much rather it is to be seen as 'a predictable and inevitable strategic response on the part of capital and the state to a deepening crisis of the capitalist profit system' (Smith, 2018: 21). It is mistaken to belive that neoliberalism, and not capitalism, is facing a crisis (Chibber, 2017). Neoliberalism is a form of crisis-ridden capitalism. Capitalism and neoliberal capitalism are both crisis-ridden.

The neoliberal state experiences internal contradictions, like the capitalist form of the state as such. There is clearly a contradiction between the declared public aims of neoliberalism (the well-being of all) and its actual effect, which is rising income and wealth inequality between the big business (top 1% or so) and the rest. As I am completing this chapter, Oxfam has just reported that in India, top 10% of the population owns 77.4% of the national wealth, and top 1% holds 51.53% of the national wealth, while bottom 60% owns merely 4.8% of the national wealth (Samuel, 2019). Additionally, there are more specific contradictions that Harvey (2005) has so well described which apply to India as well: between the need for the state to let markets function freely and the need to intervene in order to deliberately create a business climate; the need to enforce market rules in an authoritarian way and the ideas of individual freedom; the integrity of the financial system and its volatile character; between competition and monopolistic tendencies; and between individual market freedom and loss of solidarity, and so on. As a new stage in the development of capitalism emerging in the wake of the post-war boom, neoliberalism has several general traits (deregulation, privatization, liberalization, financialization, etc.) that are affecting all spheres of life, including culture, the state and everyday life.

Like all the different forms of capitalism, neoliberalism operates differently in different national contexts. A dialectical conceptualization of neoliberalism in India (where it goes by the name of New Economic Policy, or NEP) must be rooted in a general theory of neoliberalism, and it must be sensitive to the differences and similarities between the pre-1991 and post-1991 regimes in India, and to both the economic and the non-economic character of the NEP. Such a conceptualization must also see the governmental or policy aspect of the NEP as rooted in the class character of Indian society.

As in many other countries, so in India, neoliberal capitalism has meant a series of *reduction* in: corporate contributions to society/state (= reduction in taxes); the power of unions; state control over pricing of services and over business activities; state's restrictions on trade; state's support for the less-well off (e.g. farmers); the scope of state ownership of productive enterprises and of facilities (schools, etc.) and commons, and so on. As a result, there has been the opposite of this reduction: an *expansion* of the *effect* of class power of ruling class and expansion of the misery for the masses.

In any fundamental sense, there was not a time before or since independence when the Indian capitalist class did not have its power to exploit labor and dispossess small-scale producers. So neoliberalism, strictly speaking, is not the restoration of class power, as some scholars think (e.g. Harvey, Dumenil, etc.). Yet, to the extent that there was *some* restriction on its power within the political sphere (e.g. what it could produce and what it could not), neoliberalism is an *effect* of changing balance of political power between the capitalist class and the masses in the 'post-Soviet' world. On the basis of its growing economic strength, supported in many ways by the state, between the 1950s and the mid-1980s, and with support from imperialist capital and its institutions, Indian capitalist class has now been able to impose its economic will in a much more strident manner than before. NEP is a political expression of the capitalist class's 'desire' and need to bridge the gap between its economic power (in terms of its control over property) and its political power. NEP *is* a policy, but it is more than that. It is the political articulation of the interests of the Indian capitalist class in the context of a globalizing capitalism. Neoliberalism is 'capitalism without Leftist illusions' (e.g. illusions that there can be such a thing as humane capitalism on a long-term basis). India's NEP is a policy *on behalf* of capital. It is therefore a policy *of* capital, mediated and implemented by the state, at central and provincial scales. India's NEP is more than a governmental policy. It is a programme of the bourgeoisie that promotes economic growth and bestows benefits to certain relatively privileged sections of the population (e.g. IT engineers), but has devastating impacts on the toiling masses.

Neoliberalism in rural areas (or agrarian neoliberalism) in a country where 70% of the population are villagers and where almost half of the workforce depends on agriculture, is particularly ruthless in its impacts. Neoliberalism has also produced enormous spatial unevenness. Neoliberalism in India, like in the periphery as such, is also a part of the imperialist project, being implemented via burgeoning 'new compradore' elements both in the bourgeois class and outside. Given the adverse impacts of neoliberalism, it has inspired massive resistance from below, which has been countered by the state via a combination of: heavy repression; meagre concession; and mind-numbing deception (i.e. the false idea that neoliberal growth is good for all). Interestingly, if the Left has struggled for power at the regional level to alleviate sufferings of the masses, the Left has ended up, in practice, becoming, more or less, a conduit through which neoliberalism has been delivered to the detriment of the interests of the masses. Of course, this is not to say that Gujarat and Kerala are the same. They clearly are not.

If we see neoliberalism as a form of capitalism, this view has also specific political implications. India, along with other less developed countries, are often seen as countries that have less income and more absolute poverty. Instead, I argue that India (like the other less developed countries) must be fundamentally seen in class terms: as one that has suffered from aborted – or incomplete – revolutions against the propertied class. They have suffered from: aborted democratic revolution, including agrarian revolution against feudal(-type) relations, aborted national (or anti-imperialist) revolution, and untried anti-capitalist revolution. A dialectical view of neoliberalism and the NEP connects them both to the democratic and agrarian questions, the national question, and the question of socialism itself.

Consider the democratic question. There has been massive resistance to the NEP, as mentioned earlier, to which the state is responding in a most undemocratic (= repressive) manner. The state is also promoting *venal* capitalism; massive corruption in the public offices has been endemic since the 1990s, a time during which markets have been less regulated, thus refuting the argument that de-regulation reduces corruption. Corruption implies undemocratic use of public offices for private gains ('private' meaning the nexus of the business world and the state managers). The neoliberal state itself is managed by people who are increasingly and openly allied with the moneybags and money-making, while being on the payroll of the state, which is supposed to work for everyone.

Given that all the parties – including the Left parties – are forced to follow neoliberalism, the room for democratic dissent is shrunk, and this is more so now, with the election of a government in 2014 led by a Hindu-fundamentalist party with fascistic tendencies. This has a more specific implication: by making all political parties/groups equal as far as their adherence to neoliberalism is concerned, the NEP has created a situation where casteism and religious fundamentalism are used to divide the poor electorate and to garner votes. This creates conditions for the perpetuation of undemocratic relations based on religious and caste identity. This also creates a condition where capitalists can subject workers – those who belong to specific vulnerable social groups – to super-exploitation and weaken any potential resistance by dividing the masses along the lines of religion, caste, gender, etc. Given that various petty-bourgeois or regionalist parties (some of which call themselves, bizarrely, socialist) thrive by playing identity politics, it is not unusual for a party or a coalition of parties in power to buy their support for neoliberal policies by giving some material concession to identity politics (e.g. reservation in promotion for scheduled castes). Identity politics becomes a vehicle of capitalist and landlord class politics, that is to say, politics in the service of neoliberalism.

The NEP is also creating new aspects of the agrarian question, the question about peasants' property and about their miseries caused by national and international agribusiness (*not* feudal or semi-feudal landlords) and by the neoliberal state acting on behalf of agribusiness. So the democratic question broadly understood – including democratic governance, equal rights of citizens irrespective of their castes or religious backgrounds, and the agrarian question – becomes important in new ways in neoliberal times. Neoliberalism has created the need for a heightened battle for democracy.

Consider the national question. This question is no longer about fighting formal colonialism. The new national question has many elements. It is about fighting 'new imperialism', which is predominantly practiced through economic mechanisms and ultimately backed up by the threat of force. It is the imperialism of the powerful governments of the developed world, of MNCs, and of international institutions (IMF, the World Bank, MNCs, major creditors, and 'aid' agencies). This is an imperialism that is justified and sold to ordinary people through the discourse of development (as growth). It is also sold using chauvinistic ideas about India's 'superpower status', which is only as a regional subordinate of the supreme guardian of global capitalism, the USA. The post-colonial neoliberal state itself, managed by people with the neoliberal mentality ('neoliberality'), has become a new mechanism of imperialism. So, neoliberalism has heightened the need for anti-imperialist struggle and for the sovereignty of oppressed nations. As well, an important aspect of space-economy is the phenomenon of SEZs where the usual laws of the land, including labor laws do not operate. These can be compared to the princely states of colonial times, and do not contribute to national unity, and must be gotten rid of. The national question and the democratic question (i.e. the questions of the new imperialist subordination, the state and society becoming more undemocratic, and of peasants losing land) are rooted in the fact that the NEP represents capitalism in its most naked and ruthless form.

If the above assessment is broadly correct, it indicates a very different sort of solution to the national and democratic question and to the specific problems, such as mass impoverishment, spatially uneven development and agrarian crisis, that neoliberalism is creating, than what the traditional Left has been offering. The intellectual and political fight against the NEP cannot be merely about changing the dirty clothes of the state (meaning changing its policy and making it regulate the affairs of capitalism, as in 'olden times'). It cannot be about interrupting, deconstructing, and destabilizing things and narratives about neoliberalism and wider society a bit here and a bit there, although the struggle for the regulation of business is not entirely unnecessary. The idea that there is such a thing as neoliberalism (or capitalism) with a human face is, once again, based on the lie, the deception, that the basic interests of capital are fundamentally compatible with the basic interests of the toiling masses in a sustainable, contradiction-free, manner. Unregulated growth, control of society's resources by big business, the exploitation of labor, income inequality, and ecological devastation cannot be compatible with socially coordinated wealth creation, equality, solidarity, popular democracy, and satisfaction of human needs. If this critique is right, then the intellectual and political project must have the larger goal of theoretically and practically transcending the very conditions that produce the neoliberalism model itself and going beyond the content of whose form neoliberalism is.

Indicative of the hegemony of neoliberalism, in India (as elsewhere), is the fact that scholars talk about neoliberalism more than about capitalism. So a major discursive, or ideological, success of neoliberalism is that it has hidden capitalism under its *choli* (a short-sleeved blouse worn by many Indian women). Scholars often explain society's economic, social and ecological problems in terms of neoliberalism, and not capitalism. That is, when critical ideas about economy are produced, they are often against neoliberalism as such and not against capitalism per se. Form is prioritized over content.

What is problematic about neoliberalism, including neoliberal policy, is not *this or that* aspect of it (e.g. the idea that it increases poverty and inequality or the idea that restriction on short-term capital flows or shrinking government intervention is the problem). Rather, the *whole* 'thing' is the problem. So it requires a totalizing (dialectical) critique, one that situates its limited benefits in relation to its enormous costs and sees it from multiple vantage points.

There is nothing wrong with critiquing neoliberalism, and there is nothing wrong with raising anti-neoliberalism demands. The demands must be made. But the scope of this anti-neoliberalism is narrow. It remains merely a partial demand aimed at fighting for a better capitalism. The political action that is merely anti-neoliberalism fails to convert the fight against neoliberalism into a transitional demand. Anti-neoliberalism must be a transitional demand which must be made to connect the existing (lower) level of consciousness to the level of consciousness that is needed for a fundamental challenge to class relations in India.

To reiterate the point just made: much critical discourse and much progressive politics, in India (and outside India), are stuck with a critique of neoliberalism as such, in the hope for a world that is less neoliberal, rather than a world that is not capitalist. Just as a restrictive concept of capitalism discussed in Chapter 3, a concept in which capitalism exists only when there is economically advanced capitalism, has justified a capitalist politics of the Left that aims to produce a better (= more democratic) and more advanced capitalism, similarly, similarly, a critique of capitalism that, more or less, equates capitalism to neoliberalism, is bound to encourage a bourgeois politics of the masses, one that aims for a capitalism that is a little more state-directed than it is now.

4        Capitalist Class Relation, Technological Change, and Labor

We have seen that capitalism can be seen in terms of its multiple forms (e.g. forms of subsumption; neoliberalism, etc.), and we have also seen that formal subsumption can, in certain ways, be an obstacle to technological change. There is another way in which one can examine capitalism: this is to examine the ways in which technological change under capitalism does happen with potential redistributive effects on the worker. Given the importance of agriculture in a less developed country such as India, the topic of technological change in that sector is of special interest. A major form of technological-change has been the Green Revolution (GR), which has similarities with the on-going 'gene revolution' (biotechnology revolution). While the GR seems to be somewhat associated with the ratio of the rural population below the poverty line *at a point in time,* there seems to be no association between the GR and the important issue of poverty *reduction.* This is the case whether or not the population factor is held constant. The GR technology and the population factor, the twin neo-Malthusian mechanisms in which Lipton and others invest so much causal power, seem to have no statistical relation with poverty reduction (at the State level in India). Poverty reduction has taken place both with and without technological advancement. And persistence of poverty characterizes both technological advancement and the lack of it.

The real test of the relation between the GR and poverty lies in its impact on what happens to the poverty process over time (not just at a point in time) and in different States (not just in some particular places). Poverty has been, and arguably, can be, reduced without the GR (or for that matter, without any other technology or an increase in the economic output as such). And, in some cases, GR can have some favourable impact on the poor (through its impact on non-farm employment and by other means). But it is not necessary that that will be the case generally. Given the GR, poverty reduction is possible but not necessary. More generally, technology is neither a necessary nor a sufficient condition for reduction in absolute poverty. If the lack of technology was a necessary cause of poverty, one in seven people in the United States of America would not have to live below the line of absolute poverty. While the GR technology does not have any necessary poverty reduction impact, it cannot also be said that it has any necessary poverty-increasing impact, *independently* of social relations within which technology operates. There is simply no necessary relation between technology and poverty reduction, positive or negative. Much of what I have said about technology in its Green Revolution form applies to technology in its biotechnology form. A transition seems to be occurring from the Green Revolution to the gene revolution (biotechnology). The latter is linked to neoliberal capitalism. Biotechnology companies are pushing for the use of GM (genetically modified) seeds to be used on the ground that with these seeds, cultivators will increase their yields and therefore their income. The arguments in favour of the use of GM seeds are almost identical to those for the Green Revolution (HYV seeds) and therefore can be critically assessed in the way that this chapter does for the Green Revolution. Like the Green Revolution, the gene revolution is controversial, and for similar reasons (Bownas, 2016; Herring and Paarlberg, 2016). GMO seeds are extremely expensive to buy (Plahe et al., 2017; Shiva et al., 2002). These seeds have to be bought every year (a cultivator cannot save the seeds from the current year for use in the next year). The use of the seeds requires other chemicals have led to some of the farmers going into debt, and some of them are committing suicide. The effects of GMO seeds, like those of HYV seeds, will depend on the overall political-economic, or class context, in which these seeds are accessed and used (Carroll, 2017). If in India's Maharashtra State, the districts using GM cotton seeds are the districts where numerous indebted farmers have committed suicide, this points to the need to examine the GM technology in relation to the context of class relations within which it works.

The analysis of the GR–poverty relation sheds light on the relation between technology and society, or to use the terminology of Marxist political economy, the relation between social relations and productive forces (especially, technology) (Cohen, 2000; Liodakis, 1997; *Science & Society*, 2006). The analysis supports the general theoretical idea about the class character of technology, that technological change and its social consequences for people are shaped by capitalist social relations of production (Smith, 2010). Technology, as a 'thing' exists and operates, in the context of certain social relations, which shape how it produces its effects. So technology is not only a thing but is also a relationship. Technology itself cannot solve humanity's problems such as poverty, as its effects are mediated by capitalist class relations.

It is in fact no longer sufficient to define technology solely as use-values, as the equipment, techniques, etc. That definition is not false. But it fails to capture the historically specific nature of technology under *capitalist class relations*. This means that whether a technology is used and when used what its effects on common people will be, depend on whether it can remove certain natural barriers to production and exchange and increase the quantity of use-values produced. It also depends on whether the technology can generate profits (especially, in the form of extra surplus value caused by a rise in productivity of labor). Under capitalism, the fundamental aim of technological change is not to satisfy human needs. This view is contrary to technology fetishism. In the latter view, technology (whether it is mechanical, biological, electronic, etc.) holds the key to the resolution of society's problems. Harary (2018) calls such a view 'technological utopia'.

*Because* technology works in the context of social relations, technology, understood non-deterministically and dialectically, can be a window on to the understanding the structure of social relations itself. It is worth repeating Marx's point from *Capital* volume 1:

> Technology reveals the active relation of [human beings] to nature, the direct process of production of [their] life, and thereby it also lays bare the process of the production of the social relations of [their] life, and of the mental conceptions that flow from those relations.
>
> MARX, 1977: 493

While it is true that technology reveals the character of social relations of production, what is more true is that the entire 'regime' of production process – including what kind of use-values are produced and whether they are produced for the world market and how (and with what kind of techniques) – reveals the nature of social relations of production. It is useful therefore to examine the regime of production for the world market under neoliberal capitalism.

## 5    Export-Oriented Neoliberal Capitalism, Social Oppression, and Dual Metabolic Rift

In an interesting way, in policy circles, the emphasis on agricultural production and that on the neoliberal approach to development have come together in recent times. In the late 2000s, the World Bank suggested that agriculture – commercial agriculture, that is – could deliver economic development and poverty reduction in the Global South. And, internationally, neoliberal approach to development is promoted by the World Bank and other similar institutions. Neoliberalism (which is the main topic of Chapter 4), which is often known as NEP (New Economic Policy) in India, includes at least two inter-connected things. One is the state's relative withdrawal from welfare provision (which has implications for the social wage and the balance of power between capital and labor over wages, etc.). Another is the promotion of a regime of relatively de-regulated production which is enabled by trade liberalization and which is based on a politically vulnerable non-unionized (mobile) working class to produce cheap commodities for export. These two approaches – stress on agriculture and a neoliberal approach – are combined when export-oriented, de-regulated production of nontraditional agricultural goods from poorer countries such as India (to richer countries but not just to richer countries) is encouraged. Shrimp aquaculture is a very important aspect of this process. Shrimp production is a specific instance of a larger system of production. It is a form of 'New Agricultural Production' (NAP): the production of luxury (or high-value) non-traditional agri-commodities for export (Watts, 1996). NAP fits in with, and is a part of, a larger process: neoliberalism, or, agrarian neoliberalism. In India, NAP is a part of NEP.

Production of shrimp – like the production of all things – requires labor. In most cases, this labor takes the form of *wage*-labor. All wage-laborers *are the same* at one level in that they all have a specific relation with capital in terms of relations of exchange, property and production of surplus value. At another level (at a more concrete level), wage-labor *is differentiated* along lines of social relations of gender, age, location and ethnicity, so we deal with not wage-labor as such but, for example, indigenous wage-labor, child wage-labor, etc. The exploitation and domination of aqua-laborers happens in ways in which capitalist relations are mediated by place-specific relations of difference. The exploitation and domination of aqua-laborers are also shaped by the specificities of nature-dependent production (e.g. the biophysical character of labor process). Just as forces of nature such as land and water are 'exploited' in shrimp-culture, meaning that the shrimp-production process extracts a lot more out of nature than it returns to it, laborers on shrimp-farms are similarly exploited: the wage they receive to produce a 'cheap' commodity for export are less than the net value embodied in the shrimps that they produce. Akin to the metabolic rift, this is a social rift. The two rifts are parts of the same process: relation between capital and the immediate producer.

Shrimp culture is justified by the 'rhetoric of poverty alleviation'. This kind of development discourse is contradicted by the materiality of the real situation: those who produce shrimps, like millions of people performing other kinds of work, do not receive a decent wage, and are forced to experience all the three forms of LMR (Labor Metabolic Rift). The inadequacy of wages takes many forms. The 'gross wages' are low. Their *net* wages are also low because of the various hidden 'costs of work' (e.g. deductions from wages; costs of illness that is caused by work). Real wages are low in relation to laborers' basic needs. Relative wages – wages relative to the profit – earned by entrepreneurs are also low (workers are aware of this 'class inequality' in part from the lavish life style of the aqua-entrepreneurs). To Kautsky's words (1988: 385), they work 'like beasts of burden by day [and are] housed worse than beasts of burden by night'. The conditions of aqua-laborers, including the ways in which their lives in the workplace and labor market are controlled, are similar those of the workers subjected to sweatshop conditions more generally (Mezzadri, 2016, 2018; Pattenden, 2016).

The regime of low wages and poor working conditions in shrimp areas is caused and reproduced by multiple concrete mechanisms. Increasingly divorced from the means of production such as land and access to water bodies, and without savings or secure long-term employment, workers, including women and child workers, rely on this or that capitalist for their social reproduction. Each owner presumes that the workers whom they employ only for 4–5 months will somehow survive for the rest of the year from family production, meager crumbs thrown at their families in their own villages from the government (whose welfare commitment is dwindling anyway), or from the employment by other owners. If employers have to employ certain workers on a more permanent basis, they might have *some* interest in their long-term social reproduction. This is not the case. The other concrete mechanisms behind the regime of low wages and poor working conditions include: deliberate delay in, and withholding of, the payment of wages; strict labor control regimes including use of chemicals maximizing work effort; and capital's power to impose and define the 'piece' and the 'wage' in the piece-wage system, even in the face of occasional protests. Interestingly, these are some of the processes that Marx talks about in *Capital* volume 1.

There are also several subjective processes that reproduce low-wage capitalism. These include the specific form of working class consciousness that suggests a form of empathy for the 'suffering' employers. This is a form of consciousness – a bourgeois consciousness of workers – that overlies an incipient 'anti-capital' consciousness, or consciousness in its 'embryonic form' (Lenin 1977b: 113). Underlying workers' empathy for employers who pay low wages and commit what Marx would call 'fraudulent tricks' is the mistaken idea that wages are paid to a laborer out of the sale of products of her labor. According to this idea, the magnitude of wages depends on the actual price at which the employer is able to sell the shrimps, so if shrimps sell for less, wages will be less. Shared by both employers and laborers, this idea, this illusion, contributes to the reproduction of capitalist relations. It is useful to quote Marx here again:

> Wages are not a share of the worker in the commodities produced by him. Wages are that part of already existing commodities with which the capitalist buys a certain amount of productive labor-power.
> MARX, 1976: 36

The temporality of wage-form of labor – the *fact* that wages are paid *after* the product of labor is sold contributes to an *illusion* in the minds of workers.

Workers' spontaneous consciousness is generally contradictory. While there is evidence of illusion as just mentioned, there is also evidence that workers are conscious of the fact their situation is objectionable. While many workers are conscious of the need to be organized against these conditions, some show more passive resistance. The latter is indicated when some say that 'No one should work in shrimp-culture in his or her life'. What if a large number of workers believe in this? What if local branches of Left parties suddenly have their veil over their eyes removed? Unfortunately, the reality is that the locally-based Left parties have failed to do anything to mobilize workers and raise the workers' consciousness.

One can see that the processes underlying the low-wage regime discussed above are connected to the politics of wage-labor relations, i.e. to the issue of the balance of power between capital and labor. Even such economic factors as unemployment causing low wages are not just economic factors: unemployment makes political resistance against low wages difficult to launch. But employers know that workers *can* resist. That is why they take pre-emptive steps to stop any possible unity among workers.

The relations between capital and labor are being mediated by specific social relations (and cultural constructions) of gender, age, and ethnicity (one of whose local forms is aboriginality). These are utilized by employers to create a vulnerable workforce, which makes it possible to super-exploit without much political trouble. Importantly, relations between capital and labor are also mediated by the geographical character of labor. Generally, a social wage (e.g. government welfare) and local 'social capital' can tip the balance of power between the employer and the employee slightly, in favour of the employee. Migrant workers, however, are denied this advantage. At one level, capital's laborers do not have to be migrants, or indeed, women or children. But in actual practice, in a specific places and times, social difference makes a difference to capital's attempt to pocket the economic difference between (a) the value that the oppressed worker produces and the value of the wage that the worker is lucky to receive, and (b) between the value of labor power (what wages should be) and what they actually receive.

It is also important to notice how the relation between capital and labor operates through the biophysical nature of the labor process. This happens in many ways. The shrimp production process is nature-dependent: it can be affected by unpredictable rains and floods. Shrimps can catch diseases. We need to, however, connect the nature of the nature-dependent production to its social (capitalist) nature. Consider how the unpredictability of the biophysical process as well as the fact that the production process has to be continuous (i.e. shrimps have to be watched for 24 hours) contribute to a form of consent to the regime of long hours and difficult (night) work in the mind of laborers:

they (including child laborers) are made to believe that shrimps are like children, can become sick, and need to be constantly looked after through long hours of work. The biophysicality of the labor process acts as a mask to hide its capitalist character. It also acts as a form of labor control: if shrimps have not been fed well throughout the night at proper intervals, the employer will know this from a specific form of the physical movement of shrimps. Aqua-labor is controlled in other ways as well. For example, women laborers' work intensity is sought to be enhanced through the use of chemical technology when, for example, chemicals are mixed with shrimps to help the laborers de-head them faster. Ensuring the safety/health of the biological product (shrimp) is paramount; this leads the employers to hire nonlocals who are easier to discipline and who have limited ability to inflict Luddite class revenge (e.g. by harming the shrimps in the event of a labor dispute). The biophysical process also affects laborers' health, producing what Fracchia (2008) would call the 'body in pain'. The men, women and children, who produce a popular delicacy for the national and global markets, cannot even eat with their own hands the simple food (rice, etc., and not shrimp) that they can buy with their meager wages. Their hands have blisters due to the use of chemicals at the production and beheading sites. It is as if each shrimp, a commodity, records in its body the annals of low wages, unending night shifts, and long hours of work as well as the unfulfilled desire of the poor laborers to enjoy a socially acceptable level of living. The aqua-labor process signifies the production of a use-value as well as the capitalist character of that production.

Workers' conditions are of little concern to owners, however. If a worker is crippled, another can be hired. There is plenty of labor power available, whose production has no/little direct cost to individual employers. But if one shrimp is below the expected size or if it dies, what is lost is value (labor power already spent) and surplus value (profit), which have no substitute. When a use-value (e.g. edible shrimps) produced by the worker is lost, the value is also lost, and with that, any surplus value in it is also lost. So shrimps' health is of great interest to owners. If shrimps are not healthy, owners cannot sell them in the global market for an expected profit on their investment. It is human labor that produces shrimps, but shrimps become more 'valuable' than human beings and their labor.

Like many other export commodities from the countries of the periphery, shrimps are being produced dominantly under social relations of global capitalism. This is capitalism based on the formal subsumption of labor (which is the topic in Chapter 3), a mode of capitalist production based on long working days and the payment of low wages (i.e. wages that do not even cover subsistence needs). Formal subsumption of labor comprises what I called LMR 2 and LMR 3 (as well as LMR 1) in Chapter 6. Wages and the working day are touching their physical minimum and physical maximum respectively. In the context of global demands for reduced state intervention in national economies, Third World comparative advantage supposedly lies in 'cheap' environmental and labor resources. 'Cheap', however, only signifies the relationship between commodities exchanged; hidden are the material realities of production. It is also unlikely that the low-wage regime described here is specific to the spatial context under study (India). It is likely to be common to most shrimp-exporting poorer countries.

Relevant here is Marx's (1977: 164) notion of commodity fetishism where relations between commodities produced in different places replace relations between people producing these, both in reality and in our consciousness. In commodity fetishism, it appears as if being bought and sold for a profit is in the very DNA of a thing (a use-value) such as shrimp. That a dollar in the USA or Canada can buy – or that a certain amount of a product can be exchanged for – several counts of cheap foreign shrimps, this relation of exchange, is not written in the body of the commodity-shrimp, how-much-ever we may twist and turn and pinch these edible (non-human) creatures. Much rather, this relation of exchange is based on specific social relations under which the laboring human creatures producing this commodity live, work and suffer. These are the social relations of capitalist property and of production, of the class relations. And these class relations are defended by the state.

## 6     Class, Capitalism, and the Capitalist State

Yet, to do a class analysis of the state often prompts a charge of analytical bias (because the state is often assumed to work as a neutral agent), as well as the charge of economism and 'classism'. The latter charge implies that a class analysis of the state reduces the state to class relations and to its economic imperatives, and thus ignores non-class social relations such as caste and gender, etc. Those who make these charges – including those who put their faith in the state's ability to solve the fundamental problems of the majority-class, which must sell its labor power and/or small amount of products of their labor (as small-scale producers) – must answer the following: if the capitalism that India has is not particularly conductive to a sustained and systemic increase in labor productivity per hour per person and to an economic regime which is not based on making people work long hours for barely 400 Rupees a day, if whatever limited welfare benefits were provided to the lower classes are being cut or in constant danger of being cut, if technological change that has happened does not benefit the lower classes much, if export-oriented production does not help those who produce things for export, if the desperate masses have to struggle against their dispossession and against extreme forms of exploitation and oppression, and if a fascistic movement, including fascistic politicians, are curtailing democratic rights of ordinary people and are deepening the neoliberal assault on the toiling masses, what explains all this and why does the state not do anything?

It is a truism, albeit a crucial one that is defended in this book, that class relations and the attendant material conditions, constitute the most important context for all forms of intervention by the state and for the very form (territorial and political form) of the state itself. Of course, within this class context other social relations – i.e. those of caste, religion, ethnicity, region and nation – operate and influence the state and its class character. And within the limits set by class relations, state officials and politicians exercise power relations over the masses, in a way that cannot be reduced to capitalism and that benefits the officials and politicians: in India, bureaucrats and politicians-in-power behave as kings and queens with respect to the masses.

Because capitalism is the dominant mode of production in India, the state is a capitalist state, and thus an 'agent' of capitalist development, *both* in pre-neoliberal and neoliberal times, and *both* in rural and urban areas. The relation of partnership between the two arms of capital relation – the state and the capitalist class – has been justified in terms of two major ideologies: one is the ideology of state control and socialism, and another is one of free market. Ideology does not mean total lies. Ideology refers to ideas that are partly true and partly false and that contribute to the reproduction of an in-egalitarian and exploitative order (Eagleton, 1991). The ideology of state control over the business world in India in the early years of the post-1947 period was not entirely a lie. There *was* a degree of state control. There was a degree of state intervention on behalf of the masses. Even the ruling class understood from the very beginning (since the 1940s) that a small degree of state control and a small degree of pro-poor re-distribution is a remedy to potential social upheaval in the aftermath of 1917. In the neoliberal times, the other ideology, the ideology of free market has justified interventions by the state that are more blatantly in the interest of capital than before. In other words, the state has always worked, more or less, in the interest of the capitalist class. Its policies (as well its form – federal-liberal-democratic form) have been accordingly influenced by the interests and actions of the dominant classes. Of course, state policies have also been, to some extent, shaped by the lower-class struggles, actual or potential. What I say about the capitalism – state relation in India is supported by comments on the topic from Ronald Herring, a long-time critical commentator on Indian political economy: the structural power of capital is evident in the imperative facing every governmental regime of whatever nominal ideology to maintain 'business confidence', or spur investment, increase growth rates and employment, improve foreign exchange positions, or improve geopolitical security' (Herring, 2013: 131). Herring adds: 'no explicit mobilization is necessary for these outcomes; if capital is not pleased with such policies, it will move away or stop investing' (ibid.). Much discussion of class politics curiously ignores this 'most materially significant element of class power' (p. 131). Parties and governments are forced to serve capital in the national interests – and this is what Miliband (1983) refers to when he talks about the 'partnership' between capital and an 'autonomous' state elite. But these same parties and governments are not forced to serve the subordinate classes in the same national interest (Herring, 2013: 139). From the standpoint of capital and its state, these classes, the majority, are obviously not the nation, and their interest in a decent standard of living and in a democratic polity and culture, is not the national interest.

Like any capitalist state, the state in India must sustain the myth that capitalist accumulation (which goes by the name of 'growth' or 'Vikas', etc.) benefits not just the already-better-off entrepreneurs, and that the poor also gain some significant advantages from it. The myth needed is that the exploiters (misnamed as employers and wealth-creators) and the exploited, benefit from the same process. This myth legitimizes the state. As well, the legitimacy of the post-1947 state derived in no small measure from two assumptions: that, unlike colonial government which served 'foreign' interests, it would serve domestic ones; and that, to this end, it would promote economic development from which the nation as a whole would benefit. Increasingly, however, the distinction between the pre-1947 and post-1947 development projects is being eroded, as the neoliberal state not only facilitates the dispossession and exploitation of the poor by international and domestic capital, but also encourages the latter to undertake export-oriented cultivation. Farm crops are once again being seen to be produced mainly for an elite (= 'foreign') market, much as they were during the colonial era. This can contribute to the broader process of delegitimizing the state, a situation which in turn can intensify class struggle 'from below This can prompt the repressive 'from above' response by the neoliberal state protecting the interests of the capitalist class in India.

Because of a continuing failure on the part of the state to promote development in the interest of workers and small-scale producers and because of its current neoliberal policies supportive of domestic and foreign capital, this apparatus may indeed face a legitimation crisis, especially in rural areas and in urban slums. The extent to which such a legitimation crisis will be, in fact, realized depends on how the lower classes and their organizations respond to the situation theoretically and politically. And to the degree that a crisis does take shape, much will also depend on how the state responds, in particular the use of coercive power at its disposal, and how in turn lower classes respond to this. Indeed, the topic of how the lower classes fight for their rights and how the state responds, is an important one.

## 7      Lower-Class Struggles and the State Response

Relations of class (as well as caste- and gender-based social oppression that exploited classes are subjected to) have created extremely difficult conditions of living for workers and peasants, which the post-colonial capitalist state has, more or less, failed to significantly mitigate. The conjunctural combination of unjust conditions of living and state failure has created a situation ripe for *class* struggle, one instance of which is the Naxalite movement, a part of the world-wide Maoist movement.

The Naxalite movement is rooted in material conditions of existence, which are social-cultural as well as economic. It has fruitfully combined class politics (albeit in a rather limited manner) as well as those of cultural oppression. Many people within the state agencies, and many middle class people, do not fully understand Naxalites' pro-poor ideological significance. They homogenize the movement associating it exclusively with violence. They often mistakenly treat Naxalites merely/mainly as armed thugs, without any political and socio-economic program of development for the poor. However, the Naxalite movement does suffer from serious problems. This emanate from its inadequate class-based understanding and inadequate class-based practice. The material conditions of deprivation are produced dominantly by the specific ways in which capitalism works in the concrete conditions of India, which include remnants of feudalism, and liberal democracy (however distorted), within the system of global capitalism. The Naxalites have not fully and consistently understood the following: that the most important reason for rural distress, and indeed the distress of the majority of the country's population, is the *capitalist* character of the system, which is also mainly responsible for state's failure to mitigate some of the adverse effects of the system on the poor. In part because of the Naxalites' inadequate understanding of the system's dynamics, their dominant focus has been mistakenly on the rural/agrarian issue (in backward regions) and on its so-called 'semi-feudal' shell. This has meant that the movement has, more or less, been disconnected socially from the working class and spatially from urban areas, the main theatres of accumulation and exploitation by both domestic and imperialist bourgeoisie.

The *ideological* framing or representation of the Naxalite movement as terrorist, as a menace, as a security threat, as ultra-left extremism, along with state's own *political* shell (liberal-democratic form), give some legitimacy to the state to repress. In the Naxalite case, this is the fact that they are a communist movement and that a communist movement is automatically seen as a threat to the security of the capitalist state (Subramanian, 2004). This ethos, supported by many middle class people, legitimizes state repression. Further, the state has access to its own expanding *mobilizing structures:* network of police and paramilitary agencies, police informers, anti-Naxalite civilian militias that the state supports, all of which, of course, complement the private coercive means available to the propertied classes. Here it is important to mention how state-supported research calls for more state violence against Naxalism. Most importantly, the political-economic-ideological threat from Naxalites offers the *political opportunity* for repression.

There is no doubt that Naxalites use violent methods. One should also remind oneself that: landlords and some business houses use daily violence against ordinary people; government officials and politicians behave in the most rude manner with the masses, sometimes not shying away from using coercive measures; Hindu mobs burn Christians' houses, destroy mosques and massacre Muslims, with the covert/overt support of politicians; Islamic terrorists kill innocent Hindus; and higher castes also kill lower castes. Yet, Naxalite violence is seen as *the greatest* threat to the state and to the class order that the state must protect. This is *because* their violence is against: actions of specific sections of the property-owning class (e.g. landlords, traders, mining companies), the excesses of the capitalist class system, and functioning of state personnel and laws that *support* the exploitative property owners. In the case of the Naxalite movement, its violence is prompted by state violence (and by violence from the sections of the property-owning class itself). If this is the case, then the idea that the state is violent towards Naxalites just because they are violent is inadequate, if not entirely untrue. State violence is rooted in its own class *content* and in the class content (character) of the Naxalites. It does not primarily come from their *mode* of fighting. The physical threat from Naxalites is not the only reason for state violence. The state uses, and will use, violence against the Naxalite movement because the state must defend the interests of sections of the propertied class that the movement is fighting against.

Apart from challenging certain aspects of the class system, the Naxalite movement also seeks to build alternative modes of living *within* capitalism. And that is a threat to the state. In terms of its actual practice, the alternative development landscape that the Naxalites seek to produce somehow resonates with the post-Marxist (e.g. Gibson-Graham, 2006) idea of production of post-capitalist spaces within capitalism (see also Holloway, 2005). The lower classes that the movement seeks to mobilize are not just an agency of *resistance* (backed by *force* where necessary). The movement also plays a positive, albeit limited, developmental role. In a sense the Maoists are mimicking state practices of governmentality (Sundar, 2014a), or rather, what one might call 'state's developmentality'. The latter can be seen as developmental governmentality, which signifies the deployment of developmental activities and development discourse to discipline people and shape their consciousness that in turn legitimizes the capitalist state. Naxalites promote an alternative developmentality which produces consent of common people to Naxalism, and thus potentially enhances their politicization, posing a serious threat to the state. State violence is partly directed at *destroying* this consent. As Spacek (2017) says: 'force and development have become conceptually blended and hybridised in practice, leading to a colonisation of statecraft by policing and violence' (p. 176). Further: 'The police have become the developmental agents in the [Naxal] region, responsible for carrying out infrastructural and social service delivery. They are the primary agents of the state', a state that is operating on the basis of 'architectures of force and spaces of violence' (p. 176). So, in so far as carrying out developmental activities is about producing consent to the legitimacy of the state and to the class rule that the state defends, and in so far as the coercive organs are the agents of developmental activities, the boundary between coercive and consent-making state activities begins to be blurred.

The state generally functions as one arm of the structure of private – property relations, and intervenes on behalf of the propertied classes (Das, 2017a: Chapter 8). Whatever else the state is, it is, above all, an armed body of people, separate from ordinary toiling masses who are the majority (workers and poor peasants). The state is basically an institution of class violence, functioning on behalf of the ruling classes, and against the ordinary people. The state uses violence against ordinary citizens if they fight against: (a) this *structure of private property relations*, (b) the *mechanisms* through which this structure works (e.g. competitive drive for profit, rent and interest; dispossessing people of their land in order to ensure access of the business world to people's resources), (c) and the *concrete effects* of these mechanisms (e.g. extreme poverty; ecological destruction). The state uses violence against ordinary citizens if they fight against the powerful *agents* of the state (e.g. parties; officers; police) who support these relations/mechanisms. The form of political movement of the masses does not matter much. Its content – its class content – does. That is: whether ordinary people are engaged in peaceful mobilization or whether they use a degree of violence (in self-defense), is generally beside the point. And when inequality level rises, the mask of democracy that a state wears is increasingly difficult to wear. State violence against ordinary people and against those who politically mobilize them *is* an intervention on behalf of the ruling classes and their political spokespersons and managers, whether or not the mobilization of ordinary people is violent. In the internal wars against Naxalism (and other acts of resistance) the state is deploying common people against themselves: most of the people who join the security apparatuses are from working class and peasant backgrounds, desperate to earn a living, and these people, are used by the elite to kill people like themselves (i.e. people from working class and peasant backgrounds who resist exploitation and oppression and undemocratic acts of the state).[6]

The state impersonates guerilla tactics of a section of the Naxalite movement to fight it (Sundar, 2014a). By doing so, it is turning what I would call the 'homo sufferer' (working masses) into Agamben's 'homo sacer': those people who the organs of the state could kill without being guilty of committing murder. In India's so-called red corridor, there is an important contradiction: the red corridor's monetary value is multiple times the nation's annual income, and yet it contains the world's most impoverished people (especially among low castes and aboriginal communities). To 'resolve' this kind of exceptionally intense contradiction which signifies the contradiction between a small elite and the majority of the population, the state creating a (quasi-) 'state of exception', 'a legal civil war that allows for the physical elimination not only of political adversaries but of entire categories of citizens who for some reasons cannot be integrated into the political system' (Agamben, 2005: 2). This civil war is the class struggle from above against the masses, i.e. the lower classes (workers and poor peasants, including those who are from the adivasi and Dalit backgrounds).

The state is able to engage in violence against Naxalites by producing an epistemological exaggeration: a political-geographic overestimation of the threat to the state, a knowledge-claim, a ruling class ideology, which would justify the increased level of violence by the state. By saying that the Naxalite threat can be anywhere anytime, the state of exception can potentially be produced anywhere anytime within the nation. The border moves inside, so the military can be engaged, if needed. That this feeds into, and is supported by, right-wing, hyper-nationalist groups and individuals, is not surprising. The state's approach to lower classes is, more or less, the same, whether its affairs are managed by the BJP or the Congress or indeed by regional parties.

---

6  It is interesting that: in a speech in June 1975, Jayaprakash Narayan called on the police and the army to disobey what he described as illegal orders (Smith, 1979).

The post-colonial state labelling the Naxalite movement as a menace, as criminal, as unpatriotic, etc. is symbolic violence, as is its tendency to see any social justice movement as Naxalite and therefore violent. In this sense, the post-colonial state's approach to militant movements for social justice is similar to the colonial state's attitude to militant freedom fighters. In September 2018, the state arrested five well-known social justice activists, labelling them 'urban Naxals' for their alleged connection to the Naxalite movement (Hindu, 2018). The deployment of the construct of 'Urban Naxal' is a means of expanding state's battle against the Naxalite movement to the cities. This urbanization of state's fight against Naxalism which is a rural phenomenon, is also a form of an all-out war against *any form* of dissent that the state cannot cope with or tolerate. Someone who is seen as an enemy of *the state* is equated to an enemy *of the people* in order to justify penal interventions. This seeing does not see that the state works on behalf of the fundamental interests of a tiny minority of the population, propertied classes, and that it even works at the behest of certain individuals or fractions belonging to the propertied classes. The state must create its enemy, its other, to justify its own existence and to deflect attention from state's real enemy (nation of workers and peasants, the majority of the population), whose interests are antagonistic to the ruling class-minority which the state must protect. The state cannot *overtly* declare the majority of the nation as its enemy but its actions treat the majority as the enemy or as if it is the enemy: *anyone* who resists the class rule and its effects is labelled a Naxalite and can be harmed, whether or not they have anything to do with Naxalism. So the state has *de facto* launched a war against the enemy within, against the majority of the people, via its war against the localized Naxalites. Just as the state is generally a false protector of common people's interests, the enemy it constructs is also generally false, or not as true as portrayed by the state.

Symbolic violence can create a condition for 'subjective violence', which is the violence performed by 'a clearly identifiable agent' (Zizek, 2008: 1, 10). This agent can be the agent of the ruling classes (their security agents or hired hoodlums) or of the state apparatus. State's subjective violence is reinforced by, and complements, the subjective violence by the ruling class, and to which Naxalite movement responds by its own subjective violence.

Systemic violence refers to the 'catastrophic consequences of the smooth functioning of our economic and political systems' (Zizek, 2008: 2). This is the violence that prompts the other two forms of violence (symbolic and subjective forms). Class rule is behind systemic violence and the state supports the class rule. The state is launching a violent war on people because they are fighting against systemic violence (i.e. they are fighting against a war on their livelihood and on their democratic right to protest injustice). State violence against Naxalites is an instance of a general form of violence, a violence that is necessary to thwart all forms of actual/potential opposition to systemic violence (i.e. to class rule). The government claims that its coercive forces are there to counter the Naxalites, but in actuality its aim is to intimidate into silence the democratic movements such as people resisting land grabs or fighting police repression. Where are these coercive forces of the state when the propertied classes and their goons inflict violence against ordinary people and when Hindu mobs lynch innocent Muslims? By creating drastic panic among people and curtailing people's freedom, the state makes it possible for corporations to be free to 'suck out the minerals and forest resources' (Dias, in Ismi, 2013). One form of freedom comes at the expense of another. Between two equal freedoms, it is the freedom that can be backed by greater violence that wins. The money buried in the mines is much more important than the respect for democratic rights of the exploited and oppressed (in the indigenous communities).

What state violence – the *de facto* 'everywhere-endless-war' against its people fighting for justice – means is this: while a 'society' will not tolerate violence against the state, it will very easily tolerate violence against the body and soul of its common citizens, including little children who are malnourished, who have to work as bonded labor abused by labor contractors and employers (Das, 2019), and who are assaulted by security people, in Naxalite areas. Why do the counts of security personnel killed while fighting against some segments of the Naxalite movement more important than the counts of the little children dying premature death and of women dying while giving birth, because of the failure of the state to provide for better conditions of life?[7]

Someone can argue that all states, when challenged by non-state forces, will behave the same way as the Indian state is doing in response to the Naxalite challenge. He/she might ask: would a socialist state (a state that comes to exist just after a revolutionary overthrow of capitalism) allow people to challenge it in the way that the Naxalite movement does? The answer is no. But there is a difference. It is a class difference. In class divided societies, the ruling class constitute the minority, and the majority are the exploited classes. All states of class societies, including capitalism, are states of, and for, a minority (the class

---

7   '3,000 children die every day from poor diet-related illness' (Qazi, 2018). Five women die every hour during childbirth in India, according to World Health Organization (Times of India, 2016).

that controls society's productive resources) and against the majority. These states use violence to suppress the majority. That is very undemocratic. A socialist state, is different, however: it would be the first state that is the state of the majority (workers and peasants) who need the state to stop overthrown classes from returning to power and to construct a society that is democratic in economic, political and cultural spheres. Therefore, any challenge from the overthrown propertied classes, who constitute a tiny minority, will need to be crushed by the state on behalf of the people. That response of the state is not comparable to the fact that a capitalist state violently crushes an opposition to it from the masses, the majority. The question is not: how does the state respond when it faces a challenge? The question is: what is the main purpose of the state with respect to the basic classes? The class character of the state and the class character of the challenge are important to keep in mind. State violence to preserve the privilege of a minority is not the same violence that may be necessary to preserve the economic and political power of the vast majority.

One must be critical of state violence, the scope of which has been *expanding*. There is another aspect of the reality which cannot be denied. This is that the Naxalite theory and strategy are self-*limiting* (Das, 2010, 2015). This is for various reasons. Firstly, there is the fact that the Naxalite movement is *not* fundamentally against the totality of capitalist class relations. The Naxalite movement is also problematic in that, whether or not it uses violence, it mistakenly treats the peasantry (or, the rural poor) as the main revolutionary agent rather than an ally of the urban working class. The deployment of anarchic and secretive violence by certain segments of the movement is against the principle that the masses can only self-emancipate themselves and that they will do this on the basis of their political organization and organized action, and not on the basis of secretive violence. But if the state can inflict violence on a movement which is not particularly anti-capitalistic and if it does not mobilize urban workers, then one can imagine how violent the state will be in relation to a movement that is fundamentally anti-capitalistic, mobilizing the main revolutionary agent (the working class) to fight for a socialist society characterized by popular democracy in every sphere of life, and not for a better – more democratic – form of capitalism.

We have seen that state repression is particularly likely when lower-class struggles target property relations that cause ordinary citizens to suffer. Whether these movements are violent, and whether the state is a liberal-democracy is a contingent matter. The liberals' argument that democracy pacifies the state collapses when one considers how repressive the liberal-democratic Indian state is towards a movement such as the Naxalite movement, even if this movement is not seeking to go beyond capitalism. The response of the state to the Naxalite movement is symptomatic of a wider tendency across countries, including India: states are turning to authoritarian methods to suppress ideological and political dissent. This is because with rising inequalities and given the crisis-tendencies of capitalism, states are increasingly unable to buy legitimacy by granting benefits, however limited, for the benefit of the majority. The states are increasingly unable to respond to the fact that there is a fundamental contradiction between big business's interests in profit and interest, and working masses' interest in obtaining access to food, shelter, health-care, education, culture and sustainable environment. The pacifying effect of democracy that some social movement theorists stress will work if the ordinary people remain pacified and do not exercise their (class-) agency in the face of exploitation and oppression and wait indefinitely for some benefits from above (e.g. state; NGOs, etc.). Lower-class struggles show limit to liberal democracy. Liberal democracy is not pacifist but it expects lower classes to remain pacified even when they are under attack by the state. Similarly, the state itself fails to obey its own laws while killing lower class members who fight for justice and yet the state expects them to obey the rules of law in their fight for justice.

The Indian state sees the Naxalite movement, especially, the activity of the more militant section of it (CPI-Maoist), as the greatest threat to itself and to democracy, and this perception is in part because the Naxalite movement does use physical force against oppressive elements where necessary and possible. But is the Naxalite movement really the main danger to democracy? It is not. The main anti-democratic force is not the Naxalite movement (sometimes called the Far Left) but it is the Far Right.

## 8      Economic Development and Democracy under the Right-Wing Government

There has been a resurgence of the Far Right in India since the early 1990s. This tendency is represented by the Modi government installed since 2014. Under the Modi government, the overall record of development has been an epic of dismal failure. This is the case, especially if we consider the issues that affect the lives of the masses such as: unemployment and under-employment; low wages; increasing concentration of wealth and income; agrarian crisis; increasing attack on democracy and secularism and attendant communalization of society and polity, and so on. The ultra-rich has had *achhe din*. But the vast majority of people of different castes and religions live and work under economic and political conditions which, generally speaking, have not been improving.

According to the Prime Minister (or his erudite speech writer), *development* has become a vibrant *mass movement.* Development as a mass movement is a beautiful idea. Development *should* become a mass movement. It *will* become a mass movement when *masses*, democratically self-organized, *move* to take control over their lives. Development will become a mass movement when the masses (toiling workers and small-scale producers) control how nation's resources are used – i.e. when *they* are able to decide and say that nation's resources and their *own* labor are used to satisfy *their* own needs, and *not* the needs of the business class for profit, not the needs of the political class for accumulating election funding and power, and not the needs of the top and pliant bureaucratic and intellectual layers for their financial and other privileges.

Controlled by a right-wing party, the government is brazenly pro-big business and panders to a narrow, upper-middle class urban segment of highly educated technical personnel, who, in turn, churn out pro-BJP and communal propaganda meant to dupe the masses, including by using social media. The overall economic orientation of the government is indicated by 'Modinomics' (India's version of 'Reaganomics'). Modinomics is, fundamentally, an anti-people package of pro-market, pro-business policies. Its aim is to create the conditions for enabling profits for the corporates through a combination of: super-exploitation of the masses on the basis of flexible labor policies; extreme austerity; reducing corporate tax liability; and surrendering society's natural and financial resources and state-owned enterprises to private business-owners. Modinomics is a vision of the most extreme form of neo-liberal capitalism that Indian embarked on, with Manmohanomics of Dr. Manmohan Singh who served India as the Finance Minister and then as the Prime Minister. The multiple failures of the post-2014 government can be tied to its blatantly Right-wing nature. The government is right-wing for a reason: it is right for the business class, a class which is on the wrong side of history. It is right-wing because its fundamental aim is to serve the business class. It therefore cannot be expected to do much that is right for wage-earners, farmers, the poor and small-scale entrepreneurs, in any systematic, logical and long-term manner, *even if* some in government may have good intentions and even if some crumbs may fall and do fall to the people in exchange for political support.

To judge a government's policy requires one to consider, for example, the extent to which the things (or use-values) it provides its common citizens have a commodified or decommodified character (see Polanyi, 1944/2001; also Block and Polanyi, 2003). The more de-commodified the things are, the better it is for the majority, simply because the majority do not have a lot of money in their hands. One must ask: is water or education or healthcare of good quality provided to citizens in adequate amount by the government as a free use-value or, at least, at a minimal price, relative to the income of the people? From the standpoint of the majority, the purpose of a government is to provide an *antidote* to the ravages of the market, at least as far as the consumption of basic necessaries is concerned. However, true to its right-wing economic policies, what the BJP government calls 'development' is a commodity. The so-called developmental benefits are market-mediated and even corporate-mediated and constitute the mechanisms for the creation or expansion of the market for commodities. This is exactly what the neo-liberal-capitalist state does (Harvey, 2005: 2). What use are electricity wires or LPG connections if people have no money to pay for electricity and LPG? What use are roads if these roads siphon off natural resources and the surplus of an area to other places, especially, big cities, or if the roads take one to the places where there is neither decent wage-work nor free or subsidized government-provided services, or if roads allow the coercive forces to crush common people's movement for justice? A road or electricity is a 'very trivial thing' because everyone knows that it is needed by everyone but it tends to attain 'metaphysical subtleties' (Marx, 1977: 163), when it is seen in the context of the commodity-driven society that this right-wing government is intent on extending and deepening.

The impact of the existing BJP government can be seen as the sum of (a) the impact of its right-wing economic policy, (b) its communal policy of authoritarian-communalism-hyper-Hindu-nationalism, and (c) the interaction between the two. Common people are directly hurt by BJP's development policy and economic thinking, buttressed by right-wing economists, including some from the US, who had previously been marginalized. The communal-authoritarian policy that divides people and that crushes the right to dissent also directly affects the masses, in part by undermining their potential for resistance against the economic and the political elite. And given that BJP's economic policy is implemented in a context of communal-authoritarianism supported by vigilantism and mob violence, the adverse impact of the economic policy is magnified: its adverse impact is greater than what it would be if BJP was not *both* communal and economically right-wing. The Hindu-fascistic movement thrives on what I would call 'communal fetishism': just as in commodity fetishism, people are forced to live their lives as if to be bought and sold (for a profit) is a natural trait of the things they need, similarly, in communal fetishism, a Hindu with a communal consciousness lives as if a non-Hindu inherently possesses traits that are against the interests of Hindus and therefore deserves to be hated.

If you are a Dalit or from a religious minority or indeed a woman who wants to live like an ordinary citizen with all the rights that men enjoy, then your life is one of fear. Or, if you speak against the regime of unreason, religious obscurantism, and on-going attacks on secular ideals, then your life is one of fear as well. The world's largest democracy is reduced to this. The question is why? Why is this turn to the extreme right-wing thinking and practices, which are characteristic of a fascistic movement?

## 9      Capitalist Political Economy and Turn to Fascistic Tendencies

In understanding the rise of fascistic forces, one has to keep in mind Marx's theory of politics in class society. It is in 'the direct relationship of the owners of the conditions of production to the immediate producers', in which we find the hidden basis of 'the political form of the relationship of sovereignty and dependence' (Marx, 1991: 927). He also says that: 'all struggles within the state' – for example, struggles over democracy, etc. – the forms in which the struggles of the different classes are fought out (Marx and Engels, 1978: 54). Avoiding economic reductionism, Marx asserts that while politics is based on economic matters, politics also reacts back on economic matters.

The rise of the BJP is a national-scale manifestation of a global phenomenon which is the fact that the big business facing an economic and social crisis is resorting to social reaction, the politics of hatred, and authoritarianism (both authoritarianism from above – the state; and authoritarianism from below – rightwing forces on the ground). The increasing strength of right-wing forces, including the rise of the BJP as the political head of these forces in India, has been engendered by three political-economic mechanisms:

a.   The first is the crisis of global capitalism that is manifested in India. Associated with this is the crisis of post-colonial national capitalism, and the attendant crisis of the livelihood of common people. The bourgeois system of the world and India's backward capitalism operating within the influence of imperialism and imperialist institutions, have been simply incapable of meeting the basic needs of the toiling classes. Masses have been subjected to exploitation (and indeed, super-exploitation), dispossession, and immiserization in its absolute and relative forms.

b.   The combination of the mechanisms of exploitation, dispossession, and immiserization requires legitimization/ justification in the minds of the masses. To the extent that these mechanisms are not accepted by the masses, they engage in potential/actual opposition, which in turns prompts a ruling class response in the form of authoritarianism. The latter also requires justification. There is thus a need for double justification (consent from the masses): the system of exploitation/dispossession/immiserization needs justification, and the coercive response to the lower-class struggle against the system also requires justification. There is a need for actively weakening of the lower-class opposition too. The ideology of religion and associated Hindu-nationalism, apart from the use of caste-based politics, provides such justification (consider all the calls for making sacrifices – accepting austerity and low wages, etc. – in the name of the nation). It also divides the masses along the lines of religion and fake view of nationalism that considers vast sections of the population as anti-national. Deployment of religion and religion-based politics is supplemented with lies and false promises, to obtain consent to the system, and this, in a liberal-democracy, includes obtaining votes for fascistic political outfits. All in all, a structural space is created for increasing strength of fascistic forces, which have been existing in India since the 1920s.

c. Capitalism produces a class-agency for the fascistic project. It produces a reserve army of labor and pauperized small-scale producers (who are on their way to becoming completely propertyless), the elements of which, in a poor economy without social benefits (or with very limited benefits) from the government, are vulnerable to lumpenization and criminality. Having been 'spiritually destroyed and morally disoriented by the cruelties they suffer in their everyday life', these victims of (neoliberal) capitalism, not surprisingly, form the bulk of the fascist storm troopers (Ahmad, 2013: 3). There are vast sections of the population whose needs are not met by capital or the state, and they blame their situation on, for example, minorities.

## 10 Bourgeois Political System and the Fascistic Movement

Just because capitalism creates a need for fascistic forces and just because capitalism creates lumpen elements that can be used by the fascistic project, that does not necessarily mean there will be fascistic forces in *active operation*. One has to understand the politics of the fascistic tendencies and not just their necessary political-economic conditions. There are indeed bourgeois-*political* dynamics of the rise of fascistic tendencies.

The failure of bourgeois politics as well as Left politics to defend democracy and secularism is a crucial (intermediate) process contributing to the rise of the BJP. The Congress and the BJP are two faces of Indian bourgeois politics, both promoting neoliberal capitalism, and the BJP using the religious divide to distinguish itself in the election market in a much more aggressive, unabashed and overt manner than the Congress. There has indeed been a decline of the relatively secular bourgeois national party (Congress) and attendant 'capital flight' from the Congress to the BJP. One might say that: as Nehruvianism (semi-statist developmental model with very muted elements of social democracy), in part influenced by the Bombay plan, saved the Indian bourgeoisie from any communist threat, potential and actual during the post-1917 period, the fascistic threat came in its turn to liberate the bourgeoisie from Nehruvianism, in a conjuncture where a strong Left movement is not present to counter the fascistic movement.

The Left defines the current stage of Indian revolution as a democratic revolution, a stage at which an important task of the Left is to protect the democratic rights of minorities. Yet, what we see is the fiercest attack on democratic rights from communal-fascistic forces. The fascistic forces have come to constitute a very powerful obstacle to the Left movement, including in the traditional bastions of Left influence. These forces are a clear threat to the communist movement on the ground, as we have been seeing in Tripura and Kerala (and also in West Bengal), where communists and their offices are being physically attacked.

The BJP's goal is to see an India that is not only 'Congress-free' ('Congress-mukt') (because Congress has generally tried to defend secular values) but also 'Left-free' ('Left-mukt') or indeed 'Communist-mukt'. This shows that the right-wing forces are much more than mere religious-sectarian forces. Their threat is much more than the threat to secularism and bourgeois democracy. They are fundamentally capitalist, anti-proletarian, anti-communist forces whose fascistic aim is to destroy not only the democratic-secular ethos of the nation but also the organizations of the class-conscious masses, of workers and peasants of India. The BJP makes use of whatever elements of the democratic system it can use, to subvert the values of the democratic system itself in the service of a communal-bourgeois agenda and to establish a system where political power is always in the hands of the majority-religion.

A part of the blame for this tragic situation must indeed be on the Left itself: its failure to develop socialist consciousness and strong democratically-functioning socialist organizations. Indeed, much of what we see in India and elsewhere in terms of fascistic tendencies can be captured by these lines except that we are not talking about fascism but fascistic tendencies: 'Fascism is a product of ... a sharp social crisis' and 'the revolutionary weakness of the ... proletariat' (Trotsky, 1931a). The proletarian movement is in part weak due to bourgeois-reformist organizations and by the traditional communist parties which have failed 'to unite the workers under the banner of the revolution' as well as by the far left tendencies to do much to organize the workers. 'Through the fascist agency, capitalism sets in motion the masses of the crazed petty bourgeoisie, and bands of the declassed and demoralized lumpenproletariat' all of whom capitalism itself 'has brought to desperation and frenzy' (Trotsky, 1944). But during a transitional stage, when traits of fascism and liberal-capitalism are combined, such extreme measures are not yet necessary. Normal resources play the dominant role, supplemented by fascistic forces. The latter forces play not only a coercive role but also a consent-generating role: deploying myths about the past, and lies, and brainwashing people about what a nation means, about the superiority of a religion (Hindutva), and so on, in order to make people believe in the fascistic vision. The petty bourgeois fascist forces also seek to undermine ideas about labor and proletarian movement. The significance of assistance that capital mobilizes from normal resources (e.g. police personnel) relative to the assistance from fascistic forces on the ground can also change depending on the severity of the crisis and the strength of the anti-capitalist proletarian forces.

The increasing strength of right-wing forces represents a most extreme form of the latent tendency towards an attack on democracy, the tendency that exists in capitalist societies when there is massive inequality in wealth and income, under conditions of capitalist economic crisis. Fundamental to the worldview of the fascistic forces are the idolization of *free market economics* in the interest of the business class, and the deployment of *authoritarian politics.* Authoritarian politics is necessary to implement free market economics to help the property-owning classes. This is especially so in a society like India where millions of people are not only subjected to economic miseries caused by capitalist class relation and lower level of economic development under the rule of capital, but are also fighting against their miseries, and who therefore have to be suppressed/managed through authoritarian means, if the business class has to be kept happy. The ideology and practices of free market economics and authoritarian politics are dressed up by right-wing demagogic leaders. These two catchwords – development and good governance (or similar terms) – resonate with common people who are economically poor and who have also been subjected to apathy on the part of politicians and bureaucrats. These catchwords are used, along with hyper-nationalism based in the idea of the supremacy of a religion (e.g. Hinduism), to help produce/spark a *mass movement.* In short: blatant free market economic ideas and policies, rabid religious nationalism, and authoritarian intolerance towards rational dissent: all these come together, support each other, and produce a grassroots movement.

The BJP is definitely not an ordinary political party. Yet, the *perception* that it is an ordinary party has been slowly produced, over decades, by the corporate media, and sections of the middle class and of the business world. It is extra-ordinary that the BJP has in fact become an ordinary political party which one could choose from a set of parties on the ballot box. It is also an extra-ordinary fact that the views of this party and of its fascistic supporters including RSS ideologues on a given topic have become a part of polite, civilized and public discussions on television channels, and in classrooms, conferences and teas-shops, and at dinner tables. This shows how far to the right public life has moved in India.

It is less true to say that the BJP is a communal party that just happens to support the business class. It is more true to say that BJP is fundamentally a bourgeois party that makes use of communal hatred to attain political influence and in the process serves bourgeois interests (as well as some reactionary interests of a bigoted section of the citizenry). Communalism (religious-sectarian hatred), or antagonism based in religious difference, may have a degree of autonomy with respect to capitalism, if not with respect to class as such. But once it exists, capitalism makes full use of it and feeds into it.

When all parties more or less aspire to satisfy the demands of the business class, then in the competitive market for votes, it helps a party if it can make use of gimmicks such as religious pride and hyper-nationalism to package itself as a unique commodity in the electoral market. The BJP is a national party that is not only pro-business but also communally divisive, a party that crushes not only economic rights but also democratic rights of toiling masses. While the BJP government defends the interests of the top 1–10% by not restricting the greedy pursuit of profit, it hurts the economic interests of the masses *and* undermines their power to fight back. The fascistic-nationalist movement is not only profoundly pro-capitalist but also is it shamelessly subordinating the interests of toiling masses living in India to imperialism. It makes use of religion, hyper-nationalism and historical distortions in order to divide the masses. It resorts to authoritarianism to weaken those who oppose it and its policies, bypassing parliament and harassing critics. It now seems a common BJP strategy to engineer a communal riot, polarize voters and win elections based on hatred and fear. And once this communal party is in power, there are further communal attacks as the perpetrators know that they will be directly or indirectly protected by the BJP. Communal riots often give a sense of satisfaction to the economically desperate lumpen elements created by capitalism, making them believe that they can achieve something in life. But they are, generally, unaware of being mere pawns in the larger communal-corporate 'game'. They are unaware of the fact that the fascistic politics they are engaging in are the politics by the masses but against the masses, i.e. that that politics is against their own interests. When the common people are divided on the basis of sectarian hatred and distracted from real issues because of hyper-nationalist hysteria, the ruling class and its politicians benefit. If the consciousness that prompts people to politically intervene in line with their class interests that are irreconcilable with ruling class interests, is class consciousness, then fascistic consciousness that the BJP feeds into and relies on is the polar opposite of class consciousness.

The rise of the BJP represents the crisis not only of bourgeois economics but also of bourgeois politics: the bourgeois political-economic system, and therefore, the bourgeois ruling class, has, simply, failed to secure not only social rights but also democratic rights, including rights of religious minorities. So the blame for the current situation must be at the door not only of the BJP and these forces, but also the bourgeoisie itself, or the bourgeois system as a whole, and this is indicative of what can be called a great Indian consensus: mechanisms of systematic attack on democratic rights, including the rights of religious minorities, have been slowly and steadily put in place, a process which has quickened when India 'fell for' the Washington consensus (i.e. neoliberal capitalism). That is why the fascistic threat is a class project, and not merely a political-cultural project. The threat exists in the following context: while the ruling class is losing its right to be the ruling class, the masses are not yet ready to say 'we cannot take it anymore', although some stirring in their consciousness is apparent.

Controlled by a Right-wing party, the BJP government, whether now or in the future, is not, and will not be, in sync with the political culture of a country, where the vast majority of its men and women of different religions and castes do not have the means to satisfy their basic needs, and where there is a deeply-felt desire for democracy and secularism. The majority of Indians are religious. But they do not necessarily favor the political-sectarian use of religion to make one group hate another. They do not necessarily favor politicians who spread religious hatred for political gain. However contradictory and utopian religious ideas are, all religions propagate 'spiritually' uplifting ideas, even if it is the case that many religious ideas also contribute to the reproduction of unjust social arrangements, which, in turn, necessitate religious beliefs. Religious ideas express, among other things, people's desire to be much better than what they normally are and what they can be. Many religious ideas teach people to be 'spiritual', generous, loving and kind-hearted, so even if people are religious, they can oppose the misuse of religion for narrow, divisive political gains undermining the secular-democratic character of the country. Partly because of this, and partly because of the correct perception that peoples' economic needs cannot be met by religious politics,  the majority of of citizens, including, Hindus, generally speaking, have not supported the Hindu nationalist party's attempt to *unite* all Hindus to garner their votes on the basis of religion and on the basis of the utterly false notion that Hindus are under threat from Muslims or from the Muslim-majority of Pakistan.

## 11      What Is to Be Done?

The nature of the BJP's fascistic tendencies highlights the vulnerability of bourgeois democracy, of the entire bourgeois system.[8] India's democratic character can no longer be taken for granted. The bourgeois class and its political arms (parties, etc.) have failed to defend bourgeois democracy, including secularism. The 'defense' of democracy and secularism has now fallen on the shoulders of proletariat, more clearly than before. Therefore, the rise of the BJP can potentially create a fertile ground for more radical struggle against the bourgeois system itself.

Democratic politics and fascistic politics in societies dominated by bourgeois mode of production and exchange are both forms of bourgeois class rule. If ultra-right politics, like its more-democratic variant, is the political intervention of the ruling class to cope with its own crisis, then arriving at a different politics requires the political intervention of the masses of workers and petty producers, and their organic intellectuals. As Bannerji (1995: 35) puts it so eloquently: 'Misery does not automatically produce communism, and the desire for change born of suffering does not spontaneously know "what is to be done" to end oppression'. It is only their struggle, launched on the basis of sound theory (which has to be Marxist theory) and with the assistance of democratically-organized, multi-scalar, anti-capitalist, socialist, revolutionary organizations, that can ensure that every country meets the basic needs of every man, woman and child of all religions, castes, races and locations, where a culture of democracy among the ordinary toiling people prevails, and, where to quote Tagore, the Nobel Laureate:

> Where the mind is without fear and the head is held high
> Where knowledge is free
> Where the world has not been broken up into fragments by narrow domestic walls [of religion or caste, etc.] ...
> Where the clear stream of reason has not lost its way into the dreary desert sands of dead habit...
>
> TAGORE, 1913: 31; parenthesis and ellipses added

Common people must ask, and the Left and progressive forces must encourage them to ask: who is it that fears the citizens united to fight for their rights

---

8   The re-election of the BJP in 2019 with an enhanced mandate has confirmed this fear. The 2019 election happened after the completion of this book, so I do not talk about this. See Das (2019b) on this, which effectively functions as an epilogue to the book.

against the economic elite? Is it not the case that what is under attack is neither Hinduism from Islam, nor India from Pakistan or from Muslim immigrants, but 'the nation of ordinary people' (who work as wage-earners and/or
as petty-producers, and whose most basic needs are not met, from the ruling
class and its state)? Is it not true that: those who are attacking this nation of
common people are the economic elite, which controls society's resources using them for their own profit, and which is supported by the BJP's politicians
and the pliant officers who apparently constitute the steel frame and by their
subservient propagandists in academia and the media? Is there not more common ground among them (wage-earners and among small-scale producers of
different religions and castes, within India and across South Asia and the world)
than there are differences among them, including those based in religion?

People must ask: whose interests are the politicians who spread religious hatred serving? How do the oppression/domination of religious minorities and an
emotional feeling of hyper-nationalism based on Hindu identity, help a society
address problems of: unemployment, poverty, inequality, caste- and gender-
based oppression, environmental pollution, natural resources depletion, the
country's subjugation to powerful imperialist powers, localized semi-feudal
oppression, agrarian distress, and the lack of affordable health-care, housing and education? How can these problems be caused by the fact that some
people are Hindus and others are not? Is it, or is it not, the case that: when
political leaders and big business fail to solve people's major problems, they
seek to divert people's attention *from* such failure *towards* non-issues by using religion, myths, false nationalism and so on, to divide the people? Why is
it that the right-wing government feels threatened by any attempt to forge a
unity of secular political forces, prompting it to use undemocratic measures
against opposition forces? Those in the business world cannot also be allowed
to maintain their 'silence': they must be asked by the masses this question: do
they support or oppose the forces which are communal and which spread sectarian hatred and which repress any force of dissent?

Not only must one ask questions such as the ones posed above, but also
must they fight to deepen and defend their democratic rights, including the
right to practice any religion, to eat any food, to engage in any occupation or
to love anyone. And in doing this, they must be conscious of what *binds* them:
what binds them, irrespective of their different religions, is the fact that their
democratic rights (*including* secularism) and their right to a decent livelihood,
*are* under attack by this government, while the owners of big business and
their right-wing lackeys (hangers-on) in academia and media are having *achhe
din* (good times). The BJP and its authoritarian government, and all the reactionary forces on the ground supporting them, must continue to face the
collective and democratic might of the toiling masses and progressive intellectuals. There is, and there can be, no force that is more powerful than the united

force of the organized and class-conscious workers and small-scale producers. If they withdraw their labor from the farms, factories, offices, laboratories,
schools and universities, or if they do not bring the products of their labor to
the market (as small-scale producers), or if the unemployed, demanding decent jobs, join the currently employed people and/or start a non-cooperation
movement by not only boycotting elections but also stopping the movement
of commodities on roads and railway lines, then the system is in big trouble. It
is time that the masses of India (and of South Asia) begin to ask fundamental
questions about what kind of society they are living in, what kind of society
they wish to live in, and how to get there. In fact, the combination of Hindutva and nationalism keeps alive permanently the threat of a war between a
Muslim-dominated Pakistan and an increasingly Hinduized India, which, as
a potential and/or a reality is a vote-catcher for the Hindu-nationalist party.
Then there is a strong and urgent need for the common people of India and
other countries to mobilize themselves on the basis of their common class and
democratic interests, against the bourgeois system, including its right-wing
movements, and not allow them to be divided on the basis of nationality or
religion.

A struggle of the masses can start spontaneously. But to have some success,
it needs theoretical and political guidance. This is what the party of workers
and its allied organizations and organic intellectuals of the workers and peasants inside and outside the party, provide. In the fight against fascistic tendencies, which represent the extreme form of capitalist tyranny, the Left must play
a leading role. To fight against fascistic forces, it must dominantly focus on
non-electoral activities (including battles on the streets and inside the trade
unions, peasants' and women's organizations and the organizations to defend
secularism) aimed at class-based mobilization of workers and small-scale producers, much more than electoral activities. The Left should have its own mobilizational work: apart from mobilizing people against fascistic forces, the
Left must mobilize exploited men and women (a) against curtailment of democratic rights of all citizens and specific democratic rights of religious minorities, low castes, women, aboriginal peoples and other oppressed groups, and
(b) against the on-going attack on living standards. Keeping its organizational
independence vis-à-vis bourgeois-landlord forces, the Left must engage in
these two forms of struggle, on the basis of immediate and transitional demands, *as a part of* and *within the framework of*, the fight for socialism, a fight
that is local, regional, national and global. By being involved in various forms
of struggle – struggles inside and outside the workplaces (farms, factories,
mines, offices), struggles that are economic, political and ecological, the struggles for economic concessions and struggles are against social oppression of
religious and caste minorities and women and against ecological damage – the
Left can truly be the tribune of the people in the Lenin sense, fighting both

tyranny wherever it is manifested and exploitation of workers and peasants. Such Left action might produce concessions to alleviate the suffering of the oppressed and exploited people and will unite those members of its basic classes who are socially oppressed (e.g. *Dalits*) with those who traditionally are not; struggles produce – or contribute to – unity because to succeed, struggles *require* unity. The Left political intervention will also allow common people to be aware of the power of united struggle and of the limits to what is possible to accomplish in the form of improvement in their conditions, under capitalism. The truth that capitalist class relation and the capitalist state, whether in India or elsewhere, will not guarantee democratic rights and decent standard of living has to be proven in practice, one that requires prior theoretical and political preparation. The fight against the social oppression of workers and small-scale producers from Dalit and aboriginal background and the fight against oppression of female workers and female small-scale producers must be a top priority. In the process of all these different types of struggle, the working class, allied with small-scale producers, can aspire to the ideological-political hegemony, and ultimately, for the status of 'the new ruling class'. Keeping in mind the importance of 'stadiality' (Laibman, 2005) within an overall framework of uninterrupted class struggle ending in the abolition of all forms of class rule, one can imagine, not in any absolute sense though, the economic and political struggles of workers and small-scale producers as three concentric circles (or better, perhaps as a spiral or a helix), beginning, first, with the struggle around immediate economic and political demands, and 'then' struggle around transitional economic and political demands, and finally, moving on to the struggle for a workers' and small-scale producers' government. The Left's intervention cannot be shaped by and merely reflect, the present level of class consciousness (which is low), nor can it engage in ultra-leftism which assumes as if a socialist revolution around the corner right now, obviating the need for patient time-consuming political and ideological work aimed at raising the level of class consciousness.

Within the extra-electoral struggles in all these different spheres, and being fully aware of the importance of united front activities, the Left must provide tactical and critical support to the various progressive movements led by non-party Marxists and by non-Marxist radicals such as people's science movements, progressive artists and literary movements, movements against obscurantism, and ecological movements. The Left must also provide tactical and critical support to the mass movements against social oppression and for economic concessions (e.g. higher wages) that are led by non-party Marxists and by non-Marxist radicals, including those involved in temple entry movements on behalf of Dalits and the protection of democratic rights. Within the extra-electoral struggles in all these different spheres, the Left, keeping its organizational independence, must build principled *alliances* with non-communists, including progressive scientists. The Left in India (and elsewhere) must pay heed to Lenin's advice on the need for alliance between communists and non-communists and to the idea that revolution cannot be made by revolutionaries alone.

In so far as the Left parties, much more than other parties, consistently fight against communalism and call for progressive policies at the national scale, and as far as the fight against the fascistic movement is concerned, they must make sure that: workers, self-employed non-capitalist producers, class-conscious trade union members, their progressive organic intellectuals and independent activists participating in class-based social movements, come together, at local, regional and national levels, starting from a city-neighborhood and a village. These elements must form multi-religion, multi-caste, working class, anti-fascism/anti-communalism action committees (or defense guards), with the aim of struggling against the attack on democratic and social rights of these basic classes and class-fractions, in the first instance. What is needed, in India (as elsewhere in similar contexts), is a *class*-based extra-electoral 'coalition' (i.e. a 'united front' on a tactical basis) of political forces that are organizationally independent of the big-business parties, in order to struggle for secularism and democracy (and more). Such extra-electoral struggle should be a vehicle for the development of democratic consciousness and win the masses to the cause of a large-scale political project of defending and deepening democratic rights and to the cause of socialism/communism. From such struggles, will organically emerge politically advanced workers, and from them, a stratum that will show proletarian leadership ability and revolutionary intention. Of course, a top priority must be given to the development of a cadre that learns the history of communist struggles in India, South Asia and the world, and that is steeped in the Marxism of the MELLT ( Marx, Engels, Lenin, Luxemburg, Trotsky), (Das, 2017a), the theory that shapes the socialist program which in turn shapes struggles and theoretical reflections on the struggles.

Apart from extra-electoral struggle, the Left must fight the fascistic tendencies within the electoral arena, on the basis of the idea that the extra-electoral struggle is to subordinate the electoral struggle and that the main reason for electoral politics is not to try to capture power through elections and establish socialism (this is an impossibility) but to use the parliament and provincial assemblies as the political spaces where the Left can raise awareness not only about common people's problems and the failure of the capitalist system to address these, but also  about its own alternative solutions and to measure the degree of support it has from the masses. Within the electoral sphere, the Left cannot practice neutrality ('political indifferentism', in Marx's words) with respect to whether there is a secular bourgeois democratic government or a communal-fascistic bourgeois government that kills dissent in every pore of society, just as it cannot be neutral to whether a bourgeois government spends money on workers' primary education and one that does not (see Marx, 2010).

The Left itself *should not be* a part of the bourgeois-secular front against the fascistic tendencies. That would be multi-class bloc. Keeping its organizational independence, the Left should be outside of the front and exercise its autonomy to criticize and to mobilize the masses against the front on economic and other policies that may affect the masses adversely. The ultimate aim of the Left is not a liberal-democratic secular bourgeois government but a proletarian-democratic secular socialist government of workers and peasants.

It is to be stressed that the defeat of fascistic tendencies should not be equated to the electoral defeat of the BJP: the BJP may be defeated (as in provincial elections in late 2018) and yet fascistic forces will be involved in their usual ground-work, covertly and overtly, although without formal access to state power through the BJP, these forces will lose some of their force. So the fight against fascistic tendencies must be a much greater fight than the electoral fight to defeat the BJP. And no other political movement can engage in that fight more strongly than the Marxist Left can. It is also clear that when fascistic tendencies are weakened/eliminated and when the focus of Left's attention is more on class struggle against capital as such than on fascistic movements, the so-called secular parties (i.e. the Congress and its allies) are most likely to be united with those which are not (i.e. the BJP and its allies), in order to fight the Left. That is all the more reason why the fight against fascistic tendencies must be seen as a part of the fight for establishing a socialist government and why the Left must maintain its organizational independence vis-à-vis bourgeois forces, secular or not.

Mainly on the basis of the revolutionary struggle against capitalism and its state, the struggle that aims to establish a workers' state, the Left must seek to stop fascistic forces from controlling governmental power and being a great threat to class-based mobilization. The ruling class attack on secularism and growing strength of fascistic tendencies is indicative not only of the low level of consciousness and lack of unity among members of basic classes but also of the fact that the struggle against the attack on secularism is an inherent part of class struggle itself. As Yechuri (1993) says, 'The struggle against the communal forces today is, at the same time, the struggle for maintaining the unity of these classes and to that extent, is an integral aspect of the class struggle' (p. 15). In fact, the struggle against fascism must ultimately be to cut its roots in capitalism. In the process of mobilizing the masses for concessions (including economic concessions within capitalism) both during the rule of communal fascistic forces and when a secular government is in power, the Left must develop their class consciousness and gradually prepare them to demand a workers' state, supported mainly by non-exploiting small-scale producers. The fight against fascistic tendencies, initially a *defensive* fight, should be seen positively as opening a door towards socialist struggle.

Any temporary and tactical agreement with bourgeois forces that might be objectively necessary because of the relative weakness of the Left can, once again, be justified only if the genuine aim of the Left is to prepare the masses to fight for socialism, and not to just fight for a capitalism that is more democratic, more egalitarian and less neoliberal. Any temporary compromise with bourgeois secular forces, outside of the strategy for socialist revolution, would not only not contribute to the socialist movement but also would it not significantly defeat the fascistic forces. Ahmad (2013: 22) writes: 'in the context of the extremely wide dissemination of communal consciousness in the country at large, secularism has emerged as a specifically communist virtue'. The fight against communalism is to be a part of the fight for communism. The fight for communism must be taken out of the documents of communist parties/groups as a long-term goal divorced from current struggles, and be given a material expression through agitation, education and organization of masses *now*. 'A revolutionary victory can become possible only as a result of long political agitation, a lengthy period of education and organization of the masses' (Trotsky, 1934). Revolution and socialism must be parts of popular common sense: these must be *talked about* in the everyday life of the masses and of communist leaders – i.e. at the picket lines, in party meetings, on the street, in the eating places, in the Marxist and progressive reading group meetings and in the corridors of university departments where communists work, in schools, in books on comics and stories, in films, in the theatres, in the editorial board meetings of online and in-print Marxist journals. Revolution and socialism must be discussed during protests against militarism, fascistic attacks on minorities, encounter-killings, violence against women and children, police brutality against striking workers and peasants, corruption scandals involving both the business class and state officials/politicians, and cuts to funding for welfare, and indeed in *every* place where masses live their daily lives. The masses and the Left leaders and the Left intellectuals must eat, breathe, live, and fall in love with, the very idea of a more humane society, one that is democratic in every possible manner, a society which goes by this name: socialism or communism.

I have used the term Left (or Marxist Left) to denote both the existing Left and the Left that the masses need for their fight for socialism. Are these two views of the Left the same or at least similar? In fact, the actually-existing Left falls short by miles from the 'imagined' Left, even if there is much common ground between the two. The threat from the fascistic movement and the massive crisis of livelihood of the masses are reason enough for a thorough re-thinking of what kind of Left is needed. In India, there is a crisis of revolutionary leadership, a crisis of the Left. This crisis is not only one of larger more-or-less reformist communist parties/groups and their trade unions and mass organizations, but also of the smaller Far Left groups. What is definitely needed is a 'new' Left, one that is to be much to the left of the existing mainstream Left (electoralist or not) and that is much less sectarian and much more united than the small Far Left groups, whether they are based in India or not. This re-thinking involves rethinking the ways in which the small Far left groups operate, which exhibit sectarian tendencies, which remain permanently fragmented and/or are fragmenting, and which are engaged in excessive negativism in relation to other Marxist Left groups. After all, not only are theory and political programs political but also how an organization conducts itself is political. As well, there is a serious need to rethink the theory and strategy of revolution that is subscribed to by the larger communist parties that are currently operating as a political force on the ground as the actually-existing Left. Must this Left not fight to abolish capitalism rather than to fight for a better form of capitalism, and must it not take seriously the idea that reforms are more or less by-products of revolutionary struggle? Is it really the case that capitalism is not ripe, for a struggle to begin to overthrow it? As we have seen in Chapter 3, India is dominantly a capitalist society: the most general form of capitalism (i.e. the formal subsumption of labor) does exist as the dominant form of class relation in India, and the transition to a more developed form of capitalism is blocked by capitalism itself, operating in a world of imperialism. Let the Indian Left read and reflect on Lenin's *April Theses*. And the leaders of the communist movement, advanced workers and Marxist intellectuals might want to reflect in a non-sectarian way on these lines from Vladimir Lenin's most trusted comrade and the co-architect of 1917:

> All talk to the effect that historical conditions have not yet "ripened" for socialism is the product of ignorance or conscious deception. The objective prerequisites for the proletarian revolution have not only "ripened"; they have begun to get somewhat rotten. Without a socialist revolution, in the next historical period at that, a catastrophe threatens the whole culture of mankind. The turn is now to the proletariat, i.e., chiefly to its revolutionary vanguard. The historical crisis of mankind is reduced to the crisis of the revolutionary leadership.
>
> TROTSKY, 1938

Indeed, 'Without a socialist revolution, ... a catastrophe threatens the whole culture of mankind', and fascism *is* a part of that catastrophe. This is as true about the West as about the less developed capitalist countries such as India.

Capitalism exists at the level of fundamental class *relation*, which has three aspects (relation of exchange, relation of property, and relation of value and surplus value) (Das, 2017a: Chapter 7). Capitalism exists at the level of *mechanisms* that these relations set up, and at the level of the *effects* of the *mechanisms* on the masses. And, capitalist society can be (more/less) fascistic and (more/less) democratic. It is important for the Left to fight against the adverse effects of capitalist class relation for short-term progressive policies and against fascistic tendencies, on the basis of immediate and transitional demands, both in the workplaces and more widely. There is a need for civil polite polemical struggles among various Left groups with the aim of clarification of principles with respect to the theory and strategy of revolution. And, there is a need for united front type struggles on the part of independent individual communist groups and parties against the effects of capitalism on people's lives, with the aim of getting beyond the class relation of capitalism. It is from such polemical struggles and struggles against the current society that a future Left will gradually emerge. There is currently *no* Left party/group that can successfully fight against the effects of capitalism, against fascistic tendencies and against wage-slavery. Now, given the danger that fascistic tendencies pose, the secular-democratic bourgeois and petty bourgeois forces will at best want to confine their political activity to the creation of a polity that merely weakens such tendencies making the society more democratic,[9] leaving intact the capitalist class relation. Yet, that political aim, however inadequate from the Left vantage-point, does have some common ground with the Left's aim to eliminate fascistic tendencies. But there is a difference, from the Left standpoint: that fight has to be also a fight against fascists' pro-business policies and against the attack on workers and small-scale producers' living standards. And there is still more to do: fighting for democracy and for some economic concessions is not enough. It is worth repeating Marx and Engels's point on this. As socialists:

> it is our interest and our task to make the revolution permanent until all the more or less propertied classes have been driven from their ruling positions, until the proletariat has conquered state power and until the

---

9   They would do so because of the pressure of genuine secular-democratic forces on the ground whom these non-Left parties represent and because access to state power is a means of access to power and resources for the secular-democratic parties who are in a competitive relation with the BJP and its allies. From a class standpoint, the non-BJP parties' commitment to secularism and democracy will always remain wooly and vacillating, given the existence of the pressure coming from bourgeois political economy for fascistic politics.

> association of the proletarians has progressed sufficiently far – not only in one country but in all the leading countries of the world – that competition between the proletarians of these countries ceases and at least the decisive forces of production are concentrated in the hands of the workers. Our concern cannot simply be to modify private property, but to abolish it, not to hush up class antagonisms but to abolish classes, not to improve the existing society but to found a new one.
>
> MARX and ENGELS, 1850

If we apply these principles to the current context, where there is a low level of economic development along with massive poverty, and where fascistic forces are gaining strength, it will be possible to say something, in a general way, as to 'what is to be done'.

The most important thing that needs to be done is this: the political mobilization of the 400-million-plus Indian working class, *allied with* petty producers, *independent* of all bourgeois forces *as part of a South Asian and an* international working class offensive against capitalism. Such an independent socialist mobilization of the exploited and oppressed masses in India will be advanced by, and will contribute to, a similar movement in countries such as the UK and the US (where Hindutva-based fascistic tendencies are already raising their ugly head). But who will do it?

The independent mobilization of the masses on the basis of a socialist program requires that efforts be made towards a reforging and regroupment of revolutionary socialist individuals and groups to form a democratically-organized party of class conscious workers. Informed by principles of *non-sectarian* class politics and the avoidance of a left version of the personality cult and petty-bourgeois ego clashes, this reforging must bring together *all* socialists, strategically and/or tactically, who are against not only the fascistic politics of the BJP's Hindu majoritarianism but also against caste-based identity politics, the liberal democratic politics of so-called secular parties such as Congress and its regional offshoots. It must also include those who are critical of the mainstream communist parties' electoralist, reformist, stage-ist politics. The leadership of existing communist parties, given their history, theory and program shaped by Stalinism, are *incapable* of mobilizing the masses for a socialist movement. However, it is conceivable that there are rank-and-file individuals and factions within the current communist parties who can join the new socialist movement; instant hatred against everyone associated with the existing communist parties is inadequate and is a potential sign of sectarianism.

This revolutionary socialist movement requires a revolutionary theory and that can only come from what I have referred to as the Marxism of the MELLT.

The movement must encompass three inter-connected fights, as mentioned before. One is the fight for a secular-democratic society, a society without the BJP/RSS agenda and a society where the democratic questions (i.e. issues concerning social oppression, landlordism, and new forms of imperialism) are resolved. In particular, the RSS/BJP agenda must be ideologically and politically countered, as militantly as possible, by workers and semi-proletarians mobilized in *every locality*, and nationally and overseas (among the diaspora). The fight for a democratic-secular society, the fight to resolve the democratic questions, must include the support for oppressed nationalities (e.g. Kashmiris) to exercise their *right* to independence from Pakistan and India. Another is the fight for economic concessions, including those based on transitional demands. These two inter-connected fights must be fought under the leadership of the working class, *as a part of* the struggle for a socialist society in India, in South Asia and globally, a society that is democratic in every sphere of life (economic, political, cultural and at the level of the family), that is ecologically sustainable and that practises solidarity with the oppressed and the exploited in every country of the world.

The question is: to what extent do the politically advanced workers, the leaders of the Left movement from different theoretical and political traditions, and Left intellectuals in India (and elsewhere) agree with such a perspective, the perspective of Marx and Engels as well as those Marxists who have followed them critically and closely?

# Processes Influencing the Balance of Power between Capital and Labor

The first process is the *availability* – and economic affordability – of a given productivity-raising technology (which can be mechanical, chemical, bio-technical, etc.). Secondly, and in the context of nature-dependent production, favorable ecological conditions are particularly important.[1] These do not exist everywhere. Thirdly, for accumulation and struggle against employers to happen in any significant manner, there must be a substantial amount of concentration of property in the hands of a few owners. Unless there are a few property owners with a sufficient amount of means of production under their control, and even if wage-labor relations dominate, accumulation by private owners, and especially, via technological change, will be inhibited, and class struggle against the employers over wages and working conditions may not be particularly intense because of the absence of strong economic-cultural differences between laborers and property owners who are operating as relatively small-scale capitalists. Fourthly, there is the issue of inter-sectoral relations in terms of production of consumer demand: for example, the development of non-agricultural economic activities in rural areas and associated increase in the total amount of investment, expands the market for farm goods and may increase the demand for (farm-) labor. The latter can enhance labor's bargaining power resulting in higher wages, to which capital can respond by introducing technology, with the real subsumption of labor as the result. Finally, there is the issue of capitalist state interventions. Government assistance including subsidized food and employment generation on public projects – which partly reflects struggle of direct producers – leads to the tightening of the labor market and covers a part of the reproduction of labor power, including sections of the reserve army. All this enhances the bargaining power of labor. From the standpoint of capital itself, state interventions also matter. The state intervention on behalf of the working class and poor peasantry creates an internal market for capital. And by manipulating relative prices, the state can make the terms of trade between two sectors (e.g. agriculture and industry) favorable for one. This can increase the amount of capital in the hands of property owners in the favored sector and therefore may make technology

---

1   Money invested cannot be got back before a certain time period (e.g. until a crop matures), which is determined by nature's time rather than capital's time. This means that capitalists can be slow to sink money in farming, making the development of agrarian capitalism over time a slow process (Mann and Dickinson, 1978).

affordable by it. It should be noted that all these contextual factors (including the ways in which ecological conditions are made use of) are connected to the overall *capitalist* development of the country, directly or indirectly, and this overall *capitalist* nature of development indirectly defines the context within which capital-labor confrontation takes places and which affects the possibility of the transition from formal subsumption. This transition as a spatially uneven process contributes to uneven (and combined) development.

# A Suggested Research Program on Agrarian Neoliberalism

1.  Why does neoliberalism impact labor and environmental resources in rural areas?

    1.1.  How do production processes, wages, and employment differ amongst different types of subsistence and commercial farms, and between places, and why?

    1.2.  Does neoliberalism promote change from formal subsumption of labor (deployment of labor on the basis of low wages and long hours) to real subsumption of labor (deployment of labor on the basis labor-saving technology), and how?

    1.3.  Is there greater interaction between agriculture and industry and between rural and urban areas, under neoliberalism, and with what consequences for the different classes in rural areas? How do economic development processes and state interventions within a given 'city-region' (a large city and its surrounding rural areas) impact the possibilities for a political alliance between urban workers and rural non-exploiting petty-producers to demand radical concessions and to challenge capitalist relations?

    1.4.  How do agricultural production relations transform local ecologies and lead to (adverse) consequences for the environment and laboring bodies?

2.  How does neoliberalism lead to new patterns of deployment of labor and land in rural areas specifically in the form of what is called 'new agriculture'?

    2.1.  With respect to 'new agriculture', which refers to the conversion of land-use to production and export of luxury crops, how do production/labor processes differ across different types of farms, and between places, and why?

    2.2.  How closely is 'new agriculture' related to food availability, employment, wages, and poverty over time and across regions?

    2.3.  How do new agricultural production relations transform local ecologies and lead to (adverse) consequences for the environment and laboring bodies?

3.  Why does neoliberalism, promising to promote fast economic growth and benefit the masses, turn out to be a contradiction-prone and problematic development project?

3.1.  How is the state's selective 'withdrawal' from the economy under neoliberalism related to rural economic development, food security and poverty?

3.2.  How does neoliberalism create and intensify conflicts (e.g. between workers and employers; and between different users of natural resources)?

3.3.  By spatially concentrating investment and laborers, might new agriculture enable political organization of the masses over social and ecological issues?

3.4.  How do state and agribusinesses respond to various conflicts? What material and discursive strategies are employed to promote social norms supportive of agrarian neoliberalism?

3.5.  How are conflicts expressed within state institutions, and between the state and civil society at large? How does the democratic state justify support for agribusiness whilst reducing subsidies for poor populations, as under WTO rubric? Is a legitimacy crisis emergent in rural areas for a state no longer appearing as guarantor of welfare in the everyday lives of the poor? What connection might there be between agrarian neoliberalism and growing influence of fascistic tendencies among certain classes and groups in rural areas?

# Bibliography

Adduci, M. 2017. "Neoliberalism, mining and labour in the Indian state of Odisha: Outlining a political economy analysis." *Journal of Contemporary Asia* 47, no. 4: 596–614.

Agamben, G. 2005. *The state of exception.* Chicago: University of Chicago Press.

Agarwala, R. 2006. "From work to welfare: A new class movement in India." *Critical Asian Studies* 38, no. 4: 419–444.

Agarwala, R. 2013. *Informal labor, formal politics and dignified discontent in India.* Cambridge: Cambridge University Press.

Agarwala, R. 2019. "Using legal empowerment for labour rights in India." *Journal of Development Studies* 55, no. 3: 401–419.

Aguiar, L., and Herod, A., eds. 2006. *The dirty work of neoliberalism: Cleaners in the global economy.* Oxford: Blackwell.

Ahluwalia, M.S. 1978. "Rural poverty and agricultural performance in India." *Journal of Development Studies* 14, no. 3: 298–323.

Ahluwalia, M.S. 2002. "Economic reforms in India since 1991: Has Gradualism worked?" *Journal of Economic Perspectives* 16, no. 7: 67–88.

Ahmad, A. 2013. "Communalisms: Changing forms and fortunes." *The Marxist* XXIX, no. 2.

Alauddin, M., and Tisdell, C. 1991. *The Green Revolution and economic development: The process and its impacts in Bangladesh.* Basingstoke: Macmillan.

Alauddin, M., and Tisdell, C. 1995. "Labour absorption and agricultural development Bangladesh experience and predicament." *World Development* 23, no. 2: 281–295.

Alavi, H. 1965. "Peasant and Revolution." In *The Socialist Register 1965*, eds. R. Miliband and J. Saville, 241–277. London: The Merlin Press.

Alavi, H. 1972. "The State in Post-colonial Societies: Pakistan and Bangladesh." *New Left Review*, no. 74: 59–81.

Albright, M. 2018. "Will we stop Trump before it's too late?" *New York Times.* https://www.nytimes.com/2018/04/06/opinion/sunday/trump-fascism-madeleine-albright.html.

Ali, A. 2006. "Rice to shrimp: Land use land cover changes and soil degradation in Southwestern Bangladesh." *Land Use Policy* 23, no. 4: 421–435.

Allinson, J., and Anievas, A. 2009. "The uses and misuses of uneven and combined development: an anatomy of a concept." *Cambridge Review of International Affairs* 22, no. 1: 47–67.

Ambani, M. 2018. "Building a global-scale corporation in India." In *India Transformed*, ed. R. Mohan, 554–566. Washington D.C.: Brookings Institution Press.

Amin, S. 2005. "India: A great power?" *Monthly Review* 6, no. 9: 1–13.

Amsden, A. 1998. *Asia's next giant: South Korea and late industrialization.* Oxford: Oxford University Press.

Anandan, S. 2018. "4 years of Modi: Dalits are being stripped of their dignity." *National Herald.* https://www.nationalheraldindia.com/opinion/4-years-of-modi-dalits-are -being-stripped-of-their-dignity.

Anandhi, S., and Kapadia, K. 2017. *Dalit women: Vanguard of an alternative politics in India.* Abingdon, Oxon: Routledge.

Anderson, L., and Seligson, M.A. 1994. "Reformism and radicalism among peasants." *American Journal of Political Science* 38, no. 4: 944–972.

Anderson, P. 1980. *Arguments within English Marxism.* London: Verso.

Anievas, A., Saull, R., Davidson, N., and Fabry, A. 2014. *The longue durée of the far right: An international historical sociology.* London: Routledge.

Ansari, A. 2011. *Communalisation of Indian society.* Delhi: Aakar.

Arun, M. 2017. "Demonetisation shook the economy. Did it break it, or leave it healthier?" *India Today.* https://www.indiatoday.in/magazine/msn-it/story/20171113-dem onitisation-note-ban-bjp-modi-economy-arun-jaitley-gdp-1077353-2017-11-04.

Ashman, A. 2009. "Capitalism, Uneven and Combined Development and the Transhistoric." *Cambridge Review of International Affairs* 22, no. 1: 29–46.

Aston, T., and Philpin, C. 1985. *The Brenner Debate: Agrarian class structure and economic development in pre-industrial Europe.* Cambridge: Cambridge University Press.

Auvinen, J. 1997. "Political conflict in less developed countries 1981–89." *Journal of Peace Research* 34, no. 2: 177–195.

Avakian, B. 2008. *Away with gods.* Chicago: Insight Press.

Azam, J., and Bhatia, K. 2017. "Provoking insurgency in a federal state: Theory and application to India." *Public choice* 170, no. 3–4: 183–210.

Bagchi, S. 2017. "Naxalbari at 50." *The Hindu.* https://www.thehindu.com/society/naxal bari-at-50/article18514656.ece.

Bahl, V. 1995. *The making of the Indian working class: A case of the Tata Iron and Steel Company, 1880–1946.* New Delhi: Sage.

Baker, D. 2006. "The political economy of fascism: Myth or reality, or myth and reality?" *New Political Economy* 11, no. 2: 227–250.

Baker, K., and Jewitt, S. 2007. "Evaluating 35 years of the green revolution technology in villages of Bulandshahr district, western UP, north India." *Journal of Development Studies* 43, no. 2: 312–339.

Balagopal, K. 2006. "Chattisgarh: The physiognomy of violence." *Economic and Political Weekly* 41, no. 21: 2183–2186.

Banaji, J. 2003. "The fictions of free labor: Contract, coercion, and the so-called unfree labor." *Historical Materialism* 11, no. 3: 69–95.

Banaji, J. 2010. "The ironies of Indian Maoism." *International Socialism*, issue 128. http://isj.org.uk/the-ironies-of-indian-maoism/.

Banaji, J., ed. 2016a. *Fascism: essays on Europe and India,* Gurgaon: Three Essays Collective.

Banaji, J., ed. 2016b. "Preface." In *Fascism: Essays on Europe and India,* ed. J. Banaji. Gurgaon: Three Essays Collective.

Banaji, J., ed. 2016c. "Postscript." In *Fascism: Essays on Europe and India,* ed. J. Banaji. Gurgaon: Three Essays Collective.

Banaji, J., ed. 2016d. "Trajectories of fascism: Extreme-right movements in India and elsewhere." In *Fascism: Essays on Europe and India,* ed. J. Banaji. Gurgaon: Three Essays Collective.

Bandyopadhyay, D. 1994. "Reflections on Land Reforms in India since Independence." In *Industry and Agriculture in India since Independence,* ed. T. Sathyamurthy. New Delhi: Oxford University Press.

Banerjee, S. 1980. *In the wake of Naxalbari: A history of the Naxalite Movement in India.* Calcutta: Subarnarekha.

Banerjee, S. 1984. India's simmering revolution: The Naxalite uprising. London: Zed.

Banerjee, S. 1986. "Rural scene." In *Agrarian Struggles after Independence,* ed. A.R. Desai. New Delhi: Oxford University Press.

Banerjee, S. 1999. "Strategy and forms of political participation among left parties." In *Class formation and political transformation in post-colonial India,* ed. T. Sathyamurthy, 202–237. Delhi: Oxford University Press.

Banerjee, S. 2002. "Naxalbari: between past and future." *Economic and Political Weekly* 37, no. 22: 2115–2116.

Banerjee, S. 2006. "Beyond Naxalbari." *Economic and Political Weekly* 41, no. 29: 3159–3163.

Banerjee, S. 2008a. "On the Naxalite movement: a report with a difference." *Economic and Political Weekly* 43, no. 21: 10–12.

Banerjee, S. 2008b. "A Political cul-de-sac: CPI(M)'s tragic denouement." *Economic and Political Weekly* 43, no. 42: 12–15.

Banerjee, S. 2012. *Marxism and the Indian left: From 'interpreting' India to 'changing' it.* Kolkata: Purbalok.

Banerjee, S. 2017. "Half-a-century of Maoist journey in India from Naxalbari to Chhatisgarh." *Economic and Political Weekly* 52, no. 21.

Bannerji, S. 2000. "Organized business and politics in India." In *Politics in India,* ed. R. Chatterji. Kolkata: Levanta Books.

Banerjee-Guha, S. 2009. "Neoliberalising the 'urban': New geographies of power and injustice in Indian cities." *Economic and Political Weekly* 44, no. 22: 95–107.

Bannerji, H. 1995. *Thinking through: Essays on feminism, Marxism, and anti-racism.* Toronto: Women's press.

Bannerji, H. 2006. "Making India Hindu and male – cultural nationalism and the emergence of the ethnic citizen in contemporary India." *Ethnicities* 6, no. 3: 362–390.

Bansil, P. 1992. *Agricultural statistics compendium,* vols. 1–2. Technical and Economic Research Institute, New Delhi.

Barbier, E., and Suthawan, S. 2004. *Shrimp farming and mangrove loss in Thailand.* Cheltenham: Edward Elgar.

Bardhan, P. 1984. *Land, labour and rural poverty: Essays in development economics.* Oxford University Press, Delhi.

Bardhan, P. 1990. *Political Economy of Development in India.* Delhi: Oxford University Press.

Bardhan, P. 1998. *The political economy of India's development.* New Delhi: Oxford University Press.

Bardhan, P. 2005. "Nature of opposition to economic reforms in India." *Economic and Political Weekly* 40, no. 48: 4995–4998.

Barker, C. 2006. "Capital and revolutionary practice." *Historical Materialism* 14, no. 2: 55–82.

Barraclough, S., and Finger-Stich, A. 1996. *Some ecological and social implications of commercial shrimp farming in Asia.* UN Research Institute for Social Development #74, Geneva.

Basile, E. 2013. *Capitalist development in India's informal economy.* New York: Routledge.

Basole, A. 2016. "The agrarian question in India." *In contemporary readings in Marxism: A critical introduction,* ed. R. Kumar. Delhi: Aakar Books.

Basu, A. 2013. "The changing fortunes of the Bharatiya Janata Party." In *Routledge handbook of Indian politics,* eds. A. Kohli and P. Singh, 81–90. London: Routledge.

Basu, D. 2009. "Analysis of classes in India: A preliminary note on the industrial bourgeoisie and Middle class." *Sanhati* http://sanhati.com/excerpted/1919/.

Basu, P. 2002. *Towards Naxalbari.* Calcutta: Progressive Publishers.

Basu, S. 2004. *Does class matter? Colonial capital and workers' resistance in Bengal (1980–1937).* Delhi: Oxford University Press.

Basu, D., and Das, D. 2013. "The Maoist Movement in India: Some political economy considerations." *Journal of Agrarian Change* 13, no. 3: 365–381.

Basu, T., Datta, P., Sarkar, S., and Sen, S. 1993. *Khaki shorts and saffron flags.* Hyderabad: Orient Longman.

Baviskar, A., 2003. "Between violence and desire: Space, power, and identity in the making of metropolitan Delhi." *International Social Science Journal* 55, no. 175: 89–98.

Bear, L. 2017. "'Alternatives' to austerity: A critique of financialized infrastructure in India and beyond." *Anthropology today* 33, no. 5: 3–7.

Beck, T. 1995. "The green revolution and poverty in India: A case study of West Bengal." *Applied Geography* 15, no. 2: 161–181.

Beeson, M. 2009. "Developmental states in East Asia: A comparison of the Japanese and Chinese experiences." *Asian Perspective* 33, no. 2: 5–39.

Behera, C. 2002. "India: Prospects for Conflict and Peace." *Swisspeace and Swiss Agency for Development and Cooperation.* www.isn.ethz.ch/researchpub/publihouse/fast/crp/2000/crp_india_2000.htm.

Belton, B., and Little D. 2008. "The development of aquaculture in Central Thailand: Domestic demand versus export-led production." *Journal of Agrarian Change* 8, no. 1: 123–143.

Belton, B., Haque, M., and Little D. 2012. "Does size matter? Reassessing the relationship between aquaculture and poverty in Bangladesh." *Journal of Development Studies* 48, no. 7: 904–922.

Belton, B., Padiyar, A., Ravibabu G., and Rao, G. 2017. "Boom and bust in Andhra Pradesh: Development and transformation in India's domestic aquaculture value chain." *Aquaculture* 470: 196–206.

Bentall, J., and Corbridge, S. 1996. "Urban rural relations, demand politics and the new agrarianism in North West India: the Bharatiya Kisan union." *Transactions of the Institute of British Geographers* 21, no. 1: 27–48.

Bernstein, H. 1996. "Agrarian questions then and now." *Journal of Peasant Studies* 24: 22–59.

Bernstein, H. 2007. *Capital and labor from centre to margins.* Keynote address at conference on Living on the Margins. Vulnerability, Exclusion and the State in the Informal Economy, Cape Town. http://pdf.steerweb.org/WFP%20ESSAY/Bernstein_dsi.pdf.

Beteille, A. 2000. *Chronicles of our time.* Delhi: Penguin Books.

Beteille, A. 2007. *Marxism and class analysis.* New Delhi: Oxford University Press.

Berti, D., Jaoul, N., and Kanungo, P. 2011. *Cultural entrenchment of Hindutva: Local meditations and forms of convergence.* New Delhi: Routledge.

Bhaduri, A. 1973. "A study in agricultural backwardness under semi-feudalism." *The Economic Journal* 83, no. 329: 120–137.

Bhaduri, A. 1983. *The economic structure of backward agriculture.* London: Academic Press.

Bhaduri, A., Rahman, H.Z., and Arn, A. 1986. "Persistence and polarization: A study in the dynamics of agrarian contradiction." *Journal of Peasant Studies* 13, no. 3: 82–89.

Bhagwati, J. 1998. "The design of Indian development." In *India's economic reforms and development: Essays for Manmohan Singh,* eds. I.J. Ahluwalia and I.M.D. Little, 23–39. New Delhi: Oxford University Press.

Bhagwati, J. 2001. "Growth, poverty and reforms." *Economic and Political Weekly* 36, no. 10: 843–846.

Bhalla, G.S. 2007. *Indian agriculture since Independence.* Delhi: National Book Trust.

Bhalla, S. 1995. "Development, poverty and policy: The Haryana experience." *Economic and Political Weekly* 30, no. 41–42: 2619–2621, 2623–2625, 2627–2631, 2633–2634.

Bhalla, S. 1999. "Liberalisation, rural labour markets and the mobilisation of farm workers: The Haryana story in an all-India context." *Journal of Peasant Studies* 26, no. 2–3: 25–70.

Bhandari, R. 2008. "The disguises of wage-labor: Juridical illusions, unfree conditions and novel extensions." *Historical Materialism* 16, no. 1: 71–99.

Bhardwaj, A. 2015. "RSS mouthpiece defends Dadri lynching: Vedas order killing of sinners who kill cows." *The Indian Express.* https://indianexpress.com/article/india/india-news-india/rss-mouthpiece-defends-dadri-vedas-order-killing-of-sinners-who-kill-cows/.

Bharadwaj. K. 1982. "Regional Differentiation in India." *Economic and Political Weekly* 17:14–16.

Bhat, M., and Bhatta, R. 2004. "Considering aquacultural externality in Coastal Land allocation decisions in India." *Environmental & Resource Economics* 29: 1–20.

Bhatia, B. 2006. "On armed resistance." *Economic and Political Weekly* 41, no. 29: 3179–3183.

Bhatia, R. 2017. "The Year of Love Jihad in India." *New Yorker.* https://www.newyorker.com/culture/2017-in-review/the-year-of-love-jihad-in-india.

Bhattacharya, D. 2017. "50 years of Naxalbari: With Sangh in power, a new political energy needed now." *Catch News.* http://www.catchnews.com/politics-news/50-years-of-naxalbari-with-sangh-in-power-a-new-political-energy-needed-now-60954.html.

Bhattacharyya, S. 2001. "Capitalist development, peasant differentiation and the State: Survey findings from West Bengal." *The Journal of Peasant Studies* 28, no. 4: 95–126.

Bhattacharyya, S. 2013. *Two decades of market reform in India: Some dissenting views.* New York: Anthem Press.

Bhattacharyya, A., and Basu, S. 2018. *Marginalities in India: Themes and perspectives.* Singapore: Springer Verlag.

Bhelari, K. 2003. "Partners in progress: Maoist Naxals are trying out all ways to win the hearts of people." *The Week*, 22 June.

Bhowmik, S. 2014. *The state of labour: The global financial crisis and its impact.* India: Routledge.

Bidwai, P. 2015. *The Phoenix moment: Challenges confronting the Indian left.* New Delhi: Harper Collins.

Block, F., and Polanyi, K. 2003. "Karl Polanyi and the Writing of 'The Great Transformation.'" *Theory and Society* 32, no. 3: 275–306.

Bobbio, N. 2005. *Liberalism and democracy.* London: Verso.

Boer, R. 2009. *Criticism of heaven.* Chicago: Haymarket.

Boer, R. 2011. *Criticism of religion.* Chicago: Haymarket.

Boer, R. 2012. *Criticism of theology.* Chicago: Haymarket.

Boer, R. 2013. *Criticism of earth.* Chicago: Haymarket.

Boer, R. 2014. *In the vale of tears.* Chicago: Haymarket.

Bond, P. 2014. "BRICS and the tendency to sub-imperialism." *Pambazuka News.* https://www.pambazuka.org/governance/brics-and-tendency-sub-imperialism.

Bond, P., and Desai, A. 2006. *Explaining uneven and combined development in South Africa.* http://146.230.128.54/ccs/files/Bond%20Desai%20Uneven%20and%20Combined%20Development.pdf.

Bordoloi, Sudarshana, and Das, R. "Modernization Theory." In *International Encyclopedia of Geography: People, the Earth, Environment and Technology,* eds. Douglas Richardson, Noel Castree, Michael F. Goodchild, Audrey Kobayashi, Weidong Liu, and Richard A. Marston. Hoboken, NJ: John Wiley & Sons.

Borooah, V.K. 2008. "Deprivation, Violence, and Conflict: An Analysis of Naxalite Activity in the Districts of India." *International Journal of Conflict and Violence* 2, no. 2: 317–333.

Bownas, R. 2016. "Lost in transnationalism? GMOS in India and the eclipse of equitable development discourse." *Journal of South Asian Development* 11, no. 1: 67–87.

Boyd, W., Prudham, S., and Schurman, R. 2001. "Industrial dynamics and the problem of nature." *Society and natural resources* 14, no. 7: 555–570.

Brass, P.R. 1997. *Theft of an idol: Text and context in the representation of collective violence,* Princeton, NJ: Princeton University Press.

Brass, T. 1990. "Class struggle and the deproletarianization of agricultural labour in Haryana (India)." *Journal of Peasant Studies* 18, no. 1: 36–67.

Brass, T. 1994. "Some observations on unfree labor, capitalist restructuring, and de proletarianization." *International Review of Social History* 39, no. 2: 255–275.

Brass, T. 1995a. "Reply to Utsa Patnaik: If the Cap Fits..." *International Journal of Social History Review* 40, no. 1: 93–117.

Brass, T. 1995b. "The Politics of Gender, Nature and Nation in the Discourse of the New Farmers' Movements." In *New Farmers' Movements in India,* ed. T. Brass. London: Frank Cass Publishers.

Brass, T. 1999. *Towards a comparative political economy of unfree labour.* London and Portland: Frank Cass Publishers.

Brass, T. 2000. "Labour in post-colonial India: A response to Jan Breman." *The Journal of Peasant Studies* 28, no. 1: 126–146.

Brass, T. 2002. "Rural labour in agrarian transitions: The semi-feudal thesis revisited." *Journal of Contemporary Asia* 32, no. 4: 456–473.

Brass, T. 2003. "Why unfree labour is not "so-called": The fictions of Jairus Banaji." *The Journal of Peasant Studies* 31, no. 1: 101–136.

Brass, T. 2011. "Primitive accumulation, capitalist development and socialist transition: Still waiting for Godot?" *Journal of Contemporary Asia* 41, no. 1: 1–24.

Brass, T. 2012. *Labor regime change in the 21st century.* Leiden: Brill.

Brass, T. 2017a. "Class struggle and unfree labor: The (Marxist) road not taken." *Science & Society* 81, no. 2: 197–219.

Brass, T. 2017b. "Who these days is not a subaltern? The populist drift of global labor history." *Science & Society* 81, no. 1: 10–34.

Breman, J. 1985. *Of peasants, migrants and paupers: Rural labor circulation and capitalist production in West India.* Oxford: Oxford University Press.

Breman, J. 1989. "The disintegration of the Hali system." In *South Asia*, eds. H. Alavi and J. Harriss. New York: Monthly Review Press.

Breman, J. 1990. "Even dogs are better of the ongoing battle between capital and labor in the cane fields of Gujarat." *Journal of Peasant Studies* 17, no. 4: 546–608.

Breman, J. 1996. *Footloose labor: Working in India's informal economy.* Cambridge: Cambridge University Press.

Breman, J. 2003. *The labouring poor in India: Patterns of exploitation, subordination, and exclusion.* New Delhi: Oxford University Press.

Brenner, R. 1982. "The agrarian roots of European capitalism." *Past and Present* 97: 16–113.

Brenner, R. 1985. "Agrarian class structure and economic development in pre-industrial Europe." In *The Brenner Debate*, eds. T.H. Aston and C. Philipin, 10–63. Cambridge: Cambridge University Press.

Brenner, R. 1986. "The Social Basis of Economic Development." In *Analytical Marxism*, ed. J. Roemer, 23–53. Cambridge: Cambridge University Press.

Bridi, R. 2017. *The political-economy of science and (bio)technology: The emergence of agricultural biotechnology in the Canada.* (Ph.D. dissertation). York University, Toronto, Canada.

Brohman, J. 1996. "Postwar development in the Asian NICs: Does the neoliberal model fit reality?" *Economic Geography* 72, no. 2: 107–130.

Bukharin, N.I. 1933. "The theory of Capitalism." *Marxist.org.* https://www.marxists.org/archive/bukharin/works/1933/teaching/3.htm.

Burkett, P. 1996. "Value, capital and nature: some ecological implications of Marx's critique of political economy." *Science and Society* 60, no. 3: 332–359.

Burkett, P. 1999. *Marx and nature: A red and green perspective.* New York: St. Martin's Press.

Burkett, P., and Hart-Landberg, M. 2003. "A critique of 'catch-up' theories of development." *Journal of Contemporary Asia* 33, no. 2: 147–171.

Burkhart, R.E. 2002. "The capitalist political economy and human rights: Cross-national evidence." *Social Science Journal* 39, no. 2: 155–170.

Bush, S. 2008. "Contextualising fisheries policy in the Lower Mekong Basin." *Journal of Southeast Asian Studies* 39, no. 3: 329–353.

Byres, T. 1972. "The dialectic of India's Green Revolution." *South Asian Review* 5, no. 2: 99–116.

Byres, T. 1981. "The new technology, class formation and class action in the Indian countryside." *Journal of Peasant Studies* 8, no. 4: 405–454.

Byres, T. 1983. *The Green Revolution in India.* Milton Keynes: The Open University Press.

Byres, T. 1989. "Agrarian structure, the new technology and class action in India." In *South Asia,* eds. H. Alavi and J. Harriss. New York: Monthly Review Press.

Byres, T. 1991. "Agrarian question and differing forms of capitalist agrarian transition: An essay with reference to Asia." In *Rural Transformation in Asia,* eds. J. Breman and S. Mundle. Delhi: Oxford University Press.

Byres, T. 1996. *Capitalism from above and capitalism from below.* London: Macmillan.

Byres, T., ed. 1997. *The state, development planning & liberalisation in India.* Delhi: Oxford University Press.

Byres, T. 2003. "Structural change, the agrarian question and the possible impact of globalization." In *Work and well-being in the age of finance,* eds. J. Ghosh and C. Chandrasekhar, 171–211. New Dehli: Tulika.

Byres, T. 2013. "Development planning and the interventionist state versus liberalization and the neoliberal state: India, 1989–1996." In *Two decades of market reform in India: Some dissenting views,* ed. S. Bhattacharayya, 27–54. New York: Anthem Press.

Callinicos, A. 1988. *Making history: Agency, structure and change in social theory.* Cornell: Cornell University Press.

Callinicos, A. 1993. *Race and class.* London: Bookmarks.

Callinicos, A. 2004. *Making history: Agency, structure in social theory.* Leiden: Brill.

Callinicos, A. 2010. "Editor's introduction." *International Socialism.* http://isj.org.uk/the-ironies-of-indian-maoism/.

Caparaso, J., and Levine, D. 1991. *Theories of political economy.* Cambridge: Cambridge University Press.

Carchedi, G. 2010. *Behind the crisis.* Leiden: Brill.

Carling, A., and Wetherly, P., eds. 2006. "Rethinking Marx and history (a special issue)." *Science & Society* 70, no. 2: 46–154.

Carroll, M. 2017. "The sticky materiality of neoliberal neonatures: GMOs and the agrarian question." *New Political economy* 22, no. 2: 203–218.

Carter, B. 1995. "A growing divide: Marxist class analysis and the labor process." *Capital & Class* 19, no. 1: 33–72.

Castell, M. 1983. *The city and the grassroots: A Cross-cultural theory of urban social movements.* Berkeley: University of California Press.

Castree, N. 2001. "Commodity fetishism, geographical imaginations and imaginative geographies." *Environment and Planning A* 33: 1519–1525.

Castree, N. and Braun, B. 2001. *Social Nature: Theory, Practice and Politics.* Oxford: Blackwell.

Center for Monitoring Indian Economy (CMIE). 1987. *Basic statistics relating to the Indian economy,* vol. 2. Bombay.

Chacko, P. 2018. *Marketizing Hindutva: The state, society, and markets in Hindu nationalism.* Cambridge: Cambridge University Press.

Chadha, G. 1984. "The landless and the poor in green revolution regions of India." *Agricultural Situation in India* 39, no. 5.

Chadha, G. 1994. *Employment, earnings and poverty.* New Delhi: Sage.

Chakrabarti, A. 2012. "The Indian communist movement at a crossroads: A Marxian assessment." *Rethinking Marxism* 24, no. 3: 458–474.

Chakrabarti, A., and Cullenberg, S. 2003. *Transition and development in India.* New York: Routledge.

Chakrabarti, A., Chaudhury, A., and Cullenberg, S. 2009. "Global order and the new economic policy in India: The (post)colonial formation of the small-scale sector." *Cambridge Journal of Economics* 33, no. 6: 1169–1186.

Chakrabarti, S. 2009. *Red sun: Travels in Naxalite country.* New Delhi: Penguin Books.

Chakrabarty, B. 2008. *Indian politics and society since independence: Events, processes and ideology.* London: Routledge.

Chakrabarty, B. 2014. *Communism in India: Events, processes and ideologies.* New York: Oxford University press.

Chakrabarty, B. 2015. *Left radicalism in India.* Abington: Routledge.

Chakravarti, A. 2001. *Social power and everyday class relations: Agrarian transformation in North Bihar.* New Delhi: Sage.

Chakravarti, A. 2018. *Is this Azaadi? Everyday lives of Dalit agricultural laborers in a Bihar village.* Delhi: Tulka.

Chakravarty, M. 2016. "The richest 1% of Indians now own 58.4% of wealth." *Livemint.* https://www.livemint.com/Money/MML9OZRwaACyEhLzUNImnO/The-richest-1-of-Indians-now-own-584-of-wealth.html.

Chakravorty, S. 2016. "Land acquisition in India: The political-economy of changing the law." *Area Development and Policy* 1, no. 1: 48–62.

Chancel, L., and Picketty, T. 2017. "Indian income inequality, 1922–2015: From British Raj to billionaire Raj?" *World Inequality Database.* https://wid.world/document/chancelpiketty2017widworld/.

Chandan, A. 1979. "Victims of green revolution." *Economic and Political Weekly* 14, no. 25.

Chandavarkar, R. 2009. *Origins of industrial capitalism in India.* Cambridge, GBR: Cambridge University Press.

Chandra, B. 1989. *India's struggle for independence.* New Delhi: Penguin.

Chandra, B. 1992. "The Indian capitalist class and imperialism before 1947." In *Class, state and development in India,* B. Berberoglu. New Delhi: Sage.

Chandra, B. 2008. *Communalism: A primer.* Delhi: National Book Trust.

Chandra, N. 1974. "Farm efficiency under semi-feudalism – a critique of marginalist theories and some Marxist formulations." *Economic and Political Weekly* 9, no. 32–33–34.

Chandra, U., and Taghioff, D. 2016. *Staking claims: The politics of social movements in contemporary rural India.* New Delhi: Oxford University Press.

Chandramohan, C. 1998. "Political economy of agrarian conflicts in India." *Economic and Political Weekly* 33, no. 41: 2647–2653.

Chandrasekhar, C. 2018. "Neoliberal anti-populism." *Frontline* https://www.frontline .in/columns/C_P_Chandrasekhar/neoliberal antipopulism/article6279859.ece.

Chandrasekhar, C., and Ghosh, J. 2006. *The market that failed: A decade of neoliberal economic reforms in India.* New Delhi: Leftword Books.

Chandrasekhar, C., Patnaik, P., and Sen, A. 1999. "The proliferation of the bourgeoisie and economic policy." In *Class formation and political transformation in post-colonial India*, ed. T. Sathymurthy. Delhi: Oxford University Press.

Chang, D. 2003. *Demystifying the developmental state: A critique of the theories and practices of the state in the development of capital relations in Korea.* (Ph.D. thesis). University of Warwick, England.

Chang, D. 2013. "Labour and 'developmental state': A critique of the developmental state through of labour." In *Beyond the development state: Industrial policy into the twenty-first century,* eds. B. Fine, D. Tavasci, and J. Saraswati, 85–109. London: Pluto.

Chari, S. 2004. *Fraternal capital: Peasant-workers, self-made men, and globalization in provincial India.* Stanford: Stanford University Press.

Chatterjee, I. 2012. "Feminism, the false consciousness of neoliberal capitalism? Informalization, fundamentalism, and women in an Indian city." *Gender, Place and Culture* 19, no. 6: 790–809.

Chatterjee, P. 2000. "Development planning and the Indian state." In *Politics and the State in India*, ed. Z. Hasan. New Delhi: Sage.

Chatterjee, P. 2004. *The politics of the governed: Reflections on popular politics in most of the world.* New York: Columbia University Press.

Chatterjee, P. 2005. "Making autonomous geographies: Argentina's popular uprising and the unemployed workers movement." *Geoforum* 36, no. 5: 545–561.

Chatterjee, P. 2017. "Gramsci in India: Capitalist hegemony and subaltern politics." *Studi Storici* 58, no. 4: 963–986.

Chattopadhyay, B., Sharma, S.C., and Ray, A.K. 1987. "Rural/Urban terms of Trade, Primary Accumulation and the Increasing Strength of the Indian Farm Lobby." In *Food Systems and Society in Eastern India,* eds. B. Chattopadhyay and P. Spitz. Geneva: UNRISD.

Chattopadhyay, P. 1990a. "On the question of the mode of production in Indian agriculture: A preliminary note." In *Agrarian relations and accumulation: The mode of production debate in India,* ed. U. Patnaik. Delhi: Oxford University Press.

Chattopadhyay, P. 1990b. "An anti-kritik." In *Agrarian relations and accumulation: The mode of production debate in India,* ed. U. Patnaik. Delhi: Oxford University Press.

Chattopadhyaya, D. 2013. *Religion and society.* Delhi: Aakar.

Chauhan, B.R. 2003. "Village community." *The Oxford Companion to Sociology and Social Anthropology Volume 1*, ed. V. Das, 409–457. Delhi: Oxford University Press.

Chaudhuri, K. 2001. "A Naxalite Offensive in Orissa." *Frontline* 18, no. 18. https://www .frontline.in/static/html/fl1818/18180400.htm.

Chhibber, P. 2010. *Democracy without associations transformation of the party system and social cleavages in India.* Ann Arbor: University of Michigan Press.

Chhibber, P., and Nooruddin, I. 2004. "Do party systems count? The number of parties and government performance in the Indian States." *Comparative Political Studies* 37, no. 2: 152–187.

Chibber, V. 2003. *Locked in place: State building and late industrialization in India.* Princeton: Princeton University Press.

Chibber, V. 2006. "On the decline of class analysis in South Asian studies." *Critical Asian Studies* 38, no. 4: 356–387.

Chibber, V. 2017. "Our road to power." *Jacobin*. https://www.jacobinmag.com/2017/12/ our-road-to-power.

Chibber, V., and Usmani, A. 2013. "The state and the capitalist class in India." In *Routledge handbook of Indian politics,* eds. A. Kohli and P. Singh, 204–210. London: Routledge.

Chossudovsky, M. 1999. *The globalization of poverty: Impacts of IMF and World Bank Reforms.* London: Zed Books.

Clarke, K. 2017. "Social forces and regime change beyond class analysis." *World Politics.* 69, no. 3: 569–602.

Clarke, S. 1991. *The state debate.* New York: St. Martin's Press.

Cleaver, H. 1972. "The contradictions of the Green Revolution." *American Economic Review* 62, no, 2: 177–186.

Cohen, D. 2014. "Is India about to elect its Reagan?" *The Hindu.* https://www.thehindu .com/opinion/op-ed/Is-India-about-to-elect-its-Reagan/article11640720.ece.

Cohen, G. 2000 (1978). *Karl Marx's theory of history: A defence.* Princeton: Princeton University Press.

Communist Party of India (Marxist-Leninist-Liberation). 2008. "CAG audit interim report: NREGA being mocked in spirit?" *Communist Party of India (Marxist-Leninist Liberation).* http://www.cpiml.net/liberation/2008/02/cag-audit-interim-report-nr ega-being-mocked-spirit.

Cook, N. 1996. "Population and poverty in classical theory: testing a structural model for India." *Population Studies A Journal of Demography* 50, no. 2: 173–185.

Corbridge, S. 1993. "Marxisms, modernities, and moralities: Development praxis and the claims of distant strangers." *Environment and Planning D* 11, no. 4: 450–471.

Corbridge, S., and Harriss, J. 2000. *Reinventing India: Liberalization, Hindu nationalism and popular democracy.* New Delhi: Oxford University Press.

Corbridge, S., Williams, G., Srivastava, M., and Veron, R. 2004. *Seeing the State: Governance and Governmentality in Rural India.* Cambridge: Cambridge University Press.

Cox, K. 1990. "Territorial structures of the state: Some conceptual issues." *Tijdschrift voor economische en sociale geografie* 81, no. 4: 251–266.

Cowan, T. 2018. "The urban village, agrarian transformation, and rentier capitalism in Gurgaon, India." *Antipode* 50, no. 5: 1244–1266.

Cowen, M., and R. Shenton. 1996. *Doctrines of development.* London: Routledge.

CPI(M). 2017. 'Thinking together'; People's Democracy. http://peoplesdemocracy. in/2017/0402_pd/thinking-together.

CPI(M). 2018. "Press Communique. March 30." Party Central Office, New Delhi.

CPI-ML (Liberation). 2008. "CAG audit interim report: NREGA being mocked in spirit?" http://www.cpiml.net/liberation/2008/02/cag-audit-interim-report-nrega-being -mocked-spirit.

CPI(Maoist). 2014. Strategy and tactics of Indian revolution. http://www.banned thought.net/India/CPI-Maoist-Docs/Founding/StrategyTactics-pamphlet.pdf.

CPI-ML. 2011. "POSCO Project: No to corporate corruption and loot!" *Communist Party of India (Marxist-Leninist) Liberation.* http://www.cpiml.net/liberation/2011/06/ posco-project-no-corporate-corruption-and-loot.

CPI(ML). 2018. General Programme of CPI(ML); http://cpiml.net/documents/10th- party-congress/general-programme-of-cpiml.

Crowley, T. 2014. "The Many Faces of the Indian Left." *Jacobin.* https://www.jacobin mag.com/2014/05/the-many-faces-of-the-indian-left/.

D'Costa, A. 2005. *The long march to capitalism: Embourgeoisment, international and industrial transformation in India.* New York: Palgrave MacMillian.

D'Costa, A. 2011. "Geography, uneven development and distributive justice; The political economy of IT growth in India." *Cambridge Journal of Regions Economy and Society* 4, no. 2: 237–251.

D'Costa, A. 2013. "Globalization, the middle class and the transformation of the Indian state in the new economy." In *Two decades of market reform in India: Some dissenting views,* ed. S. Bhattacharyya, 125–142. New York: Anthem Press.

D'Costa, A. 2017. *The land question in India: State, dispossession, and capitalist transition.* Oxford: Oxford University Press.

D'Mello, B. 2018. *India after Naxalbari: Unfinished history.* New York: Monthly Review Press.

Da Corta, L., and Venkateshwarlu, D. 1999. "Unfree relations and the feminisation of agricultural labour in Andhra Pradesh, 1970–95." *Journal of Peasant Studies* 26, no. 2–3: 71–139.

Dale, G. 2010. Karl Polanyi: The limits of the market. Cambridge: Polity Press.

Damas, M. 1991. *Approaching Naxalbari.* Calcutta: Radical Impression.

Damodaran, H. 2018. "Labour markets: The 'puzzle' of rural wages." *Indian Express.* https://indianexpress.com/article/india/labour-markets-the-puzzle-of-rural-wages -5019670/.

Dantawala, M. 1987. "Growth and equity in agriculture." *Indian Journal of Agricultural Economics* 42, no. 2.

Das, A.N. 1982. *Agrarian movements in India: Studies on 20th century Bihar.* London: Frank Cass.

Das, A.N. 1997. *Swami and Friends: Sahajananda Saraswati and Those who Refuse to Let the Past of Bihar's Peasant Movements Become History.* Paper for the Peasant Symposium, University of Virginia, May 1997. Charlottesville, Virginia.

Das, G. 2012. *India grows at night: A liberal case for a strong state.* New Delhi: Penguin.

Das, K. 2000. "Informal Sector." In *Alternative Economic Survey.* Delhi: Rainbow Publishers.

Das, R. [Raju]. 1995. "Poverty and agrarian social structure: A case-study in rural India." *Dialectical Anthropology* 20, no. 2: 169–192.

Das, R. [Raju]. 1996. "State theories: A critical analysis." *Science and Society* 60, no. 1: 27–57.

Das, R. [Raju]. 1998a. "The green revolution, agrarian productivity and labour." *International Journal of Urban and Regional Research* 22, no. 1: 122–135.

Das, R. [Raju]. 1998b. "The social and spatial character of the Indian state." *Political Geography* 17, no. 7: 787–808.

Das, R. [Raju]. 1999a. "Politicism and idealism in state theory." *Science and Society* 63, no. 1: 97–104.

Das, R. [Raju]. 1999b. "Geographical unevenness of India's green revolution." *Journal Contemporary Asia* 29, no. 2: 167–186.

Das, R. [Raju]. 1999c. "The spatiality of class and state power: The case of India's land reforms." *Environment and Planning A* 31, no. 12: 2103–2216.

Das, R. [Raju]. 2000. "The state society relations: The case of an anti-poverty policy." *Environment and Planning C* 18, no. 6: 631–650.

Das, R. [Raju]. 2001a. "The political economy of India." *New Political Economy* 6, no. 1: 103–117.

Das, R. [Raju]. 2001b. "The spatiality of social relations: An Indian case-study." *The Journal of Rural Studies* 17, no. 3: 347–362.

Das, R. [Raju]. 2001c. "Class, capitalism and agrarian transition: A review and critique of some recent arguments." *Journal of Peasant Studies* 29, no. 1: 155–174.

Das, R. [Raju]. 2002. "The Green Revolution and poverty: A theoretical and empirical examination of the relation between technology and society." *Geoforum* 33, no. 1: 55–72.

Das, R. [Raju]. 2004. "Social capital and poverty of wage labourers: Problems with the social capital theory." *Transactions Institute of British Geographers* 29, no. 1: 27–45.

Das, R. [Raju]. 2005. "Rural society, the state and social capital in Eastern India: A critical investigation." *Journal of Peasant Studies* 32, no. 11: 48–87.

Das, R. [Raju]. 2006. "Marxist theories of the state." In *Alternative theories of the state,* ed. S. Pressman, 64–90. New York: Palgrave Macmillan.

Das, R. [Raju]. 2007. *"Looking, but not seeing: State* and/as class in rural India." *Journal of Peasant Studies* 34, no. 3–4 (Special issue on Peasant, State and Class): 408–440.

Das, R. [Raju]. 2009. "What's the Left to do in India." *A Socialist Project Review,* no. 26: 58–61.

Das, R. [Raju]. 2010. "Radical peasant movements and rural distress in India: A Study of the Naxalite Movement." In *India's New Economic Policy,* eds. W. Ahmad, A. Kundu, and R. Peet, 281–306. New York: Routledge.

Das, R. [Raju]. 2012a. "From labor geography to class geography: Reasserting the Marxist theory of class." *Human Geography: A New Radical Journal* 5, no. 1: 19–35.

Das, R. [Raju]. 2012b. "Academia as a site of class struggle." *Radical Notes.* http://radical notes.com/journal.

Das, R. [Raju]. 2012c. "Reconceptualizing capitalism: Forms of *subsumption of* labor, class struggle, and uneven development." *Review of Radical Political Economics* 44, no. 2: 178–200.

Das, R. [Raju]. 2012d. "The dirty picture of neoliberalism." *Links: International Journal of Socialist Renewal.* http://links.org.au/node/2818.

Das, R. [Raju]. 2013a. "The relevance of Marxist academics." *Class, Race and Corporate Power* 1, no. 1.

Das, R. [Raju]. 2013b. "Capitalism and regime change in the (globalizing) world of labour." *Journal of Contemporary Asia* 43, no. 4: 709–723.

Das, R. [Raju]. 2013c. "The market for education, civil servants and the India state." *Sanhati.* http://sanhati.com/excerpted/8813/.

Das, R. [Raju]. 2015. "Critical observations on neoliberalism and India's New Economic Policy." *Journal of Contemporary Asia* 45, no. 4: 715–726.

Das, R. [Raju]. 2016. "The attack on democracy and secularism in India." *Bullet: Socialist Project E-Bulletin, No. 1252.* http://www.socialistproject.ca/bullet/1252.php.

Das, R. [Raju]. 2017a. *Marxist class theory for a sceptical world.* Leiden/Boston: Brill.

Das, R. [Raju]. 2017b. "David Harvey's Theory of Accumulation by Dispossession: A Marxist Critique." *World Review of Political Economy* 8, no. 4: 590–616.

Das, R. [Raju]. 2017c. "David Harvey's theory of uneven geographical development: A Marxist critique." *Capital and Class* 41, no. 3: 511–536.

Das, R. [Raju]. 2018a. "Contradictions of India's Right-wing Government, and Growing Disenchantment." *Journal of Contemporary Asia* 49, no. 2: 313–328.

Das, R. [Raju]. 2018b. "A Marxist perspective on sustainability: Brief reflections on ecological sustainability and social inequality." *Links: International Journal of Socialist Renewal.* http://links.org.au/marxism-ecological-sustainability-social-inequality.

Das, R. [Raju]. 2019. "Politics of Marx as non-sectarian revolutionary class politics: An interpretation in the context of the 20th and 21st centuries." *Class, Race and Corporate Power*, March issue.

Das, R.J. and Chen, A. 2019. "Towards a Theoretical Framework for Understanding Capitalist Violence Against Child Labour." *World Review of Political Economy* 10, no. 2: 191–219.

Das, R. [Raju], and Mishra, D. 2019. "Industrialization and Geographically Uneven Development." Unpublished manuscript.

Das, R. [Ritanjan]. 2018. Neoliberalism and the transforming left in India: A contradictory manifesto. London: Routledge.

Das, T. 2018. "Changing colours of government-business relations." In *India Transformed*, ed. R. Mohan, 224–236. Washington, DC: Brookings Institution Press.

Das, R. [Ritanjan], and Mahmood, Z. 2015. "Contradictions, Negotiations and Reform: The Story of Left Policy Transition in West Bengal." *Journal of South Asian Development* 10, no. 2: 199–229.

Das Gupta, C. 2016. *State and capital in independent India: Institutions and accumulations.* Cambridge: Cambridge University Press.

Das Gupta, M., Grandvoinnet, H., and Romani, M. 2004. "State-community synergies in community-driven development." *Journal of Development Studies* 40, no. 3: 27–58.

Dasgupta, A. 2012. "Reverse pessimistic climate and boost investor sentiment." *The Hindu.* https://www.thehindu.com/business/Economy/reverse-pessimistic-climate -and-boost-investor-sentiment-pm/article3577372.ece.

Dasgupta, A. 2018. "Technological change and political turnover: The democratizing effects of the Green Revolution in India." *American Political Science Review* 112, no. 4: 918–938.

Dasgupta, B. [Biblab]. 1977. *Agrarian change and the new technology in India united nations research institute for social development.* Geneva: United Nations Research Institute for Small Development.

Dasgupta, B. [Biblab]. 1998. *Structural adjustment, global trade and the new political economy of development.* New Delhi: Vistaar.

Dasgupta, B. [Byasdeb]. 2017. "Flexible labour and capital accumulation in a post-colonial country." In *Accumulation in post-colonial capitalism,* eds. I.K. Mitra, R. Samaddar, and S. Sen, 27–57. Singapore: Springer.

Dasgupta, A., Gawande, K., and Kapur, D. 2017. "(When) do antipoverty programs reduce violence? India's rural employment guarantee and Maoist conflict." *International organization* 71, no. 3: 605–632.

Datt, G., and Ravallion, M. 2010. "Shining for the poor too." *Economic and Political Weekly* XLV, no. 7: 55–60.

Datta, A., 1998. *Land and labour relations in Southwest Bangladesh.* London: Macmillan.

Davenport, C. 2004. "The promise of democratic pacification: An empirical assessment." *International Studies Quarterly* 48, no. 3: 539–560.

Davey, B. 1974. *The economic development of India.* Nottingham: Spokesman Books.

Davidson, R. 2012. *The emotional life of your brain.* New York: Hudson Street Press.

Davidson, R. 2016. "The Four Keys to Well-Being." *Greater Good Magazine.* https://greatergood.berkeley.edu/article/item/the_four_keys_to_well_being.

De, S., and Saha, P. 2002. "BJP's politics of expediency: permeating Hindutva and legislating neo-liberal reforms." In *Class, ideology, and political parties in India,* ed. A. Jana and B. Sarmah. New Delhi: South Asian Publishers.

De Angelis, M. 2004. "Separating the doing and the deed: capital and the continuous character of enclosures." *Historical Materialism* 12, no. 2: 57–87.

De Zwart, F. 2000. "The logic of affirmative action: Caste, class and quotas in India." *Acta Sociologica* 43, no. 3: 235–249.

Demeritt, D. 2002. "What is the 'social construction of nature'? A typology and sympathetic critique", *Progress in Human Geography* 26, no. 6: 767–790.

Della Porta, D. 1995. *Social movements, political violence, and the state: A comparative analysis of Italy and Germany.* New York: Cambridge University Press.

Della Porta, D. 2014. "On violence and repression: A relational approach." *Government and Opposition* 49, no. 2: 159–187.

Desai, A.R. 1975. *State and Society in India.* Bombay: Popular Prakashan.

Desai, A.R., ed. 1986. *Agrarian struggles in India since Independence.* Delhi: Oxford University Press.

Desai, A.R. 1989. "Rural development and human rights in Independent India." *Economic and Political Weekly* 12, no. 31: 1291–1296.

Desai, M. 2003. "From movement to Party to Government: Why social policies in Kerala and West Bengal are so different." In *States, Parties and Social Movements,* ed. J. Goldstone, 170–196. Cambridge: Cambridge University Press.

Desai, R. 2002. *Slouching towards Ayodhya.* Gurgaon: Three Essays Collective.

Desai, R. 2011. "Gujarat's Hindutva of capitalist development." *South Asia: Journal of South Asian Studies* 34, no. 3: 354–381.

Deshmane, A. 2017. "Selling spirituality." *Frontline.* https://frontline.thehindu.com/the-nation/selling-spirituality/article9870620.ece?homepage=true.

Dev, S.M. 2000. "Economic reforms, poverty, income distribution and employment." *Economic and Political Weekly* 35, no. 10: 823–835.

Dhanagare, D.N. 1991. *Peasant movements in India, 1920–1950.* Delhi: Oxford University Press.

Dhar, A. 2007. "The approach to planning should change." *The Hindu.* https://www.thehindu.com/todays-paper/tp-opinion/ldquoThe-approach-to-planning-should-changerdquo/article14829064.ece.

Dhar, A. 2009. "Atrocities on SCs/STs disturbing." *The Hindu.* https://www.thehindu.com/todays-paper/tp-national/Atrocities-on-SCsSTs-disturbing-Manmohan/article16510646.ece.

Dhawale, A. 2000. "The Shiv Sena: Semi-fascism in action." *The Marxist* 16, no. 2. https://www.cpim.org/marxist/200002_marxist_sena_dhawle.htm.

Ding, X., and Ying, X. 2015. "The uneven and crisis-prone development of capitalism: A review of the tenth forum of world association for political economy." *World Review of Political Economy* 6, no. 4: 583–601.

Dias, W. 2005. "One-day general strike in India exposes need for socialist-internationalist strategy." *World Socialist Web Site.* http://www.wsws.org/en/articles/2005/09/indi-s29.html.

Dirlik, A. 2014. "Mao Zedong thought and the Third World/Global South." *Interventions-International Journal of Postcolonial Studies* 16, no. 2: 233–256.

Djurfeldt, G., and Sircar, S. 2017. *Structural transformation and agrarian change in India.* London: Taylor & Francis Group.

Dixon, C., 1990. *Rural Development in the Third World.* London: Routledge.

Dobkowski, M., and Walliman, I., eds. 2003. *Radical perspectives on the rise of fascism in German.* Kharagpur (India): Cornerstone (Original work published in 1989, by New York: MR Press).

Dollar, D., and Kraay, A. 2000. "Growth is good for the poor." *World Bank.* http://www.worldbank.org/research/growth/absddolakray.htm.

Donnelly, J. 1989. "Repression and development: The political contingency of human rights tradeoffs." In *Human Rights and Development: International Views,* ed. D.P. Forsythe, 305–328. New York: St. Martin's Press.

Doshi, S., and Ranganathan, M. 2017. "Contesting the unethical city: Land dispossession and corruption narratives in urban India." *Annals of the American Associations of Geographers* 107, no. 1: 183–199.

Draper, H. 1977. *Karl Marx's theory of revolution: State and bureaucracy.* New York: Monthly Review Press.

Dreze, J., Sen, A. 1995. *India: Economic development and social opportunity.* Delhi: Oxford University Press.

Dreze, J., Sen, A. 2002. *India: Development and participation.* Delhi: Oxford University Press.

Dryzek, J.S. 1996. "Political inclusion and the dynamics of democratization." *American Political Science Review* 90, no. 3: 475–487.

Dudley, R., and Miller, R.A. 1998. "Group Rebellion in the 1980s." *Journal of Conflict Resolution* 42, no. 1: 77–96.

Duménil, G., and Lévy, D. 2005. "The neoliberal (counter-)revolution." In *Neoliberalism: A critical reader,* eds. A. Saad-Filho and D. Johnston, 9–19. London: Pluto Press.

Dutta, A. 2018. "BJP Is trying hard to undercut Congress's soft Hindutva in Madhya Pradesh." *The Wire.* https://thewire.in/politics/bjp-is-trying-hard-to-undercut-congresss-soft-hindutva-in-madhya-pradesh.

Dutta, M. 2018. "Against All Odds: Tracing the Struggles of Workers to Form a Union Inside a Special Economic Zone in Tamil Nadu, India." In *Workers' movements and strikes in the twenty-first century: A global perspective,* eds. J. Nowak, M. Dutta, and P. Birke, 97–114. London: Rowman and Littlefield International.

Dyer, G. 1997. "Output per acre and size of holding: The logic of peasant agriculture under semi feudalism." *Journal of Peasant Studies* 24, no. 1–2: 103–131.

Eagleton, T. 1999. *Ideology.* London: Verso.

Earl, J. 2003. "Tanks, tear gas, and taxes: Toward a theory of movement repression." *Sociological Theory* 21, no. 1: 43–68.

Earl, J., Soule, S.A., and McCarthy, J.D. 2003. "Protest under fire? Explaining the policing of protest." *American Sociological Review* 68, no. 4: 581–606.

Earl, J., Martin, A., McCarthy, J., and Soile. S. 2004. "The use of newspaper data in the study of collective action." *Annual Review of Sociology* 30: 65–80.

Echeverri-Gent, J. 1995. *The state and the poor: Public policy and political development in India and the United States.* New Delhi: Vistaar Publications.

Eicher, C.K. 1995. "Zimbabwe maize based green revolution preconditions for replication." *World Development* 23, no. 5: 805–818.

Engels, F. 1883. "Frederick Engels' Speech at the Grave of Karl Marx." *Marxists.org.* https://www.marxists.org/archive/marx/works/1883/death/burial.htm.

Engels, F. 1848. "Principles of communism." In *Communist Manifesto,* K. Marx and F. Engels. https://www.marxists.org/archive/marx/works/download/pdf/Manifesto.pdf.

Engels, F. 1890. "Letter to J. Bloch." *Marxists.org.* https://www.marxists.org/archive/marx/works/1890/letters/90_09_21.htm.

Engels, F. 1894/1951. "The Peasant Question in France and Germany." In *Selected Works,* vol. 2, K. Marx and F. Engels. Moscow: Foreign Languages Publishing House.

Escobar, A. 1992. "Imagining a post-development era? Critical thought, development and social movements." *Social Text,* no. 31/32: 20–56.

Farid, H. 2005. "Indonesia's original sin: Mass killings and capitalist expansion, 1965–66." *Inter-Asia Cultural Studies* 6, no. 1: 3–16.

Ferguson, J. 1994. *The anti-politics machine: 'Development', depoliticisation and bureaucratic power in Lesotho.* Cambridge: Cambridge University Press.

Fernandes, L. 1994. "Contesting class- gender, community, and the politics of labor in a Calcutta jute mill." *Bulletin of Concerned Asian Scholars* 26, no. 4: 29–43.

Fernandes, L. 2014. *Routledge handbook of gender in South Asia.* Routledge: Milton Park.

Fernandes, L. 2016. "India's middle classes in contemporary India." In *Routledge handbook of contemporary India,* ed. K.A. Jacobsen, 232–242. London: Routledge.

Fernandez, B. 2018. "Dispossession and the depletion of social reproduction." *Antipode* 50, no. 1: 142–163.

Fields, G. 1995. "Income distribution in developing economies: conceptual, data and policy issues in broad based growth." In *Critical issues in Asian development: Theories, experience and policies*, ed. M.G. Quibria. New York: Oxford University Press.

Financial Express. 2018a. "Modi's minister makes bizarre claim; PM never said demonetisation was about black money, says MoS Shukla." *Financial Express*. https://www.financialexpress.com/economy/modis-minister-makes-bizarre-claim-pm-never-said-demonetisation-was-about-black-money-says-mos-shukla/1297529/.

Financial Express. 2018b. "Ease of doing business ranking 2019: know what worked for India and what didn't in its 23 notch leap to 77th slot." *Financial Express*. https://www.financialexpress.com/economy/ease-of-doing-business-ranking-2019-know-what-worked-for-india-and-what-didnt-in-23-notch-leap-to-77th-slot/1368596/.

Findlay, A. 1995. "Population crises: The Malthusian spectre." In *Geographies of global change,* eds. R. Johnston, P. Taylor, and M. Watts. Oxford: Blackwell.

Fine, B. 2001. *Social capital versus social theory: Political economy and social science at the turn of the millennium.* London: Routledge.

Fine, B., and Saad-Filho, A. 2017. "Thirteen things you need to know about neoliberalism." *Critical Sociology* 43, no. 4–5: 685–706.

Flaherty, M., and Karnjanakesorn, C. 1995. "Marine shrimp aquaculture and natural resource degradation in Thailand." *Environmental Management* 19, no. 1: 27–37.

Flaherty, M., Vandergeest, P., and Miller, P. 1999. "Rice paddy or shrimp pond: Tough decisions in rural Thailand." *World Development* 27, no. 12: 2045–2060.

Foley, B. 2018. "Intersectionality: A Marxist Critique." *Science & Society* 82, no. 2: 269–275.

Fominaya, C.F., and Wood, L., eds. 2011. "Repression and Social Movements." *Interface: A Journal for and About Social Movements* 3, no. 1: 1–11.

Foucault, M. 1979. *Discipline and punish: The birth of the prison.* New York: Vintage Books. Translated from the French by Alan Sheridan.

Fracchia, J. 2008. "The capitalist labour-process and the body in pain: The corporeal depths of Marx's concept of immiseration." *Historical Materialism* 16, no. 4: 35–66.

Franke, R., and Chasin, B. 1991. "Kerala state, India: Radical reform as development." *Monthly Review* 42, no. 8: 1–23.

Frankel, F. 1971. *India's Green Revolution: Economic gains and political costs.* Princeton: Princeton University Press.

Frankel, F. 1990. "Caste, land and dominance in Bihar: Breakdown of the Brahminical order." In *Dominance and state power,* vol. 1, eds. F. Frankel and M. Rao, 46–132. Delhi: Oxford University Press.

Frankel, F. 1994. *Dominance and state power in modern India: Decline of a social order,* volume 1. Delhi: Oxford University Press.

Frankel, F. 2005. *India's political economy, 1947–2004 The gradual revolution.* New Delhi: Oxford India.

Freebairn, D. 1995. "Did the green revolution concentrate incomes? A quantitative study of research reports." *World Development* 23, no. 2: 265–279.

Friedmann, H. 1993. "The political economy of food: A global crisis." *New Left Review* 197: 29–56.

Frontier. (n.d.). www.frontierindia.scriptmania.com/V15PAGE5.htm.

Fuller, C., and Véronique, B., eds. 2001. *The everyday state and society in Modern India.* London: Hurst.

Gabriel, M. *Love and capital.* New York: Back Bay Books.

Ghertner, D.A. 2014. "India's urban revolution: Geographies of displacement beyond gentrification." *Environment and Planning A* 46, no. 7: 1554–1571.

Ghose, D. 2018. "Rahul Gandhi tests 'soft Hindutva' in poll-bound Madhya Pradesh as Congress borrows heavily from BJP's electoral strategy." *Firstpost.* https://www.first post.com/politics/rahul-gandhi-tests-soft-hindutva-in-poll-bound-madhya-pradesh-as-congress-borrows-heavily-from-bjps-electoral-strategy-5283511.html.

Ghosh, J. 1998. "Liberalization Debates." In *The Indian economy since independence,* ed. T. Byres. New Delhi: Oxford University Press.

Gibson-Graham, J.K. 2006. *A post-capitalist politics.* Minneapolis: Minnesota University Press.

Giddens, A. 1981. *A contemporary critique of historical materialism.* London: Macmillan.

Gidwani, V. 2008. *Capital, interrupted: Agrarian development and the politics of work in India.* Minneapolis: University of Minneapolis Press.

Gill, S. 1988. "Contradictions of Punjab model of growth and search for an alternative." *Economic and Political Weekly* 23, no. 42: 2167–2173.

Gill, S. 1994. "The farmers movement and agrarian change in the green revolution belt of North West India." *Journal of Peasant Studies* 21, no. 3–4: 195–211.

Gimenez, M. 2005. "Capitalism and the oppression of women: Marx revisited." *Science & Society* 69, no. 1: 11–32.

Gimenez, M. 2017. "Intersectionality." *Science & Society* 81, no. 2: 261–269; no. 3: 450–452.

Gimenez, M. 2018. Intersectionality: Marxist critical observations. *Science & Society* 82, no. 2: 261–269.

Goldman, A., and Smith, J. 1995. "Nature of green revolutions." *World Development* 23, no. 2.

Gomes, J. 2015. "The political economy of the Maoist conflict in India: An empirical analysis." *World Development* 68: 96–123.

Gonzalez, O., Beltran, L., Caceres-Martinez, C., Ramirez, H., Hernandez-Vazquez, S., Troyo-Dieguez, E., and Ortega-Rubio, A. 2003. "Sustainability Development Analysis of Semi-Intensive Shrimp Farms in Sonora, Mexico." *Sustainable Development* 11, no. 4: 213–222.

Goss, J., Burch, D., and Rickson, R. 2000. "Agri-food restructuring and Third World transnationals: Thailand, the CP Group and the Global Shrimp Industry." *World Development* 28, no. 3: 513–530.

Goss, J., Skladany, M., and Middendorf, G. 2001. "Dialogue: Shrimp aquaculture in Thailand: A response to Vandergeest, Flaherty, and Miller." *Rural Sociology* 66, no. 3: 451–460.

Goodman, D., and Watts, M., eds. 1997. *Globalising food: Agrarian questions and global restructuring.* London: Routledge.

Government of India. 1969. "Home ministry, research and policy division, 1969." In *The Causes and Nature of Current Agrarian Tensions*, ed. A. Desai. New Delhi.

Government of India. 1986. "The Causes and Nature of Current Agrarian Tension." In *Agrarian struggles in India since Independence,* ed. A.R. Desai. Delhi: Oxford University Press.

Government of India. 1998. *Rural Development Statistics, 1998.* Hyderabad: National Institute of Rural Development.

Government of India. 1998. Union Home Minister Shri L.K. Advani's Speech. The High Level Meeting of Chief Ministers and Police Chiefs on Naxalism, Hyderabad, June 15, 2009.

Government of India. 2003. India: *Rural Development Statistics, 2002–2003.* Hyderabad: National Institute of Rural Development.

Government of India. 2005. *India: Rural Development Report.* Hyderabad: National Institute of Rural Development.

Government of India. 2007. *Rural Development Statistics: 2005–2006.* Hyderabad: National Institute of Rural Development.

Government of India. 2008. *Rural Development Statistics: 2007.* Hyderabad: National Institute of Rural Development.

Government of India. 2015. "Ministry of labour and employment. Annual Report." *Government of India.* https://labour.gov.in/sites/default/files/Chapter%20-%204.pdf.

Grabowski, R. 2005. "Agricultural revolution, political development, and long-run economic growth." *Canadian Journal of Development Studies* 26, no. 3: 393–408.

Griffin, K. 1974. *The political economy of agrarian change: An essay on the Green Revolution.* London: Macmillan.

Griffin, K. 1989. *Alternative strategies for economic development.* New York: St. Martin's Press.

Grossman, H. 1929. *Law of the accumulation and breakdown.* https://www.marxists.org/archive/grossman/1929/breakdown/

Gudavarthy, A. 2005. "Dalit and Naxalite Movements in AP: Solidarity or Hegemony?" *Economic and Political Weekly* 40, no. 51: 5410–5418.

Guha, R. 1983. *Elementary aspects of peasant insurgency in colonial India*. Delhi: Oxford University Press.

Guha, R. 2002. "Chipko: Social history of an 'environmental' movement." In *Social movements and the state,* ed. G. Shah. Delhi: Sage.

Guha, R. 2006. "The guru of hate." *The Hindu.* https://www.thehindu.com/todays-paper/tp-features/tp-sundaymagazine/the-guru-of-hate/article3232784.ece.

Guha, R. 2007. "Adivasis, Naxalites and democracy." *Economic and Political Weekly* 42, no. 32: 3305–3312.

Guha, R. 2012. *Patriots and partisans.* New Delhi: Penguin Books.

Gupta, A. 2000. "Blurred boundaries: The discourse of corruption, the culture of politics and the imagined state." In *Politics and the State in India,* ed. Z. Hasan. New Delhi: Sage.

Gupta, A., and A. Sharma, 2006. "Globalization and Postcolonial States." *Current Anthropology* 47, no. 2.

Gupta, A. and Sivaramakrishnan, K. 2011. "Introduction: The state in India after liberalization." In *The State in India after Liberalization: Interdisciplinary Perspectives*, eds. A. Gupta, and K. Sivaramakrishnan, 1–28. New York: Routledge.

Gupta, D., and Sriram, K. 2018. "Impact of security expenditures in military alliances on violence from non-state actors: evidence from India." *World Development* 107: 338–357.

Gupta, T.D. 2003. "Recent developments in the Naxalite movement – Communists in India." *Monthly Review* 45, no. 4: 8–24.

Gupta, T.D. 2006. "Maoism in India." *Economic and Political Weekly* 41, no. 29: 3172–3176.

Gurr, T. 1986. "Persisting Patterns of Repression and Rebellion: Foundations for a General Theory of Political Coercion." In *Persistent Patterns and Emergent Structures in a Waning Century*, ed. M. Karns, 149–170. New York: Praeger.

Gurr, T. 1988. "War, revolution, and the growth of the coercive state." *Comparative Political Studies* 21, no. 1: 45–65.

Habib, I. 2014. "Major historical problems in the light of Marxism." In *Marx, Gandhi and Modernity*, ed. A. Bilgrami. Delhi: Tulika Books.

Habib, I. 2015. *Religion in Indian history.* Delhi: Tulika Books.

Habib, I. 2017. "Seventy years on, India cannot allow the divisive forces to triumph again." *The Wire.* https://thewire.in/history/bjps-fascist-character-grave-danger-democracy-civil-rights-india.

Hale, A., and Opondo, M. 2005. "Humanizing the cut flower chain: Confronting the realities of flower production for workers in Kenya." *Antipode* 37, no. 2: 301–323.

Hansda, R. 2017. "Small-scale farming and gender-friendly agricultural technologies: the interplay between gender, labour, caste, policy and practice." *Gender, Technology, and Development* 21, no. 3: 189–205.

Haragopal, G. 2017. "Maoist Movement: Context and Concerns." *Economic & Political Weekly* 52, no. 21.

Hardin, C. 2014. "Finding the 'neo' in neoliberalism." *Cultural Studies* 28, no. 2: 199–221.

Harris, R., and Seid, M., eds. 2000. *Critical perspectives on globalization and neoliberalism in the developing countries.* Leiden: Brill.

Harriss, J. 1988. "A review of South Asian studies." *Modern Asian Studies* 22, no. 1: 43–56.

Harriss, J. 1991. "The green revolution in North Arcot: Economic trends, household mobility, and the politics of an awkward class." In *The Green Revolution Reconsidered,* eds. P.B. Hazell and C. Ramaswamy. Baltimore: The John Hopkins University Press.

Harriss, J. 1992. "Does the 'Depressor' Still Work? Agrarian Structure and Development in India: A Review of Evidence and Argument." *Journal of Peasant Studies* 19, no. 2: 189–227.

Harriss, J. 2011a. "What is Going on in India's 'Red Corridor'? Questions about India's Maoist Insurgency-Literature Review." *Pacific Affairs* 84, no. 2: 309–327.

Harriss, J. 2011b. "How far have India's economic reforms been 'guided by compassion and justice'? Social policy in the neoliberal era." In *Understanding India's New Political Economy: A Great Transformation?*, eds. S. Ruparelia, S. Reddy, J. Harriss, and S. Corbridge, 127–140. New York: Routledge.

Harriss, J. 2011c. "'New politics' and the governmentality of the post-liberalization state in India: an ethnographic perspective." In *The state in India after liberalization: Interdisciplinary perspectives,* eds. A. Gupta and L. Sivaramakrishnan, 91–108. London: Routledge.

Harriss, J. 2013. "Politics and redistribution in India." In *Routledge handbook of Indian politics*, eds. A. Kohli and P. Singh. London: Routledge.

Harriss White, B., and Janakarajan, S. 1997. "From green revolution to rural industrialization in South India." *Economic and Political Weekly* 32, no. 25: 1469–1477.

Harriss-White, B., and Janakarajan, S. 2004. *Rural India facing the twenty-first century: Essays on long-term village change and recent development policy.* London: Anthem Press.

Harvey, D. 1974. "Population, resources, and the ideology of science." *Economic Geography* 50, no. 3: 256–277.

Harvey, D. 1978. "The urban process under capitalism." *International Journal of Urban and Regional Research* 2, no. 1–4: 101–131.

Harvey, D. 1982. *Limits to capital.* Chicago: Chicago University Press.

Harvey, D. 1990. "Between space and time: Reflections on the geographical imagination." *Annals of the Association of American Geographers* 80, no. 3: 418–434.

Harvey, D. 1996. "Justice, nature and the geography of difference." Oxford: Blackwell.

Harvey, D. 1998. "The body as an accumulation strategy." *Environment and Planning D: Society and Space* 16, no. 4: 401–421.

Harvey, D. 2000. *Spaces of hope*. Edinburgh: Edinburgh University Press.

Harvey, D. 2003. *The New Imperialism*. Oxford: Oxford University Press.

Harvey, D. 2005. *A brief history of neoliberalism*. New York: Oxford University Press.

Harvey, D. 2006. *Spaces of global capitalism*. London: Verso.

Harvey, D. 2016. "Neoliberalism is a political project (an interview)." *Jacobin*. https://www.jacobinmag.com/2016/07/david-harvey-neoliberalism-capitalism-labor-crisis-resistance/.

Harwood, J. 2013. "Development policy and history: Lessons from the green revolution." *History and Policy*. http://www.historyandpolicy.org/policy-papers/papers/development-policy-and-history-lessons-from-the-green-revolution.

Heble, A. 1979. "The green revolution: its social and economic consequences." *How*.

Heller, P. 1995. "From class struggle to class compromise: redistribution and growth in a South Indian state." *Journal of Development Studies* 31, no. 5: 645–672.

Heller, P. 1999. *The labor of development: Workers and the transformation of capitalism in Kerala, India*. Ithaca & London: Cornell University Press.

Heller, P., and Fernandes, L. 2006. "Hegemonic aspirations: New middle class politics and India's democracy in comparative perspective." *Critical Asian Studies* 38, no. 4: 495–522.

Heller, P., and Fernandes, L. 1996. "Social capital as a product of class mobilization and state intervention: Industrial workers in Kerala, India." *World Development* 24, no. 6: 1055–1071.

Heller, P., and Fernandes, L. 1999. *The labour of development: Workers and the transformation of capitalism in Kerala, India*. Ithaca: Cornell University Press.

Henderson, C.W. 1991. "Conditions affecting the use of political repression." *Journal of conflict resolution* 35, no. 1: 120–142.

Herath, G., and Jayasuriya, S. 1996. "Adoption of HYV technology in Asian countries." *Asian Survey* 36, no. 12: 1184–1200.

Herod, A. 1994. "On workers' theoretical (in)visibility in the writing of critical urban geography: A comradely critique." *Urban Geography* 15, no. 7: 681–693.

Herod, A. 1999. "Reflections on interviewing foreign elites: Praxis, positionality, validity, and the cult of the insider." *Geoforum* 30, no. 4: 313–327.

Herring, R. 1999. "Embedded Particularism: India's failed developmental state." In *The developmental state*, ed. M. Woo-Cumings. Ithaca, NY: Cornell University Press.

Herring, R. 2006. "Why did "operation cremate Monsanto" fail? Science and class in India's great terminator-technology hoax." *Critical Asian Studies* 38, no. 4: 467–493.

Herring, R. 2013. "Class politics in India: Euphemization, identity, and power." In *Routledge handbook of Indian politics*, eds. A. Kohli and P. Singh. London: Routledge.

Herring, R.J., and Agarwala, R. 2006. "Introduction – Restoring to class: Puzzles from the subcontinent." *Critical Asian Studies* 38, no. 4: 323–356.

Herring, R., and Paarlberg, R. 2016. "The political economy of biotechnology." *Annual Review of Resource Economics* 8: 397–341.

Hess, D., and Martin, B. 2006. "Repression, backfire, and the theory of transformative events." *Mobilization* 11, no. 2: 249–267.

Hilton, R., ed. 1978. *The transition from feudalism to capitalism*. London: Verso.

Hindustan Times. PTI. 2002. "Major Naxalite Outfits." *Hindustan Times*. https://www .hindustantimes.com/india/major-naxalite-outfits/story-oveBIOPZoV4Hd B5La2w7dM.html.

Holloway, J. 2005. "No." *Historical Materialism* 13, no. 4: 265–284.

Houston, I., and Pulido, L. 2000. "The work of performativity." *Environment and Planning D: Society and Space* 20, no. 4: 401–424.

Houtzager, P. 2000. "Social movements amidst democratic transitions: Lessons from the Brazilian countryside." *Journal of Development Studies* 36, no. 5: 59–88.

Hristov, J. 2005. "Indigenous Struggles for land and culture in Cauca, Colombia." *Journal of Peasant Studies* 32, no. 1: 88–117.

Huang, Y. 2015. "Can capitalist farms defeat family farms? The dynamics of capitalist accumulation in shrimp aquaculture in South China." *Journal of Agrarian Change* 15, no. 3: 392–412.

Huitric, M., Folke, C., and Kautsky, N. 2002. "Development and government policies of the shrimp farming industry in Thailand in relation to mangrove ecosystems." *Ecological Economics* 40, no. 3: 441–455.

Human Rights Watch. 1999a. *Broken People: Caste violence against India's 'untouchables'.* New York: Human Rights Watch.

Human Rights Watch. 1999b. "The pattern of abuse: Rural violence in Bihar and the state's response." *Human Rights Watch*. http://www.hrw.org/reports/1999/india/In dia994-06.htm.

Ilaiah, K. 2000. "Caste, or class or caste-class: a study in Dalitbahujan consciousness and struggles in Andhra Pradesh in 1980s." In *Class, caste, and gender*, ed. M. Mohanty, 227–255. Delhi: Sage.

India Together. 2007. "NREGA battling cancerous corruption in Orissa." *India Together*. http://www.india together.org/2007/oct/gov-nregs.htm.

Indian Aquaculture Authority (IAA). 2001. "Shrimp Aquaculture and the Environment." http://aquaculture.tn.nic.in/pdf/farming.pdf.

Indian Express. 2017. "BJP-RSS new enemies of Naxalite movement, say leaders." *The Indian Press*. https://indianexpress.com/article/india/bjp-rss-new-enemies-of-nax alite-movement-say-leaders-4678690/.

Indian National Congress. 2017. "Modi govt. diluting MNREGA." *Indian National Congress*. https://www.inc.in/en/in-focus/the-systematic-strangulation-of-mgnre ga-under-modi-s-watch.

International Communist League. 2014. "India: Hindu far right sweeps elections: For a socialist federation of South Asia!" *International Communist League*. https://www .icl-fi.org/english/wh/227/india.html.

Islam, M. 2008. "In search of "white gold": Environmental and agrarian changes in rural Bangladesh." *Society and Natural Resources* 22, no. 1: 66–78.

Ismi, A. 2013. "Maoist Insurgency Spreads to Over 40% of India. Mass Poverty and Delhi's Embrace of Corporate Neoliberalism Fuels Social Uprising." *Global Research*. http://www.globalresearch.ca.

Jacob, S. 2015. "Towards a comparative subnational perspective on India." *Studies in Indian Politics* 3, no. 2: 229–246.

Jaffrelot, C. 2011. *Religion, caste, and politics in India.* New York: Columbia University Press.

Jaffrelot, C. 2013. "Caste and political parties in India." In *Routledge handbook of Indian politics*, eds. A. Kohli and P. Singh. London: Routledge.

Jain, H.K. 2010. *Green revolution: history, impact and future.* Houston: Studium Press.

Jairath, V. 2014. "Studying communal riots in India: Some methodological issues." In *Political sociology of India,* ed. A. Kumar. Delhi: Sage.

Jal, M. 2014. *The new militants.* Delhi: Aakar.

Jalal, A. 1995. *Democracy and authoritarianism in South Asia.* Cambridge: Cambridge University Press.

Jamieson, M. 2002. "Ownership of sea-shrimp production and perceptions of economic opportunity in a Nicaraguan Miskitu Village." *Ethnography* 41, no. 3: 281–298.

Jamil, G. 2017. *Accumulation by segregation: Muslims localities in Delhi.* Delhi: Oxford University Press.

Jannuzi, F. 1996. *India's persistent dilemma: The political economy of agrarian reform.* London: Orient Longman.

Jawed, S. 2017. "Fact check: Are rural roads constructed in 2016–17 at an all-time high as claimed by BJP?" *Altnews*. https://www.altnews.in/fact-check-rural-roads-construc ted-2016-17-time-high-claimed-bjp/.

Jeffrey, C. 1997. "Richer farmers and agrarian change in Meerut District, Uttar Pradesh, India." *Environment and Planning A* 29, no. 12: 2113–2127.

Jeffrey, C., Jeffery, P., and Jeffery, R. 2005. "Reproducing difference? Schooling, jobs, and empowerment in Uttar Pradesh, India." *World Development* 33, no. 12: 2085–2101.

Jeffrey, C., and Lerche, J. 2000. "Stating the difference: State, discourse and class reproduction in Uttar Pradesh, India." *Development and Change* 31, no. 4: 857–878.

Jenkins, S. 2011. "The politics of India's special economic zones." In *Understanding India's new political economy*, eds. S. Ruparelia, S. Reddy, J. Harriss, and S. Corbridge. London: Routledge.

Jessop, B. 2002. *The future of the capitalist state.* Cambridge: Polity Press.

Jha, A., Gupta, S., and Ramaswamy, S. 2017. "India risk survey 2017." *Pinkerton/FICCI.* http://www.ficci.in/Sedocument/20416/India-Risk-Survey-2017-Report.pdf.

Jha, S.K. 2003. "Jharkhand: Anti-naxal strategy and use of POTA." *Institute for Conflict Management,* no. 1021, 2003. http://www.ipcs.org/article/naxalite-violence/jharkh and-anti-naxal-strategy-and-use-of-pota-1021.html.

Jodhka, S., Rehbein, B., and Souza, J. 2017. *Inequality in capitalist societies.* London: Routledge.

Jones, H. 1990. *Population geography.* London: Paul Chapman.

Jones, K. 2018. "Indian court dismisses Maruti Suzuki workers' bail application." *World Socialist Website.* https://www.wsws.org/en/articles/2018/10/23/mswu-o23.html.

Jones, S. 2014. "US corporate profits soar as productivity rises and wages stagnate." https://www.wsws.org/en/articles/2014/12/04/wage-do4.html.

Jose, A. 1988. "Agricultural wages in India." *Economic and Political Weekly* 23.

Josh, B. 2011. *A history of the Indian communists: from united front to left front.* New Delhi: Sage.

Judge, P., ed. 2014. *Towards sociology of Dalits.* Delhi: Sage.

Kallis, A. 2003. *The fascism reader.* London: Routledge.

Kannan, K. 1999. "Rural labour relations and development dilemmas in Kerala: Reflections on the dilemmas of a socially transforming labour force in a slowly growing economy." *Journal of Peasant Studies* 26, no. 2–3: 140–181.

Kapadia, K. 1997. "Mediating the meaning of market opportunities – Gender, caste and class in rural South India." *Economic and Political Weekly* 32, no. 52: 3329–3235.

Kapadia, K. 2002. *The violence of development: The politics of identity, gender and social inequalities in India.* London: Zed.

Kar, G. 2018. "The enduring prevalence of semi-feudal agrarian relations in India." *Journal of Labour and Society* 21, no. 2: 193–213.

Karat, P. 1992. "BJP: A reactionary response." *The Marxist* x, no. 3.

Karat, P. 2000. "CPI(M) programme: Basic strategy reiterated." *The Marxist* 16, no. 3. http://www.cpim.org/marxist/200003_marxist_progrm_pk.htm.

Karat, P. 2004. "Implications of BJP rule: The election battle ahead." *The Marxist* 20, no. 1.

Karat, P. 2014. "The rise of Narendra Modi: A joint enterprise of Hindutva and big business." *The Marxist* xxx, no. 1.

Kautsky, K. 1988. *The Agrarian Question.* Winchester, Massachusetts: Zwan Publications.

Kaviraj, S. 1988. "A critique of the passive revolution." *Economic and Political Weekly* 23, no. 45/47: 2429–2433, 2436–2441, 2443–2444.

Kaviraj, S. 1991. "On state, society and discourse in India." In *Rethinking Third World Politics,* ed. J. Manor, 72–99. Harlow: Longman.

Kaviraj, S. 2011. "On the enchantment of the state: Indian thought on the role of the state in the narrative of modernity." In *The state in India after liberalization: Interdis-*

*ciplinary perspectives,* eds. A. Gupta and L. Sivaramakrishnan, 31–48. London: Routledge.

Kennedy, J., and Purushotham. S. 2012. "Beyond Naxalbari: A comparative analysis of Maoist insurgency and counterinsurgency in Independent India." *Comparative Studies in Society and History* 54, no. 4: 832–862.

Kerswell, T., and Pratap, S. 2019. *Worker Cooperative in India.* Singapore: Springer Singapore.

Khanna, G., and Zimmerman, L. 2017. "Guns and butter? Fighting violence with the promise of development." *Journal of Development Economics* 124: 120–141.

Khatkhate, D. 2006. "Indian economic reform, a philosopher's stone." *Economic and Political Weekly* 41, no. 22: 2203–2205.

Khera, R. 2008. "Empowerment guarantee act." *Economic and Political Weekly* 43, no. 35: 8–10.

Khilnani, S. 2017. *The idea of India.* New York: Farrar, Straus and Girour.

Kishor, C.S. 1998. "Poverty alleviation after post liberalisation: Study of a tribal block in Orissa." *Economic and Political Weekly* 33, no. 28: 1846–1851.

Klak, T., and Myers, G. 1997. "The discursive tactics of neoliberal development in small third world countries." *Geoforum* 28, no. 2: 133–149.

Kodras, J.E. 1997. "The changing map of American poverty in an era of economic restructuring and political realignment." *Economic Geography* 73, no. 1: 67–93.

Kohli, A. 1987. *The state and poverty in India: The politics of reform.* Cambridge: Cambridge University Press.

Kohli, A. 2012. *Poverty amid plenty in the new India.* Delhi: Cambridge University Press.

Kosambi, D. 1957. *Exasperating essays: Exercises in the dialectical method.* Poona: Bhagawat.

Kotovsky, G. 1964. *Agrarian Reforms in India.* New Delhi: People's Publishing House.

Krishna, A. 2002. "Enhancing Political Participation in Democracies – What is the Role of Social Capital?" *Comparative Political Studies* 35, no. 4: 437–460.

Krishna, C. 2003. *Fascism in India: Faces, fangs, and facts.* New Delhi: Manak Publications.

Krishna, S. 2015. "Number fetish: Middle-class India's obsession with the GDP." *Globalizations* 12, no. 6: 859–871.

Krishnan, S. 2017. "The engineering India's middle-class politics." *Contemporary South Asia* 25, no. 4: 364–379.

Kruks-Wisner, G. 2018. "The pursuit of social welfare: citizens claim making in rural India." *World Politics* 70, no. 1: 122–163.

Kujur, R. 2006. "Under development and Naxal movement." *Economic and Political Weekly* 41, no. 7: 557–559.

Kumar, A. 1999. "Massacres by landlord militia rock India's second most populous state." *World Socialist Website.* http://www.wsws.org/articles/1999/feb1999/ind2-f24.shtml.

Kumar, A. 2008. "Dissonance between economic reforms and democracy." *Economic and Political Weekly* 43, no. 1: 54–60.

Kumar, C. 2018. "India lost 11.73 lakh man days to strikes in 2017." *Times of India.* https://timesofindia.indiatimes.com/india/india-lost-11-73-lakh-man-days-to-strikes-in-2017/articleshow/62539692.cms.

Kumar, S. 2017. "After silent revolution: Most marginalized Dalits and local democracy in Uttar Pradesh, North India." *Studies in India Politics* 5, no. 1: 18–31.

Kumar, V. 2002. "Dalits." *Alternative economic survey.* New Delhi: Rainbow Publishers.

Kumara, K. 2017. "Indian economy in a downward spiral." *World Socialist Website.* https://www.wsws.org/en/articles/2017/10/11/inec-o11.html.

Kumara, K. 2018a. "India: Modi government accelerates anti-worker privatization drive." *World Socialist Website.* https://www.wsws.org/en/articles/2018/04/09/modi-a09.html.

Kumara, K. 2018b. "Indian Prime Minister Modi to tout pro-business record at World Economic Forum." *World Socialist Website.* https://www.wsws.org/en/articles/2018/01/23/modi-j23.html.

Kumara, K. and Kumar, A. 2016. "Indian government's demonetisation causes mass hardship and economic chaos." *World Socialist Website.* https://www.wsws.org/en/articles/2016/11/21/inde-n21.html.

Kumbamu, A. 2019. "The Naxalite movement, the oppressive state, and the revolutionary struggle in India." In *The Palgrave handbook of social movements, revolution, and social transformation,* ed. B. Berberoglu, 233–247. Cham: Palgrave.

Kundu, S. 2018. "RBI Working Paper Series No. 03 Rural Wage Dynamics in India: What Role does Inflation Play?" *Reserve Bank of Canada.* https://www.rbi.org.in/Scripts/PublicationsView.aspx?id=18117#C7.

Kunnath, G. 2006. "Becoming a Naxalite in rural Bihar: Class struggle and its contradictions." *Journal of Peasant Studies* 33, no. 1: 89–123.

Kunnath, G. 2013. "Anthropology's ethical dilemmas reflections from the Maoist fields of India." *Current Anthropology* 54, no. 6: 740–752.

Lebowitz, M. 2003. *Beyond Capital: Marx's political economy of the working class.* New York: Palgrave Macmillan.

Lebowitz, M. 2005. "The politics of assumption and the assumption of politics." *Historical Materialism* 14, no. 2: 29–487.

Leftwich, A. 2000. *States of development: On the primacy of politics in development.* Cambridge: Polity.

Lenin, V. 1899. The *development of capitalism in Russia, volume of collected works.* Moscow: Progress Publishers.

Lenin, V. 1901. "What is to be done?" *Marxists.org.* https://www.marxists.org/archive/lenin/works/1901/witbd/iii.htm.

Lenin, V. 1908. "Marxism and revisionism." *Marxists.org.* https://www.marxists.org/archive/lenin/works/1908/apr/03.htm.

Lenin, V. 1913. "The three sources and three component parts of Marxism." *Marxists. org.* https://www.marxists.org/archive/lenin/works/1913/mar/x01.htm.

Lenin, V. 1914a. "Tactics of the class struggle of the proletariat." https://www.marxists .org/archive/lenin/works/1914/granat/ch05.htm.

Lenin, V. 1914b. "Summary of dialectics." *Marxists.org.* https://www.marxists.org/ar chive/lenin/works/1914/cons-logic/summary.htm.

Lenin, V. 1917. "On compromises." *Marxists.org.* https://www.marxists.org/archive/len in/works/1917/sep/03.htm.

Lenin, V. 1918. "The proletarian revolution and the renegade Kautsky." Marxists.org. https://www.marxists.org/archive/lenin/works/1918/prrk/democracy.htm

Lenin, V. 1919a. "A great beginning." *Marxists.org.* https://www.marxists.org/archive/ lenin/works/1919/jun/19.htm.

Lenin, V. 1919b. "The state." *Marxists.org.* https://www.marxists.org/archive/lenin/ works/1919/jul/11.htm.

Lenin, V. 1920. ""Left-wing" communism: An infantile disorder: No compromises." *Marxists.org.* https://www.marxists.org/archive/lenin/works/1920/lwc/ch08.htm.

Lenin, V. 1921. "Once again on the trade unions: The current situation and the mistakes of Trotsky and Buhkarin." *Marxists.org.* https://www.marxists.org/archive/lenin/ works/1921/jan/25.htm.

Lenin, V. 1922. "On the Significance of Militant Materialism." *Marxists.org.* https:// www.marxists.org/archive/lenin/works/1922/mar/12.htm.

Lenin, V. 1977a. *Selected Works*, vol. 1. Moscow: Progress Publishers.

Lenin, V. 1977b. *The state and revolution.* Moscow: Progress Publishers.

Lenin, V. 1977c. *Selected works*, vol. 3. Moscow: Progress Publishers.

Lenin, V. 1978. *Revolutionary adventurism*. Moscow: Progress Publishers.

Lerche, J. 1999. "Politics of the poor: Agricultural labourers and political transforma- tions in Uttar Pradesh." *Journal of Peasant Studies* 26, no. 2–3: 182–241.

Lerche, J., Shah, A., and Harriss-White, B. 2013. "Introduction: Agrarian questions and left politics in India." *Journal of Agrarian Change* 13, no. 3: 337–350.

Levien, M. 2011. "Special economic zones and accumulation by dispossession in India." *Journal of Agrarian Change* 11, no 4: 454–483.

Levien, M. 2012. "The land question: Special economic zones and the political economy of dispossession in India." *Journal of Peasant Studies* 39, no. 3–4: 933–969.

Levien, M. 2013. "Regimes of dispossession: From steel towns to special economic zones." *Development and Change* 44, no. 2: 381–407.

Levien, M. 2017. "Gender and land dispossession: A comparative analysis." *Journal of Peasant Studies* 44, no. 6: 1111–1134.

Levien, M. 2018. *Dispossession without development: Land grabs in neoliberal India.* Ox- ford: Oxford University Press.

Liberation. 2003. "Women agricultural labour struggles: Key issues." http://www.cpiml .org/liberation/year_2003/february/aadhi%20zameen%202.htm.

Liodakis, G. 1997. "Technological change in agriculture: A Marxist critique" *Sociologia Ruralis* 37, no. 1: 61–78.

Lipton, M. 1989. *New seeds and poor people.* London: Unwin Hyman.

Lockwood, D. 2014. The *Indian bourgeoisie: A political history of the Indian capitalist class in the early twentieth century.* London: I.B. Tauris.

Lofgren, H. 2016. "The Communist Party of India (Marxist) and the Left government in West Bengal, 1977–2011: Strains of governance and socialist imagination." *Studies in Indian Politics* 4, no. 1: 102–115.

Lokniti. 2018. "Lokniti-CSDS-ABP News Mood of The Nation Survey-3." http://www .lokniti.org/pdf/Lokniti-ABP-News-Mood-of-the-Nation-Survey-Round-3-May-2018 .pdf.

Louis, P. 2000. "Shankarbigha revisited." *Economic and Political Weekly* 35, no. 7: 507–509.

Louis, P. 2005. "Jehanabad II: Viewing Bihar." *Economic and Political Weekly* 40, no. 51: 5371–5372.

Lowy, M. 2010. *The politics of combined and uneven development.* Chicago, IL: Haymarket Books.

Luxemburg, R. 2009. *The Rosa Luxemburg Reader*, eds. P. Hudis and K. Anderson. New York: MR Press.

MacCulloch, R. 2005. "Income Inequality and the Taste for Revolution." *Journal of Law & Economics* 48, no. 1: 93–123.

Mackel, K.A. 2010. "Fascism: A political ideology of the past." *Inquiries Journal* 2, no. 11. http://www.inquiriesjournal.com/articles/317/fascism-a-political-ideology-of-the -past.

Maitra, K. 2012. *Marxism in India: From decline to debacle.* New Delhi: Lotus Collection.

Maitra, P. 1997. "Globalization of capitalism, agriculture and the negation of nation states." *International Journal of Social Economics* 24: 237–254.

Mallick, C. 2018. "Public-private discord in the land acquisition law: Insights from Rajarhat in India." *Singapore Journal of Tropical Geography* 39, no. 3: 401–420.

Mallick, R. 1994. *Indian communism: Opposition, collaboration, and institutionalization.* Oxford: Oxford University Press.

Malreddy, P.K. 2014. "Domesticating the 'New Terrorism': The case of the Maoist insurgency in India." *European Legacy-Toward New Paradigms* 19, no. 5: 590–605.

Mandel, E. 1969. "Marxist theory of the state." *Marxists.org.* https://www.marxists.org/ archive/mandel/1969/xx/state.htm.

Mandel, E. 2002. "Anticipation and hope as categories of historical materialism." *Historical* Materialism 10, no. 4: 245–259.

Mander, H. 2016. "The poor have been forgotten more and more." *Governance Now.* https://www.governancenow.com/views/columns/the-poor-have-been-gotten-more-more- harsh-mander-economic-reforms.

Mann, M. 2004. *Fascists*. Cambridge: Cambridge University Press.

Mann, S.A., and Dickinson, J.M. 1978. "Obstacles to the development of a capitalist agriculture." *Journal of Peasant Studies* 5, no. 4: 466–481.

Mannathukkaren, N. 2011. "Redistribution and recognition: Land reforms in Kerala and the limits of culturalism." *The Journal of Peasant Studies* 38, no. 2: 379–411.

Mao T. 1926. "Analysis of classes in Chinese society." *Marxists.org.* https://www.marxists.org/reference/archive/mao/selected-works/volume-1/mswv1_1.htm.

Mao T. 1961. "Selected Works." *Marxists.org.* https://www.marxists.org/reference/archive/mao/selected-works/index.htm.

Martinez-Alier, J. 2001. "Ecological conflicts and valuation: Mangroves versus shrimps in the late 1990s." *Environment and Planning C: Government and Policy* 19, no. 5: 713–728.

Marx, K. 1843. "A contribution to the critique of Hegel's philosophy of right: Introduction." *Marxists.org.* https://www.marxists.org/archive/marx/works/1843/critique-hpr/intro.htm.

Marx, K. 1845. "Theses on Feuerbach." *Marxists.org.* https://www.marxists.org/archive/marx/works/1845/theses/theses.htm.

Marx, K. 1873. "Political Indifferentism." *Marxists.org.* https://www.marxists.org/archive/marx/works/1873/01/indifferentism.htm.

Marx, K. 1967. *The eighteenth Brumaire of Louis Napoleon*. Moscow: Progress.

Marx, K. 1976. *Wage-labour and capital*. New York: International Publishers.

Marx, K. 1977. *Capital,* vol. 1. New York: Vintage.

Marx, K. 1991. *Capital,* vol. 3. London: Penguin Books.

Marx, K. 2000. *Selected Writings*, ed. by D. McLellan. New York: Oxford University Press.

Marx, K. 2010. *The first international and after.* London: Verso.

Marx, K., and Engels, F. 1845. "Theses on Feuerbach." *Marxists.org.* https://www.marxists.org/archive/marx/works/1845/theses/theses.htm.

Marx, K., and Engels, F. 1848. "The Communist Manifesto." *Marxists.org.* https://www.marxists.org/archive/marx/works/download/pdf/Manifesto.pdf.

Marx, K., and Engels, F. 1850. "Address of the central committee to the Communist League." *Marxists.org.* https://www.marxists.org/archive/marx/works/1847/communist-league/1850-ad1.htm.

Marx, K., and Engels, F. 1964. *On religion,* ed. R. Niebuhr. Atlanta: Scholars Press.

Marx, K., and Engels, F. 1976. *Collected works,* vol. 6. New York: International Publishers.

Marx, K., and Engels, F. 1977. *Selected works*. Moscow: Progress Publishers.

Marx, K., and Engels, F. 1978. *The German Ideology,* ed. C. Arthur. New York: International Publishers.

Marx, K., and Engels, F. 1982. *Selected correspondence*. Moscow: Progress Publishers.

Mason, T. 1995. *Nazism, Fascism and the working class*. Cambridge: Cambridge University.

Mazumdar, S. 2016. "Theorizing the capitalist state." In *Contemporary readings in Marxism*, ed. R. Kumar. Delhi: Aakar.

Mazzadri, A. 2017. *The sweatshop regime: Labouring bodies, exploitation, and garments made in India.* Cambridge: Cambridge University Press.

McAdam, D., McCarthy, J.D., and Zald, M.N., eds. 1996. *Comparative perspectives on social movements: Political opportunities, mobilizing structures, and cultural framings.* New York: Cambridge University Press.

McCartney, M. 2013. "Going, going, but not yet quite gone: the political economy of the Indian intermediate classes during the era of liberalization." In *Two decades of market reform in India: Some dissenting views,* ed. S. Bhattacharyya. New York: Anthem Press.

McDowell, L. 2001. "Father and Ford revisited: gender, class and employment change in the new millennium." *Transactions of the Institute of British Geographers* 26, no. 4: 448–464.

McDowell, L. 2008. "Thinking through class and gender in the context of working class Studies." *Antipode* 40, no. 1: 20–24.

McMichael, P. 2000. "A global interpretation of the rise of the East Asian food import complex." *World Development* 28, no. 3: 409–424.

Mehta, J. 2002. "Give poverty a face, please." *Alternative Economic Survey: 2000–2001,* 29–34. Delhi: Rainbow Publishers.

Menon. N., ed. 1999a. *Gender and politics in India.* Delhi: Oxford University Press.

Menon, N., ed. 1999b. "Introduction." In *Gender and politics in India,* ed. N. Menon. Delhi: Oxford University Press.

Meyer, R. 2016. "Precarious workers' movements and the neoliberal state." *Working USA – The Journal of Labor and Society* 19, no. 1: 37–55.

Mezzadri, A. 2016. "Class, gender and the sweatshop: On the nexus between labour commodification and exploitation." *Third World Quarterly* 37, no. 10: 1877–1900.

Mezzadri, A. 2017. *The sweatshop regime: Labouring bodies exploitation, and garments made in India.* Cambridge: Cambridge University Press.

Mezzadri, A., and Fan, L. 2018. "'Classes of labour' at the margins of global commodity chains in India and China." *Development and Change* 49, no. 4: 1034–1063.

Mies, M. 2012. *The lace makers of Narsapur: Indian housewives produce for the world market.* Victoria, Australia: Spinifex Press.

Miliband, R. 1983. "State power and class interests." *New Left Review* 1/138, March–April.

Miller, B.A. 2000. *Geography and Social Movements.* Minneapolis: University of Minnesota Press.

Misra, A. 1994. "Bihar changing peasant struggle." *Economic & Political Weekly* 29, no. 19.

Misra, V., and Hazell, P. 1996. "Terms of trade, rural poverty, technology and investment: the Indian experience, 1952–53 to 1990–91." *Economic and Political Weekly* 31, no. 13: A2-A13.

Mitra, S. 2011. *Politics in India: Structure, process and policy.* London: Routledge.

Mittal, S. 2018. "Rise of the new entrepreneurial classes and the emergence of a high-growth economy." In *India Transformed,* ed. R Mohan, 567–574. Washington, DC: Brookings Institution Press.

Miyamura, S. 2010. "Diverse trajectories of industrial restructuring and labor organising in India." *Third World Quarterly* 37, no. 10: 1921–1941.

Moberg, L. 2015. "The political economy of special economic zones." *Journal of Institutional Economics* 11, no. 1: 167–190.

Mohammad, N. 2018. "How Many jobs are really being created by the Modi govt's Mudra Scheme?" *The Wire.* https://thewire.in/labour/modi-mudra-loan-scheme-job-creation-reality.

Mohanty, M. 1977. *Revolutionary violence: A Study of the Maoist Movement in India.* New Delhi: Allied.

Mohanty, M. 2004. "Introduction: Dimensions of power and social transformation." In *Class, caste, and gender,* ed. M. Mohanty. Delhi: Sage.

Mohanty, M. 2006. "Challenges of revolutionary violence." *Economic and Political Weekly* 41, no. 29: 3163–3168.

Mohanty, M. 2017. "Adivasi Swaraj is the answer to violence." *Economic and Political Weekly* 52, no. 21.

Moore, B. 1993. *Social origins of dictatorship and democracy: Lord and peasant in the making of the modern world.* Boston: Beacon Press.

Morris, A. 2000. "Charting futures for sociology: Reflections on social movement theory." *Contemporary Sociology – A Journal of Reviews* 29, no. 3: 445–454.

Mosse, D. 2018. "Caste and development: Contemporary perspectives on a structure of discrimination and advantage." *World Development* 110: 422–436.

Mukherjee, A. 2015. "Imperialism, nationalism and the making of the Indian capitalist class, 1920–1947." In *SAGE series in modern Indian history,* eds. B. Chandra, M. Mukherjee, and A. Mukherjee. Los Angeles: Sage.

Mukherjee, M. 2004. *Peasants in India's non-violent revolution: Practice and theory.* New Delhi: Sage.

Mukherji, N. 2012. *The Maoists in India: Tribal under siege.* London: Pluto.

Mukherji, P. 1984/2000. "Naxalbari movement and the peasant Revolt in North Bengal." In *Social movements in India,* ed. M.S.A. Rao, 17–90. Delhi: Manohar.

Mukherji, P. 2014. "The Indian state in crisis? Nationalism and nation-building." In *Sociology of India,* ed. A. Kumar. Delhi: Sage.

Mukherji, R. 2008. "The political economy of India's economic reforms." *Asian Economic Policy Review* 3, no. 2: 315–331.

Mukherji, R. 2017. "Governance reform in a weak state: Thirty years of Indian experience." *Governance – An International Journal of Policy Administration and Institutions* 30, no. 1: 53–58.

Mullings, B. 1999. "Insider or outsider, both or neither: Some dilemmas of interviewing
in a cross-cultural setting." *Geoforum* 30, no. 4: 337–350.

Murali, K. 2002. "Andhra Pradesh: Continuing militancy in Telengana." *Economic and
Political Weekly* 37, no. 8: 692–695.

Murali, K. 2017. *Caste, class, and capital: The social and political origins of economic
policy in India.* Cambridge: Cambridge University Press.

Murphy, J. 2011. "Indian call centre workers: Vanguard of a global middle class?" *Work
Employment and Society* 25, no. 3: 417–433.

Murphy, J., and Jammaulamadaka, N. 2017. *Governance, resistance and the post-colonial
state: Management and state building social movements.* New York: Routledge.

Murthy, N. 2018. "The impact of the 1991 economic reforms on Indian businesses." In
*India Transformed,* ed. R. Mohan, 609–618. Washington, DC: Brookings Institution
Press.

Nadkarni, M. 1976. "Tenants from the dominant class: A developing contradiction in
land reforms." *Economic and Political Weekly* 11, no. 52: A137, A139–A146.

Nadkarni, M. 1991. "Review: The mode of production debate: A review article." *Indian
Economic Review* New Series 26, no. 1: 99–104.

Nag, P.K., and Nag, A. 2004. "Drudgery, accidents and injuries in Indian agriculture."
*Industrial Health* 42, no. 2: 149–162.

Naher, F. 1997. "Green revolution in Bangladesh production stability and food self- suf-
ficiency." *Economic and Political Weekly* 32, no. 26: A84–A89.

Nair, S. 2018. "Farmers badly hit by demonetisation, admits Agriculture Ministry." *The
Hindu.* https://www.thehindu.com/news/national/farmers-badly-hit-by-demoneti
sation-admits-agriculture-ministry/article25550924.ece?homepage=true.

Nanda, M. 1995. "Transnationalization of third world state and undoing of Green Revolution." *Economic and Political Weekly* 30, no. 4: PE 20–30.

Nanda, M. 2005. *The wrongs of the religious Right.* Gurgaon: Three Essays Collective.

Nanda, M. 2007. *Postmodernism and religious fundamentalism.* Pondicherry: Navayana.

Nanda, P. 2015. "Industrial strikes and lockouts see steep decline in India." *Livemint.*
https://www.livemint.com/Politics/tjP4DiG7Uro95iNCiebrAO/Industrial-strikes-
and-lockouts-see-steep-decline-in-India.html.

Nandy, A. 2003. *The romance of the state and the fate of dissent in the tropics.* New Delhi:
Oxford University Press.

Naruzzaman, M. 2005. "Economic liberalization and poverty in the developing countries." *Journal of Contemporary Asia* 35, no. 1: 109–127.

Naseemullah, A. 2016. "The contested capacity of the Indian state." *Indian Review* 16,
no. 4: 407–432.

Nathan, D. 1999. "Agricultural labour and poor peasant movement in India." In *Class Formation and Political Transformation in Post-colonial India*, ed. T. Sathyamurthy. New Delhi: Oxford University Press.

Navlakha, G. 2006. "Maoists in India." *Economic and Political Weekly* 41, no. 22: 2186–2189.

Nayar, B. 2001. *Globalization and nationalism: The changing balance in India's economic policy 1950–2000*. New Delhi: Sage Publications.

Nayyar, R. 1996. "New initiatives for poverty alleviation in rural India." In *Economic reforms and poverty alleviation in India,* eds. C. Rao and H. Linnemann. New Delhi: Sage.

NCRB. 2016. "Crime in India." *National Crime Records Bureau.* http://ncrb.gov.in/Stat Publications/CII/CII2016/pdfs/NEWPDFs/Crime%20in%20India%20-%202016% 20Complete%20PDF%20291117.pdf.

Neiberg, M. 2018. *Fascism.* London: Routledge.

Neiland, A., Soley, N., and Varley, J. 2001. "Shrimp aquaculture: economic perspectives for policy development." *Marine Policy* 25, no. 4: 265–279.

Nelson, L. 2003. "Decentering the movement: Collective action, place, and the 'sedimentation' of radical political discourses." *Environment and Planning D-Society and Space* 21, no. 5: 559–581.

Niclas- Tölle, B. 2015. *The socialist opposition in Nehruvian India, 1947–1964.* Frankfurt am Main: Peter Land Edition.

Nielsen, K.B. 2016. "The everyday politics of India's "land wars" in rural eastern India." *Focaal-Journal of Global and Historical Anthropology* no. 75: 105–118.

Nielsen, K.B., and Nilsen, A.G. 2016. *Social movements and the state in India: Deepening democracy?* London: Palgrave Macmillan.

Nigam, A. 2006. *The insurrection of little selves: The crisis of secular-nationalism in India.* Delhi: Oxford University Press.

Nilsen, A.G. 2008. "Political economy, social movements and state power: A Marxian perspective on two decades of resistance to the Narmada dam projects." *Journal of Historical Sociology* 21, no. 2–3: 303–330.

Nilsen, A.G. 2010. *Dispossession and resistance in India: The river and the rage.* London: Routledge.

Nilsen, A.G., and Roy, S. 2015. *New subaltern politics: Reconceptualizing hegemony and resistance in contemporary India.* New Delhi: Oxford University Press.

O'Connor, J. 2017. "Marxism and the three movements of neoliberalism." *Critical Sociology* 36, no. 5: 691–715.

Oberoi, R. 2018. "4 years of Modi govt: 8 charts that show why the euphoria is gone & next big positive missing." *Economic Times.* https://economictimes.indiatimes.com/ markets/stocks/news/4-years-of-modi-8-charts-that-show-why-the-euphoria-is-gone-next-big-positive-missing/articleshow/64314349.cms.

O'Brien, P. 2007. "Global economic history as the accumulation of capital through a process of combined and uneven development: an appreciation and critique of Ernest Mandel." *Historical Materialism* 15, no. 1: 75–108.

Odisha Government. 2004. *Odisha human development report.* Bhubaneswar: Odisha Government: Planning and Coordination Department.

Odisha Government. 2005. *District statistical handbook: Puri.* Bhubaneswar: Odisha Government: Directorate of Economics and Statistics.

Ollman, B. 1993. *Dialectical Investigations.* New York: Routledge.

Ollman, B. 2003. *Dance of the dialectic.* Urbana: University of Illinois Press.

Omvedt, G. 1993. *Reinventing revolution: New social movements and the socialist tradition in India.* Armonk, NY: M.E. Sharpe.

Ondetti, G.A. 2006. "Repression, opportunity, and protest: Explaining the take-off of Brazil's landless movement." *Latin American Politics and Society* 48, no. 2: 61–94.

Oommen, T.K. 1971. "Green revolution and Agrarian conflict." *Economic and Political Weekly* 6, no. 26: A99, A101–A103.

Oseland, E., Håvard Haarstad, H., and Fløysand, A. 2012. "Labor agency and the importance of the national scale: Emergent aquaculture unionism in Chile." *Political Geography* 31, no. 2: 94–103.

Oslender, U. 2004. "Fleshing out the geographies of social movements: Colombia's Pacific Coast black communities and the 'aquatic space.'" *Political Geography* 23, no. 8: 957–985.

Ostry, J., Loungani, P., and Furceri, D. 2016. "Neoliberalism: Oversold?" *IMF: Finance and Development.* https://www.imf.org/external/pubs/ft/fandd/2016/06/pdf/ostry.pdf.

Otsuka, K., Gascon, F., and Asano, S. 1994. "Green revolution and labour demand in rice farming the case of Central Luzon, 1966–1990." *Journal of Development Studies* 31, no. 1: 82–109.

Oxfam. 2018. "Richest 1 percent bagged 73 percent of wealth created last year." OXFAM *India.* https://www.oxfamindia.org/pressrelease/2093.

Oya, C. 2005. "Agrarian neoliberalism." In *Neoliberalism: A critical Reader*, ed. A. Saad-Filho. London: Pluto.

Page, B. 1993. *Marxism and spirituality: An international anthology.* Westport, Connecticut, and London: Bergin and Garvey.

Paige, J.M. 1975. *Agrarian revolution.* New York: Free Press.

Palmer-Jones, R. 1993. "Agricultural wages in Bangladesh what the figures really show." *Journal of Development Studies* 29, no. 2: 277–300.

Palshikar, S., Kumar, S., and Lodha, S. 2017. *Electoral politics in Indi: The resurgence of the Bharatiya Janata Party.* London: Routledge, Taylor and Francis.

Panitch, L., and Albo, G., eds. 2016. *Socialist Register 2016: The politics of the right.* London: Merlin Press.

Parker, J. 2012. "Unravelling the neoliberal paradox with Marx." *Journal of Australian Political Economy* 70, no. 70: 193–213.

Parthasarathy, D. 2015. "The poverty of (Marxist) theory: peasant classes, provincial capital, and the critique of globalization in India." *Journal of Social History* 48, no. 4: 816–841.

Parthasarathy, G. 1987. "Changes in the incidence of rural poverty." *Indian Journal of Agricultural Economics* 42, no. 1.

Parthasarathy, G. 1995. "Public intervention and rural poverty: case of non-sustainable reduction in Andhra Pradesh." *Economic and Political Weekly* 30, no. 41/42: 2573–2575, 2577–2581, 2583–2586.

Parsai, G. 2007. "Manmohan to head land reforms council." *The Hindu.* https://www.thehindu.com/todays-paper/Manmohan-to-head-land-reforms-council/article14866257.ece.

Patel, R., and McMichael, P. 2008. "Third worldism and the lineages of global fascism: The regrouping of the global South in the neoliberal era." *Third World Quarterly* 25, no. 1: 231–254.

Pathy, J. 1998. "Contemporary struggles of the tribal peoples of India." *Indian Journal of Social Work* 59, no. 1.

Patnaik, P. 1995. *Whatever happened to Imperialism.* New Delhi: Tulika.

Patnaik, P. 2010. "The state under neo-liberalism." *MRZine.* http://mrzine.monthlyreview.org/2010/patnaik100810.html.

Patnaik, P. 2011. "Future of Marxism." In *Another millennium?,* ed. R. Thapar. New Delhi: Penguin.

Patnaik, P. 2016. "Nationalism, Hindutva and the assault on thought." *Communist Party of India: Marxist,* XXXII 1. http://www.cpim.org/content/nationalism-hindutva-and-assault-thought.

Patnaik, P. 2017a. "Neoliberalism and inequality are inseparable." *News Click.* https://newsclick.in/neoliberalism-and-inequality-are-inseparable.

Patnaik, P. 2017b. "Why India needs the Left." *The Wire.* https://thewire.in/196923/india-left-future-economy-social-policy/.

Patnaik, P. 2018a."The dramatic rise in wealth inequality." *People's Democracy.* http://peoplesdemocracy.in/2018/0128_pd/dramatic-rise-wealth-inequality.

Patnaik, P. 2018b. "The state under neoliberalism." http://citeseerx.ist.psu.edu/viewdoc/download?doi=10.1.1.527.9907&rep=rep1&type=pdf.

Patnaik, U. 1972. "Development of capitalism in agriculture – I." *Social Scientist* 1, no. 2: 15–31.

Patnaik, U. 1983. "Classical theory of rent and its application to India: Some preliminary thoughts on sharecropping." *Journal of Peasant Studies* 10, no. 2–3: 71–87.

Patnaik, U. 1986. "The agrarian question and development of capitalism in India." *Economic and Political Weekly* 21, no. 18: 781–793.

Patnaik, U. 1990a. *Agrarian relations and accumulation: The mode of production debate in India.* Delhi: Oxford University Press.

Patnaik, U. 1990b. "Capitalist development in agriculture: Note." In *Agrarian relations and accumulation: The mode of production debate in India*, ed. U. Patnaik. Delhi: Oxford University Press.

Patnaik, U. 1990c. "Capitalist development in agriculture: Further comment." In *Agrarian relations and accumulation: The mode of production debate in India*, ed. U. Patnaik. Delhi: Oxford University Press.

Patnaik, U. 1990d. "On the mode of production in Indian agriculture: Reply." In *Agrarian relations and accumulation: The mode of production debate in India*, ed. U. Patnaik. Delhi: Oxford University Press.

Patnaik, U. 1990e. "Some economic and political consequences of the green revolution in India." In *The Food Question: Profits versus people,* eds. H. Bernstein, B. Crow, M. McKintosh, and C. Martin. New York: Monthly Review Press.

Patnaik, U. 1991. "Food availability and famine: a longer view." *The Journal of Peasant Studies* 19, no. 1: 1–25.

Patnaik, U. 1995. "On capitalism and agrestic unfreedom." *International Review of Social History* 40, no. 1: 77–92.

Patnaik, U. 1999. *The long transition: Essays on political Economy.* New Delhi: Tulika.

Patnaik, U. 2002. "Deflation and Deja vu: India's Agriculture in the World Economy." In *Agrarian studies: Essays on agrarian relations in less developed countries*, eds. V. Ramachandran and M. Swaminathan. New Delhi: Tulika.

Patnaik, U. 2003. "On the inverse relation between primary exports and food absorption in developing countries under liberalized trading regimes." In *Work and wellbeing in the age of finance*, eds. J. Ghosh and C. Chandrasekhar, 256–287. New Delhi: Tulika.

Patnaik, U. 2007. *The republic of hunger.* Gurgaon: Three Essays Collective.

Patnaik, U. 2013. "Theorizing food security and poverty in the era of economic reforms." In *Two decades of market reform in India: Some dissenting views*, ed. S. Bhattacharyya, 93–124. New York: Anthem Press.

Patnaik, U. 2016. "Growing inequalities in the South in the Present Era of primitive capitalist accumulation." *Studies in Peoples History* 3, no. 1: 59–70.

Patnaik, P., Chandrasekhar, C.P., and Ghosh, J. 2004. "The political economy of the economic reform strategy: The role of the Indian capitalist class." In *Class, caste, and gender*, ed. M. Mohanty. Delhi: Sage.

Pattenden, J. 2011. "Gatekeeping as accumulation and domination: Decentralization and class relations in rural south India." *Journal of Agrarian Change* 11, no. 2: 164–194.

Pattenden, J. 2016. "Working at the margins of global production networks: local labour control regimes and rural-based labourers in South India." *Third World Quarterly* 37, no. 10: 1809–1833.

Pattenden, J. 2018. "The politics of classes of labour: Fragmentation, reproduction zones and collective action in Karnataka, India." *Journal of Peasant Studies* 45, no. 5–6: 1039–1059.

Paul, S. 1990. "Green revolution and poverty among farm families in Haryana, 1969/70–1982/83." *Economic and Political Weekly* 25, no. 39: 1809–1833.

Paul, S, and Sarma, V. 2017. "Industrialization-led displacement and long term-welfare: Evidence from West Bengal." *Oxford Development Studies* 45, no. 3: 240–259.

Paulini, T. 1979. *Agrarian movements and reforms in India: The case of Kerala.* Breitenbach: Verlag Stuttgart.

Paxton, R. 2004. *The anatomy of Fascism.* New York: Vintage.

Pearse, A. 1980. *Seeds of plenty, seeds of want: Social and economic implications of the Green Revolution.* London: Clarendon Press.

Peck, J., and Theodore, N. 2001. "Contingent Chicago: Restructuring the spaces of temporary labor." *International Journal of Urban and Regional Research* 25, no. 3: 471–496.

Peck, J., and Tickell, A. 2002. "Neoliberalizing space." *Antipode* 34, no. 3: 380–404.

Pedersen, J.D. 1992. "State, bureaucracy and change in India." *Journal of Development-Studies* 28, no. 4: 616–639.

Peet, R. 1983. "Relations of production and the relocation of United States manufacturing industry since 1960." *Economic Geography* 59, no. 2: 112–143.

People's Democracy. 2017. "Thinking together." *People's Democracy.* https://peoplesdemocracy.in/2015/0712_pd/thinking-together.

Pereira, A. 2016. "BJP tops list of reelected MPs in terms of assets and criminal cases." *Firstpost.* https://www.firstpost.com/politics/bjp-tops-list-of-reelected-mps-in-terms-of-assets-and-criminal-cases-1557703.html.

Petras, J. 1997. "Imperialism and NGOs in Latin America." *Monthly Review* 49, no. 7.

Petras, J., and Veltemeyer, H. 2007. "The 'development state' in Latin America: Whose development, whose state?" *Journal of Peasant Studies* 34, no. 3–4: 371–407.

Phyne, P. 2010. "A comparative political economy of rural capitalism salmon aquaculture in Norway, Chile and Ireland." *Acta Sociologica* 53, no. 2: 160–180.

Pillai, P. 2003. *Left Movement and Agrarian Relations, 1920–1995.* New Delhi: South Asian Publishers.

Plahe, J., Wright, S., and Marmbo, M. 2017. "Livelihood crises in Vidarbha, India: Food sovereignty through traditional farming systems as a possible solution." *South Asia: Journal of South Asian Studies* 40, no. 3: 600–618.

Plekhanov, G. 1971. *Fundamental problems of Marxism.* New York: International Publishers.

Poe, S.C., and Tate, C.N. 1994. "Repression of human rights to personal integrity in the 1980s." *American Political Science Review* 88, no. 4: 853–872.

Pokrant, B., and Reeves, P. 2007. "Work and labor in the Bangladesh brackish-water shrimp export sector." *South Asia: Journal of South Asian Studies* 26, no. 3: 359–389.

Polanyi, K. 1944/2001. *The great transformation: The political and economic origins of our time*, 2nd ed. Boston: Beacon Press.

Post, C. 1999. "Ernest Mandel and the Marxist theory of bureaucracy." In *The Legacy of Ernest Mandel*, ed. G. Achcar. London: Verso.

Poulantzas, N. 1968. *Political Power and Social Classes*. London: New Left Books (cited from the English Translation, NLB, London, 1973).

Pradhan, D., and Flaherty, M. 2008. "National initiatives, local effects: Trade liberalization, shrimp aquaculture, and coastal communities in Odisha, India." *Society & Natural Resources* 21, no. 1: 63–76.

Pramanik, S., and Nandi, N. 2001. Women fishworkers and their role in the inshore fishing areas of Sundarban. *Man in India* 81, no. 1: 169–177.

Prasad, P. 1989. *Lopsided growth: Political economy of Indian development*. Delhi: Oxford University Press.

Prasad, P. 1990. "Reactionary role of usurer's capital in Rural India." In *The mode of production debate in India*, ed. U. Patnaik. Delhi: Oxford University Press.

Prasad-Aleyamma, M. 2018. "Cards and carriers: migration, identification and surveillance in Kerala, South India." *Contemporary South Asia* 26, no. 2: 191–205.

Prashad, V. 2015. *No free left: The futures of Indian communism*. New Delhi: Leftword.

Pratt, G. 2004. *Working Feminism*. Edinburgh: Edinburgh University Press.

Pred, A. 1984. "Place as historically contingent process: Structuration and the time-geography of becoming places." *Annals of the American Association of Geographers* 74, no. 2: 279–297.

Premchand, A. 2017. *Contemporary India: Society and its governance*. Milton: Taylor and Francis.

Pressman, S., ed. 2006. *Alternative theories of the State*. New York: Palgrave.

Pushpendra. 2000. "Liberalization and Agrarian reforms: some recent controversies." In *Land reforms in India: Volume 5*, eds. B.N. Sinha, and Pushpendra, 45–63. New Delhi: Sage.

Qazi, M. 2018. "Malnutrition ravages India's children." *The Asian Age*. http://www.asianage.com/india/all-india/030118/malnutrition-ravages-indias-children.html.

Radice, H. 2008. "The developmental state under global neoliberalism." *Third World Quarterly* 29, no. 6: 1153–1174.

Rahul, N. 1995. "Green revolution and subsistence agriculture you reap as you sow." *Economic and Political Weekly* 32, no. 18: 930–932.

Rai, P. 2007. "NREGA battling cancerous corruption." *India Together*. http://www.indiatogether.org/nregs-government--2.

Rao, C. 1994. *Agricultural growth, Rural poverty and environmental degradation in India*. Delhi: Oxford University Press.

Rao, J.M. 1998. "Agricultural development under state planning." In *The State, Development Planning and Liberalisation in India*, ed. T. Byres. Delhi: Oxford University Press.

Rao, J.M. 1999. "Agrarian power and unfree labour." *Journal of Peasant Studies* 26, no. 2–3: 242–262.

Rao, S. 2018. "Gender and class relations in rural India." *Journal of Peasant Studies* 45, no. 5–6: 950–968.

Ram, N. 1972. "Development of Capitalism in Agriculture." *Social Scientist,* vol. 1, no. 5: 51–57.

Ramakrishnan, V. 1999. "A history of massacres." *Frontline* 16, no. 5. https://www.front line.in/static/html/fl1605/16050300.htm.

Ranganathan, S. 2018. *Hinduism: A contemporary philosophical investigation.* New York: Routledge.

Ray, R. 2002. *The Naxalites and their ideology.* Delhi: Oxford University Press.

Rediff. 2006. "Naxalism single biggest internal security challenge: PM." *Rediff India Abroad.* http://www.rediff.com/news/2006/apr/13naxal.htm.

Renton, D. 2007. *Fascism: Theory and practice.* Delhi: Aakar (originally published by Pluto).

Rieman, R. 2018. *To fight against this age: Fascism and humanism.* New York: W.W. Norton & Company.

Rigg, J. 1989. "The green revolution and equity: Who adopts the new rice varieties and why?" *Geography* 74, no. 2: 144–150.

Roberts, D. 2011. "Reconsidering Gramsci's interpretation of Fascism." *Journal of Modern Italian Studies* 16, no. 2: 239–255.

Roberts, M. 2016. *The long depression.* Chicago: Haymarket.

Roberts, M. 2017. "Modi rules, Harvard doesn't." *Michael Roberts Blog.* https://thenext recession.wordpress.com/2017/03/14/modi-rules-harvard-doesnt/.

Roberts, M. 2018. "China workshop: Challenging the misconceptions." *Michael Roberts Blog.* https://thenextrecession.wordpress.com/2018/06/07/china-workshop -challenging-the-misconceptions/.

Robinson, W., and Barrera, M. 2012. "Global capitalism and twenty-first century fascism: a US case-study." *Race and Class* 53, no. 3: 4–29.

Ronnback, P., Troell, M., Zetterstrom, T., and Babu, D. 2003. "Mangrove dependence and socio-economic concerns in shrimp hatcheries of Andhra Pradesh, India." *Environmental Conservation* 30, no. 4: 344–352.

Routledge, P. 1997. "Space, mobility, and collective action: India's Naxalite movement." *Environment and Planning A* 29, no. 12: 2165–2189.

Roy, A. 2011. *Broken republic.* New Delhi: Penguin Books.

Roy, A. 2009. "The heart of India is under attack." *The Guardian.* https://www.theguard ian.com/commentisfree/2009/oct/30/mining-india-maoists-green-hunt.

Roy, B. 2002. "Naxalite violence: Legacy of another era." *Times of India.* https://timeso findia.indiatimes.com/edit-page/Naxalite-Violence-Legacy-of-Another-Era/article show/15602206.cms.

Roy, I. 2018. *Politics of the poor: Negotiating democracy in contemporary India.* Cambridge: Cambridge University Press.

Roy, M.S. 2011. *Gender and radical politics in India: Magic moments of Naxalbari (1967–1975).* New York: Routledge.

Roy, T. 2005. *Rethinking economic change in India: Labour and livelihood.* London: Routledge.

Roy Chowdhury, S. 2015. "Bring class back in: Informality in Bangalore." *Socialist Register* 51: 73–92.

Rubin, I. 1973. *Essays on Marx's theory of value.* Montreal: Black Rose Books.

Rudolph, L.I., and Rudolph S.H. 1987. *In pursuit of Lakshmi: The political economy of the Indian State.* Chicago: Chicago University Press.

Rudra, A. 1983. "Mode of production in Indian agriculture." *Economic and Political Weekly* 18, no. 12: 421.

Rudra, A. 1988. "Emerging class structure in rural India." In *Rural poverty in South Asia,* eds. T. Srinivasan and P. Bardhan. New York: Columbia University Press.

Rudra, A., Majid, A., and Talib, B. 1990 (1969–70). "Big farmers of Punjab." In *Agrarian Relations and Accumulation: The mode of production debate in India,* ed. U. Patnaik. Delhi: Oxford University Press.

Rukmini, S. 2017. "On religious hostilities, India ranked just slightly better than Syria: Pew study." *Huffpost.* https://www.huffingtonpost.in/2017/04/13/on-religious-hostilities-india-ranked-just-slightly-better-than_a_22037994/.

Rummel, R.J. 1984. "Libertarianism, violence within states, and the polarity principle." *Comparative Politics* 16, no. 4: 443–462.

Ruparelia, S., Reddy, S., Harriss, J. and Corbridge, S., eds. 2011. *Understanding India's new political economy,* London: Routledge.

Rutherford, T. 2010. "De/Re-centering work and class?: A review and critique of labor geography." *Geography Compass* 4, no 7: 768–777.

Rutherford, T., and Gertler, M. 2002. "Labor in lean times: geography, scale and national trajectory of work place change." *Transactions of the Institute of British Geographers* 27, no. 2: 195–212.

Sackley, N. 2015. "The road from serfdom: economic storytelling and narratives in the rise of neoliberalism." *History and Technology* 31, no. 4: 397–419.

Sagar. 2006. "The spring and its thunder." *Economic and Political Weekly* 41, no. 29: 3176–3178.

Sahay, S. 2006. *The Indian working class movement during freedom struggle.* Patna: Janaki Prakashan.

SAHRDC (South Asia Human Rights Documentation Centre). 2002. "Emerging state of insecurity: India's war against Itself." *SAHRDC.* www.hrdc.net/sahrdc/hrfeatures/HRF51.htm.

Sainaith, P. 2001. "Age of inequality." In *India: Another millennium?*, R. Thapar, 152–168. New York: Penguin.

Sainaith, P. 2009. "Neo-liberal terrorism in India: The largest wave of suicides in history." *Counterpunch*. http://www.counterpunch.org/sainath02122009.html.

Sainaith, P. 2013. "Farmers' suicide rates soar above the rest." *The Hindu*. https://www.thehindu.com/opinion/columns/sainath/farmers-suicide-rates-soar-above-the-rest/article4725101.ece.

Samal, K. 2003. "Fishing communities on Chilika Lake." *Economic and Political Weekly* 38, no. 31: 3319–3325.

Samanta, A. 1984. *Left extremist movement in West Bengal*. Calcutta: Firma KLM Private Ltd.

Samuel, V. 2019. "What is inequality?" *Oxfam India*. https://www.oxfamindia.org/blog/what-inequality.

Sanchez, A., and Strumpell, C. 2014. "Anthropological and historical perspectives on India's working classes." *Modern Asian Studies* 48, no. 5: 1233–1241.

Sanyal, K. 2013. *Rethinking capitalist development: Primitive accumulation, governmentality and post-colonial capitalism*. London: Routledge.

Sarangi, A. 2017. "State formation and political economy of India: The Rudolphian paradigm." *Indian Review* 16, no. 3: 344–356.

Sarkar, R., and Sarkar, A. 2016. "The rebel's resource curse: A theory of insurgent-civilian dynamics." *Studies in Conflict and Terrorism* 40, no. 10: 870–898.

Sarkar, S. 1983. *Modern India: 1885–1947*. Delhi: Macmillan.

Sarkar, S. 2016. "The fascism of the Sangh Parivar." In *Fascism: Essays on Europe and India,* ed. J. Banaji. Gurgaon: Three Essays Collective.

Sarmah, B., and Baurua, J., eds. 2014. *Neoliberal state and its challenges*. Delhi: Aakar.

Sass, R. 2000. "Agricultural 'killing fields': The poisoning of Costa Rican Banana Workers." *International Journal of Health Services* 30, no. 3: 491–514.

Sathyamurthy, T. 1996. "State and society in a changing political perspective." In *Class formation and political transformation in post-colonial India,* ed. T.V. Sathyamurthy. Delhi: Oxford University Press.

Saul, J. 1974. "The State in postcolonial societies: Tanzania." In *The Socialist Register 1974,* eds. R. Miliband and J. Saville. London: The Merlin Press.

Saull, R. 2015. "Capitalist development and the rise and 'Fall' of the far-right." *Critical Sociology* 41, no. 4–5: 619–639.

Saxton, A. 2007. *Religion and the human impact*. Delhi: Aakar.

Sayer, A. 1992. *Method in social science: A realist approach*. London: Routledge.

Sayer, A. 2000. *Realism and social science*. London: Sage.

Schatzman, C. 2005. "Political challenge in Latin America: Rebellion and collective protest in an era of democratization." *Journal of Peace Research* 42, no. 3: 291–310.

Schiller, B. 1998. *The economics of poverty and discrimination*. Eaglewood Cliffs: Prentice Hall.

Schultz, K. 2018. "Indian children's book lists Hitler as leader 'who will inspire you.'" *The New York Times*. https://www.nytimes.com/2018/03/17/world/asia/india-hitler-childrens-book.html.

Science & Society. 2018. "Intersectionality: A symposium." *Science & Society* 82, no. 2: 248–291.

Sen, A. [Amartya]. 1999. *Development as Freedom*. New Delhi: Oxford University Press.

Sen, A. [Amartya]. 2005. *The argumentative India: Writings on Indian history, culture and identity*. London: Allen Lane.

Sen, A. [Anupam]. 2017. *The state, industrialization and class formations in India: A Neo-Marxist perspective on colonialism, underdevelopment and development*. London: Routledge.

Sen, A. [Arindam]. 2017. "The movement-party dialectics: Tebhaga-Telangana to Naxalbari-CPI(ML)." *Economic and Political Weekly* 52, no. 21.

Sen, S., Debabrata, P., and Lahiri, A. 1978. *Naxalbari and after: A frontier anthology*. Calcutta: Kathashilpa.

Sengupta, M. 2008. "How the state changed its mind: Power, politics & the origins of India's market reforms." *Economic & Political Weekly* 43, no. 21: 35–42.

Shah, A. 2006. "Markets of protection – The terrorist Maoist Movement and the state in Jharkhand, India." *Critique of Anthropology* 26, no. 3: 297–314.

Shah, A. 2013. "The agrarian question in a Maoist guerrilla zone: Land, labour and capital in the forests and hills of Jharkhand, India." *Journal of Agrarian Change* 13, no. 3: 424–450.

Shah, A. 2017. "Humaneness and Contradictions: India's Maoist-inspired Naxalites." *Economic and Political Weekly* 52, no. 21.

Shah, A., and Jain, D. 2017. "Naxalbari at its golden jubilee: Fifty recent books on the Maoist movement in India." *Modern Asian Studies* 51, no. 4: 1165–1219.

Shah, G. 1988. "Grass-roots mobilization in Indian politics." In *India's democracy*, ed. A. Kohli, 262–304. Hyderabad: Orient Longman.

Shah, G. 2004. *Social movements in India*. New Delhi: Sage.

Shah, G., Mander, H., Thorat, S., Deshpande, S., and Beviskar, A. 2006. *Untouchability in rural India*. Delhi: Sage.

Shakir, M. 1986. *State and politics in contemporary India*. New Delhi: Ajanta Publications.

Shantha, S. 2018. "In Dantewada's Naxal area, 'political participation' looks completely different." *The Wire*. https://thewire.in/politics/chhattisgarh-elections-dantewada-naxals.

Shariff, A. 1999. *India: Human development report*. New Delhi: Oxford University Press.

Sharma, D. 2017. "Farm output may have increased in three years, but farmers welfare has not." *The Wire*. https://thewire.in/agriculture/modi-three-years-farmers-agriculture.

Sharma, H.R. 1992. "Agrarian relations in India since independence." *Journal of Indian School of Political Economy* 4, no. 2: 201–262.

Sharma, T. 1992. *Technical change, income distribution and rural poverty*. New Delhi: Shirpa Publications.

Sharma, U. 2002. *Caste*. Delhi: Viva Books.

Sharma, R., and Poleman, T. 1993. *The new economics of India's Green Revolution: Income and employment diffusion in Uttar Pradesh*. Ithaca: Cornell University Press.

Sheth, N. 2014. "Trade unions in India: A sociological approach." In *Political sociology of India*, ed. A. Kumar. Delhi: Sage.

Shiva, V. 1991. *The violence of the green revolution: Third world agriculture, ecology and politics*. London: Zed Books Ltd.

Shiva, V. 2000. *Stolen harvest: The hijacking of the global food supply*. Cambridge: South End Press.

Shiva, V., Jafri, A., Emani, A., and Pande, M. 2002. *Seeds of suicide: The ecological and human costs of globalisation of agriculture*. New Delhi: Navdanya.

Shrestha, N., and Patterson, J., 1990. "Population and poverty in dependent states Latin America considered." *Antipode* 22, no. 2: 121–155.

Shrimali, R. Forthcoming. *Corporate hijack of agriculture: Case of contract farming in India*. Singapore: Palgrave.

Simeon, D. 1986. "Communalism in modern India: a theoretical examination." *Mainstream*. http://www.sacw.net/article2760.html.

Simeon, D. 2016. "The law of killing: A brief history of Indian fascism." In *Fascism: essays on Europe and India*, ed. J. Banaji. Gurgaon: Three Essays Collective.

Singer, W. 2012. *Independent India, 1947–2000*. London: Pearson.

Singh, H. 2014. *Recasting Caste: From the sacred to the profane*. New Delhi: Sage.

Singh, I. 1990. *The great ascent: The rural poor in South Asia*. Baltimore: The John Hopkins University Press.

Singh, P. 1995. *The Naxalite Movement in India*. Delhi: Rupa Publication.

Singh, R. 2010. *On nationalism and communalism in India*. Delhi: Aakar.

Singh, S. 2002. "Agricultural labourers." In *Alternative economic survey*. New Delhi: Rainbow Publishers.

Singh, S. [Supriya]. 2017. *Commercialization of Hinterland and dynamics of class, caste and gender in rural India*. Newcastle: Cambridge Scholars Publishing.

Singhal, S., and Nilakantan, R. 2016. "The economic effects of a counterinsurgency policy in India: a synthetic control analysis." *European Journal of Political Economy* 45: 1–17.

Singharoy, D. 2004. *Peasant movements in post-colonial India*. New Delhi: Sage.

Sinha, A. 2011. "An institutional perspective on the liberalization state in India." In *The state in India after liberalization: Interdisciplinary perspectives*, eds. A. Gupta and K. Sivaramakrishnan, 49–68. London: Routledge.

Sinha, A. 2016. "A distinctive Indian political economy: New concepts and a synthesizing framework." *Studies in Indian Politics* 4, no. 2: 266–273.

Sinha, S. 2009. "Workers and working classes in contemporary India." In *Beyond Marx: Theorizing the global relations of the 21st century*, eds. M. van der Linden and K. Roth. Leiden: Brill.

Sinha, S. 2017. "Histories of power, the 'Universalization of Capital' and India's Modi government: Between and beyond Marxism and post-colonial theory." *Critical Sociology* 43: 4–5.

Sitton, J. 1996. *Recent Marxian theory.* Albany: State University of New York Press.

Skocpol, T. 1982. "What makes peasants revolutionary?" *Comparative Politics* 14, no. 3: 351–375.

Smith, J. 2016. *Imperialism in the twenty-first century: Globalization, super-exploitation, and capitalism's final crisis.* New York: Monthly Review Press.

Smith, J. 1979. "Jayprakash Narayan dies." *Washington Post.* https://www.washington post.com/archive/local/1979/10/09/jayaprakash-narayan-dies/5a363a02-4138-49e2-8a4e-d977f8304104/?utm_term=.caef13d50dbe.

Smith, M. 2018. *Invisible leviathan: Marx's law of value in the twilight of capitalism.* Leiden: Brill.

Smith, N. 2007. "Nature as an accumulation strategy." In *The Socialist Register 2007*, eds. C. Leys and L. Panitch. London: The Merlin Press.

Smith, T. 2010. "Technological change in capitalism: Some Marxian themes." *Cambridge Journal of Economics* 34, no. 1: 203–212.

So, A. 2007. "Peasant conflict and the local predatory state in the Chinese countryside." *Journal of Peasant Studies* 34, no. 3–4: 560–581.

Song, H. 2013. "Marxist critiques of the developmental state and the fetishism of national development." *Antipode* 45, no. 5: 1254–1276.

Spacek, M. 2017. "Internal borderlands: Architectures of force and state expansion in India's central 'frontier'." *Conflict Security and Development* 17, no. 2: 163–182.

Spivak, G. 2000. "Discussion: An afterword on the new subaltern." In *Subaltern Studies 11*, eds. P. Chatterjee and P. Jeganathan, 305–334. New Delhi: Permanent black.

Sreeraj, A.P., and Vakulabharanam, V. 2015. "High growth and rising inequality in Kerala since the 1980s." *Oxford Development Studies* 44, no. 4: 367–383.

Srinivas, N. 1998. "Explaining small scale organization forms in Kerala fisheries." In *Entrepreneurship and Innovation: Models of Development*, ed. R. Kanungo. Delhi: Sage.

Srinivas, M.N. 2012. "Sociology in India and its future." In *Indian sociology: Issues and Challenges*, ed. L. Bhai. Delhi: Sage.

Srivastava, A. 1997. "Bihar to check leak of government funds to Naxals." *Indian Express.*

Srivastava, R. 1999. "Rural labour in Uttar Pradesh: Emerging features of subsistence, contradiction and resistance." *Journal of Peasant Studies* 26, no. 2–3: 263–315.

Srujana, B. 2017. "British Raj to billionaire Raj—India's journey into neoliberalism." *Newsclick.* https://newsclick.in/british-raj-billionaire-raj-indias-journey-neoliberalism.

Stanley, D. 2003. "The economic impact of mariculture on a small regional economy." *World Development* 31, no. 1: 191–210.

Steger, M., and Roy. 2010. *Neoliberalism: A very short introduction.* Oxford: Oxford University Press.

Stern, R. 2000. *Democracy and dictatorship in South Asia: Dominant classes an political outcomes in India, Pakistan, and Bangladesh.* Santa Barbara: ABC-CLIO.

Stern, R. 2011. *Changing India: Bourgeois revolution on the subcontinent.* Cambridge: Cambridge University Press.

Steur, L. 2014. "An 'expanded' class perspective: Bringing capitalism down to earth in the changing political lives of Adivasi workers in Kerala." *Modern Asian Studies* 48, no. 5: 1334–1357.

Stonich, S. 1995. "The environmental-quality and social-justice implications of shrimp mariculture development in Honduras." *Human Ecology* 23: 143–168.

Stonich, S., Bort, J., and Ovares, L. 1997. "Globalization of shrimp mariculture: The impact on social justice and environmental quality in Central America." *Society & Natural Resources* 10, no. 2: 161–179.

Storper, M. and Walker, R. 1989. *The capitalist imperative.* New York: Blackwell.

Subadevan, S., and Naqvi, I. 2017. "Contesting urban citizenship: the urban poor's strategies of state engagement in Chennai, India." *International development planning review* 39, no. 1: 77–95.

Subramanian, A., ed. 2008. *India's turn: Understanding the economic transformation.* New Delhi: Oxford University Press.

Subramanian, D. 2015. "No room for class struggle in these undertakings: Providing social welfare for Indian state sector industrial workers (circa 1950–2000)." *Modern Asian Studies* 49, no. 5: 1526–1579.

Subramanian, K. 2004. "The Naxalite Movement and government response: A critical assessment." *Mainstream* XLII, no. 52.

Subramanian, S. 1998. "Combating Naxalite violence." http://www.aapssindia.org/articles/art2/naxalite.html.

Subramanian, S. 2008. "Control and access: The everyday dimensions of property." *Contributions to Indian Sociology* 42, no. 1: 93–122.

Sud, N. 2014. "The state in the era of India's sub-national regions: liberalisation and land in Gujarat." *Geoforum* 51: 233–242.

Sugden, F. 2017. "A mode of production flux: the transformation and reproduction of rural class relations in lowland Nepal and North Bihar." *Dialectical Anthropology* 41, no. 2: 129–161.

Sugden, F., and Punch, S. 2014. "Capitalist expansion and the decline of common property ecosystems in China, Vietnam and India." *Development and Change* 45, no. 4: 656–684.

Sundar, N. 2006. "Bastar, Maoism and Salwa Judum." *Economic and Political Weekly* 41, no. 29: 3187–3192.

Sundar, N. 2011. "The rule of law and the rule of property: law-struggles and the neoliberal state in India." In *The state in India after liberalization: Interdisciplinary perspectives,* eds. A. Gupta and L. Sivaramakrishnan, 175–194. London: Routledge.

Sundar, N. 2014a. "Mimetic sovereignties, precarious citizenship: state effects in a looking-glass world." *Journal of peasant Studies* 41, no. 4: 469–490.

Sundar, N. 2014b. "No surprises here: Modi's Naxalite policy." http://nandinisundar .blogspot.ca/2014/09/no-surprises-here-modis-naxalite-policy.html.

Sunilraj, B., and Heath, O. 2017. "The historical legacy of party system stability in Kerala." *Studies in Indian Politics* 5, no. 2: 193–204.

Surjeet, H.S. 1986. *What the AIKS Stands For.* New Delhi: All India Kisan Sabha.

Surjeet, H.S. 1992. *Land reforms in India.* New Delhi: National Book Centre.

Swaminathan, M. 2000. "Consumer food subsidies in India: Proposals for reform." *The Journal of Peasant Studies* 27, no. 3: 92–114.

Sweezy, P.M. 1986. "Feudalism-to-Capitalism revisited." *Science & Society* 50, no. 1: 81–84.

Tagore, R. 1913. *Gitanjali.* http://www.spiritualbee.com/media/gitanjali-by-tagore.pdf.

Teitelbaum, E. 2006. "Was the Indian labor movement ever co-opted? Evaluating standard accounts." *Critical Asian Studies* 38, no. 4: 389–417.

Teitelbaum, E. 2013. "Labour regulation, trade unions and unemployment." In *Routledge handbook of Indian politics*, eds. A. Kohli and P. Singh. London: Routledge.

Teltumbde, A. 2010. *The persistence of caste.* Delhi: Navayana.

Teltumbde, A. 2016. *Dalits: Past, present and future.* Abingdon, Oxon: Taylor and Francis.

Tendulkar, S., and Bhavani, T. 2007. *Understanding reforms.* New Delhi: Oxford University Press.

Tendulkar, S., and Jain, L. 1995. "Economic reforms and poverty." *Economic and Political Weekly* 30, no. 23: 1373–1375, 1377.

Teubal, M. 2000. "Structural adjustment and social disarticulation: The case of Argentina." *Science and Society* 64, no. 4: 460–489.

Thapar, R. 2016. *Indian society and the secular.* Gurgaon: Three essays collective.

Thara, K. 2016. "Protecting caste livelihoods on the western coast of India: An intersectional analysis of Udupi's fisherwomen." *Environment and Urbanization* 28, no. 2: 423–436.

The Economic Times. 2008. "Jyoti Basu supports Buddhadeb's view on capitalism." *The Economic Times.* https://economictimes.indiatimes.com/jyoti-basu-supports-bud dhadebs-view-on-capitalism/articleshow/2676957.cms?from=mdr.

The Hindu. 2017. "'Unforgiveable': The Hindu's editorial on December 7, 1992 on Babri Masjid demolition." *The Hindu.* https://www.thehindu.com/news/national/unfor givable-editorial-on-the-babri-masjid-demolition-published-by-the-hindu-on-de cember-7-1992/article21272508.ece.

The Hindu. 2018a. "Who is an urban Naxal, asks Romila Thapar." *The Hindu.* https:// www.thehindu.com/news/national/who-is-an-urban-naxal-asks-romila-thapar/ar ticle25088465.ece.

The Hindu. 2018b. "Need for an employment policy to solve jobless growth." *The Hindu.* https://www.thehindu.com/news/national/need-for-an-employment-policy-to- solve-jobless-growth/article25041745.ece.

The Indian Express. 2018. "Why a new report agrees with Piketty on inequality, blames policy." *The Indian Express.* https://indianexpress.com/article/explained/pay-gap -income-inequality-policy-sc-st-religion-bias-5074635/.

Thompson, E.P. 1966. *The making of the English working class.* New York: Vintage Books.

Thorner, A. 1982. "Semi-feudalism or capitalism: Contemporary debate on classes and modes of production in India." *Economic and Political Weekly* 17, no. 51: 2061–2066.

Thorner, D. 1969. "Maliks and money-lenders – Their role." In *Rural Sociology in India,* ed. A.K. Desai. Bombay: Popular Prakashan.

Thorner, D. 1973. *Agrarian prospect in India.* Delhi: Allied Publishers.

Tilly, C. 2005. "Repression, mobilization and explanation." In *Repression and mobiliza- tion,* eds. C. Davenport, H. Johnston, and C. Muller, 211–226. Minneapolis: University of Minnesota Press.

Times of India. 2016. "Five women die every hour during childbirth, according to World Health Organization." *Times of India.* https://timesofindia.indiatimes.com/india/5- women-die-every-hour-during-childbirth-in-India-WHO/articleshow/52781552. cms.

Times of India. 2018. "Shashi Tharoor warns of 'Hindu Pakistan' under BJP rule, Sambit Patra hits back." *Times of India.* https://timesofindia.indiatimes.com/india/if-bjp- wins-2019-ls-polls-it-will-pave-the-way-for-creation-of-hindu-pakistan-shashi-thar oor/articleshow/64951115.cms.

Tisdell, C., Maitra, P., eds. 2018. *Technological change, development, and the environ- ment: Socio-economic perspectives.* Milton: Routledge.

Tiwana, B., and Singh, P. 2015. "Nation state, marketization of social services and uncer- tainty of livelihood in India." *World Review of Political Economy* 6, no. 1: 33–57.

Toye, J., and Jackson, C. 1996. "Public expenditure policy and poverty reduction: Has the world bank got it right?" *Institute of Development Studies Bulletin* 27, no. 1: 56–66.

Trotsky, L. 1928. "The Third International after Lenin: 11. Strategy and tactics in the imperialist epoch (Part 3)." *Marxists.org.* https://www.marxists.org/archive/trotsky/ 1928/3rd/ti06.htm#p2-08.

Trotsky, L. 1929. "Leon Trotsky's Writings on Britain: The Anglo-Russian Committee: Trotsky on the struggle in Britain in retrospect." *Marxists.org*. https://www.marxists .org/archive/trotsky/britain/v2/cho2g.htm.

Trotsky, L. 1930. "The Turn in the Communist International and the Situation in Germany." *Marxists.org*. https://www.marxists.org/archive/trotsky/germany/1930/3009 26.htm.

Trotsky, L. 1931a. "Germany, the key to the international situation." *Marxists.org*. https:// www.marxists.org/archive/trotsky/germany/1931/311126.htm.

Trotsky, L. 1931b. "Permanent Revolution." *Marxists.org*. https://www.marxists.org/ar chive/trotsky/1931/tpr/prge.htm.

Trotsky, L. 1932a. "Bourgeoisie, petty bourgeoisie and proletariat." *Marxists.org*. https:// www.marxists.org/archive/trotsky/1932/08/onlyroad2.htm.

Trotsky, L. 1932b. "Bureaucratic ultimatism." *Marxists.org*. https://www.marxists.org/ archive/trotsky/1932/01/whatnext5.htm.

Trotsky, L. 1932c. "Centrism 'in general' and the centrism of the Stalinist bureaucracy." *Marxists.org*. https://www.marxists.org/archive/trotsky/1932/01/whatnext9.htm.

Trotsky, L. 1932d. "Democracy and fascism I." *Marxists.org*. https://www.marxists.org/ archive/trotsky/1932/01/whatnext2.htm.

Trotsky, L. 1932e. "Democracy and fascism II." *Marxists.org*. https://www.marxists.org/ archive/trotsky/1932/01/whatnext3.htm.

Trotsky, L. 1932f. "Germany: The Only Road (Part 1)." *Marxists.org*. https://www.marx ists.org/archive/trotsky/germany/1932/onlyroad1.htm.

Trotsky, L. 1932g. "Germany: The Only Road (Part 2)." *Marxists.org*. https://www.marx ists.org/archive/trotsky/germany/1932/onlyroad2.htm#s9.

Trotsky, L. 1932h. "Strike strategy." *Marxists.org*. https://www.marxists.org/archive/ trotsky/1932/01/whatnext11.htm.

Trotsky, L. 1932i. "What next? Vital questions for the German proletariat. Part I." *Marx ists.org*. https://www.marxists.org/archive/trotsky/germany/1932-ger/next01.htm.

Trotsky, L. 1932j. "What next? Vital questions for the German proletariat. Part II." *Marxists.org*. https://www.marxists.org/archive/trotsky/germany/1932-ger/next02 .htm.

Trotsky, L. 1932k. "What next? Vital questions for the German proletariat. Part III." *Marxists.org*. https://www.marxists.org/archive/trotsky/germany/1932-ger/next03 .htm.

Trotsky, L. 1932l. "What they say in Prague about the united front." *Marxists.org*. https:// www.marxists.org/archive/trotsky/1932/09/onlyroad7.htm.

Trotsky, L. 1933a. "The German Catastrophe: The Responsibility of the Leadership." *Marxists.org*. https://www.marxists.org/archive/trotsky/germany/1933/330528.htm.

Trotsky, L. 1933b. "What is national socialism?" *Marxists.org*. https://www.marxists.org/ archive/trotsky/germany/1933/330610.htm.

Trotsky, L. 1934a. "Bonapartism and fascism." *Marxists.org.* https://www.marxists.org/archive/trotsky/germany/1934/340715.htm.

Trotsky, L. 1934b. "Whither France." *Marxists.org.* https://www.marxists.org/archive/trotsky/1936/whitherfrance/choo.htm.

Trotsky, L. 1938. "Transitional program." *Marxists.org.* https://www.marxists.org/archive/trotsky/1938/tp/transprogram.pdf.

Trotsky, L. 1939. "Three conceptions of the Russian Revolution." *Marxists.org.* https://www.marxists.org/archive/trotsky/1939/xx/3concepts.htm.

Trotsky, L. 1940. "Bonapartism, fascism and war." *Marxists.org.* https://www.marxists.org/archive/trotsky/1940/08/last-article.htm.

Trotsky, L. 1944. "Fascism what it is and how to fight it." *Marxists.org.* https://www.marxists.org/archive/trotsky/works/1944/1944-fas.htm.

Trotsky, L. 1974. *Writings of Leon Trotsky*: 1938–1939. New York: Pathfinder.

Ullrich, O. 1992. "Technology." In *Development Dictionary*, ed. E. Sachs. London: Orient Longman.

Upadhya, C. 1997. "Social and cultural strategies of class formation in coastal Andhra Pradesh." *Contributions to Indian Sociology* 31, no. 2: 169–193.

Upadhyay, S. 2018. "Workers and the right wing: The situation in India." *International Labor and Working-class History* 93: 79–90.

Vaddiraju, A.K. 1999. "Emergence of backward castes in South Telengana agrarian change and grass roots politics." *Economic Political Weekly* 34, no. 7: 425–430.

Vaidyanathan, A. 1986. "Labour use in rural India: A study of spatial and temporal variations." *Economic and Political Weekly* 21, no. 52: A130–A146.

Vakulabharanam, V., and Motiram, S. 2011. "Political economy of agrarian distress in India since the 1990s." In *Understanding India's new political economy,* ed. S. Ruparelia, S. Reddy, and S. Corbridge. London: Routledge.

Vakulabhranam, V., Zhong, W. and X. Jinjun. 2009. "Patterns of Wealth Disparities in India during the Era of Liberalization." Working Paper, Graduate Economics Research Center, Nagoya University.

Vanaik, A. 1990. *The painful transition: Bourgeois democracy in India.* London: Verso.

Vanaik, A. 2011. "Subcontinental strategies." *New Left Review*, no. 70.

Vanaik, A. 2017. *The rise of Hindu authoritarianism: Secular claims, communal realities.* London: Verso.

Vanaik, A. 2018. "India's two hegemonies." *New Left Review*, 112. https://newleftreview.org/II/112/achin-vanaik-india-s-two-hegemonies.

Vanden, E. 2018. "Targets of violence: evidence from India's Naxalite conflict." *Economic Journal* 128, no. 609: 887–916.

van der Linden, M. 2007. "The 'law' of uneven and combined development: some underdeveloped thoughts." *Historical Materialism* 15, no. 1: 145–165.

Vandergeest, P., Flaherty, M., and Miller, P. 1999. "A political ecology of shrimp aquaculture in Thailand." *Rural Sociology* 64, no. 4: 573–596.

Varadarajan, S. 2009. "Modi's 'action-reaction' quote." *Reality, one bite at a time: India, Asia and the World.* http://svaradarajan.blogspot.com/2009/10/modis-action-reaction-quote.html.

Varma, S. 2018a. "Indian millionaires up 20%, while 670 million Indians' income rises 1%." *News Click.* https://newsclick.in/indian-millionaires-20-while-670-million-indians-income-rises-1.

Varma, S. 2018b. "Glimpses of four years of Modi's Achche Din." *News Click.* https://newsclick.in/glimpses-four-years-modis-achche-din.

Varma, S. 2019. "Agri workers' wages grew just 3% per year during Modi rule." *News Click.* https://www.newsclick.in/agri-workers-wages-grew-just-3-year-under-modi-rule.

Varshney, A. 1993. "Self-limited empowerment: Democracy, economic development and rural India." *Journal of Development Studies* 29, no.4: 177–215.

Varshney, A. 1994/1998. *Democracy, development and the countryside: Urban rural struggles in India.* Cambridge: Cambridge University Press.

Vasudevan, R. 2008. "Accumulation by dispossession in India." *Econmomic and Political Weekly* 43, no. 11: 41–43.

Velaskar, P. 2016. "Theorising the interaction of caste, class and gender: A feminist sociological approach." *Contributions to Indian Sociology* 50, no. 3: 389–414.

Veltmeyer, H. 1997. "New social movements in Latin America." *Journal of Peasant Studies* 25, no. 1: 139–169.

Veltmeyer, H., Petras, J., and Vieux, S. 1997. *Neoliberalism and class conflict in Latin America: A comparative perspective on the political economy of structural adjustment.* New York: St. Martin's Press.

Verma, H.S. 2005. *The OBCs and the ruling classes in India.* Jaipur: Rawat Publications.

Veron, R., Williams, G., Corbridge, S., and Srivastava, M. 2006. "Decentralized Corruption or Corrupt Decentralization? Community Monitoring of Poverty-alleviation Schemes in Eastern India." *World Development* 34, no. 11: 1922–1941.

Vicol, M. 2019. "Potatoes, Petty Commodity Producers and Livelihoods: Contract farming and agrarian change in Maharashtra, India." *Journal of Agrarian Change* 19, no. 1: 135–161.

Vidyasagar, K. 2005. *Communist politics in India: Struggle for survival.* Delhi: Academic Excellence.

Vidyasagar, R. 1999. "New agrarianism and the challenges of the left." In *Class formation and political transformation in post-colonial India,* ed. T. Sathyamurthy, 202–237. Delhi: Oxford University Press.

Vijayabaskar, M., and Menon, A. 2018. "Dispossession by neglect: Agricultural land sales in southern India." *Journal of Agrarian Change* 18, no. 3: 571–587.

Vogel, L. 2014. *Marxism and social oppression.* Leiden/Boston: Brill.

Volodin, A. 2018. "The logic of directed development in postcolonial India." *Herald of the Russian Academy of Sciences* 88, no. 1: 96–103.

Vyas, V.S., and Bhargava, P. 1995. "Public intervention for poverty alleviation." *Economic and Political Weekly* 30, no. 41/42: 559–2561, 2563–2565, 2567–2569, 2571–2572.

Walker, K. 2008. "Neoliberalism on the ground in rural India: predatory growth, agrarian crisis, internal colonization, and the intensification of class struggle." *Journal of Peasant Studies* 35, no. 4: 557–620.

Wallace, H.S. 2017. "American Fascism, in 1944 and Today." *The New York Times*. https://www.nytimes.com/2017/05/12/opinion/american-fascism-trump.html.

Watts, M. 1996. "Development III: The global agrofood system and late twentieth-century development, (or Kautsky redux)." *Progress in Human Geography*, 20, no. 2: 230–245.

Webster, N. 1990. "Agrarian relations in Burdwan District, West Bengal: From the economics of Green Revolution to the politics of Panchayat Raj." *Journal of Contemporary Asia* 20, no. 2: 177–211.

Weeks, J. 1981. *Capital and exploitation*. Princeton: Princeton University Press.

Weeks, P. 1992. "Fish and people: Aquaculture and the social sciences." *Society & Natural Resources* 5, no. 4: 345–357.

Whitehead, J. 2007. "Hegemony and the decline of the Narmada Bachao Andolan in Gujarat, 1998–2001." *Critical Asian Studies* 39, no. 3: 399–421.

Whitehead, J. 2010. *Development and dispossession in the Narmada Valley*. Delhi: Pearson.

Wickremasinghe, N., and Jones, K. 2004. "India: Stalinists to promote Congress power bid." *World Socialist Web Site*. http://www.wsws.org/en/articles/2004/05/ind-m13.html.

Williams, G. 2004. "Evaluating participatory development: Tyranny, power and (re-) politicisation." *Third World Quarterly* 25, no. 3: 557–578.

Williams, M. 2009. *The roots of participatory democracy: Democratic communists in South Africa and Kerala, India*. New York: Palgrave Macmillan.

Wilson, K. 1999. "Patterns of accumulation and struggles of rural labour: Some aspects of agrarian change in central Bihar." *Journal of Peasant Studies* 26, no. 2–3: 316–354.

Witsoe, J. 2011. "Corruption as power: Caste and the political imagination of the postcolonial state." American Ethnologist 38, no. 11: 73–85.

Wood, E. 1995. *Democracy against capitalism*. New York: Cambridge University Press.

Wood, E. 1997. "The non-history of capitalism." *Historical Materialism* 1, no. 1: 5–21.

Wood, E. 2003. *The empire of capital*. Delhi: Leftword.

Wood, E. 2007. "A reply to critics." *Historical Materialism* 15: 143–170.

World Bank. 1997. *India: Achievements and challenges in reducing poverty*. The World Bank, Washington.

World Bank. 2007. *World development report: Agriculture for development.* The International Bank for Reconstruction and Development/The World Bank, Washington.

World Economic Forum. 2018. "The inclusive development index." *World Economic Forum.* http://www3.weforum.org/docs/WEF_Forum_IncGrwth_2018.pdf.

Wright, E. 1995. "The class analysis of poverty." *International Journal of Health Services* 25, no. 1: 85–100.

Wright, E. 2015. *Understanding class.* London: Verso.

Yapa, L.S. 1979. "Ecopolitical economy of the green revolution." *Professional Geographer* 31, no. 4: 371–376.

Yapa, L.S. 1993. "What are improved seeds: An epistemology of improved seeds." *Economic Geography* 69, no. 3: 254–273.

Yapa, L.S. 1996. "What causes poverty? A postmodern view." *Annals of the Association of American Geographers* 86, no. 4: 707–728.

Yechury, S. 1993. "Communalism, religion and Marxism." *The Marxist* 10, no. 4; 11, no. 1.

Yuval, N.H. 2018. *21 lessons for the 21st century.* London: Jonathan Cape.

Zizek, S. 2008. *Violence.* New York: Picador.

# Index

Keywords below include concepts that reflect social processes at a more general level and in the Indian context.